America's
TEST KITCHEN

America's
TEST KITCHEN

Cooking
for Two

2009

THE YEAR'S BEST RECIPES CUT DOWN TO SIZE

BY THE EDITORS OF
AMERICA'S TEST KITCHEN

PHOTOGRAPHY BY
CARL TREMBLAY, KELLER + KELLER, AND DANIEL J. VAN ACKERE

AMERICA'S TEST KITCHEN
17 Station Street, Brookline, MA 02445

Library of Congress Cataloging-in-Publication Data
The Editors at America's Test Kitchen

AMERICA'S TEST KITCHEN COOKING FOR TWO 2009:
The Year's Best Recipes Cut Down to Size

1st Edition

Hardcover: $35 US/$45 CAN
ISBN-13: 978-1-933615-43-1   ISBN-10: 1-933615-43-5
1. Cooking. 1. Title
2009

Manufactured in the United States of America

10 9 8 7 6 5 4 3 2 1

Distributed by America's Test Kitchen
17 Station Street, Brookline, MA 02445

EDITORIAL DIRECTOR: Jack Bishop
EXECUTIVE EDITOR: Elizabeth Carduff
FOOD EDITOR: Julia Collin Davison
SENIOR EDITOR: Rachel Toomey
ASSOCIATE EDITORS: Elizabeth Emery, Kate Hartke, and Suzannah McFerran
TEST COOKS: Adelaide Parker, Megan Wycoff, and Dan Zuccarello
EDITORIAL ASSISTANT: Elizabeth Pohm
DESIGN DIRECTOR: Amy Klee
ART DIRECTOR: Greg Galvan
DESIGNERS: Erica Lee and Matthew Warnick
STAFF PHOTOGRAPHER: Daniel J. van Ackere
ADDITIONAL PHOTOGRAPHERS: Christopher Churchill, Keller + Keller, and Carl Tremblay
FOOD STYLING: Marie Piraino and Mary Jane Sawyer
PRODUCTION DIRECTOR: Guy Rochford
SENIOR PRODUCTION MANAGER: Jessica Quirk
TRAFFIC AND PROJECT MANAGER: Alice Carpenter
COLOR AND IMAGING SPECIALIST: Andrew Mannone
PRODUCTION AND IMAGING SPECIALISTS: Judy Blomquist and Lauren Pettapiece
COPYEDITOR: Barbara Wood
PROOFREADER: Jeffrey Schier
INDEXER: Elizabeth Parson

PICTURED ON THE FRONT COVER: Stir-Fried Beef with Snap Peas and Red Pepper (page 17)
PICTURED OPPOSITE TITLE PAGE: Roast Cornish Game Hens with Couscous Stuffing (page 109)
PICTURED ON BACK OF JACKET: Lasagna (page 59), Herb-Roasted Prime Rib with Potatoes (page 104), French-Style Pot Roast (page 186), and Raspberry-Nectarine Pie (page 265)

Contents

Introduction

MANY THINGS ARE BEING DOWNSIZED these days, including the family dinner table, which reminds me of the story of an editor of a country newspaper who saw his circulation drop dramatically, year after year. Suddenly, he looked up from his desk to see a funeral procession going by the window. He took one look at the hearse, threw up his hands in despair, and exclaimed, "There goes my subscriber!"

Yes, times have changed. As a kid, I was used to finding a crowd around the table in the Yellow Farmhouse when we sat down to noon dinner. In those days, the mark of a good cook was being able to serve large numbers of last-minute neighbors. Leftovers were never a problem. The worst-case scenario was feeding odds and ends to Bonnie, the mutt, or Dixie, the collie. Most times, however, leftovers were headed for the supper or breakfast table.

And so, when many of our readers began asking for a cookbook designed for just two people, not the usual four to six, I have to admit to a bit of philosophic hesitation. After all, isn't cooking about feeding the multitudes, the modern version of loaves and fishes? Sure, but the reality of the home kitchen is that kids grow up and move out, or, for a variety of other reasons, many home cooks are preparing supper for themselves and just one other. It's cozy, to be sure, but it raises a multitude of culinary issues.

You might simply say, "Just cook for four and eat the leftovers the next day." Sounds reasonable (and this was my first reaction), but many dishes don't reheat well, many cooks want something freshly cooked each night, and there is always the issue of not using up produce and other ingredients, even when cooking for larger numbers. (What does one do with half a head of cabbage?) When we started work in the test kitchen, we found that "cooking for two" was quite a different thing entirely; there are different rules and approaches that truly change the way one cooks.

The first issue was using up ingredients. Pita bread, for example. One of my favorite recipes in the book is for a Greek-style pita sandwich—but leftover pita goes stale quickly, so we included a great recipe for homemade pita chips that take but a few minutes to bake. Or how about canned white beans? A bit less than a cup goes into our Whole Wheat Pasta with Greens, Beans, Pancetta, and Garlic Bread Crumbs, and then the rest can be used to make Rosemary–White Bean Spread. The "Use It Up" recommendations go on and on—from avocado to egg yolks, from mango to kidney beans.

Some of the chapters are what you might expect— Everyday Main Dishes, Pasta for Dinner, Fancy Dinners, Side Dishes, and Desserts—but we've included a few unexpected surprises as well: Skillet Meals; Last-Minute Suppers from the Pantry; and One Big Roast, Three Great Meals. Some recipes are exercises in scaling back quantities (e.g., how to make lasagna in a loaf pan), some are surprising in their simplicity (a frittata from pantry ingredients), and others introduce a whole new way of cooking (start with Pan-Roasted Turkey Breast and then use leftovers for White Turkey Chili, Skillet Turkey Pot Pie, or Turkey Curry). And we even tackle the problem of downsizing big desserts, from cakes and pies to crisps and crumbles.

For those of you who have struggled through conventional cookbooks for years, trying to cut recipes in half, reuse leftovers with a bit of flair, or repurpose half-cans of this and that: *Cooking for Two* has been written, tested, and edited just for you. It's a combination of common sense, a frugal approach to the culinary arts, and an abiding love of good food. Best of all, these recipes will make you want to step right back into the kitchen, facing the stove and looking forward to what is on the menu for tonight.

CHRISTOPHER KIMBALL
Founder and Editor,
Cook's Illustrated and *Cook's Country*
Host, *America's Test Kitchen* and
Cook's Country from America's Test Kitchen

THE SMART SHOPPER'S GUIDE

MAKING THE MOST OF THE RECIPES IN THIS BOOK

LET'S FACE IT—WE ALL WASTE FOOD. And when you're cooking for two, this is an even bigger problem. Sure, there are some stores where you can buy loose leafy greens or a handful of Brussels sprouts, but usually you're stuck with prepackaged produce sold in large quantities. The same is true for canned goods and many other items used in everyday recipes. So what's the solution to this problem? Careful planning and shopping. To that end, we've prepared this guide to key ingredients, both perishable and canned, that are used throughout the book. So if you're making one recipe with bagged spinach or half a can of kidney beans, you can see which other recipes in the book call for them so you don't have to toss the extras.

ASPARAGUS	AMOUNT	PAGE
Chicken with Orzo and Asparagus	½ bunch	8
Steamed Sole and Vegetable Bundles	½ bunch	140

AVOCADO		
Pan-Seared Shrimp with Chipotle Sauce	½	85
Creamy Avocado-Herb Dressing	½	85

BEANS, CANNED CANNELLINI		
Rosemary–White Bean Spread	¾ cup	54
Whole Wheat Pasta with Greens and Beans	¾ cup	54
Provençal Vegetable Soup with Pistou	¾ cup	153
Pasta e Fagioli	¾ cup	169
Rustic Pork and White Bean Stew	¾ cup	193

BEANS, CANNED KIDNEY		
Kidney Bean Salad	¾ cup	134
Turkey Chili	¾ cup	135

CABBAGE		
Creamy New York Deli Coleslaw	¾ head	217
Grilled Fish Tacos with Corn on the Cob	¼ head	219

CAULIFLOWER		
Roasted Cauliflower	½ head	241
Cauliflower Gratin	½ head	244

CHERRIES, JARRED MORELLO		
Cherry Clafouti	¾ cup	260
Cherry Sauce	1¼ cups	260

CHERRY TOMATOES		
Quick Tomato Salsa	1 cup	70
Simple Chicken Bake with Fennel, Tomatoes, and Olives	1 cup	71
Pasta with Garden Vegetable Sauce	½ cup	148
Pasta Salad with Summer Vegetables	½ cup	149
Grilled Bone-In Chicken Breasts with Cherry Tomatoes	2 cups	197
Cherry Tomato Salad with Basil and Fresh Mozzarella	1 cup	232
Cherry Tomato Salad with Tarragon and Blue Cheese	1 cup	233

COCONUT MILK		
Steamed Mussels in Coconut Milk	¾ cup	90
Coconut Rice Pudding	1 cup	90

CUCUMBER		
Stone Pot–Style Korean Mixed Rice	½	21
Creamy Dill Cucumber Salad	½	21
Greek-Style Lamb Pita Sandwiches	¼	27
Sesame Noodles with Shredded Chicken	½	67
Spicy Cucumber Relish	½	88

FETA CHEESE		
Chicken with Israeli Couscous, Spinach, and Feta	2 ounces	7
Marinated Feta with Lemon and Shallot	4 ounces	8
Greek-Style Lamb Pita Sandwiches	1 ounce	27
Spinach Salad with Radishes, Feta, and Pistachios	2 tablespoons	235

HEAVY CREAM		
Shrimp and Grits	½ cup	35
Shrimp and Grits with Bacon	½ cup	36

STOCKING THE COOKING-FOR-TWO KITCHEN

IN GENERAL, WHEN YOU'RE COOKING FOR TWO, you really don't need special equipment—the usual battery of pots, pans, knives, and tools will work just fine. (Although if your kitchen isn't stocked with smaller skillets—8- and 10-inch—or a small saucepan, you'll need them for a variety of recipes in this book.) But for some scaled-down casseroles and desserts, we found we needed smaller baking dishes, cake pans, and more. Some casseroles worked with common cookware—a loaf pan, we found, makes a great vessel for smaller lasagna or shepherd's pie. But for other recipes, like our gratins and many desserts, special equipment was necessary. Fortunately, these dishes are inexpensive and are widely available both online and at many retail stores. Plus, you'll never need more than two (and sometimes just one will suffice). Here's a list of the cookware we found most useful in this book.

SQUARE BAKING DISHES

We use an 8-inch square baking dish to cook entrées like our Chicken and Vegetable Bakes (pages 71–72).

SMALL SHALLOW BAKING DISHES

Small baking dishes with low sides (no more than 2 inches high to expose the surface of the food) are useful for a variety of recipes. We use an 8½ by 5½-inch ceramic baking dish to make scaled-down gratins (pages 239–244) and certain desserts, but a dish of a comparable size or of a different material could be used instead.

SMALL BAKING PAN

When you want to make a small sheet cake (see our Lemon Buttermilk Sheet Cake on page 268), this 7¼ by 5¼-inch pan works perfectly since its capacity is about one-third that of a 13 by 9-inch baking pan.

LOAF PANS

Loaf pans (either 9- or 8-inch) are the perfect vessels for baking some small casseroles, such as our Lasagna (page 59) and Shepherd's Pie (page 189).

SMALL CAKE PANS

With two 6-inch round cake pans, you can make a perfectly sized layer cake for two people (see our Fluffy Yellow Layer Cake with Chocolate Frosting on page 275).

SMALL PIE PLATE

We found that a 6-inch pie plate works perfectly when you want to bake a pie that serves two (see our Raspberry-Nectarine Pie on page 265).

RAMEKINS

Ramekins are handy for making a number of savory and sweet dishes. In our testing, we found that 6-ounce ramekins were the perfect size for making Flan (page 285) and 12-ounce ramekins were ideal for making individual Cheese Soufflés (page 173), Blueberry Crumbles (page 255), and Pear Crisps (page 258).

SMALL SPRINGFORM PANS

We turned to 4½-inch springform pans to downsize a variety of cakes, including our Almond Cake (page 277) and New York Cheesecake (page 283).

INDIVIDUAL BUNDT PANS

These 1-cup pans are ideal for making our individually-sized Rich Chocolate Bundt Cakes (page 272).

EGGPLANT PARMESAN

CHAPTER 1

SKILLET MEALS

PAN-ROASTED CHICKEN AND VEGETABLES

ROASTED CHICKEN AND ROOT VEGETABLES are a classic combination. But roasting a whole chicken in the oven takes a little more time than we'd like on a weeknight, so when we want to prepare a simple chicken dinner for two, we turn to pan-roasting—a common restaurant technique in which food is browned on the stovetop in a skillet that is then placed directly in the oven. Besides being a relatively quick technique, pan-roasting is an easy way to ensure crisp, nicely browned chicken skin. Browning the chicken in the skillet also leaves behind rich, caramelized drippings, or fond, which is ideal for flavoring the vegetables. Best of all, we thought roast chicken and vegetables for two would fit perfectly in one skillet, eliminating the need to dirty multiple pots and pans.

Bone-in chicken breasts are particularly well suited to pan-roasting: The initial stovetop time helps create a crispy-skinned exterior and also shortens the oven time so the interior stays juicy.

After browning the chicken on both sides, we transferred it to a plate and added our vegetables (tasters favored a simple combination of potatoes, carrots, and shallots) to the skillet, then topped the vegetables with the seared chicken. To streamline the dish further, we opted for red potatoes over other types of potatoes because their tender skin doesn't require peeling, and baby carrots for the same reason, thus saving us some prep time. We then transferred the skillet to the oven to allow everything to finish cooking together. We tested oven temperatures ranging from 375 to 500 degrees. The highest temperatures caused profuse smoking from the singed drippings, and temperatures on the lower end meant protracted cooking times, defeating our goal of a quick weeknight supper. At 450 degrees, however, the skin was handsomely browned and crackling crisp, and the meat cooked swiftly (about 18 minutes for 12-ounce breasts) to an internal temperature of 160 degrees. The vegetables, however, were another story: The potatoes were burnt on the outside and raw in the middle, and the carrots posed a similar problem—they were crunchy in the middle and lacked the sweetness that usually comes from roasting. Only the shallots emerged perfectly cooked. Clearly, the potatoes and carrots were not spending enough time in the oven.

The solution to our problem with the vegetables was to use the microwave to parcook them. While the chicken browned, we popped the potatoes and carrots into the microwave to give them a head start, and by the time the chicken was ready for the oven, the potatoes and carrots were ready to finish up in the skillet, where they could soak up the flavorful fond. This time, they emerged from the oven with deeply caramelized exteriors and creamy, tender interiors.

As a final touch, we infused olive oil with lemon juice, garlic, red pepper flakes, and thyme, then drizzled it over the chicken and vegetables just before serving. With this boldly flavored sauce, no one missed the pan juices from traditional roast chicken.

Pan-Roasted Chicken and Vegetables
SERVES 2

If using kosher chicken, do not brine. If brining the chicken, do not season with salt in step 2. We prefer to use small or medium potatoes (1 to 3 inches in diameter) because they are easier to cut into uniform pieces, but regardless of what size potatoes you use, be sure to cut them into uniform wedges to ensure even cooking.

- 8 ounces small red potatoes (about 3), cut into 1-inch wedges (see note)
- 4 ounces baby carrots (about 14)
- 3½ tablespoons olive oil
  Salt and pepper
- 2 (12-ounce) bone-in, skin-on split chicken breasts, trimmed (see page 7) and brined if desired (see note; see page 76)
- 2 shallots, peeled and quartered
- 4½ teaspoons fresh lemon juice
- 1 garlic clove, minced
- 1 teaspoon minced fresh thyme
  Pinch red pepper flakes

1. Adjust an oven rack to the middle position and heat the oven to 450 degrees. Toss the potatoes and carrots with 1½ teaspoons of the oil, ⅛ teaspoon salt, and a pinch of pepper in a microwave-safe bowl. Microwave on high, uncovered, until the vegetables soften but still hold their shape, about 5 minutes, gently stirring once during cooking.

2. Meanwhile, pat the chicken dry with paper towels and season with salt and pepper. Heat 1 tablespoon more oil in a 12-inch ovensafe nonstick skillet over medium-high heat until just smoking. Carefully lay the chicken breasts, skin-side down, in the skillet and cook until well browned, 6 to 8 minutes. Flip the chicken and continue to brown lightly on the second side, about 3 minutes.

3. Remove the chicken from the pan, add the shallots and microwaved vegetables, then place the chicken, skin-side up, on top of the vegetables. Transfer the skillet to the oven and bake until the thickest part of the breast registers 160 to 165 degrees on an instant-read thermometer, 15 to 20 minutes.

4. Using potholders (the skillet handle will be hot), remove the skillet from the oven. Transfer the chicken and vegetables to a serving platter, tent loosely with foil, and let rest for 10 minutes. Meanwhile, whisk the remaining 2 tablespoons oil, lemon juice, garlic, thyme, and pepper flakes together in a small bowl, and season with salt and pepper to taste. Drizzle the oil-lemon mixture over the chicken and vegetables before serving.

NOTES FROM THE TEST KITCHEN

TRIMMING SPLIT CHICKEN BREASTS

Using kitchen shears, trim off the rib sections from each breast, following the vertical line of fat from the tapered end of the breast up to the socket where the wing was attached.

CHICKEN DINNERS

IT'S NO WONDER THAT BONELESS, SKINLESS CHICKEN breasts are so popular—they are widely available, easy to prepare, and quick-cooking. They can be purchased individually, but they are most often sold in packs of four, so you can cook two and freeze two for another night. We wanted to incorporate this convenient cut of chicken into a simple yet satisfying skillet supper for two. Cooking boneless breasts in a skillet is easy enough; our challenge would be making an entire meal in one skillet, complete with a starch and a vegetable.

Because boneless chicken breasts are so lean, we found that flouring the chicken before sautéing helped protect the meat from drying out—a problem that's of particular concern when the breasts are being served simply

(we planned to place them atop a bed of grains and vegetables just before serving). We cooked the breasts until they were golden brown on both sides and registered an internal temperature of 160 to 165 degrees. This took about 12 minutes for smaller breasts and up to 16 minutes for larger breasts. Once the chicken was cooked through, we transferred it to a 200-degree oven to keep warm while we focused on the rest of our meal.

Couscous is a quick-cooking grain, so we thought it would be an ideal addition to our skillet chicken supper. We decided to use Israeli couscous, which is larger than traditional couscous and therefore must be simmered. We found that toasting the small pearls before simmering them kept the grains distinct and added a pleasant nuttiness. Like most other grains, couscous is well suited to a variety of flavors, and although simmering it in chicken broth was adequate, we seized the opportunity to incorporate some other ingredients for added complexity. A bold combination of shallot, garlic, red pepper flakes, and lemon zest was just what this dish needed.

Now we just needed a vegetable component to complete the dish. After experimenting with leafy greens such as Swiss chard and kale, we settled on spinach, because tasters liked its flavor more than that of chard and because it was far more tender than kale, which tasters also felt had an overpowering flavor. We opted for packaged baby spinach because it's ready to use and requires very little cooking; incorporating it was as easy as opening the package and stirring the spinach into the hot couscous, where it wilted in a matter of minutes. A little lemon juice added a brightness, and tangy feta cheese was the perfect finishing touch, contributing a little richness. We liked this recipe so much that we developed a version with orzo, asparagus, and Parmesan cheese, for a variation that is equally simple yet flavorful.

Chicken with Israeli Couscous, Spinach, and Feta
SERVES 2

Israeli couscous is larger than traditional couscous and therefore must be simmered. Orzo can be substituted for the couscous. See page 8 for a recipe to use up the leftover feta.

¼ **cup unbleached all-purpose flour**
2 **(6 to 8-ounce) boneless, skinless chicken breasts, trimmed**

    Salt and pepper

3   tablespoons olive oil

¾   cup Israeli couscous (see note)

1   shallot, minced (about 3 tablespoons)

3   garlic cloves, minced (about 3 teaspoons)

½   teaspoon grated lemon zest plus

    2 tablespoons fresh lemon juice

¼   teaspoon red pepper flakes

1¾ cups low-sodium chicken broth

6   ounces baby spinach (about 6 cups)

2   ounces feta cheese, crumbled (about ½ cup)

1. Adjust an oven rack to the middle position and heat the oven to 200 degrees. Place the flour in a shallow dish. Pat the chicken dry with paper towels and season with salt and pepper. Working with one breast at a time, dredge the chicken in the flour, shaking off the excess.

2. Heat 1 tablespoon of the oil in a 10-inch non-stick skillet over medium-high heat until just smoking. Carefully lay the chicken breasts in the skillet and cook until well browned on the first side, 6 to 8 minutes. Flip the chicken breasts, reduce the heat to medium, and continue to cook until the thickest part of the breast registers 160 to 165 degrees on an instant-read thermometer, 6 to 8 minutes longer. Transfer the chicken to a plate, tent loosely with foil, and let rest in the warm oven while preparing the couscous.

3. Wipe out the skillet with a wad of paper towels. Add 1 tablespoon more oil and the couscous to the skillet and toast over medium heat until light golden, about 2 minutes. Stir in the shallot, 2 teaspoons of the garlic, ¼ teaspoon of the lemon zest, and ⅛ teaspoon of the pepper flakes and cook until fragrant, about 30 seconds.

4. Stir in the broth and bring to a simmer, then reduce the heat to medium-low and cook, stirring often, until the liquid is absorbed and the couscous is al dente, 8 to 10 minutes.

5. Meanwhile, whisk 1 tablespoon of the lemon juice, remaining 1 tablespoon oil, remaining 1 teaspoon garlic, remaining ¼ teaspoon lemon zest, and remaining ⅛ teaspoon pepper flakes together in a small bowl.

6. Stir the spinach, one handful at a time, into the skillet and cook until wilted, about 5 minutes. Off the heat, stir in the feta and remaining 1 tablespoon lemon juice and season with salt and pepper to taste. Divide the couscous between two plates and top with the chicken. Drizzle with the lemon juice mixture and serve.

USE IT UP: FETA

Marinated Feta with Lemon and Shallot

MAKES ABOUT 1 CUP

Serve with wedges of warm pita bread or slices of baguette. The marinated feta can be refrigerated in an airtight container for up to 1 week; before serving, let sit at room temperature until the oil liquefies, about 1 hour. This recipe can easily be doubled or tripled.

½   cup extra-virgin olive oil

1   shallot, sliced thin

¼   teaspoon dried oregano

2   teaspoons grated lemon zest

⅛   teaspoon red pepper flakes

4   ounces feta cheese, cut into ½-inch cubes

1. Cook ¼ cup of the oil, shallot, oregano, lemon zest, and pepper flakes in a small saucepan over low heat until the shallot is softened, about 12 minutes.

2. Remove the saucepan from the heat and gently stir in the feta. Cover and let sit until the mixture reaches room temperature, about 1½ hours.

3. Stir in the remaining ¼ cup oil and serve.

Chicken with Orzo, Asparagus, and Parmesan

SERVES 2

Israeli couscous can be substituted for the orzo.

¼   cup unbleached all-purpose flour

2   (6 to 8-ounce) boneless, skinless chicken breasts, trimmed

    Salt and pepper

3   tablespoons olive oil

¾   cup orzo (see note)

1   shallot, minced (about 3 tablespoons)

3   garlic cloves, minced (about 3 teaspoons)

1   teaspoon minced fresh thyme

½   teaspoon grated lemon zest plus

    2 tablespoons fresh lemon juice

1¾ cups low-sodium chicken broth

½   bunch asparagus (about 8 ounces), tough ends trimmed, cut into 1-inch lengths

1   ounce Parmesan cheese, grated (about ½ cup)

CHICKEN WITH ISRAELI COUSCOUS, SPINACH, AND FETA

1. Adjust an oven rack to the middle position and heat the oven to 200 degrees. Place the flour in a shallow dish. Pat the chicken dry with paper towels and season with salt and pepper. Working with one breast at a time, dredge the chicken in the flour, shaking off the excess.

2. Heat 1 tablespoon of the oil in a 10-inch non-stick skillet over medium-high heat until just smoking. Carefully lay the chicken breasts in the skillet and cook until well browned on the first side, 6 to 8 minutes. Flip the chicken breasts, reduce the heat to medium, and continue to cook until the thickest part of the breast registers 160 to 165 degrees on an instant-read thermometer, 6 to 8 minutes longer. Transfer the chicken to a plate, tent loosely with foil, and let rest in the warm oven while preparing the orzo.

3. Wipe out the skillet with a wad of paper towels. Add 1 tablespoon more oil and the orzo to the skillet and toast over medium heat until light golden, about 2 minutes. Stir in the shallot, 2 teaspoons of the garlic, ½ teaspoon of the thyme, and ¼ teaspoon of the lemon zest and cook until fragrant, about 30 seconds.

4. Stir in the broth and bring to a simmer, then reduce the heat to medium-low and cook, stirring often, for 4 minutes. Stir in the asparagus, cover, and continue to cook until the liquid is absorbed, the orzo is al dente, and the asparagus is crisp-tender, 4 to 6 minutes longer.

5. Meanwhile, whisk 1 tablespoon of the lemon juice, the remaining 1 tablespoon oil, remaining 1 teaspoon garlic, remaining ½ teaspoon thyme, and remaining ¼ teaspoon lemon zest together in a small bowl.

6. Off the heat, stir the Parmesan and remaining 1 tablespoon lemon juice into the skillet and season with salt and pepper to taste. Divide the orzo between two plates and top with the chicken. Drizzle with the lemon juice mixture and serve.

CHICKEN FAJITAS

FAJITAS, A SIMPLE COMBINATION of grilled meat, onions, and peppers tucked into flour tortillas, are easy to make and quick-cooking by design. But although the heaping platter of meat and vegetables accompanied by a mountain of toppings at most restaurants may be intended for two people, it could easily feed a crowd. We wanted a recipe for fajitas that really does serve two, with no leftovers in sight. And we thought the confines of a skillet might be just the place to start.

The skirt steak in classic beef fajitas doesn't need a marinade to add juiciness or flavor, but boneless chicken breasts need all the help they can get. Starting with a mixture of lime juice, vegetable oil, salt, and pepper as our base, we tried several marinating methods. Soaked in the marinade over an extended time, the chicken breasts exuded too much liquid, which prevented them from developing a nicely browned exterior. Also, marinating the chicken any longer than 15 minutes in our lime juice–heavy marinade meant that the meat actually started to "cook" in the acid. Although we've encountered this problem with any marinade containing an acid component, it's a problem that's amplified when marinating such a small amount of meat (we needed only two breasts). We also tried brining—soaking the chicken in a saltwater solution. This seasoned the chicken and kept it juicy, but tasters found the meat too moist—waterlogged, even. Instead, we decided to flavor the chicken after cooking, sautéing it plain and tossing the cooked strips in the marinade afterward. This method yielded the best results: tender, browned chicken with a bright, unadulterated tang.

Our post-marinade's high acid content added fresh citrus notes to the chicken that tasters approved of, but because fajita meat is often grilled, we missed the smoky complexity. After trying numerous unsuccessful flavor additions, we finally hit upon Worcestershire sauce. Though an unlikely choice for chicken, Worcestershire sauce has a savory quality that was just what our chicken needed. A mere teaspoonful added a layer

of saltiness and smokiness. A bit of brown sugar helped round out the flavors of our marinade, and cilantro added freshness.

Bell pepper and onion are requisite components of any fajitas recipe, adding sweetness and textural contrast. While the chicken rested, we sautéed the pepper and onion in the same skillet, taking advantage of the flavorful fond left by the meat. A little water added to the pan helped the process along. Though the fond lent the vegetables a full flavor that needed minimal enhancement, we experimented with a variety of spices and settled on chili powder, which added a characteristically Southwestern touch.

All that was left to do was warm the tortillas and pull together our favorite toppings, which we could now use to complement—not cover up—our full-flavored chicken fajitas.

Chicken Fajitas

SERVES 2

To make these fajitas spicy, add a sliced jalapeño along with the bell pepper. Serve with salsa, sour cream, chopped avocado, shredded cheese, shredded lettuce, and lime wedges.

- 2 **(6 to 8-ounce) boneless, skinless chicken breasts, trimmed**
  Salt and pepper
- 2 **tablespoons vegetable oil**
- 1 **red, yellow, or orange bell pepper, stemmed, seeded, and sliced into ½-inch-wide strips**
- 1 **small red onion, halved and sliced thin**
- 2 **tablespoons water**
- 1 **teaspoon chili powder**
- 2 **tablespoons fresh lime juice**
- 1 **tablespoon chopped fresh cilantro**
- 1 **teaspoon Worcestershire sauce**
- ½ **teaspoon brown sugar**
- 6 **(6-inch) flour tortillas, warmed (see page 190)**

1. Adjust an oven rack to the middle position and heat the oven to 200 degrees. Pat the chicken dry with paper towels and season with salt and pepper.

2. Heat 1 tablespoon of the oil in a 10-inch non-stick skillet over medium-high heat until just smoking. Carefully lay the chicken breasts in the skillet and cook until well browned on the first side, 6 to 8 minutes. Flip the chicken breasts, reduce the heat to medium, and continue to cook until the thickest part of the breast registers 160 to 165 degrees on an instant-read thermometer, 6 to 8 minutes longer. Transfer the chicken to a plate, tent loosely with foil, and let rest in the warm oven while preparing the vegetables.

3. Add the bell pepper, onion, water, chili powder, and ¼ teaspoon salt to the skillet and cook over medium heat until the vegetables are softened, 5 to 7 minutes. Transfer to a serving platter and tent loosely with foil.

4. Meanwhile, whisk the lime juice, cilantro, Worcestershire, brown sugar, remaining 1 tablespoon oil, and ¼ teaspoon salt together in a large bowl and set aside.

5. Slice the chicken into ¼-inch-thick pieces, and toss with the lime juice mixture. Arrange the chicken on the platter with the vegetables and serve with the warm tortillas.

NOTES FROM THE TEST KITCHEN

THE BEST SUPERMARKET FLOUR TORTILLAS

It's no surprise that the best flour tortillas are freshly made to order. But those of us without a local tortilleria must make do with the packaged offerings at the local supermarket. To find out which ones taste best, we rounded up every 6-inch flour tortilla we could find (usually labeled "fajita size") and headed into the test kitchen to taste them.

Tasters immediately zeroed in on texture, which varied dramatically from "doughy and stale" to "thin and flaky." The thinner brands were the hands-down winners, with **Tyson Mexican Original Flour Tortillas, Fajita-Style,** being tasters' clear favorite. We recommend buying these unless, of course, you can find locally made tortillas.

KEEPING HERBS FRESH LONGER

We use a lot of fresh herbs in the test kitchen, so we know firsthand that their shelf life is short—a particular problem when you're cooking for two and using small quantities. To get the most life out of your herbs, gently rinse and dry them (a salad spinner works perfectly), and then loosely roll them in a few sheets of paper towels. Put the roll of herbs in a zipper-lock bag and place it in the crisper drawer of your refrigerator. Stored in this manner, your herbs will be fresh, washed, and ready to use for a week or longer. (See page 213 for a recipe to use up any leftover herbs.)

TORTILLA CASSEROLE

WE'RE BIG FANS OF CASSEROLES. Not only are they incredibly satisfying, but they are also the ultimate one-dish meal. Plus, it's a preparation that's well suited to an endless variety of flavor and ingredient combinations. One of our favorites is tortilla casserole, a rich and hearty combination of tortillas layered with a spicy chile sauce, tender shredded chicken, vegetables, and cheese; the result is something like a Mexican lasagna. Unfortunately, like lasagna, this dish can take a long time to assemble and often disappoints; overcooked chicken bathed in canned cream soup and congealed cheese were the results of several recipes we tried. And, of course, there's another problem—casseroles are meant to feed a crowd. Could we capture all that we love about this dish in a simple skillet dinner for two?

We started by browning boneless, skinless chicken breasts in a skillet, then set them aside to build a sauce. We knew what not to put in our sauce—canned cream of chicken soup. But as for the rest of the ingredients, recipes varied widely. We cooked shallot and garlic with chipotle chile in adobo sauce, which lent the dish smokiness and heat, and then added chicken broth to form the base of the sauce. As for vegetable additions, tasters didn't care for olives, mushrooms, or green bell peppers—all ingredients we noted in our research. Some recipes actually had so many vegetables and beans that the tortillas became lost in the mix. Still other recipes turned to using jarred salsa, which resulted in a soggy mess. Our skillet casserole for two needed simplicity, so in the end, tasters liked a single fresh tomato, which cut through the richness of the cheese.

But the tortillas were still soggy no matter how few ingredients we used. Instead, we turned to tortilla chips. We stirred half of the tortilla chips into the sauce, nestled in the chicken breasts, and simmered the mixture until the chicken was cooked through and the tortilla chips broke down and thickened the sauce. We then shredded the chicken and stirred it back into the sauce, along with the chopped tomato, cilantro, and the remaining tortilla chips. The sauce coated the newly added tortilla chips just enough to moisten them, but they retained some of their texture and crunch.

For the cheese, we tried Monterey Jack, cheddar, and sharp cheddar cheese. The Monterey Jack was a bit mild, its flavor getting lost in the sauce. Cheddar was better, but the sharp cheddar proved our best option—its strong flavor held its own without overpowering the other ingredients. We topped the casserole with more shredded cheese and broiled it briefly to melt the cheese quickly without drying out the casserole. To bring a little color to the finished dish, we added a sprinkling of fresh cilantro. We now had a simple skillet tortilla casserole for two that's just as satisfying as any casserole meant to feed a crowd.

Tortilla Casserole

SERVES 2

To make the casserole spicier, add the greater amount of chipotle chile. Some brands of tortilla chips can be quite salty, so season sparingly with salt when cooking. Serve with sour cream.

- **2 (6 to 8-ounce) boneless, skinless chicken breasts, trimmed**
   Salt and pepper (see note)
- **2 tablespoons vegetable oil**
- **1 shallot, minced (about 3 tablespoons)**
- **2 garlic cloves, minced**
- **1–2 teaspoons minced chipotle chile in adobo sauce (see note)**
- **1¾ cups low-sodium chicken broth**
- **5 ounces tortilla chips, broken into 1-inch pieces (about 5 cups)**
- **1 tomato, cored, seeded, and chopped medium**
- **4 ounces sharp cheddar cheese, shredded (about 1 cup)**
- **2 tablespoons chopped fresh cilantro**

1. Adjust an oven rack to be about 6 inches from the broiler element, and heat the broiler. Pat the chicken dry with paper towels and season with salt and pepper. Heat 1 tablespoon of the oil in a 10-inch ovensafe skillet over medium-high heat until just smoking. Add the chicken and cook until lightly browned on both sides, about 5 minutes. Transfer to a plate and set aside.

2. Add the remaining 1 tablespoon oil, shallot, garlic, chipotle, and ¼ teaspoon salt to the skillet and cook over medium heat until fragrant, about 30 seconds.

Stir in the broth and bring to a simmer, scraping up any browned bits.

3. Stir in half of the tortilla chips. Nestle the chicken into the broth and chips, cover, and cook over medium-low heat until the thickest part of the breast registers 160 to 165 degrees on an instant-read thermometer, about 10 minutes. Transfer the chicken to a carving board. When the chicken is cool enough to handle, shred it into bite-sized pieces following the photo.

4. Return the shredded chicken to the skillet along with the tomato, ½ cup of the cheese, and 1 tablespoon of the cilantro. Stir in the remaining tortilla chips until moistened.

5. Sprinkle the remaining ½ cup cheese over the top and broil until golden, 5 to 10 minutes. Using potholders (the skillet handle will be hot), remove the skillet from the oven. Let the casserole cool for 5 minutes, then sprinkle with the remaining 1 tablespoon cilantro and serve.

NOTES FROM THE TEST KITCHEN

SHREDDING CHICKEN

Hold one fork in each hand, with the tines facing down. Insert the tines into the chicken and gently pull the forks away from each other, breaking the meat apart and into long, thin strands.

THE BEST TORTILLA CHIP

With an overwhelming array of tortilla chips lining supermarket aisles, how do you pick the best of the bunch? Despite their being made from just a handful of ingredients—cornmeal, oil, and salt—we found great variation in flavor among the different samples that we tried. As a general rule, we favored finer-textured chips and chips with a higher salt content. Our favorite tortilla chips are Santitas Authentic Mexican Style and **Tostitos 100 Percent White Corn Restaurant Style** tortilla chips.

POT-ROASTED STEAKS WITH ROOT VEGETABLES

A GOOD POT ROAST BY DEFINITION entails the transformation of a tough (read cheap), nearly unpalatable cut of meat into a tender, rich, flavorful roast by means of a slow, moist cooking process called braising. It should not be sliceable, but rather so tender that it falls apart at the touch of a fork—comfort food, pure and simple. Could we get the same soul-satisfying results with a smaller cut of meat, creating a warm and inviting winter supper for two?

The meat for pot roast should be well marbled with fat and connective tissue to provide the dish with the necessary flavor and moisture. Recipes typically call for roasts from the sirloin (or rump), round (leg), or chuck (shoulder). So for our smaller "pot roast," we tested cube steaks, top round steaks, bottom round steaks, chuck steaks, and blade steaks. Since we were using a small cut of meat, we found we could do our pot-roasting in a covered skillet, without having to lug out the Dutch oven. The cube steaks emerged from the oven surprisingly dry, and the top and bottom round cuts were both stringy and difficult to chew. The chuck steak had good flavor, but the intramuscular fat and sinew were unappealing. The unanimous choice for this dish was blade steak, which was praised for its meaty flavor and moist, tender texture. (There is a small line of fat that runs through this steak, but it is nearly undetectable after braising.)

Because pot roast is cooked with liquid at a low temperature, the exterior of the meat will not brown sufficiently unless it is first seared on the stovetop. High heat and a little oil were all that we needed to caramelize the exterior of the beef and boost both the flavor and the appearance of the dish.

Using water as the braising medium, we started with a modest ¼ cup and allowed the steaks to braise in the oven for up to two hours (an adequate amount of time to tenderize most any tough cut of meat). This produced meat that was unacceptably fibrous, even after two hours of cooking. After increasing the amount of liquid incrementally, we found that the moistest meat was produced when we added enough liquid to come halfway up the sides of the steaks, about 1½ cups. Flipping the meat halfway through cooking ensured that the steaks cooked evenly and became tender throughout.

Next we tested different liquids, hoping to give both the steaks and the sauce a flavor boost. In addition to the water, we tried chicken broth, beef broth, and red wine. Each failed to win tasters over completely when used on its own, but a combination of water, chicken broth, and red wine was just right. We found we needed to add the wine after the steaks were removed from the skillet; when added any earlier, its flavor penetrated the meat too deeply. Some sautéed celery, onion, and garlic added another layer of flavor to the sauce, and baby carrots and red potatoes required little prep and made our dish into a meal.

Some pot roast recipes call for thickening the sauce with a mixture of equal parts butter and flour; others use a slurry of cornstarch mixed with a little braising liquid. But both techniques made the sauce gravy-like—fine for a large roast but a little overwhelming for our steaks. Instead we chose to remove the steaks from the skillet once they had finished cooking, then we reduced the liquid over medium-high heat until the flavors were concentrated and the sauce thickened.

We now wondered if our smaller skillet pot roast could be cooked right on the stovetop. However, after a few rounds of stovetop cooking, we felt that it was too difficult to maintain a steady temperature and constant low simmer. Turning back to the oven, we found that 350 degrees was just right—high enough to keep the liquid at a bare simmer but low enough to prevent the meat from drying out. In just over an hour, our "pot roast" emerged rich, tender, and utterly satisfying.

Pot-Roasted Steaks with Root Vegetables

SERVES 2

A $7 to $10 bottle of medium-bodied red table wine made from a blend of grapes, such as a Côtes du Rhône, will work well here. The vegetables in the braising liquid do not get strained out before serving, so be mindful to cut them into fairly even pieces. Feel free to substitute 4 ounces parsnips for the carrots.

2 (8-ounce) top blade steaks, ¾ to 1 inch thick
   Salt and pepper
2 tablespoons vegetable oil

4 ounces baby carrots (about 14) (see note)
1 small onion, minced (about ½ cup)
1 celery rib, chopped medium
2 garlic cloves, minced
½ teaspoon sugar
1 teaspoon minced fresh thyme
1 cup low-sodium chicken broth
½ cup water
8 ounces small red potatoes (about 3), cut into 1-inch pieces
2 tablespoons dry red wine (see note)

1. Adjust an oven rack to the lower-middle position and heat the oven to 350 degrees. Pat the steaks dry with paper towels and season with salt and pepper. Heat 1 tablespoon of the oil in a 12-inch ovensafe non-stick skillet over medium-high heat until just smoking. Carefully lay the steaks in the skillet and cook until well browned on the first side, 3 to 5 minutes. Flip the steaks and continue to cook until well browned on the second side, 3 to 5 minutes longer. Transfer the steaks to a plate.

2. Add the remaining 1 tablespoon oil to the skillet and heat over medium heat until shimmering. Add the carrots, onion, and celery and cook, stirring often, until the onion is softened, 3 to 5 minutes. Stir in the garlic, sugar, and thyme and cook until fragrant, about 30 seconds. Stir in the broth and water and bring to a simmer.

3. Nestle the potatoes and browned steaks, along with any accumulated juice, into the skillet and bring to a simmer. Cover the skillet, transfer to the oven, and cook until a dinner fork slips easily in and out of the steaks, about 1¼ hours, flipping them halfway through cooking.

4. Using potholders (the skillet handle will be hot), remove the skillet from the oven. Transfer the steaks to a platter, tent loosely with foil, and let rest while finishing the sauce.

5. Being careful of the hot skillet handle, bring the cooking liquid left in the skillet to a simmer over medium-high heat and cook until it is slightly thickened, 5 to 7 minutes. Stir in the wine and continue to simmer for 1 minute longer. Season the sauce with salt and pepper to taste. Spoon the sauce and vegetables over the meat and serve.

BEEF AND VEGETABLE STIR-FRIES

A STIR-FRY IS AN IDEAL QUICK and easy weeknight meal for two—both protein and vegetables, cut into small pieces, are cooked quickly over high heat, then tossed together with a flavorful sauce and served over rice. There is nothing overly complicated about stir-fries; the key is plenty of intense heat. The pan must be hot enough to caramelize sugars, deepen flavors, and evaporate unnecessary juices all in a matter of minutes. Because a stir-fry comes together so quickly, it is critical to get all the ingredients organized ahead of time.

The piece of cookware you use is critical to success. We found that a large (12-inch) nonstick skillet is key; although a stir-fry for two doesn't require a huge quantity of ingredients, you want to avoid crowding them in the pan.

Most stir-fries start with some sort of protein. We decided we'd focus on one type of meat—a lean cut of beef—and create several flavor combinations. We found that freezing the beef for at least 15 minutes made it easier to cut the meat into wide, flat slices that would cook quickly and brown nicely. A simple yet flavorful marinade (tasters liked a combination of soy sauce and sugar) enhanced the meat without overpowering it.

With the preparation of our meat determined, we moved on to the cooking process. We browned one side of the beef without stirring, then stirred once to quickly brown the second side. Although choosing not to "stir-fry" seems counterintuitive and goes against the constant stirring suggested in many recipes, we found the continuous motion detracted from browning.

After the beef was cooked, we quickly removed it from the pan and added the vegetables in a single batch. We found that many vegetables cooked quickly over such high heat, but tougher vegetables needed a little extra help. We steamed snow peas and green beans by adding a bit of water to the pan and covering with a lid; once the vegetables were crisp-tender, the cover came off so the excess water could evaporate. We found the combinations of vegetables to be limitless, from snap peas and red bell pepper to green beans and shiitake mushrooms. Once you become comfortable with the techniques of stir-frying and learn how long each vegetable takes to cook, you can mix and match most any combination to your liking.

In most stir-fry recipes, the aromatics (typically garlic, ginger, and scallions) are added at the outset of the cooking process, when the pan is empty. But in batch after batch, by the time the stir-fry was done our aromatics had burned. We found we could avoid this by cooking the aromatics after the vegetables. When the vegetables were done, we pushed them to the sides of the pan, added the aromatics and some oil to the center, and cooked until they were fragrant but not colored, about 20 seconds. We then stirred the aromatics into the vegetables.

Finally, we turned to the sauce. We found that chicken broth makes the best base because it is not overpowering (though in one variation we substitute fresh tangerine juice for a unique flavor boost). Soy, oyster, and black bean sauces, as well as sesame oil, are great flavor enhancers, but moderation is key—a little goes a long way.

Determining our options for flavoring the sauce was fairly easy, but the sauce consistency needed work—most of the sauces we tried were too thin. The solution

STIR-FRIED BEEF WITH SNAP PEAS AND RED PEPPER

was as simple as adding a little cornstarch, which helped the sauce cling to the meat and vegetables.

Our components and process were set: We made the sauce, cooked the beef, and then cooked the vegetables and aromatics. We then added the beef back to the pan along with the sauce and cooked the whole dish just until the sauce thickened, which took all of about 30 seconds. Incredibly quick and simple, any of these stir-fries makes a perfect meal for two.

Stir-Fried Beef with Snap Peas and Red Pepper
SERVES 2

Freezing the beef for 15 minutes before slicing makes it easier to cut thin slices.

- 6 ounces flank steak, cut into 2-inch-wide strips with the grain, then cut across the grain into ⅛-inch-thick slices (see note)
- 1 tablespoon soy sauce
- 2 teaspoons sugar
- ¼ cup low-sodium chicken broth
- 2 tablespoons oyster sauce
- 1 tablespoon dry sherry
- ½ teaspoon cornstarch
- 1 garlic clove, minced
- 1½ teaspoons grated or minced fresh ginger
- 1 tablespoon vegetable oil
- 6 ounces sugar snap peas (about 2 cups), ends trimmed and strings removed
- ½ red bell pepper, stemmed, seeded, and sliced into ¼-inch-wide strips
- 1 tablespoon water

1. Toss the beef with the soy sauce and ½ teaspoon of the sugar in a medium bowl and let marinate for at least 10 minutes, or up to 1 hour. In a separate bowl, whisk the remaining 1½ teaspoons sugar, broth, oyster sauce, sherry, and cornstarch together. In another bowl, combine the garlic, ginger, and ½ teaspoon of the oil.

2. Drain the beef, discarding the marinade. Heat 1 teaspoon more oil in a 12-inch nonstick skillet over high heat until just smoking. Add the beef in a single layer, breaking up any clumps. Cook without stirring for 1 minute, then stir and continue to cook until the meat is browned, 1 to 2 minutes. Transfer the beef to a clean bowl.

3. Add the remaining 1½ teaspoons oil to the skillet and heat over high heat until just smoking. Add the snap peas and bell pepper and cook, stirring often, until the vegetables begin to brown, 3 to 4 minutes. Add the water, cover the skillet, and cook until the vegetables are crisp-tender, about 1 minute longer.

4. Uncover and clear the center of the skillet. Add the garlic mixture to the clearing and cook, mashing the mixture into the pan, until fragrant, 15 to 30 seconds. Stir the garlic mixture into the vegetables.

5. Return the beef, along with any accumulated juice, to the skillet and stir to combine. Whisk the broth mixture to recombine and add it to the skillet. Cook, stirring constantly, until thickened, about 30 seconds, and serve.

USE IT UP: RED BELL PEPPER

Romesco Sauce
MAKES ABOUT ½ CUP

This Spanish sauce is excellent spooned over grilled chicken or fish, or used as a dipping sauce for crudités. You can substitute sherry vinegar for the red wine vinegar.

- ½ red bell pepper, stemmed and seeded
- 1 plum tomato, cored, halved, and seeded
- 3 tablespoons slivered almonds, toasted (see page 226)
- 1 tablespoon extra-virgin olive oil
- 1 teaspoon red wine vinegar
- 1 garlic clove, minced
- Pinch cayenne pepper
- Salt and pepper

1. Adjust an oven rack to be about 3 inches from the broiler element and heat the broiler. Arrange the pepper and tomato on a foil-lined baking sheet, cut-sides down, and broil until their skins are charred but the flesh is still firm, about 9 minutes. Let the vegetables cool slightly, then peel off the charred skin and cut the vegetables into large chunks.

2. Process the almonds in a food processor until finely ground, about 15 seconds. Add the skinned pepper and tomato pieces, oil, vinegar, garlic, cayenne, and ¼ teaspoon salt and continue to process until the mixture is smooth, about 1 minute. Season with salt and pepper to taste before serving.

Stir-Fried Beef with Tangerine, Onion, and Snow Peas

SERVES 2

An orange can be substituted for the tangerines. If available, substitute ½ teaspoon toasted and ground Sichuan peppercorns for the red pepper flakes. Freezing the beef for 15 minutes before slicing makes it easier to cut thin slices.

- 6 **ounces flank steak, cut into 2-inch-wide strips with the grain, then cut across the grain into ⅛-inch-thick slices (see note)**
- 2 **tablespoons soy sauce**
- 2 **teaspoons light brown sugar**
- 6 **tablespoons fresh tangerine juice plus ½ teaspoon grated tangerine zest from 2 tangerines (see note)**
- ½ **teaspoon cornstarch**
- ½ **teaspoon toasted sesame oil**
- 1 **tablespoon vegetable oil**
- 1½ **teaspoons black bean sauce**
- 1½ **teaspoons grated or minced fresh ginger**
- 1 **garlic clove, minced**
- ⅛ **teaspoon red pepper flakes (see note)**
- 1 **small onion, halved and cut into ½-inch wedges**
- 5 **ounces snow peas (about 2 cups), ends trimmed and strings removed**
- 1 **tablespoon water**

1. Toss the beef with 1 tablespoon of the soy sauce and ½ teaspoon of the sugar in a medium bowl and let marinate for at least 10 minutes, or up to 1 hour. In a separate bowl, whisk the remaining 1 tablespoon soy sauce, remaining 1½ teaspoons sugar, tangerine juice, cornstarch, and sesame oil together. In another bowl, combine the tangerine zest, ½ teaspoon of the vegetable oil, black bean sauce, ginger, garlic, and pepper flakes.

2. Drain the beef, discarding the marinade. Heat 1 teaspoon more vegetable oil in a 12-inch nonstick skillet over high heat until just smoking. Add the beef in a single layer, breaking up any clumps. Cook without stirring for 1 minute, then stir and continue to cook until the meat is browned, 1 to 2 minutes. Transfer the beef to a clean bowl.

3. Add the remaining 1½ teaspoons vegetable oil to the skillet and heat over high heat until just smoking. Add the onion and cook, stirring often, until beginning to brown, 2 to 4 minutes. Add the snow peas and cook until spotty brown, about 2 minutes. Add the water,

cover the skillet, and cook until the vegetables are crisp-tender, about 1 minute longer.

4. Uncover and clear the center of the skillet. Add the garlic mixture to the clearing and cook, mashing the mixture into the pan, until fragrant, 15 to 30 seconds. Stir the garlic mixture into the vegetables.

5. Return the beef, along with any accumulated juice, to the skillet and stir to combine. Whisk the tangerine juice mixture to recombine, and add it to skillet. Cook, stirring constantly, until thickened, about 30 seconds, and serve.

Teriyaki Stir-Fried Beef with Green Beans and Shiitakes

SERVES 2

You can substitute ½ tablespoon white wine or sake mixed with ½ teaspoon sugar for the mirin. Freezing the beef for 15 minutes before slicing makes it easier to cut thin slices.

- 6 **ounces flank steak, cut into 2-inch-wide strips with the grain, then cut across the grain into ⅛-inch-thick slices (see note)**
- 2 **tablespoons soy sauce**
- 3½ **teaspoons sugar**
- ¼ **cup low-sodium chicken broth**
- 1½ **teaspoons mirin (see note)**
- ½ **teaspoon cornstarch**
- ⅛ **teaspoon red pepper flakes**
- 1 **tablespoon vegetable oil**
- 1½ **teaspoons grated or minced fresh ginger**
- 1 **garlic clove, minced**
- 4 **ounces shiitake mushrooms, stemmed and cut into 1-inch pieces**
- 6 **ounces green beans, trimmed and halved**
- 2 **tablespoons water**
- 1 **scallion, halved lengthwise and cut into 1½-inch lengths**

1. Toss the beef with 1 tablespoon of the soy sauce and ½ teaspoon of the sugar in a medium bowl and let marinate for at least 10 minutes, or up to 1 hour. In a separate bowl, whisk the remaining 1 tablespoon soy sauce, remaining 1 tablespoon sugar, broth, mirin, cornstarch, and pepper flakes together. In another bowl, combine ½ teaspoon of the oil, ginger, and garlic.

2. Drain the beef, discarding the marinade. Heat 1 teaspoon more oil in a 12-inch nonstick skillet over high heat until just smoking. Add the beef in a single layer, breaking up clumps. Cook without stirring for 1 minute, then stir and continue to cook until the meat is browned, 1 to 2 minutes. Transfer the beef to a clean bowl.

3. Add the remaining 1½ teaspoons oil to the skillet and heat over high heat until just smoking. Add the mushrooms and cook until beginning to brown, about 2 minutes. Add the green beans and cook, stirring often, until spotty brown, 2 to 4 minutes. Add the water, cover the skillet, and cook until the beans are crisp-tender, about 2 minutes longer.

4. Uncover and clear the center of the skillet. Add the garlic mixture to the clearing and cook, mashing the

mixture into the pan, until fragrant, 15 to 30 seconds. Stir the garlic mixture into the vegetables.

5. Return the beef, along with any accumulated juice, to the skillet, add the scallion, and stir to combine. Whisk the broth mixture to recombine and add it to the skillet. Cook, stirring constantly, until thickened, about 30 seconds, and serve.

STONE POT–STYLE KOREAN MIXED RICE

IN KOREA, A POPULAR SPIN on the basic stir-fry with white rice is *bibimbap*—tender yet chewy short-grain rice heaped into bowls and topped with an array of sautéed vegetables, beef, and a fried egg, each component arranged individually on the rice. Just before serving, this steaming bowl of rice is drizzled with sesame oil, and the egg yolk is broken and stirred throughout the mixture. Typically served in a hot stone bowl, the rice develops a lightly browned crust where it rests against the bowl, adding crispness to the rice's chewy texture.

Recipes for bibimbap can vary dramatically. Some rely heavily on leftovers, and others use fresh components. Whatever path is chosen, the technique is largely the same: The ingredients are sautéed separately to retain individual textures and flavors, and then these ingredients are spooned into separate portions on top of the rice. Given the time involved in preparing and combining the many different ingredients, we figured bibimbap would be much easier to prepare just for two people rather than for a crowd (the number of fried eggs alone would make it a challenge). Still, because it requires an extensive list of ingredients, we hoped to pare it down to the essentials and make it an even more suitable dish for two. And by cooking it in a skillet, we hoped to replicate the stone-bowl crust on the rice.

We started with the rice. Short-grain rice, we found, requires a different cooking technique from the long-grain rice that we most commonly use in the test kitchen, which needs a bit more liquid in order to soften correctly. But add too much liquid to short-grain rice, and it takes on a creamy, risotto-like texture. Testing a variety of water-to-rice ratios, we found a 1-to-1 ratio to be ideal. We simply brought the rice and water to a boil together in a skillet, reduced the heat to a simmer

TRIMMING BLADE STEAKS

1. Halve each steak lengthwise, leaving the gristle on one half.

2. Cut away the gristle from the half to which it is still attached.

RINSING RICE

To remove excess starch and prevent rice from becoming creamy, rinse the rice under cold water until the water runs clear.

HOW TO SEED A CUCUMBER

Peel and halve the cucumber lengthwise. With a spoon, use just enough pressure to scoop away the seeds and surrounding liquid.

WHAT IS KIMCHI?

Kimchi is a pickled vegetable condiment found at nearly every meal in Korea. It is also a common ingredient in many Korean stews and fried rice dishes. The type of kimchi available depends on the seasonality of ingredients and the region. There are more than 100 different varieties of kimchi; however, the most popular variety consists primarily of napa cabbage, scallions, garlic, and ground chiles in brine. It is packed in jars where it is allowed to ferment and build its spicy and pungent flavor.

for just a few minutes, then covered and removed the skillet from the heat to allow the rice to finish cooking. This gentle, three-step cooking technique yielded the rice we were looking for—tender grains with a slight chew.

To mimic the crust achieved in the hot stone bowl, we returned the skillet of cooked rice to medium-high heat for just under 10 minutes. Peeking beneath our large "pancake" of rice, we were delighted to find a perfectly golden crust. We divided the rice between two bowls and transferred them to a 200-degree oven to keep warm while we focused on our toppings.

Since our research uncovered dozens of combinations of toppings, we picked our favorites, starting with beef and shiitake mushrooms. In a hot skillet, the beef began to release its liquid while the mushrooms immediately soaked it up, keeping the pan dry and allowing the beef to caramelize. We then began the layering process, transferring the beef and shiitakes to the bowls of rice in the oven while we prepared the rest of the ingredients.

Sautéed spinach with garlic was another favorite topping, offering color, contrasting texture, and clean flavor. Using the same skillet, we added more oil, toasted the garlic for a moment, sautéed the spinach until wilted, and transferred it to the rice bowls in the oven.

Carrots, cucumbers, and mung bean sprouts were also plentiful in many recipes. We chose to pickle these remaining vegetables, freeing up the skillet to fry our eggs. The pickled vegetables offered a crisp, bright flavor to our bibimbap—and were appropriate, since bibimbap is often served with *kimchi* (Korean pickled vegetables). We simply grabbed a bottle of seasoned rice vinegar and tossed some with the vegetables. After 30 minutes the vegetables were well seasoned and crisp-tender.

Now we were ready to turn to the final component—the fried eggs, which are the crowning touch for bibimbap. Just before eating, each diner breaks the soft, runny egg yolk and stirs it throughout the rice, meat, and vegetables; the egg adds richness to an otherwise very lean dish. We cracked two eggs into our skillet, reduced the heat to low, and covered the skillet until the whites were cooked through and tender, and the yolks were hot but still runny. The eggs slid easily out of our nonstick skillet and into each bowl. We then gave the dish a final flourish with a drizzle of rich, nutty sesame oil.

Stone Pot–Style Korean Mixed Rice

SERVES 2

You can substitute sushi rice for the short-grain rice. You can also substitute medium- or long-grain rice; however, you will need to increase the amount of water to 1½ cups and simmer until the grains are tender, 18 to 20 minutes, before letting the rice sit off the heat in step 2. Freezing the beef for 15 minutes before slicing makes it easier to cut thin slices. Serve with kimchi (see page 20) and hot sauce.

PICKLED VEGETABLES

- ½ cup bean sprouts
- 1 carrot, peeled and grated on the large holes of a box grater
- ½ cucumber, peeled, halved lengthwise, and seeded, sliced ¼ inch thick
- ½ cup seasoned rice vinegar

RICE, BEEF, SPINACH, AND EGGS

- 1 cup short-grain white rice (see note), rinsed
- 1 cup water
- 4 ounces blade steak, trimmed (see page 20) and cut into ⅛-inch-thick slices (see note)
- 1 tablespoon soy sauce
- 4 teaspoons vegetable oil
- 4 ounces shiitake mushrooms, stemmed and sliced ¼ inch thick
- 2 garlic cloves, minced
- 5 ounces baby spinach (about 5 cups)
  Salt and pepper
- 2 large eggs, cracked into 2 small bowls
- 1½ teaspoons toasted sesame oil

1. **FOR THE PICKLED VEGETABLES:** Toss the sprouts, carrot, cucumber, and vinegar together in a medium bowl. Press lightly on the vegetables to submerge in the vinegar as much as possible, then cover with plastic wrap and refrigerate for 30 minutes, or up to 24 hours. Drain the vegetables, discarding the vinegar, and set aside.

2. **FOR THE RICE, BEEF, SPINACH, AND EGGS:** Adjust an oven rack to the middle position, place two individual serving bowls on the rack, and heat the oven to 200 degrees. Bring the rice and water to a boil in a 10-inch nonstick skillet over high heat, then cover, reduce the heat to low, and cook for 7 minutes. Remove the rice from the heat, and let sit, covered, until tender, about 15 minutes.

USE IT UP: CUCUMBER

Creamy Dill Cucumber Salad

SERVES 2

This refreshing salad is a great accompaniment to poached or grilled salmon or pan-roasted chicken breasts.

- ½ cucumber, peeled, halved lengthwise, and seeded (see page 20), sliced thin
- 1 small shallot, sliced thin
  Salt
- 3 tablespoons sour cream
- 1 tablespoon minced fresh dill
- 1 teaspoon cider vinegar
  Pinch sugar
  Pepper

Toss the cucumber and shallot with ¼ teaspoon salt in a colander and let drain for at least 15 minutes, or up to 1 hour. Whisk the sour cream, dill, vinegar, and sugar together in a small bowl. Stir in the drained cucumbers and shallot, season with salt and pepper to taste, and refrigerate until chilled before serving.

3. Return the skillet of rice to medium-high heat and cook, uncovered, until the rice forms a brown crust on the bottom, 7 to 9 minutes. Divide the rice between the bowls in the oven, and cover with foil. Wipe out the skillet with a wad of paper towels.

4. Toss the beef and soy sauce together in a medium bowl. Heat 2 teaspoons of the vegetable oil in the skillet over medium-high heat until just smoking. Add the beef, with any accumulated juice, and mushrooms and cook until the beef is cooked through and the mushrooms are soft, about 3 minutes. Divide the mixture between the bowls in the oven.

5. Add 1 teaspoon more vegetable oil and garlic to the skillet and return to medium-high heat until the garlic is sizzling and fragrant, about 30 seconds. Stir in the spinach and cook, tossing constantly, until wilted, about 1 minute. Season with salt and pepper to taste, and divide between the bowls in the oven.

6. Wipe out the skillet with a wad of paper towels. Add the remaining 1 teaspoon vegetable oil to the skillet, and return to medium-high heat until shimmering. Slide the eggs into the skillet from opposite sides of the

pan and season with salt and pepper. Cover and cook until the whites are set but the yolks are still runny, 2 to 3 minutes.

7. Uncover the eggs and remove the skillet from the heat. Remove the bowls of rice from the oven, and slide one egg on top of each bowl. Drizzle with the sesame oil, add the pickled vegetables, and serve immediately.

PAN-FRIED PORK CHOPS WITH SUCCOTASH

PAN-FRIED PORK CHOPS ARE A SOUTHERN CLASSIC. When they're done right, a crispy exterior gives way to moist, juicy pork. And pan-frying is an ideal cooking technique for a small number of people—you can fit the chops in the skillet all at once, eliminating the need for extra oil and multiple batches. But when things go wrong, a whole host of problems can occur—from soggy and chewy chops to those that are burnt on the outside and raw in the middle. The key to these chops lies in the exactitude of the technique. Our goal was to find the perfect ratio of crispy pork chop exterior to moist interior. And while we were at it, we wanted to make these pork chops a complete skillet meal for two. We thought succotash—the classic American vegetable blend of lima beans, corn, and red or green peppers—would be a good complement to our pork chops. With its sweet flavors and blend of textures—crisp, starchy, and soft—succotash makes an ideal foil to crunchy pork chops.

Our first task was choosing the right pork chop. After testing boneless and bone-in chops, we settled on boneless chops, simply because they proved to be easier to work with and faster-cooking. We also noted that the thickness of the chops should not exceed ½ inch, or we risked burning the exterior before the interior could finish cooking. Pressing on the chops with our hands helped to flatten them slightly, giving them more surface area for the breading to adhere to and giving us more crunch per chop.

As for the breading, we were presented with a whole host of options. A lot of Southern-style dishes (pork chops with milk gravy, for example) use only a light dusting of highly seasoned flour. Although tasty, these chops are far from crispy. A batter coating might work for deep-frying in a large pot, but not for the shallow-fry

we were attempting in our skillet. We focused on bread crumbs and turned to the test kitchen's standard breading method of dusting with flour, dipping in beaten egg, and rolling in bread crumbs. Tasters unanimously favored fresh bread crumbs over prepared store-bought crumbs because they had more flavor. We also found that fresh crumbs absorbed less oil than dried crumbs, because of their moisture content. We processed the fresh crumbs with garlic powder and cayenne in addition to the standard salt and pepper, and this gave them a nice flavor boost.

But we were having a little trouble making the breading adhere to the chops. Our research turned up a recipe that used mustard in addition to eggs to make the crumbs stick. We tried it and were happy to find that the mustard not only improved the holding power of the eggs but also added a welcome flavor boost. Tasters like the spicy, tangy complexity of Dijon.

We wondered how far we could take this method, and on the advice of a fellow test cook, we whisked a few tablespoons of flour into our mustard-egg mixture with the hope of making an even stickier coating on the pork chops, all the better for the bread crumbs to adhere to. The tip paid off, and we now had a flavorful and crispy bread-crumb coating that stuck to our pork chops, not to the pan.

With our chops resting in a 200-degree oven, we wiped out the remaining oil in the skillet so we had a clean canvas for building our succotash. We began by briefly sautéing minced red bell pepper—green peppers tasted unpleasantly bitter—and onion in butter, which would add an element of sweetness and depth. Having had success using frozen corn and lima beans in other recipes, we tried them here with good results—and using frozen vegetables was ideal because there was no prep work involved and we could use only what we needed. Both benefited from a bit of sautéing to intensify their mild flavor, so after the onion had softened we added the corn and lima beans to the skillet, cooking them both until softened, about five minutes.

With the foundation for our succotash in place, we just needed to add a little extra flavor. Tasters favored a modest amount of tarragon; its mild anise flavor added depth to the succotash and we knew it would complement the pork. We transferred the succotash to a platter and topped it with our warm pork chops, and tasters dug in with smiles on their faces.

PAN-FRIED PORK CHOPS WITH SUCCOTASH

Pan-Fried Pork Chops with Succotash

SERVES 2

If the pork is "enhanced" (see page 80 for more information), do not brine. If brining the pork, do not season the chops with salt in step 2. Fresh corn, cut from the cob, can be substituted for the frozen corn if desired; the cooking time will be the same. Feel free to substitute fresh parsley, cilantro, or basil for the tarragon. See page 17 for a recipe to use up the leftover red bell pepper.

PORK CHOPS

- 7 tablespoons unbleached all-purpose flour
- 2 large eggs
- 2 tablespoons Dijon mustard
- 2 slices high-quality white sandwich bread, torn into 1-inch pieces
- ½ teaspoon garlic powder
  Salt and pepper
- ⅛ teaspoon cayenne pepper
- 2 (5 to 6-ounce) boneless pork chops, trimmed, sides slit (see photo), and brined if desired (see note; see page 76)
- ½ cup vegetable oil

SUCCOTASH

- 2 tablespoons unsalted butter
- 1 small onion, minced (about ½ cup)
- ½ red bell pepper, stemmed, seeded, and minced
- ¾ cup frozen baby lima beans (about 3 ounces), thawed
- ¾ cup frozen corn (about 3 ounces), thawed (see note)
- 2 teaspoons minced fresh tarragon (see note)
  Salt and pepper
  Lemon wedges, for serving

1. FOR THE PORK CHOPS: Adjust an oven rack to the middle position and heat the oven to 200 degrees. Place ¼ cup of the flour in a shallow dish. In a second shallow dish, whisk the eggs and mustard until combined, then whisk in the remaining 3 tablespoons flour until almost smooth, with just a few pea-sized lumps. Pulse the bread, garlic powder, ¼ teaspoon salt, ¼ teaspoon pepper, and cayenne together in a food processor until coarsely ground, about 8 pulses, then transfer the mixture to a third shallow dish.

2. Pat the pork chops dry, then flatten them to an even ½-inch thickness by pressing on them firmly with your hand, and season with salt and pepper. Dredge the pork chops in the flour and shake off the excess. Using tongs, coat the chops with the egg mixture, allowing the excess to drip off. Coat all sides of the chops with a thick layer of bread crumbs, pressing on the crumbs to help them adhere.

3. Heat the oil in a 12-inch nonstick skillet over medium heat until shimmering. Gently place the pork chops in the skillet and cook until well browned on both sides, 6 to 8 minutes, flipping them halfway through cooking. Transfer the chops to a wire rack set over a rimmed baking sheet, and let rest in the warm oven until the center of the chops registers 150 degrees on an instant-read thermometer.

4. FOR THE SUCCOTASH: Meanwhile, pour off any oil left in the skillet and wipe it clean with a wad of paper towels. Add 1 tablespoon of the butter to the skillet and melt over medium-high heat. Add the onion and bell pepper and cook, stirring occasionally, until softened, 3 to 5 minutes. Stir in the lima beans and corn and cook until heated through and softened, about 5 minutes.

5. Off the heat, stir in the remaining 1 tablespoon butter and tarragon, and season with salt and pepper to taste. Serve the pork chops with the succotash and lemon wedges.

NOTES FROM THE TEST KITCHEN

NO MORE CURLED PORK CHOPS

To prevent your pork chops from curling in a hot pan, cut two slits, about 2 inches apart, through one side of each chop. This method works for both boneless and bone-in chops.

GREEK-STYLE LAMB PITA SANDWICHES

LAMB, WITH ITS ULTRA-RICH FLAVOR, offers the home cook a welcome break from the same old chicken, pork, and beef. One of our favorite ways to enjoy lamb is in Greek-style sandwiches called *gyros*. What's not to love about marinated lamb, tomato, lettuce, and a cooling cucumber-yogurt sauce stuffed inside a soft pita? But the traditional cooking method—one that involves layering and stacking several pounds of marinated sliced leg of lamb onto an electric vertical rotisserie to form a tightly packed cylinder of meat which is then cooked for hours and sliced—is clearly not suited to the home cook, much less a weeknight dinner for two. We'd have to find another way to cook the meat.

Flipping through cookbooks revealed that others had the same dilemma: how to cook the gyro's defining ingredient, the meat. One recipe called for quickly sautéing thin strips of marinated lamb. Trimming and slicing the fatty roast into thin strips required quite a bit of effort, and the end result resembled a bad stir-fry. A similar broiled version wasn't much better. Another recipe produced a lamb meat loaf sliced into thin strips—a novel approach, but one that took too long to prepare and yielded an odd, spongy texture.

We decided to try one last recipe: pan-fried ground lamb patties flavored with oregano and onion. Although these patties sure didn't look like gyros, the texture was close, and we didn't need to buy an entire roast. We'd found our jumping-off point.

To add flavor to the ground lamb, we used traditional Greek ingredients—oregano, chopped onion, and minced garlic—before rolling the mixture into balls and flattening them into small disks. But once the seasoned pan-fried patties were cooked through, tasters thought their texture was too dense and dry. Taking a cue from a recipe for well-done hamburgers, we incorporated a modified panade (a paste of fresh bread crumbs and milk) to make the meat juicier. But now tasters found the patties a little too mushy. At the supermarket, all we'd been able to find were pocketed pitas with tops that needed to be cut off before they could be filled. What if we replaced the white bread crumbs with crumbs from this drier bread? This gave the patties a sturdier structure and more savory flavor.

In order to achieve the meat's traditional duality of texture—crisp outside, moist inside—we tried cooking the patties in a large oiled skillet over medium-high heat. Even though they didn't look like typical chipped gyro meat, they fooled our tasters' taste buds into believing what their eyes did not.

Just because we had nicely warmed pitas and well-seasoned meat didn't mean we were done. What's a

NOTES FROM THE TEST KITCHEN

THE BEST WHOLE-MILK YOGURT

If you cannot find Greek yogurt, you can use plain whole-milk yogurt in our Tzatziki Sauce. It has three times as much fat as low-fat yogurt and far more flavor, making it the most suitable replacement for Greek yogurt. Of the four national brands of whole-milk yogurt that we tasted, two were too sour. Tasters preferred the whole-milk yogurts with the most fat—**Brown Cow Cream Top Plain Yogurt** and Stonyfield Farm Organic Whole Milk Plain Yogurt. Brown Cow's slightly richer flavor profile made it the overall winner.

STORING ICEBERG LETTUCE

We tried four storage methods to see which was most effective at keeping cored and washed iceberg lettuce fresh: wrapped in moist paper towels and stored in a plastic shopping bag, kept in its original perforated cellophane bag, wrapped in moist paper towels and stored in a zipper-lock plastic bag, and wrapped tightly in plastic wrap.

After a week, all the samples were still mostly fresh and crisp. At the two-week mark, the differences were more apparent. The two samples wrapped in moist paper towels retained the crispest leaves, which makes sense because moisture loss is often to blame when lettuce goes bad. But the winner turned out to be the sample wrapped with paper towels and stored in the shopping bag. The flimsy, porous shopping bag allowed some airflow, preventing the buildup of too much moisture and delaying spoilage.

FETA CHEESE

Within the European Union, only cheese made in Greece from a mixture of sheep's and goat's milk can be legally called feta, but most of the feta in American supermarkets is made from pasteurized cow's milk that has been curdled, shaped into blocks, sliced, and steeped in brine. Feta can range from soft to semihard and has a tangy, salty flavor. Feta dries out quickly when removed from its brine, so always store it in the brine in which it is packed (we do not recommend buying precrumbled "dry" feta).

GREEK-STYLE LAMB PITA SANDWICHES WITH TZATZIKI SAUCE

gyro sandwich without the tzatziki sauce? The cooling combination of yogurt, garlic, cucumber, dill or mint, and lemon juice is more than just a condiment; it's an essential component of this dish. Greek yogurt is dense and rich, making it ideal for this sauce, but we also had good results with plain whole-milk yogurt, which closely approximates the creamy texture of the real stuff if drained for 30 minutes in a lined strainer. Salting the cucumber first also reduced excess moisture.

With our components ready, all we had to do now was assemble the sandwich. Taking one warmed pita at a time, we spread half of the sauce on one side before adding three lamb patties and filling the rest of the space with tomatoes, shredded lettuce, and an unconventional but welcome addition of feta cheese. A single bite confirmed that this was an excellent alternative to the usual weeknight dinner.

USE IT UP: PITA BREAD

Pita Chips
MAKES 24 CHIPS

Pita bread can go stale quickly, so pita chips are a great way to use up the extras. This recipe can be doubled. The chips can be stored in an airtight container for up to 3 days. If necessary, briefly recrisp in a 350-degree oven for a few minutes before serving.

- 2 (8-inch) pita breads, split open, each round cut into 6 wedges
- 2 tablespoons olive oil
- ½ teaspoon salt

1. Adjust an oven rack to the middle position and heat the oven to 350 degrees. Spread the pita triangles, smooth-side down, over a rimmed baking sheet. Brush the top of each chip lightly with oil and sprinkle with salt.

2. Bake the wedges until they begin to crisp and brown lightly, 6 to 8 minutes. Flip the chips smooth-side up, switch and rotate the baking sheet, and continue to bake until the chips are fully toasted, 6 to 8 minutes longer.

3. Remove the baking sheet from the oven and cool the chips before serving.

Greek-Style Lamb Pita Sandwiches with Tzatziki Sauce
SERVES 2

If you cannot find Greek yogurt, you can substitute plain whole-milk yogurt that has been drained: Line a fine-mesh strainer with 3 paper coffee filters or a triple layer of paper towels and set it over a bowl. Spoon the yogurt into the lined strainer, cover, and refrigerate for 30 minutes. If using pocketless pitas, heat them in a single layer on a baking sheet in a 350-degree oven for 5 minutes. Do not cut the top quarters off the pocketless pitas; instead, use a portion of a third pita to create the pieces in step 3. See page 8 for a recipe to use up the leftover feta.

TZATZIKI SAUCE

- ¼ cucumber, peeled, halved, and seeded (see page 20), chopped fine (about ½ cup) Salt
- ½ cup Greek yogurt (see note)
- 2 teaspoons fresh lemon juice
- 1 small garlic clove, minced
- 2 teaspoons chopped fresh mint or dill

PITA SANDWICHES

- 2 (8-inch) pita breads (see note)
- 1 small onion, chopped coarse (about ½ cup)
- 2 teaspoons fresh lemon juice
- 2 teaspoons minced fresh mint or dill
- 1 garlic clove, minced
- ¼ teaspoon salt
- ⅛ teaspoon pepper
- 8 ounces ground lamb
- 2 teaspoons vegetable oil
- 1 small tomato, sliced thin, for serving
- 1 cup shredded iceberg lettuce, for serving
- 1 ounce feta cheese, crumbled (about ¼ cup), for serving

1. FOR THE TZATZIKI SAUCE: Toss the cucumber with ⅛ teaspoon salt in a colander set over a bowl and let drain for 30 minutes.

2. Combine the yogurt, drained cucumber, lemon juice, garlic, and mint in a bowl and season with salt to taste.

3. FOR THE PITA SANDWICHES: Adjust an oven rack to the middle position and heat the oven to 350 degrees. Trim the top quarter off each pita bread, then tear the trimmed quarters into 1-inch pieces. (You should have about ⅓ cup pita pieces.) Stack the pitas and wrap tightly with foil.

4. Process the onion, lemon juice, mint, garlic, salt, pepper, and pita bread pieces in a food processor to make a smooth paste, about 30 seconds, then transfer to a medium bowl. Add the lamb and gently mix with your hands until thoroughly combined. Divide the mixture into 6 equal portions and roll into balls. Gently flatten the balls into round disks, about ½ inch thick and 2½ inches in diameter.

5. Place the foil-wrapped pitas directly on the oven rack and heat for 10 minutes. Meanwhile, heat the oil in a 12-inch nonstick skillet over medium-high heat until just smoking. Add the patties and cook until well browned and a crust forms, 3 to 4 minutes.

6. Flip the patties, reduce the heat to medium, and cook until well browned and a crust forms on the second side, about 5 minutes longer. Transfer the patties to a paper towel–lined plate.

7. Spread ¼ cup of the tzatziki sauce inside each pita. Divide the patties evenly among the pitas and add half of the tomato slices, ½ cup shredded lettuce, and 2 tablespoons feta to each sandwich. Serve.

POACHED COD

IN CLASSIC FRENCH COOKING, the term *à la nage* (literally, "in the swim") refers to poaching food—often scallops, shrimp, or a fin fish—in a flavorful liquid, which is then reduced and served over the seafood. We thought cooking fish using this method would make a great dinner for two, but we wanted to put our own twist on it. Our goals were to streamline the technique and to add some vegetables to create a more substantial dish.

Our first step was to decide what type of fish we wanted to use. After trying a variety of fish fillets, tasters favored flaky, mild fish because it allowed the delicate flavors of the poaching liquid to take center stage. Cod became our first choice for its flavor and texture, although haddock and halibut were close seconds.

Determining the exact technique for cooking the fish was our next challenge. After experimenting with various heat levels and liquid amounts, we learned that the keys to this cooking method are twofold: Use low

heat (so that the fish cooks gently) and a skillet with a tight-fitting lid (to trap the heat so that the fish partially simmers and partially steams). We also found that for two fish fillets, we didn't need a whole lot of liquid. Just ⅔ cup was all it took to cook the fish and yield a broth to serve it in.

With the poaching method down, we turned our attention to the poaching liquid. Instead of the classic French components of broth, white wine, and herbs, we decided to incorporate some Asian flavors for a more modern twist. Mirin took the place of the wine, soy sauce added depth, and miso—a fermented paste of soybeans and rice, barley, or rye—contributed a salty, rich, savory flavor. With such bold flavors, we determined that water, not broth, made the best possible cooking liquid.

To round out the dish and make it a meal, we wanted to add some vegetables. Earthy shiitake mushrooms seemed like a natural pairing with our Asian-inspired poaching liquid; to intensify their flavor, we sautéed them in the skillet before cooking the fish. And, in keeping with the Japanese theme, shelled edamame (green soybeans) became the second addition—we simmered them in the broth with the fish.

Tasters liked the flavors of this dish, but they felt it was a little too one-dimensional. A sprinkling of toasted sesame oil did the trick, lending a rich, nutty flavor to the broth. For a finishing touch of flavor and color, we added thinly sliced scallion. Served in shallow bowls, this dish is so impressive-looking, you'll be surprised at how simple it is to make.

NOTES FROM THE TEST KITCHEN

ALL ABOUT MISO

Miso is the Japanese word for "bean paste." Commonly found in Asian—most notably Japanese—cuisines, miso is a fermented bean paste of soybeans and rice, barley, or rye. Miso paste is incredibly versatile, suitable for use in soups, braises, dressings, and sauces, as well as for topping grilled foods. This salty, deep-flavored paste ranges in strength and color from a mild, pale yellow (referred to as white) to stronger-flavored red or brownish-black, depending on the fermentation method and ingredients. Avoid miso labeled "light," as this is an American low-sodium product whose flavor pales in comparison to the real thing. Miso can be found in well-stocked grocery stores and Japanese or Asian markets. It will keep for up to a year in the refrigerator.

Poached Cod with Miso, Shiitakes, and Edamame

SERVES 2

Haddock or halibut can be substituted for the cod. You can substitute white, brown, barley, or brown rice miso for the red miso, but do not substitute "light" miso; its flavor is too mild. In step 2, adjust the heat as needed to maintain a very gentle simmer.

    2   teaspoons vegetable oil
    4   ounces shiitake mushrooms, stemmed
        and sliced ¼ inch thick
    1   cup shelled frozen edamame (about 4 ounces),
        thawed
    ⅔   cup water
    2   teaspoons soy sauce
    2   teaspoons mirin
    2   garlic cloves, smashed and peeled
    1   (1-inch) piece fresh ginger, peeled, sliced
        into ¼-inch-thick coins, and smashed
    2   (6-ounce) cod fillets, 1¼ inches thick (see note)
        Salt and pepper
    2   teaspoons red miso paste (see note)
    ½   teaspoon toasted sesame oil
    1   scallion, sliced thin

1. Heat the vegetable oil in a 10-inch skillet over medium heat until shimmering. Add the mushrooms and cook until they have released their liquid and are lightly browned, 3 to 4 minutes. Transfer the mushrooms to a bowl.

2. Combine the edamame, water, soy sauce, mirin, garlic, and ginger in the skillet. Pat the cod dry with paper towels and season with salt and pepper. Gently nestle the cod into the skillet, spooning some of the liquid over the top. Bring to a gentle simmer, cover, and cook over medium-low heat until the flesh is opaque and flakes apart when gently prodded with a paring knife, 5 to 7 minutes.

3. Using a slotted spatula, gently transfer the fish to shallow individual serving bowls. Remove and discard the garlic and ginger. Stir the mushrooms, miso, and sesame oil into the cooking liquid and allow to warm through, about 30 seconds.

4. Using a slotted spoon, transfer the vegetables to the bowls with the fish. Pour the hot broth over the fish, sprinkle with the scallion, and serve.

POACHED SALMON

POACHED SALMON MAKES FOR A SPEEDY DINNER with minimal cleanup, as it requires just one pot. Add a simple sauce, and the dish is even more flavorful. All too often, though, salmon is overcooked and has a washed-out flavor that not even the richest sauce can redeem. We were determined to do it right and sought a way to achieve great texture and flavor in the salmon.

Typical recipes for poached salmon call for a poaching broth made up of water, wine, herbs, vegetables, and aromatics. The broth's strong flavors are absorbed by the fish, which helps compensate for the rich salmon flavor that leaches out into the liquid. This method produces flavorful results for a simple dinner for two, but to us, it seemed wasteful to use fresh onions, carrots, celery, leeks, and parsley, only to dump them and the stock down the drain at the end.

Determined to use and waste less broth, we poached the salmon in just enough liquid to come ½ inch up the sides of the fillets. Ironically, the flavor of our fish was now coming out better than when it was poached in more liquid. Given this fact, we could skip making the poaching broth in advance and create just a simple broth of water, wine, minced shallot, herbs, and lemon juice. Because we were cooking two fillets, we needed just ½ cup of liquid in a 10-inch skillet. The flavor of our poached salmon was now light, fresh, and delicate. Next, we could focus on keeping the texture soft and not dried out.

To preserve the salmon's supple texture, we knew to remove it from the poaching broth just a few degrees before it was done so it could finish cooking while it rested and we made the sauce. When it reached 125 degrees, we set the salmon aside. Unfortunately, we encountered a problem we had seen before—the fillets were cooked just right, with the exception of the bottoms, which had been in direct contact with the hot pan and were overcooked. To elevate the fish, we placed thin lemon slices on the bottom of the skillet, then placed the fillets on top. Poaching the salmon this way meant we could infuse the poaching broth with lemon flavor (and skip the lemon juice) while also raising the fillets to prevent the bottoms from overcooking. Our salmon was now perfectly cooked.

It was time to focus on the vinaigrette. With the salmon cooked and resting, we just enhanced the remaining

POACHED SALMON WITH HERB AND CAPER VINAIGRETTE

broth by reducing and straining it, then mixing in a bit more shallot and fresh herbs. We also added a tablespoon each of capers and olive oil; the capers enhanced the brininess of the fish, and the olive oil added some much needed richness.

We had made a simple vinaigrette that paired exceptionally well with our poached salmon—all without losing valuable flavor or wasting ingredients.

Poached Salmon with Herb and Caper Vinaigrette

SERVES 2

If you can't find skinless salmon at the store, you can easily remove the skin yourself, following the photos on page 33.

- 1 lemon
- 1 tablespoon chopped fresh parsley, stems reserved
- 1 tablespoon chopped fresh tarragon, stems reserved
- 1 shallot, minced (about 3 tablespoons)
- ¼ cup dry white wine
- ¼ cup water
- 2 (6-ounce) skinless center-cut salmon fillets, about 1½ inches thick (see note)
- 1 tablespoon capers, rinsed and coarsely chopped
- 1 tablespoon extra-virgin olive oil
- 1½ teaspoons honey
  Salt and pepper

1. Trim the top and bottom off the lemon, then cut it into about eight ¼-inch-thick slices. Arrange the lemon slices in a single layer over the bottom of a 10-inch skillet. Scatter the parsley stems, tarragon stems, and 1 tablespoon of the shallot over the lemon slices and add the wine and water.

2. Lay the salmon fillets in the skillet, skinned-side down, on top of the lemons. Set the pan over high heat and bring to a simmer. Reduce the heat to low, cover, and cook until the sides of the salmon are opaque and the thickest parts register 125 degrees on an instant-read thermometer, 10 to 15 minutes. Remove the pan from the heat and, using a spatula, carefully transfer the salmon and lemon slices to a paper towel–lined plate. Tent the salmon loosely with foil and let rest while making the vinaigrette.

3. While the salmon rests, return the pan to medium-high heat and continue to simmer the cooking liquid until it has reduced to 1 tablespoon, 3 to 5 minutes. Meanwhile, combine the remaining 2 tablespoons shallot, chopped parsley, chopped tarragon, capers, olive oil, and honey in a medium bowl. Strain the reduced cooking liquid through a fine-mesh strainer into the bowl with the shallot-herb mixture, whisk to combine, and season with salt and pepper to taste.

4. Season the salmon lightly with salt and pepper. Using a spatula, carefully transfer the salmon fillets to individual serving plates, discarding the lemon slices, and serve with the vinaigrette.

TERIYAKI-GLAZED SALMON FILLETS

BECAUSE SALMON IS SO RICH AND SATISFYING— and almost always available at the fish counter—we felt it would be ideal as the basis for another skillet supper for two. We sought a cooking method that would make use of the fish's high oil content and natural moistness while also indulging our love for fish fillets that come out of the pan with a crisp, deeply golden crust. Pan-searing seemed like the obvious route, and we wanted to add a glaze—one that would form a glossy, deeply caramelized crust and permeate the flesh of the fish. First we would focus on cooking the fish, then we would turn our attention to creating a flavorful glaze.

Cooking the salmon was easy. Using skinless fillets, we seared the fish in a nonstick skillet for about 5 minutes per side, which developed a nice crust. We found that the fish, like most cuts of meat, had the best texture when we removed it from the pan before it was cooked through and allowed it to finish cooking as it rested.

Tasters wanted an Asian-inspired glaze full of bold flavors, and our thoughts turned to teriyaki sauce. The salty-sweet sauce is a staple at most Japanese restaurants, where it is served with a variety of meats and fish. Our plan was to reduce the sauce to a syrupy glaze that would coat the salmon.

Bottled teriyaki was uniformly rejected in favor of a homemade sauce, which took just five minutes to prepare. Working with various amounts of soy sauce, sugar, and mirin (a sweetened Japanese rice wine that tasters

Tart and Tangy Slaw

SERVES 2

This crisp, flavorful salad is a lively alternative to basic coleslaw.

- ½ small head napa cabbage (about 8 ounces), cored and shredded (about 4 cups)
- 1 carrot, peeled and shredded
  Salt
- 2 tablespoons raisins
- 2 tablespoons cider vinegar
- 1 tablespoon vegetable oil
- 1 teaspoon Dijon mustard
- 1½ teaspoons sugar
  Pinch red pepper flakes

1. Toss the cabbage and carrot with ½ teaspoon salt in a colander set over a medium bowl. Let sit until wilted, about 1 hour. Rinse the cabbage with cold water, then drain and dry well with paper towels. Transfer to a large bowl.

2. Bring the raisins, vinegar, oil, mustard, sugar, and pepper flakes to a boil in a small saucepan over medium heat. Pour the mixture over the cabbage and toss to coat. Serve warm or cover and refrigerate until chilled, at least 1 hour or up to 1 day.

preferred to sake), we achieved the best balance of sweetness and saltiness with ¼ cup each of soy sauce and sugar and just 1 tablespoon of mirin.

After searing the salmon on one side, we flipped it, added the sauce ingredients, and allowed the fish to finish cooking through while the sauce reduced to a sticky glaze. But getting the glaze consistency just right was difficult—no matter how closely we watched it as it simmered, it was either as thick as molasses or so thin and watery that it didn't adhere to the salmon at all. A minimal amount of cornstarch (1 teaspoon) quickly solved this problem, but other problems remained: Trying to achieve simultaneously just the right degree of doneness for the fish as well as the right consistency for the glaze was nearly impossible, and the glaze had a tendency to develop an unpleasant fishy flavor when cooked directly with the salmon. The solution turned out to be a simple one—cooking the glaze and the

salmon separately. After searing the salmon, we set it aside before adding the sauce to the skillet to reduce to a syrupy glaze.

We now wanted a quick and fresh-tasting side dish to accompany our salmon, one that could be made in the same skillet. A quick-cooking stir-fry of cabbage and shiitakes seemed like the perfect match for the teriyaki glaze. Cooking the mushrooms alone for 2 minutes encouraged browning and gave them a head start on the cabbage. The cabbage was next into the skillet, and it wilted in about 5 minutes. To build the flavor of the cabbage and mushroom mixture, we stirred in garlic, ginger, scallions, and sesame oil.

An unbeatable combination of flavors and textures (salty and sweet, tender and crunchy), our skillet teriyaki-glazed salmon fillets make a satisfying meal any night of the week.

Teriyaki-Glazed Salmon Fillets with Stir-Fried Cabbage and Shiitakes

SERVES 2

If you can't find skinless salmon at the store, you can easily remove the skin yourself by following the photos.

- ¼ cup soy sauce
- ¼ cup sugar
- 1 tablespoon mirin
- 1 teaspoon cornstarch
- 2 scallions, sliced thin
- 2 garlic cloves, minced
- 1 teaspoon sesame oil
- ½ teaspoon grated or minced fresh ginger
- 4 teaspoons vegetable oil
- 6 ounces shiitake mushrooms, stemmed and sliced ¼ inch thick
- ½ small head napa cabbage (about 8 ounces), cored and cut into 1-inch pieces (about 4 cups)
  Salt and pepper
- 2 (6-ounce) skinless center-cut salmon fillets, about 1½ inches thick (see note)

1. Adjust an oven rack to the middle position and heat the oven to 200 degrees. Whisk the soy sauce, sugar, mirin, and cornstarch together in a small bowl. In a separate bowl, combine the scallions, garlic, sesame oil, and ginger.

2. Heat 1 tablespoon of the vegetable oil in a 12-inch nonstick skillet over medium-high heat until shimmering. Add the mushrooms and cook until they soften and just begin to brown, about 2 minutes. Stir in the cabbage and cook until wilted, about 5 minutes.

3. Clear the center of the skillet, add the scallion mixture, and cook, mashing the mixture into the pan, until fragrant, about 30 seconds. Stir the scallion mixture into the vegetables. Season with salt and pepper to taste, and transfer the mixture to a platter. Tent loosely with foil and keep warm in the oven while preparing the salmon.

4. Pat the salmon dry with paper towels and season with salt and pepper. Wipe out the skillet with a wad of paper towels, add the remaining 1 teaspoon oil, and heat over medium-high heat until just smoking. Place the salmon, skinned-side up, in the skillet and cook until well browned on the first side, about 5 minutes. Flip the fish and continue to cook until the flesh is opaque and flakes apart when gently prodded with a paring knife, 3 to 5 minutes longer. Transfer the fish to the platter with the cabbage in the oven while preparing the sauce.

5. Wipe out the skillet with a wad of paper towels. Whisk the soy sauce mixture to recombine, add it to the skillet, and bring to a simmer over medium heat. Cook until the sauce is a thick, syrupy glaze, about 2 minutes. Spoon the glaze over the salmon and serve.

NOTES FROM THE TEST KITCHEN

HOW TO SKIN A SALMON FILLET

1. Insert the blade of a sharp boning knife just above the skin about 1 inch from the end of the fillet. Cut through the nearest end, away from yourself, keeping the blade just above the skin.

2. Rotate the fish and grab the loose piece of skin. Run the knife between the flesh and the skin, making sure the knife is just above the skin, until the skin is completely removed.

SHRIMP AND GRITS

A STAPLE OF THE SOUTHERN TABLE, grits are a nutritious and substantial addition to any meal. They appear in many guises, including simmered and sweetened with maple syrup or molasses; cooked to a thick consistency, cooled, and fried in slices; and, our favorite, enriched with cheese and spices and served with plump shrimp. The shrimp and grits should share equal billing in this dish. And since this recipe is typically meant to serve a group, scaling back all the components and getting the ratio of shrimp to grits just right is key.

We started by cooking the grits. There are three kinds of grits: instant, which cook in 5 minutes; quick grits, which cook in 7 to 9 minutes; and old-fashioned, which cook in 15 minutes. In a side-by-side tasting, most tasters thought the instant grits were too creamy and tasted overprocessed. The old-fashioned grits were creamy yet retained a slightly coarse texture. Quick grits had a creamy yet substantial texture and didn't take long to cook, so they were our first choice.

To add richness without relying solely on butter, as many recipes do, we cooked the grits in milk rather than water—a technique we've used with success before. But because we were using such a small amount of grits, their flavor disappeared behind the lactose-heavy milk flavor. Even when we diluted the milk significantly, the grits tasted too heavily of cooked milk. We then tried a small amount of heavy cream and water mixed together. Everyone liked this batch—the grits were rich, but without an overwhelming dairy flavor. We were surprised to find that cooked cream does not develop the same strong "cooked" flavor as milk. This is because the extra fat in cream keeps the milk proteins from breaking down when heated. After a few more batches of varying proportions, we found that 1 part cream to 3 parts water provided the best flavor.

To improve on things, we tried a few simple additions that would deepen the flavor of the grits without overpowering them. One small minced onion cooked in the skillet before adding the liquid brought depth and a touch of sweetness. Many tasters liked a little garlic as well, but we decided to add it with the shrimp. Hot sauce added a piquancy that cut through the richness.

With the grits cooked, we needed a cheese to fold in. Monterey Jack and pepper Jack cheeses made the

SHRIMP AND GRITS

grits taste sour, although the jalapeños in the cheese were appreciated and led us to increase the amount of hot sauce. Regular cheddar was bland, but the flavor was getting there. Extra-sharp cheddar proved to be the winner. The flavor was assertive and complemented the subtle corn flavor.

Now it was time for the shrimp. In most recipes the shrimp are sautéed or even grilled before joining the grits, but our skillet was already filled with the grits and we didn't want to dirty (and clean) another pan. At first, we simply stirred the shrimp into the grits and allowed them to cook from the heat of the grits. But because we were using only half a pound of shrimp, they quickly disappeared into the grits once mixed in. On a second attempt, we scattered the shrimp over the top of the finished grits, placed the lid on top of the skillet, and waited. And waited. The shrimp never did quite cook all the way through, and we were left scratching our heads. Frustrated, we threw the skillet in the oven to finish cooking the shrimp. This method worked beautifully, cooking the shrimp to perfection. What's more, the grits had loosened slightly from the additional moisture released by the shrimp and gained a creamy texture that tasters loved.

Finally, to build the flavor of the shrimp, we marinated it in a simple mixture of oil, salt, pepper, cayenne, and garlic. A sprinkle of scallions gave our shrimp and grits both a colorful contrast and a fresh burst of flavor. We had finally succeeded in re-creating this Southern classic, with minimal effort, and all in just one skillet.

Shrimp and Grits

SERVES 2

Do not substitute instant grits or old-fashioned grits for the quick-cooking grits in this recipe, as they require different amounts of liquid for cooking. To make this dish easier to eat, we suggest peeling the shrimp completely, including the tail shells.

8   ounces large shrimp (31 to 40 per pound),
    peeled and deveined (see photos)
1   tablespoon olive oil
1   garlic clove, minced
    Pinch cayenne pepper
    Salt and pepper
1   tablespoon unsalted butter
1   small onion, minced (about ½ cup)

NOTES FROM THE TEST KITCHEN

SIZING SHRIMP

Shrimp are sold by size (small, medium, large, and so on) as well as by the number needed to make 1 pound, usually given in a range. Choosing shrimp by the numerical rating is more accurate than choosing by a size label, which varies from store to store. Here's how the two systems line up.

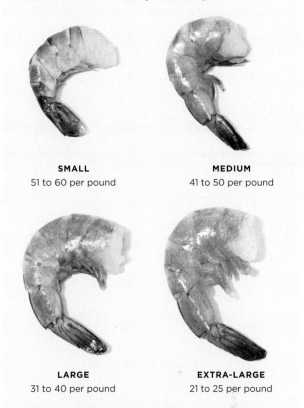

SMALL
51 to 60 per pound

MEDIUM
41 to 50 per pound

LARGE
31 to 40 per pound

EXTRA-LARGE
21 to 25 per pound

DEVEINING SHRIMP

1. Hold the shelled shrimp between your thumb and forefinger and cut down the length of its back, about ⅛ to ¼ inch deep, with a sharp paring knife.

2. If the shrimp has a vein, it will be exposed and can be pulled out easily. Once you have freed the vein with the tip of a paring knife, just touch the knife to a paper towel and the vein will slip off the knife and stick to the towel.

1½ cups water

½ cup heavy cream

½ teaspoon hot sauce

½ cup quick grits (see note)

4 ounces extra-sharp cheddar cheese, shredded (about 1 cup)

1 scallion, sliced thin

1. Adjust an oven rack to the middle position and heat the oven to 375 degrees. Toss the shrimp with the oil, garlic, and cayenne and season with salt and pepper. Cover and refrigerate while preparing the grits.

2. Melt the butter in a 10-inch skillet over medium heat. Add the onion and cook, stirring often, until softened, 3 to 5 minutes. Stir in the water, cream, hot sauce, ½ teaspoon salt, and ¼ teaspoon pepper and bring to a boil. Slowly whisk in the grits, reduce the heat to low, and cook, stirring often, until the grits are thick and creamy, 5 to 7 minutes.

3. Off the heat, whisk in the cheddar until combined. Lay the shrimp on their sides in a pinwheel formation over the grits, then press on them lightly to submerge about halfway. Transfer the skillet to the oven and bake until the shrimp are cooked through, 5 to 7 minutes. Sprinkle with the scallion before serving.

VARIATIONS

Shrimp and Grits with Chipotle Chile

Follow the recipe for Shrimp and Grits, substituting 1 to 2 teaspoons minced chipotle chile in adobo sauce for the hot sauce.

Shrimp and Grits with Bacon

Follow the recipe for Shrimp and Grits, substituting 2 slices bacon, chopped fine, for the butter. Cook the bacon over medium heat until crisp, about 8 minutes. Transfer the bacon to a paper towel–lined plate, and discard all but 1 tablespoon of the bacon fat left in the skillet. Continue to cook the onion, as directed, in the bacon fat. Sprinkle the dish with the crisp bacon along with the scallion before serving.

SKILLET POLENTA DINNER

POLENTA IS TYPICALLY SERVED AS A SIDE DISH in this country, but in Italy it is often served topped with a robust Bolognese sauce for a complete meal. This preparation seemed ideal for a dinner for two, except for one problem: Making meat sauce is typically an all-day affair and results in enough sauce to feed a hungry family. Could we streamline the cooking process, without sacrificing flavor, and make this a weeknight meal?

The long simmering time for Bolognese serves to concentrate flavors and, more importantly, break down the meat, giving it a soft, lush texture. Quick versions of meat sauce (in which ground beef, onions, garlic, and canned tomatoes are thrown together in a pot and cooked for half an hour) may be just that, but their lackluster flavor and rubbery meat bear no resemblance to the real thing. We were after the convenience of a quick-cooking sauce that had the complex flavor of one that had been cooked all day.

The best Bolognese recipes don't call for browning the meat, but instead cooking the ground meat just until it loses its raw color, then adding the liquid ingredients one by one, slowly reducing each and building flavor before adding the next. One of the first liquids in the pot is usually some form of dairy, an ingredient that imparts a sweet creaminess to the dish that is the hallmark of good Bolognese.

We started off by sautéing onion and garlic in the pan before adding the ground beef. After breaking up the meat, we added ½ cup of milk. The results were disappointing: Some of the meat was tender and moist, but most of it was tough and mealy, and the overall flavor was dull. Without sufficient time to reduce, the milk actually overpowered the meat flavor in the sauce. We needed to find another way to flavor and tenderize the meat.

Meat tenderizer made the beef spongy. Soy sauce, which tenderizes meat by helping it retain its moisture, had virtually no impact on tiny bits of ground beef. Finally we tried a panade. This paste of bread and milk is often blended into meatballs and meat loaf to help them hold their shape and retain moisture during cooking. Using a fork, we mashed up a piece of bread with some milk until we had a smooth paste and mixed it into the ground beef until well combined. We then proceeded as usual with the rest of the recipe: adding the beef mixture to the sautéed onion and garlic, adding the tomatoes, and simmering for a short period of time. We noticed a difference in the sauce even before we ladled it over polenta for tasters. The meat looked moister and, sure enough, tasters confirmed that it was.

Tasters were pleased with the meat's tenderness but complained that the sauce was too chunky, more like chili than a silky Bolognese. Pulsing the meat and panade together in the food processor created finer pieces of meat and a smoother sauce, as did pureeing the canned diced tomatoes. Incorporating a modest amount of white mushrooms boosted the beefy flavor of the meat, and a little grated Parmesan contributed a welcome nutty flavor. With a dash of red pepper flakes and some oregano, we were done with our sauce. Thanks to a few tricks, we now had a sauce with ultra-tender meat that was almost as complex and full-bodied as a sauce that had simmered for hours.

Finally, we moved on to the polenta. First of all, we knew that the polenta must be added very slowly to boiling salted water to prevent clumping. To give the flavor of the polenta a boost, we tried cooking it in boiling milk. The milk rounded out the flavor of the polenta nicely, but it also added an unpleasant texture. Using a combination of milk and water, we were able to add some flavor to the polenta without ruining its creamy texture. It took about 10 minutes over moderate heat to fully cook the polenta. We finished it with a little butter, which helped keep it smooth and soft, and a bit of garlic.

Simple and easy to prepare, this quick-cooked skillet dish is short on time but long on flavor. True, no one would mistake our polenta dinner for authentic Italian fare—but no one would believe it all came from one skillet either.

Polenta Dinner with Italian Meat Sauce

SERVES 2

This recipe uses traditional dried polenta (which looks like coarse-ground cornmeal), often found alongside the rice and grains in the supermarket; do not substitute pre-made polenta in a tube or instant polenta. When stirring the polenta, make sure to scrape the sides and bottom of the skillet to ensure even cooking.

MEAT SAUCE

3 white mushrooms, broken into rough pieces
½ slice high-quality white sandwich bread, torn into quarters
2 teaspoons milk
Salt and pepper
8 ounces 85 percent lean ground beef
1 (14.5-ounce) can diced tomatoes
2 teaspoons olive oil
1 small onion, minced (about ½ cup)
2 garlic cloves, minced
¼ teaspoon dried oregano
Pinch red pepper flakes
1 tablespoon grated Parmesan cheese, plus extra for serving

POLENTA

1⅔ cups water
½ cup whole milk
Salt
½ cup polenta (see note)
2 tablespoons unsalted butter
1 garlic clove, minced
Pepper

1. FOR THE MEAT SAUCE: Adjust an oven rack to the middle position and heat the oven to 200 degrees. Pulse the mushrooms in a food processor until finely chopped, about 5 pulses, then transfer to a small bowl. Pulse the bread, milk, ¼ teaspoon salt, and ¼ teaspoon pepper in the food processor to form a paste, about 5 pulses, then add the beef and continue to pulse until well combined, about 6 pulses; transfer to a separate bowl. Process the tomatoes in the food processor until finely chopped, about 15 seconds, then transfer to a separate bowl.

2. Heat the oil in a 10-inch nonstick skillet over medium-high heat until shimmering. Add the onion and processed mushrooms and cook, stirring often, until the mixture begins to brown, 5 to 7 minutes. Stir in the garlic, oregano, and pepper flakes and cook until fragrant, about 30 seconds. Stir in the processed meat mixture and cook, breaking the meat into small pieces with a wooden spoon, until the beef loses its raw color but does not brown, 2 to 4 minutes.

3. Stir in the processed tomatoes and bring to a simmer. Reduce the heat to low and simmer gently until the sauce has thickened and the flavors have blended, about 15 minutes. Stir in the Parmesan and season with salt and pepper to taste. Transfer the sauce to a bowl, cover, and keep warm in the oven while preparing the polenta.

4. FOR THE POLENTA: Wipe out the skillet with a wad of paper towels. Add the water and milk to the skillet and bring a boil over medium–high heat. Stir in ½ teaspoon salt, then very slowly pour the polenta into the boiling liquid while stirring constantly in a circular motion with a wooden spoon.

5. Reduce the heat to low and simmer the polenta, stirring often, until all of the liquid has been absorbed, the mixture is uniformly smooth, and it no longer has a raw cornmeal flavor, 10 to 12 minutes. Off the heat, stir in the butter and garlic and season with salt and pepper to taste. Portion the polenta into individual serving bowls, top with the meat sauce, and serve, passing the additional grated Parmesan separately.

SEAFOOD RISOTTO

SEAFOOD RISOTTO IS PERHAPS THE KING of all Italian rice dishes. An ideal seafood risotto is an elegant mix of flavors, shapes, and textures. The seafood is nestled in the creamy risotto, perfectly cooked and richly flavored, and the surrounding rice is infused with the sweet and briny flavors of the seafood. But seafood isn't cheap, and making this dish for a group can be prohibitively expensive (nor is it a dish that makes for good leftovers), so we thought it would be an ideal recipe to scale down to serve two people.

Our first step was to choose the seafood. Most of the recipes we found were from Venice and capitalized on the seemingly endless variety of seafood caught in the nearby waters. Even the best American fishmonger offers only a fraction of what is routinely available in Venetian markets, so we focused on seafood that is readily available here. We immediately ruled out shellfish such as lobster and crab (they require more work than we wanted for this dish) and flaky fish (which falls apart easily).

For their color and firm, meaty texture, shrimp were a must. After trying several sizes, we deemed medium shrimp to be just right for this dish. Squid was our next choice, but we had a hard time getting it to cook just right, and it usually emerged with an unpleasant chewy texture, so we scratched it from our list. For a big, briny hit of flavor, we hoped to add shellfish like clams and mussels, but their shells made the risotto difficult to eat—the rice tenaciously clung to the shells. We had much better luck with scallops, which contributed brininess and characteristic sweetness. Because small bay scallops can be difficult to find, we chose to use larger sea scallops and cut them into smaller pieces; this way, they cooked quickly and easily fit on a fork with a bite of rice.

With the seafood chosen (two types were plenty for our purposes), we turned our attention to the broth. Diluted chicken stock—what we normally use for making risotto—was quickly ruled out because it overwhelmed the subtle flavor of the seafood. We came across one recipe that suggested using plain water for seafood risotto, but our tasters disagreed, arguing that the resulting risotto tasted thin and bland. Bottled clam juice diluted with water tasted bland, too, but was more promising. To add backbone to the clam juice, we combined it with some chicken broth. This combination gave the risotto body and a distinct, but not overpowering, seafood flavor.

After we made several batches of risotto with this broth, we realized that a little more depth was needed to balance the sweetness of the seafood. The combination of seafood reminded one taster of bouillabaisse, which is flavored with saffron. A small pinch of this proved to be just what the risotto needed; it tied together the flavors and imparted a warm golden hue to the rice. Again borrowing from bouillabaisse, we added some basil and tomato for both color and fresh flavor.

With the flavors in order, we aimed to refine the cooking time to achieve perfectly cooked seafood. Throughout testing, we had been adding the seafood roughly five minutes before we thought the rice would be cooked through, but occasionally this led to overcooking, as Arborio rice, from batch to batch, may take several minutes longer than expected to soften. Then a fellow test cook suggested stirring the seafood into the risotto, reducing the heat to low, and covering the risotto, essentially poaching the seafood in gentle heat. The subtle heat and a lid provided enough heat to cook the seafood without overcooking the rice.

Except in rare situations, fish and cheese are never combined in Italian cooking. To add richness and body to this cheeseless risotto, we employed an Italian technique called *mantecare*, which roughly translates as "to beat" and involves rigorously stirring in butter once the rice has finished cooking. The grains become coated with the fat, giving the dish a rich, silky texture. Although we found that the additional butter is superfluous in cheese-enriched risotto recipes, it made a real difference in this dish.

Seafood Risotto

SERVES 2

To make this dish easier to eat, we suggest peeling the shrimp completely, including the tail shells.

- 1¾ cups low-sodium chicken broth
- 1 (8-ounce) bottle clam juice
- 2 tablespoons unsalted butter
- 1 small onion, minced (about ½ cup)
  Salt
- ⅔ cup Arborio rice
  Pinch saffron threads
- ½ cup dry white wine
- 6 ounces medium shrimp (41 to 50 per pound), peeled and deveined (see page 35)
- 6 ounces sea scallops, muscle removed (see page 115), quartered if large, halved if small
- 1 tomato, cored, seeded, and chopped fine
- 2 tablespoons chopped fresh basil
  Pepper

1. Combine the chicken broth and clam juice in a large microwave-safe measuring cup, cover, and microwave on high until hot, 1 to 3 minutes; set aside.

2. Melt 1 tablespoon of the butter in a 10-inch skillet over medium heat. Add the onion and ¼ teaspoon salt and cook, stirring occasionally, until softened, 3 to 5 minutes. Stir in the rice and saffron and cook, stirring often, until the ends of the rice kernels are transparent, about 2 minutes. Stir in the wine and cook until it has been completely absorbed, 1 to 2 minutes.

3. Stir in 1 cup of the hot broth mixture and continue to simmer, stirring every few minutes, until the liquid is absorbed and the bottom of the pan is almost dry, 7 to 9 minutes.

4. Stir in ½ cup more broth mixture every few minutes as needed to keep the pan bottom from drying out (you may not need all of the broth mixture), and cook, stirring often, until the rice is al dente, 10 to 12 minutes.

5. Vigorously stir in the remaining 1 tablespoon butter until melted, then gently fold in the shrimp, scallops, tomato, and basil. Cover the skillet, reduce the heat to low, and cook until the seafood is cooked through, 6 to 8 minutes, stirring once halfway through cooking. Season with salt and pepper to taste and serve immediately.

EGGPLANT PARMESAN

EGGPLANT PARMESAN IS FAMILY-FRIENDLY comfort food, a large and satisfying casserole meant to serve a crowd. But it is notoriously tedious to make, and even after we scaled down a traditional recipe to serve two it still seemed like a lot of work. Add to this the fact that most versions turned out disappointingly greasy after all the work, and we understood why most people would rather not bother. Could we streamline it, fix the greasiness problem, and scale it down so it represented a reasonable amount of work? Seemed like a tall order, but we were willing to give it a try. And since we would be making a small amount, we wondered if we could do it all in one skillet—first fry the eggplant, then combine it with layers of sauce and cheese.

We settled on using a globe eggplant, and for the best appearance, taste, and texture, we opted for unpeeled, ¼-inch-thick crosswise slices, not lengthwise planks.

This allowed us to easily get the pieces in the skillet for frying and for building the casserole.

In our first effort at frying the eggplant, we dispensed with the breading altogether, frying naked eggplant slices. The resulting eggplant earned negative comments from tasters—clearly we had taken our streamlining approach too far. We concluded that breading was essential and ticked off a list of possibilities. Flour alone wasn't substantial enough. Eggplant coated in a flour and egg batter and then bread crumbs was thick and tough. A standard single breading (dipping the eggplant first in egg, then bread crumbs) was too messy—the egg slid right off the eggplant, leaving the crumbs nothing to adhere to. A double, or bound, breading proved superior. Dipping the eggplant first in seasoned flour, then egg, then bread crumbs created a substantial (but not heavy) and crisp coating that brought the mild flavor and tender texture of the eggplant to the fore.

The initial coating of flour in a bound breading creates a dry, smooth base to which the egg and bread crumbs can cling. We seasoned the bread crumbs with generous amounts of Parmesan, salt, and pepper. We'd been using fresh bread crumbs and wondered whether we should toast them to improve their flavor or if we could get away with using store-bought crumbs. The answers were no and no. Toasted crumbs baked up too hard and tended to burn, and store-bought crumbs were so fine that they disappeared under blankets of tomato sauce and cheese.

We were able to fry the eggplant slices in two quick batches, about 2 minutes per side. With this technique, we turned out crisp, golden brown disks of eggplant, expending a minimum of effort.

Eggplant Parmesan couldn't be called such without Parmesan cheese, so that was a given. We had already used some for breading the eggplant, and a little extra browned nicely on top of the casserole. Mozzarella is another standard addition, but simply reducing the amount proportionally for two people didn't work—the cheese was now overwhelming the dish. A modest amount (4 ounces) kept the casserole from becoming soggy and weighed down.

A minced clove of garlic, a sprinkling of salt, and some olive oil pureed with a can of whole tomatoes made a quick tomato sauce. One can of whole tomatoes yielded about 1½ cups of tomato sauce, just enough to cover the bottom of the skillet, forming a saucy base, but still providing enough to moisten and flavor the eggplant from above.

Because breading softens beneath smothering layers of sauce and cheese, we overlapped the fried eggplant pieces in a spiral in the skillet, leaving a 1-inch border of the eggplant exposed as we dolloped the sauce and sprinkled the cheese over the top. This ensured crispy bites mixed in with saucy and cheesy bites. Another benefit of this technique was that without excess moisture, the casserole would be easy to cut into tidy pieces. With the eggplant fully cooked, the dish needed only a brief stay in a hot oven to melt the cheese. A handful of fresh basil leaves sprinkled on top was a final flourish, and in the end, we had drastically reduced the amount of attention and time required to prepare this dish, making it a surprisingly ideal meal for two—without sacrificing flavor.

Eggplant Parmesan

SERVES 2

Be sure to leave the outer edges of the eggplant slices unsauced in step 5 so that they remain crisp once baked.

TOMATO SAUCE

- 1 (14.5-ounce) can whole peeled tomatoes, drained, juice reserved
- 1 tablespoon extra-virgin olive oil
- 1 garlic clove, minced
- ¼ teaspoon salt

EGGPLANT

- 4 slices high-quality white sandwich bread, torn into quarters
- 1½ ounces Parmesan cheese, grated (about ¾ cup)
  Salt and pepper
- 2 large eggs
- ½ cup unbleached all-purpose flour
- 1 small globe eggplant (about 12 ounces), sliced into ¼-inch-thick rounds
- ½ cup vegetable oil
- 4 ounces mozzarella cheese, shredded (1 cup)
- ¼ cup chopped fresh basil (optional)

1. FOR THE TOMATO SAUCE: Process the drained tomatoes, olive oil, garlic, and salt together in a food processor until pureed, about 15 seconds. Transfer the mixture to a liquid measuring cup, and add the reserved tomato juice as needed until the sauce measures 1½ cups. (Wash and dry the bowl of the food processor before making the bread crumbs.)

2. FOR THE EGGPLANT: Adjust an oven rack to the lower-middle position and heat the oven to 425 degrees. Pulse the bread in the food processor to fine, even crumbs, about 15 pulses (you should have about 4 cups). Transfer the crumbs to a pie plate and stir in ½ cup of the Parmesan, ¼ teaspoon salt, and ¼ teaspoon pepper. Beat the eggs in a second pie plate. Combine the flour and ½ teaspoon pepper in a large zipper-lock bag.

3. Place the eggplant slices in the bag of flour, shake the bag to coat the eggplant, then remove the eggplant from the bag and shake off the excess flour. Using tongs, coat the floured eggplant with the egg mixture, allowing the excess to drip off. Coat all sides of the eggplant with the bread crumbs, pressing on the crumbs to help them adhere. Lay the breaded eggplant slices on a wire rack set over a rimmed baking sheet.

4. Heat the oil in a 12-inch ovensafe nonstick skillet over medium-high heat until shimmering. Add half the breaded eggplant slices to the skillet and cook until well browned on both sides, about 4 minutes, flipping them halfway through cooking. Transfer the cooked eggplant to a wire rack and repeat with the remaining breaded eggplant.

5. Pour off the oil left in the skillet and wipe out the skillet with a wad of paper towels. Spread 1 cup of the tomato sauce over the bottom of the skillet. Following the photos, layer the eggplant slices evenly into the skillet, overlapping them slightly. Dollop the remaining ½ cup sauce on top of the eggplant and sprinkle with the remaining ¼ cup Parmesan and mozzarella, leaving the outer 1 inch of the eggplant slices clean.

6. Transfer the skillet to the oven and bake until bubbling and the cheese is browned, 13 to 15 minutes. Let the eggplant cool for 5 minutes, then sprinkle with the basil (if using) and serve.

THE BEST CANNED WHOLE TOMATOES

A ripe, fresh tomato should balance elements of sweetness and tangy acidity. Its texture should be somewhere between firm and pliant—certainly not mushy. Ideally, canned tomatoes, which can be a better option than fresh because they are packed at the height of ripeness, should reflect the same combination of characteristics. But with so many brands of canned tomatoes available, which one tastes best?

First, we looked at how canned tomatoes are processed; they are steamed to remove their skins, then they are packed in tomato juice or puree. Overall, we prefer tomatoes packed in juice, because they generally have a fresher, livelier flavor than tomatoes packed in puree, which imparts a slightly stale taste. We tasted whole tomatoes both straight from the can and in a simple tomato sauce. **Progresso Whole Peeled Tomatoes with Basil** finished at the head of the pack, with a bright flavor and firm texture. Be sure to buy the tomatoes packed in juice; Progresso has another, similar-looking can of whole peeled tomatoes packed in puree.

PASTA WITH CHICKEN, BROCCOLI, AND SUN-DRIED TOMATOES

PASTA FOR DINNER

PASTA WITH CHICKEN BOLOGNESE

TRADITIONAL BOLOGNESE GETS ITS BIG FLAVOR and tender texture from braising ground beef, pork, and veal with milk, wine, and tomatoes for upward of three hours. We wanted to update this classic northern Italian dish using ground chicken; since it's more tender than ground meat, ground chicken would need less time to simmer, helping us transform this Sunday night supper into a quick weeknight dinner for two people. But after making a few batches in the kitchen, we wondered if we really could achieve the same rich flavor and tender texture from ground chicken. Our first tests left us with rubbery and bland chicken floating in a subpar tomato sauce. To get that rich, meaty flavor in a quarter of the time, this recipe would need some work.

Off the bat, we tried adding other ingredients to boost the flavor of the chicken, such as pancetta, prosciutto, and even porcini mushrooms. Prosciutto was out, owing to its overly salty flavor, but pancetta was a perfect fit—a little went a long way, adding a subtle depth of flavor. And porcini mushrooms had such an amazingly beefy impact on the sauce that we just couldn't refuse them.

Our favorite three-hour recipe calls for celery, carrots, and shallot, but we found that celery could go by the wayside, thereby streamlining our vegetable prep. Garlic found a home, but tasters thought herbs were distracting. Either butter or olive oil could be used to sauté the vegetables, but we chose butter for its richer flavor. Tomatoes add sweetness to the sauce, and their juice is used to braise the meat. We tried all kinds—whole, crushed, diced, sauce—and in the end liked juicy canned diced tomatoes pulsed briefly in the food processor. To provide deeper, slow-cooked tomato flavor, we added some tomato paste.

In a true Bolognese, liquids are reduced slowly, one at a time, to tenderize the meat and develop the characteristic sweetness of the sauce. Because chicken is relatively lean, we knew that we had to find a quicker method—the chicken wouldn't withstand the lengthy simmering time required to achieve such sweetness. To sweeten the sauce, we added a half teaspoon of sugar. But it wasn't until we started thinking outside the box and tried sweeter white wines like Riesling and Gewürztraminer in place of the traditional dry Sauvignon Blanc that our sauce achieved the proper flavor. We even tried a white

Zinfandel—the "other" white wine—often snubbed for its grapey-sweet flavor. Guess what? It worked beautifully. By reducing the wine in a skillet and then using the same skillet to build the sauce, we eliminated the need for extra pots and pans.

Now meaty, sweet, and fast, this 45-minute sauce had everything going for it—well, almost. The chicken still presented itself in the form of little rubber pellets, and no sauce, however good, could mask that.

A hint of an answer came when we thought about the milk. In Italian cooking (and in traditional Bolognese recipes), milk and meat are often braised together, producing very tender results. What if we soaked the ground chicken in milk before cooking? We tried it. After sautéing the vegetables, we added the milk-soaked chicken to the hot pan and watched as it disintegrated into grainy, mushy bits. Clearly this was not the perfect solution, but at least the chicken wasn't tough.

Next, we added the chicken directly to the pan along with the milk (no soaking). Same as before, the chicken fell apart into bits, but this time, no mush. Sure that we were on the right track, the next time we added the chicken to the pan, we quickly broke it into large pieces (letting it spend no more than a minute in the pan alone) and then added the milk. We stirred the two together to break up the meat and—success! This chicken was incredibly tender. Because we weren't browning the chicken, it never obtained that tough crust that takes

---

hours upon hours to return to its tender state; as a result, we had a sauce that was rich and meaty, sweet and bold, luxuriously tender, and on the table in 45 minutes.

Pasta with Chicken Bolognese

SERVES 2

Other pasta shapes can be substituted for the rigatoni; however, their cup measurements may vary (see page 51). Slightly sweet white wines such as Gewürztraminer, Riesling, and even white Zinfandel work especially well with this sauce. Be diligent about breaking the ground chicken into small pieces in step 3, or the sauce will be too chunky.

- 1 (14.5-ounce) can diced tomatoes
- ⅔ cup white wine (see note)
- 2 tablespoons unsalted butter
- 2 ounces pancetta, cut into ¼-inch pieces (about ⅓ cup)
- 3 tablespoons minced carrot
- 1 large shallot, minced (about ¼ cup)
- ⅛ ounce dried porcini mushrooms, rinsed and minced
  Salt
- 1 garlic clove, minced
- ½ teaspoon sugar
- 8 ounces ground chicken
- ¾ cup whole milk
- 1 tablespoon tomato paste
  Pepper
- ½ pound rigatoni (about 3 cups; see note)
  Grated Parmesan cheese, for serving

1. Pulse the tomatoes, with their juice, in a food processor until chopped fine, about 6 pulses; set aside. Simmer the wine in a 10-inch nonstick skillet over medium-low heat until it has reduced to about 1 tablespoon, about 12 minutes; transfer to a small bowl and set aside.

2. Add the butter to the skillet and melt over medium-high heat. Add the pancetta and cook, stirring frequently, until well browned, about 2 minutes. Reduce the heat to medium, stir in the carrot, shallot, porcini mushrooms, and ⅛ teaspoon salt, and cook until the vegetables are softened, about 4 minutes. Stir in the garlic and sugar, and cook until fragrant, about 30 seconds.

3. Add the ground chicken and cook for 1 minute, breaking up the meat into small pieces (some chicken will still be pink). Stir in the milk, bring to a simmer, and continue to cook, breaking up the meat into small pieces, until most of the liquid has evaporated and the meat begins to sizzle, about 10 minutes.

4. Stir in the tomato paste and cook for 1 minute. Stir in the processed tomatoes, ⅛ teaspoon salt, and ⅛ teaspoon pepper, bring to a simmer, and continue to cook until the sauce is thickened but still moist, about 7 minutes. Stir in the reduced wine and continue to cook until the flavors are blended, about 5 minutes.

5. Meanwhile, bring 4 quarts water to a boil in a large pot. Add the pasta and 1 tablespoon salt, and cook, stirring often, until al dente. Reserve ½ cup of the cooking water, then drain the pasta and return it to the pot.

6. Add the sauce to the pasta and toss to combine, adjusting the sauce consistency with the reserved cooking water as desired. Season with salt and pepper to taste and serve with the Parmesan.

PASTA WITH CHICKEN AND VEGETABLES

CHICKEN AND PASTA ARE A GREAT MATCH. Add some vegetables to the mix, and you have a complete dinner. Unfortunately, this simple pairing often produces disappointing results—tough meat, bland pasta, and drab-looking vegetables are usually hiding beneath a thick cream sauce with little flavor. We knew we could do better. We wanted to develop a foolproof method for cooking the chicken, pair it with a clean-flavored sauce that complemented the other elements without overwhelming them, and then develop a few recipes with vegetable, cheese, and flavor variations.

We decided that boneless, skinless chicken breasts were the best choice (they're easy to prepare and you can either buy them one at a time or buy more and freeze the rest for later use) and tested various cooking methods, including microwaving, broiling, sautéing, and poaching. Not surprisingly, microwaving produced bland chicken with a steamed taste, and the timing was tricky. Broiling and sautéing produced meat with the most flavor, but the nicely seared edges of the chicken turned tough and stringy after being tossed with the pasta and sauce. Poaching the chicken—in the pasta water or the simmering sauce—produced meat that was tender and juicy, but the flavor was washed out.

Wanting the flavor provided by a sauté and the tenderness that comes with poaching, we hoped to combine these methods without making our recipe unnecessarily complicated. We cooked the chicken lightly with a little butter in a skillet until golden, then removed it from the pan when it was still underdone. After building a sauce in the now-empty skillet, we returned the chicken to the pan and let it simmer in the sauce until fully cooked. That did the trick; we now had flavorful, tender chicken.

REVIVING LIMP BROCCOLI
We tried reviving limp broccoli by standing stalks overnight in three different liquids: plain water, sugar water, and salt water. The sugar, we thought, might provide food that would revive the vegetable, and the salt might work like a brine, adding moisture and seasoning. The next day, we examined the broccoli raw and then pan-roasted it. The broccoli placed in sugar water was nearly as limp as before, and the broccoli from the salted water was even more dehydrated. In both the cooked and raw states, the broccoli left standing in plain water was the clear winner. So, to keep your broccoli fresh, simply trim the stalk, stand it in an inch of water, and refrigerate it overnight.

PREPARING BROCCOLI

1. Place the head of broccoli upside down on a cutting board. Trim the florets very close to their heads and cut into 1-inch pieces.

2. Trim and square off the broccoli stalks, removing the tough outer ⅛-inch layer.

3. Slice the trimmed stalks crosswise into ¼-inch-thick pieces.

Turning our attention next to the additional ingredients, we found that some, such as mushrooms, bacon, and caramelized onions, could be cooked in the pan before building the sauce. When it came to cooking the broccoli, we found that it was best to blanch it, given that there was already a pot of boiling water going for the pasta. We simply transferred the broccoli to a paper towel–lined plate to drain while we boiled the pasta.

Up until now, we had been making a sauce by thickening heavy cream with flour and butter (called a *roux*), and we had determined that garlic, pepper flakes, herbs, and white wine were all crucial for flavor. But in scaling this recipe down to serve two people, we had reduced these ingredients too much, and tasters wanted more. We increased the amount of garlic and wine, which helped, but it wasn't enough. We tried omitting the roux and letting the cream simmer and thicken on its own, but this produced a sauce that was too fatty. We then tried replacing portions of the cream with chicken broth and were relieved to finally hear positive comments from tasters.

The flavors of the wine, garlic, and herbs were no longer muted by the heavy sauce, and, as an added bonus, the broth gave our dish a significant boost in chicken flavor. Incrementally increasing the amount of broth and decreasing the amount of cream, we made sauce after sauce, each one better than the last, until the cream was entirely eliminated. Instead, we rounded out the dish with a tablespoon of butter, a handful of cheese, and some fresh herbs. Now the sauce had serious flavor, and we had a few simple chicken and pasta dishes that were bound to become staples in our weeknight repertoire.

Pasta with Chicken, Broccoli, and Sun-Dried Tomatoes
SERVES 2

Other pasta shapes can be substituted for the ziti; however, their cup measurements may vary (see page 51). Parmesan cheese can be substituted for the Asiago.

- **3 tablespoons unsalted butter**
- **1 (8-ounce) boneless, skinless chicken breast, trimmed and sliced thin**
- **1 small onion, minced (about ½ cup)**
  Salt
- **3 garlic cloves, minced**
- **¼ teaspoon dried thyme**

1 teaspoon unbleached all-purpose flour

⅛ teaspoon red pepper flakes

1 cup low-sodium chicken broth

½ cup dry white wine

½ bunch broccoli (about ¾ pound), florets cut into 1-inch pieces, stalks peeled and sliced ¼ inch thick (see page 46)

⅓ pound ziti (about 1⅔ cups; see note)

1 ounce Asiago cheese (see note), grated (about ½ cup), plus extra for serving

½ cup oil-packed sun-dried tomatoes, patted dry and cut into ¼-inch strips

1 tablespoon chopped fresh parsley

Pepper

1. Melt 1 tablespoon of the butter in a 10-inch non-stick skillet over high heat until beginning to brown. Add the chicken, break up any clumps, and cook without stirring until it begins to brown, about 1 minute. Stir the chicken and continue to cook until it is almost cooked through, about 2 minutes longer. Transfer the chicken to a bowl, cover, and set aside.

2. Melt 1 tablespoon more butter in the skillet over medium heat. Add the onion and ⅛ teaspoon salt, and cook until softened and lightly browned, 5 to 7 minutes. Stir in the garlic, thyme, flour, and pepper flakes, and cook until fragrant, about 30 seconds. Stir in the broth and wine, and simmer until the sauce has thickened slightly and reduced to about ⅔ cup, about 10 minutes. Set aside and cover to keep warm.

3. Meanwhile, bring 4 quarts water to a boil in a large pot. Add the broccoli florets and stalks and 1 table-spoon salt, and cook, stirring often, until the florets are crisp-tender, about 2 minutes (do not overcook). Using a slotted spoon, transfer the broccoli to a paper towel–lined plate and set aside.

4. Return the water to a boil, add the pasta, and cook, stirring often, until al dente. Reserve ½ cup of the cooking water, then drain the pasta and return it to the pot.

5. Return the chicken to the skillet along with the remaining 1 tablespoon butter, Asiago, and sun-dried tomatoes, and continue to simmer the sauce until the chicken is cooked through, about 1 minute.

6. Add the chicken mixture, cooked broccoli, and parsley to the pasta and toss to combine, adjusting the sauce consistency with the reserved cooking water as desired. Season with salt and pepper to taste and serve with extra Asiago.

Pasta with Chicken, Caramelized Onion, and Red Bell Pepper

SERVES 2

Other pasta shapes can be substituted for the ziti; however, their cup measurements may vary (see page 51). Parmesan cheese can be substituted for the Asiago.

4 tablespoons (½ stick) unsalted butter

1 (8-ounce) boneless, skinless chicken breast, trimmed and sliced thin

1 large onion, halved and sliced thin

Salt

1 red bell pepper, stemmed, seeded, and sliced into ¼-inch strips

3 garlic cloves, minced

¼ teaspoon dried thyme

1 teaspoon unbleached all-purpose flour

⅛ teaspoon red pepper flakes

1 cup low-sodium chicken broth

½ cup dry white wine

⅓ pound ziti (about 1⅔ cups; see note)

1 ounce Asiago cheese (see note), grated (about ½ cup), plus extra for serving

¼ cup shredded fresh basil (see page 52)

Pepper

1. Melt 1 tablespoon of the butter in a 10-inch nonstick skillet over high heat until beginning to brown. Add the chicken, break up any clumps, and cook without stirring until it begins to brown, about 1 minute. Stir the chicken and continue to cook until it is almost cooked through, about 2 minutes longer. Transfer the chicken to a bowl, cover, and set aside.

2. Melt 1 tablespoon more butter in the skillet over medium heat. Add the onion and ⅛ teaspoon salt, and cook until softened and well browned, about 10 minutes. Stir in the bell pepper and cook until softened, about 3 minutes. Transfer to the bowl with the chicken.

3. Melt 1 tablespoon more butter in the skillet over medium heat. Add the garlic, thyme, flour, and pepper flakes, and cook until fragrant, about 30 seconds. Stir in the broth and wine, and simmer until the sauce has thickened slightly and reduced to ⅔ cup, about 10 minutes. Set aside and cover to keep warm.

4. Meanwhile, bring 4 quarts water to a boil in a large pot. Add the pasta and 1 tablespoon salt, and cook, stirring often, until al dente. Reserve ½ cup of the cooking water, then drain the pasta and return it to the pot.

5. Return the chicken and vegetables to the skillet along with the remaining 1 tablespoon butter and Asiago, and continue to simmer until the chicken is cooked through, about 1 minute.

6. Add the chicken-vegetable mixture and basil to the pasta and toss to combine, adjusting the sauce consistency with the reserved cooking water as desired. Season with salt and pepper to taste and serve with extra Asiago.

Pasta with Chicken, Bacon, Peas, and Gorgonzola
SERVES 2

Other pasta shapes can be substituted for the campanelle; however, their cup measurements may vary (see page 51). You can substitute 2 ounces fontina cheese, shredded (about ½ cup), for the Gorgonzola.

- 2 tablespoons unsalted butter
- 1 (8-ounce) boneless, skinless chicken breast, trimmed and sliced thin
- 2 slices bacon, chopped medium
- 1 small onion, minced (about ½ cup)
  - Salt
- 3 garlic cloves, minced
- ¼ teaspoon dried thyme
- 1 teaspoon unbleached all-purpose flour
- ⅛ teaspoon red pepper flakes
- 1 cup low-sodium chicken broth
- ½ cup dry white wine
- ⅓ pound campanelle (about 2 cups; see note)
- ½ cup frozen peas (about 2 ounces)
- 1 ounce Gorgonzola cheese (see note), crumbled (about ¼ cup)
- 1 tablespoon minced fresh chives
  - Pepper

1. Melt 1 tablespoon of the butter in a 10-inch non-stick skillet over high heat until beginning to brown. Add the chicken, break up any clumps, and cook without stirring until it begins to brown, about 1 minute. Stir the chicken and continue to cook until it is almost cooked through, about 2 minutes longer. Transfer the chicken to a bowl, cover, and set aside.

2. Add the bacon to the skillet and cook over medium-low heat until crisp, about 7 minutes. Transfer the bacon to a paper towel–lined plate, leaving 1 tablespoon of the fat in the pan.

3. Add the onion and ⅛ teaspoon salt to the skillet, and cook over medium-high heat until softened and lightly browned, 5 to 7 minutes. Stir in the garlic, thyme, flour, and pepper flakes, and cook until fragrant, about 30 seconds. Stir in the broth and wine, and simmer until the sauce has thickened slightly and reduced to ⅔ cup, about 10 minutes. Set aside and cover to keep warm.

4. Meanwhile, bring 4 quarts water to a boil in a large pot. Add the pasta and 1 tablespoon salt, and cook, stirring often, until al dente. Reserve ½ cup of the cooking water, then drain the pasta and return it to the pot.

5. Return the chicken to the skillet along with the remaining 1 tablespoon butter and peas, and continue to simmer until the chicken is cooked through, about 1 minute.

6. Add the chicken mixture, bacon, Gorgonzola, and chives to the pasta, and toss to combine, adjusting the sauce consistency with the reserved cooking water as desired. Season with salt and pepper to taste and serve.

PASTA CAPRESE

LEGEND HAS IT THAT THE POPULAR CAPRESE trio of garden tomatoes, fresh mozzarella, and basil leaves was introduced in the 1950s at Trattoria da Vincenzo, a beachside restaurant on the Italian island of Capri. According to creator Margherita Cosentino, the red, white, and green salad of local produce and cheese allowed ladies to "have a nice lunch while still fitting into their bikinis." Swimsuit season or not, the combination became so popular that cooks everywhere took to mixing it with hot pasta, minced garlic, and extra-virgin olive oil for a 15-minute entrée that captures the flavors of summer.

Truth be told, we were skeptical that a recipe would really be required for such a clear-cut dish. Still, we gathered a representative sampling and went into the kitchen. The outcome? Instead of collecting the praise we had expected from our colleagues, we joined them for a few chuckles. The tomatoes, pasta, and basil weren't problems, but the cheese was. In each recipe test, it had clumped into an intractable softball-sized wad, leaving one serving with no cheese at all and the other with an unwieldy amount.

For these first tests, we had purchased fresh mozzarella—the kind that comes immersed in plastic tubs of water and is shaped into irregular-sized balls—at the supermarket.

PASTA CAPRESE

What if we used regular block-style mozzarella (the low-moisture version often shredded for pizza) instead? It melted nicely and didn't turn chewy, but this inauthentic substitution cheated the dish of its star ingredient, and tasters complained about blandness.

For our next test, we took a big step in the opposite direction and tried water buffalo–milk mozzarella (*mozzarella di bufala*) from a specialty cheese shop. Much softer than the commercial fresh cheese, this handmade mozzarella melted into tender pillows when combined with the pasta—there were no rubbery bits to be found. In addition to the lovely consistency, tasters praised its flavor, which was dripping with milkiness and tang. The next day, we prepared pasta Caprese using handmade cow's-milk mozzarella and achieved the same impressive results.

So the problem was solved, as long as we had time to go to the cheese store and were willing to pay the big bucks for handmade cheese, which can easily top $9 per pound. Everyone in the test kitchen agreed this wasn't an acceptable solution, especially for what we wanted to be a convenient and quick meal for two. We needed to find a way to use fresh mozzarella from the supermarket.

Our first thought was to thoroughly coat diced mozzarella cubes with olive oil before adding the steaming pasta. This was a step in the right direction, as the oil prevented sticking—initially. After a few minutes, however, the nasty clumping problem reemerged.

We wondered what would happen if we put the diced supermarket cheese in the freezer for a few minutes before combining it with the pasta. Could chilling the cheese keep it from melting fully and clumping into wads like bubble gum? We gave this approach a trial run, dicing the mozzarella and chilling it in the freezer for 10 minutes. We then proceeded as usual, combining the firmed-up cheese with the pasta and tomatoes. Success: When added to hot pasta, the cheese softened but did not fully melt, making the unattractive elastic ropes a thing of the past. It turns out that the proteins in fresh mozzarella begin to melt at about 130 degrees. As the temperature climbs past 130 degrees, the proteins clump together. Freezing the cheese kept it from overheating when tossed with the hot pasta.

With the cheese conundrum solved, we fine-tuned the rest of the recipe, starting with the tomatoes. Juicy, garden-ripe beauties need no adornment, but a sprinkle of sugar can replace the gentle sweetness that is often missing in less-than-perfect specimens. And although

Italians would never add an acidic component to a true Caprese recipe, a squirt of fresh lemon juice did a great job of boosting the flavor of lackluster tomatoes.

In recipes that use raw olive oil, the fruity and spicy nuances of extra-virgin oil make a difference, and this dish is no exception. We added a healthy drizzle of the test kitchen's favorite extra-virgin olive oil, then stirred in some minced shallot, a sprinkle of salt, and a few twists of black pepper. Allowing the tomatoes to marinate while the pasta cooked infused them with fruity and subtle garlic flavors. Lengthy marinating times aren't recommended, however (especially with a relatively small amount of tomatoes), as more than 45 minutes yielded mealy, broken-down tomatoes. Freshly shredded basil was the finishing touch to pasta that tasted just like summer.

Pasta Caprese

SERVES 2

Other pasta shapes can be substituted for the penne; however, their cup measurements may vary (see page 51). The flavor of this dish depends on ripe tomatoes and high-quality extra-virgin olive oil. If using handmade buffalo- or cow's-milk mozzarella, don't freeze it, and add it to the marinating tomatoes in step 1.

- 2 **tablespoons extra-virgin olive oil (see note)**
- 1–2 **teaspoons fresh lemon juice**
- 1 **garlic clove, minced**
- 1 **small shallot, minced (about 1 tablespoon)**
  Salt and pepper
- 2 **ripe tomatoes, cored, seeded, and cut into ½-inch pieces (see note)**
- 6 **ounces fresh mozzarella cheese, cut into ½-inch cubes (see note)**
- ½ **pound penne (about 2½ cups; see note)**
- 2 **tablespoons shredded fresh basil (see page 52)**
- ½ **teaspoon sugar (optional)**

1. Whisk the oil, 1 teaspoon of the lemon juice, garlic, shallot, ¼ teaspoon salt, and ⅛ teaspoon pepper together in a large bowl. Add the tomatoes and gently toss to combine; set aside for at least 10 minutes but no longer than 45 minutes. Place the mozzarella on a plate and freeze until slightly firm, about 10 minutes.

2. Meanwhile, bring 4 quarts water to a boil in a large pot. Add the pasta and 1 tablespoon salt, and cook, stirring often, until al dente. Drain well.

3. Add the pasta and partially frozen mozzarella to the tomato mixture and gently toss to combine. Let stand for 5 minutes. Stir in the basil and season with salt, pepper, the remaining 1 teaspoon lemon juice, and sugar (if using) to taste. Serve immediately.

NOTES FROM THE TEST KITCHEN

THE BEST EXTRA-VIRGIN OLIVE OIL

For most cooked dishes we're perfectly happy reaching for supermarket olive oil, but sometimes only a good-quality extra-virgin olive oil will do. Typically produced in Italy, Greece, and Spain, extra-virgin oils range wildly in price, color, and packaging, so it's hard to know what you're really purchasing. Many things can impact the quality and flavor of olive oil, but the type of olive, the harvest (earlier means greener, more bitter, and pungent; later, milder and more buttery), and processing are the most important factors. The best-quality oil comes from olives picked at their peak and processed as soon as possible, without heat (which can coax more oil from the olives but at the expense of flavor). Our favorite oils were produced from a blend of olives and, thus, were well rounded—no one element came on too strong. Out of those tasted, we most liked **Columela Extra Virgin Olive Oil from Spain** ($22 for 25.4 ounces) for its fruity flavor and excellent balance.

MEASURING SHAPED PASTA

Guessing how much pasta you *really* need to cook can be tricky when cooking for just two people. Of course you can always judge by how full the box is (most pasta is packaged in 1-pound boxes), but we think it's easier to simply measure shaped pasta using dry measuring cups. Here are the cup measurements of the most common short pasta shapes:

PASTA TYPE	⅓ POUND	½ POUND
Campanelle, Farfalle, Medium Shells, Cavatappi, Fusilli, and Rigatoni	2 cups	3 cups
Penne, Ziti, Orecchiette, Small Shells	1⅔ cups	2½ cups
Macaroni	1½ cups	2 cups

KEEPING TOMATOES FRESH

Storing tomatoes stem-end down at room temperature is the best way to prolong their shelf life. That's because the scar left on the tomato where the stem once grew provides both an escape for moisture and an entry point for mold and bacteria. Placing a tomato stem-end down prevents moisture from exiting and air from entering its scar, prolonging shelf life.

PASTA WITH CREAMY TOMATO SAUCE

PASTA WITH A CREAMY TOMATO SAUCE is a naturally quick meal for two, but even such a simple sauce can require a careful balancing act. The best creamy tomato sauces balance the acidity of fruity tomatoes with the richness of dairy; the worst deliver instant heartburn and make you wish the two components had never met. What's the best way to merge these seemingly incompatible ingredients in a sauce that brings out the best in each?

After researching creamy tomato sauce recipes, we started our testing with *soffrito*, a blend of aromatics—such as onion, carrot, celery, garlic, and parsley—sautéed in olive oil, upon which traditional Italian sauces (as well as most Italian soups and stews) are built. For the richest-flavored sauce, we assumed that more was more—even when scaling down the recipe—and started with the full list of classic ingredients. As testing progressed, however, we were repeatedly confronted with the criticism that the sauce tasted too vegetal. Prepping small amounts of several vegetables for a dinner for two also seemed unnecessary. Perhaps in this case, less was more. We cooked a batch of soffrito without celery, and tasters unanimously approved. Next we eliminated carrot, and the reaction was again positive. Left with just garlic and onion to cook, we were able to reduce the cooking time to just a quick sauté.

Since we wanted a smooth sauce we could make year-round, fresh tomatoes didn't make much sense. Canned crushed tomatoes are smooth but are hard to find in cans smaller than 28 ounces—much more than needed when cooking for two. Tomato sauce, the smoothest canned tomato product, is easy to find in smaller cans, but tasters found its tomato flavor too mild in this sauce. Pureeing a can of diced tomatoes in the food processor, however, yielded a smooth sauce with bright tomato flavor.

The addition of a tablespoon of tomato paste contributed depth to the canned tomatoes. Simply stirring it into the bubbling sauce left the paste tasting raw, so we cooked it with the softened aromatics until it darkened to brick red and its flavor developed. But tasters demanded still more tomato flavor. After sifting through a list of options, we landed on sun-dried tomatoes, whose bold flavor enlivened the sauce and cut through the sweetness of the cream. A pinch of red pepper flakes and a few tablespoons of wine further intensified the sauce and rounded out its flavors.

In our initial testing, we had tried a recipe that included pancetta. Though the meat lent the sauce an undeniable body and depth, we ruled it out as too assertive—a little goes a long way in such a simple sauce, even when making a large amount. Thinking that perhaps milder prosciutto might work for our smaller quantity of sauce, we minced a couple of paper-thin slices and added them to the pan along with the onion. This sauce was hands down the best yet.

We liked how the sun-dried tomatoes softened and the sauce's flavors melded after half an hour of slow simmering. But tasters thought the sauce could use an extra punch of flavor, so we reserved a splash of the wine and a small amount of the pureed tomatoes to add at the end. Both contributed a welcome acidity, and the combination of the two cut through the dairy and brought the sauce's ingredients into sharp relief. For the cream, all we had to do was stir it into the finished tomato sauce along with the extra wine and tomatoes.

Up to this point, we had pureed each of the finished sauces to a velvety texture, thinking that smoothness was the best way to highlight creaminess. And the sauce did taste good when smooth, but it was one-dimensional. On a whim, we left a batch unpureed, and tasters loved the bits of chewy sun-dried tomatoes, soft minced onion, and pulpy pureed tomato that punctuated the otherwise silky consistency. This was finally it: a dynamic sauce in which tomatoes and cream boosted each other's flavors and that packed enough complexity to keep us coming back for more.

NOTES FROM THE TEST KITCHEN

SHREDDING BASIL

To shred basil or other leafy herbs and greens, simply stack several leaves on top of one another, roll them up, and slice. In the case of basil, we have found that rolling the leaves from tip to tail minimizes bruising and browning.

Pasta with Creamy Tomato Sauce

SERVES 2

Other pasta shapes can be substituted for the fusilli; however, their cup measurements may vary (see page 51).

- 1 (14.5-ounce) can diced tomatoes
- 2 tablespoons unsalted butter
- 2 thin slices prosciutto, minced (about ½ ounce)
- 1 small onion, minced (about ½ cup)
- 1 bay leaf
    Pinch red pepper flakes
    Salt
- 2 garlic cloves, minced
- 1 tablespoon tomato paste
- 1½ tablespoons coarsely chopped oil-packed sun-dried tomatoes, patted dry
- 3 tablespoons dry white wine or vermouth
- ½ pound fusilli (about 3 cups; see note)
- ¼ cup heavy cream
    Pepper
- 2 tablespoons shredded fresh basil (see photo)
    Grated Parmesan cheese, for serving

1. Process the diced tomatoes, with their juice, in a food processor until smooth, about 10 seconds. Measure out and reserve 1 tablespoon of the tomatoes for finishing the sauce.

2. Melt the butter in a medium saucepan over medium heat. Add the prosciutto, onion, bay leaf, pepper flakes, and ⅛ teaspoon salt, and cook, stirring occasionally, until the onion is softened and lightly browned, 5 to 7 minutes. Stir in the garlic and cook until fragrant, about 30 seconds. Stir in the tomato paste and sun-dried tomatoes, and cook until slightly darkened, about 1 minute. Stir in 2 tablespoons of the wine and cook until evaporated, about 1 minute.

3. Stir in the processed tomatoes and bring to a simmer. Reduce the heat to low, partially cover, and cook, stirring occasionally, until the sauce is thickened (a spoon should leave a trail when dragged through the sauce), 10 to 12 minutes.

4. Meanwhile, bring 4 quarts water to a boil in a large pot. Add the pasta and 1 tablespoon salt, and cook, stirring often, until al dente. Reserve ½ cup of the cooking water, then drain the pasta and return it to the pot.

5. Remove the bay leaf from the sauce and discard. Stir in the cream, reserved 1 tablespoon processed tomatoes, and remaining 1 tablespoon wine. Season with salt and pepper to taste. Add the sauce to the cooked pasta and toss to combine, adjusting the sauce consistency with the reserved cooking water as desired. Stir in the basil and serve with the Parmesan.

PASTA WITH GREENS AND BEANS

ITALIANS HAVE A KNACK FOR TRANSFORMING HUMBLE ingredients into remarkable meals, and the rustic trio of pasta, hearty greens, and beans is no exception: When carefully prepared, the combination is sublime. But making something out of almost nothing takes time. In this case, dried cannellini (white kidney) beans are gently simmered until tender, then garden-fresh greens are cleaned, cooked, and seasoned. Tossed together with al dente pasta and a sprinkling of Parmesan, the result is rich and satisfying. If we could find a few shortcuts yet retain the complex flavors of the Italian original, this dinner could become a regular in our midweek repertoire.

The hearty greens that Italians usually mix with pasta and beans include turnip, dandelion, chicory, mustard, broccoli rabe, collards, and kale. And there's a five-step approach for reducing the bitterness most of them possess: Blanch, shock (dunk in ice water), squeeze dry, chop, and sauté. The upside? When handled this way, the bitterness is tamed and the resulting greens are robust but not overpowering. The downside is that the whole process demands precious time and multiple pieces of kitchen equipment—we were never going to make this meal for just two people if we had to dirty multiple pots and pans; after all, at heart it is just a simple pasta dish.

Upon closer inspection of our greens options, two of the choices, kale and collard greens, were absolute standouts. Tasters noted their appealing vegetal and mineral qualities but made not one mention of bitterness, giving us new hope for a straightforward cooking method. Sure enough, a simple sauté tasted great, but even with a recipe scaled down to make just two servings we would have to cook the greens in more than one batch. We found our solution in a sauté/braise combination. We quickly wilted the greens in a hot pan with olive oil, aromatic onions and garlic, and spicy red pepper flakes, then poured in chicken broth to serve as the braising liquid; 10 minutes (and only one pan and one batch) later, tender, flavorful greens were ours.

As for the pasta, we'd run across a few references to whole wheat spaghetti and decided to try it. We prepared a batch, served it up, and braced for the reactions. Surprise: Tasters unanimously preferred the nutty flavor of whole wheat pasta to traditional semolina pasta for this dish. In fact, the more potent dimension of flavor provided by the whole wheat pasta was the missing link, adding complexity that brought the beans and greens into a pleasing harmony.

NOTES FROM THE TEST KITCHEN

THE BEST WHOLE WHEAT PASTA
A coarse, gummy texture and out-of-place "oatmeal" flavor plagued too many of the whole wheat pastas we've tried in years past. But the options available have multiplied dramatically, so we decided to take another look. Eight of the 10 contenders were made from whole durum wheat, the notably hard, dense wheat from which semolina, the primary ingredient in traditional pasta, is processed. Though texture has improved overall since previous tastings, several of the pastas were almost as gritty and gluey as we remembered. Our top finisher, **Ronzoni Healthy Harvest Whole Wheat Blend Pasta,** blends regular semolina with wheat bran and wheat fiber or whole durum wheat—so it's not 100 percent "whole" wheat. But the combination of a pleasantly chewy texture and wheaty flavor is worth the nutritional trade-off.

OUR FAVORITE TRADITIONAL SKILLET
We use our skillets all the time, for everything from pan-roasting chicken breasts to cooking burgers and steaks. While nonstick skillets can be purchased at a reasonable price (see page 15), when it comes to traditional skillets, the variation in price is dizzying—pans can cost anywhere from $30 to $150 or more. Preliminary tests of traditional skillets confirmed our suspicions that cheap was not the way to go, but how much do you really need to spend? We zeroed in on a group of eight pans from well-known manufacturers. All of the pans tested had flared sides, and most had uncoated stainless steel cooking surfaces, which we prize for promoting a fond (the browned, sticky bits that cling to the interior of the pan when food is sautéed and that help flavor sauces).

We concluded that medium-weight pans (not too heavy and not too light) are ideal—they brown food beautifully, and most testers handled them comfortably. These pans have enough heft for heat retention and structural integrity, but not so much that they are difficult to manipulate. For its combination of excellent performance, optimum weight and balance, and overall ease of use, the **All-Clad Stainless Steel Fry Pan,** which comes in 8-inch ($85), 10-inch ($100), and 12-inch ($135) sizes, was the hands-down winner. (See page 82 for more information on skillet sizes.)

The obvious shortcut to soaking dried beans was to use canned ones, so to compensate for the flavor deficiency we worked in some heavy-hitting ingredients: hearty pancetta and earthy fontina cheese. Though we think pancetta's hearty flavor is overwhelming for some recipes that we've scaled down to serve two, here it stands up well to the hearty beans and greens. Still more garlic, in the form of bread crumbs, contributed headiness and welcome crunch, making this a simple and satisfying weeknight meal.

Whole Wheat Pasta with Greens, Beans, Pancetta, and Garlic Bread Crumbs
SERVES 2

To measure spaghetti without a scale, bundle it into a tight, round bunch and measure the diameter with a ruler; ½ pound of spaghetti should measure 1¼ inches. Prosciutto can be substituted for the pancetta.

- 1 slice high-quality white sandwich bread, torn into pieces
- 4 teaspoons olive oil
- 3 garlic cloves, minced (about 3 teaspoons)
  Salt and pepper
- 1½ ounces pancetta (see note), cut into ½-inch pieces (about ¼ cup)
- 1 small onion, minced (about ½ cup)
- ⅛ teaspoon red pepper flakes
- ½ large bunch kale or collard greens, stems trimmed, leaves chopped into 1-inch pieces (about 7 cups)
- ¾ cup low-sodium chicken broth
- ½ pound whole wheat spaghetti (see note)
- ¾ cup drained and rinsed canned cannellini beans
- 2 ounces fontina cheese, shredded (about ½ cup)

1. Pulse the bread in a food processor to coarse crumbs, about 7 pulses. Heat 1 tablespoon of the oil in a 12-inch skillet over medium-high heat until shimmering. Add the bread crumbs and cook, stirring frequently, until beginning to brown, about 3 minutes. Stir in 1 teaspoon of the garlic and continue to cook until the bread crumbs are dark golden brown, about 1 minute. Season with salt and pepper to taste and transfer to a small bowl. Wipe out the skillet with paper towels.

2. Add the remaining 1 teaspoon oil and pancetta to the skillet and cook over medium heat until the pancetta is crisp, about 5 minutes. Transfer the pancetta to a small bowl, leaving the fat in the skillet. Add the onion and ¼ teaspoon salt to the skillet and cook over medium heat until softened and lightly browned, 5 to 7 minutes.

3. Stir in the remaining 2 teaspoons garlic and pepper flakes, and cook until fragrant, about 30 seconds. Add the greens to the pan and toss with tongs until they begin to wilt, about 2 minutes. Add the broth, cover, and simmer, tossing the greens occasionally, until they are tender, 10 to 15 minutes.

4. Meanwhile, bring 4 quarts water to a boil in a large pot. Add the pasta and 1 tablespoon salt, and cook, stirring often, until al dente. Reserve ½ cup of the cooking water, then drain the pasta and return it to the pot.

5. Stir the beans into the greens and let warm through, 1 to 2 minutes. Add the greens mixture and fontina to the pasta and toss to combine, adjusting the sauce consistency with the reserved cooking water as desired. Season with salt and pepper to taste and serve, sprinkling individual portions with the bread crumbs.

USE IT UP: CANNELLINI BEANS

Rosemary–White Bean Spread
MAKES ABOUT 1 CUP

Serve with pita chips or toasted baguette slices.

- ¾ cup drained and rinsed canned cannellini beans
- 2 tablespoons extra-virgin olive oil
- 2 tablespoons water
- 1½ teaspoons fresh lemon juice
- ½ small garlic clove, minced
- ⅛ teaspoon minced fresh rosemary
  Salt and pepper

Process the beans, oil, water, lemon juice, garlic, and rosemary in a food processor until smooth, about 15 seconds. Season with salt and pepper to taste and serve.

PASTA WITH SAUTÉED MUSHROOMS

TRANSFORMING AN ORDINARY BOX OF PASTA and a package of mushrooms into something special is weeknight cooking at its best: quick, simple, and delicious. All you need is the right recipe. Our first step was to choose the mushrooms. Not willing to shell out $18 per pound for exotic mushrooms, we limited ourselves to cultivated mushrooms that could be purchased for modest prices at the supermarket. The list included white button mushrooms, portobellos, cremini, and shiitakes. A quick taste test confirmed the obvious: White button mushrooms add substance but little flavor—unacceptable for the star ingredient. We also found that portobellos are tasty, but they darken sauces unless the gills are removed, a tedious process. We settled on a combination of cremini and shiitakes; tasters enjoyed the rich and meaty nature of cremini, and shiitakes have a hearty flavor and a pleasant chewy texture.

From experience, we knew the basics of cooking mushrooms: They leach liquid a few minutes after exposure to high heat and then, after moisture evaporates, they brown. Before they exude liquid, however, mushrooms have a lot of volume. This sometimes requires browning them in multiple batches, but because we were preparing pasta for only two, we were able to fit them all in one 10-inch skillet. We cranked up the heat on the stove and added some butter, followed by very thinly sliced mushrooms. The mushrooms quickly absorbed all of the butter and burned slightly. We started over, adding a good drizzle of olive oil to reduce the risk of burning, but keeping some butter for flavor, and slicing the mushrooms thicker. This time, they cooked the way we expected them to, ending up lightly browned.

We then looked at other variables in order to refine our technique. We use salt to draw moisture out of many vegetables, and we suspected this technique might work with mushrooms as well. In a side-by-side test, mushrooms salted at the onset of sautéing released more liquid than an unsalted batch, which was a bonus: The more juices that were released, the more deeply the mushrooms browned (dry food always browns more readily than moist). Because shiitakes contain more moisture than cremini, we gave them a quick head start in the pan. (Note that it is easy to overcook mushrooms; we learned to keep them in the skillet just until they are browned—any longer, and they become tough and rubbery.) A traditional skillet is our usual choice for sautéing, but we wondered if a nonstick pan was better for delicate mushrooms. A head-to-head test proved that the traditional skillet was better, since the resulting *fond* (the browned bits on the bottom of the pan) contributed flavor to the sauce.

Garlic and thyme have a natural affinity with mushrooms, so we added generous amounts of both, saving other herbs for variations. We were happy to note that dried thyme worked just fine here, which meant we didn't need to buy a large bunch of the herb only to use a fraction of it. We also experimented with a variety of choices from the onion family and settled on mild shallots, which didn't compete with the mushrooms.

We knew from the first recipes we tested that we wanted a light, creamy sauce. We removed the mushrooms from the skillet and made a quick sauce by deglazing the pan with chicken broth, then tested a few additions. Sour cream caused the sauce to separate, and it was too tangy. A swirl of heavy cream, however, did the trick, creating a smooth, mild sauce. We also needed an acidic element (alcohol, citrus, or vinegar) to sharpen and refine the other flavors. We tried small amounts of white wine, vermouth, Marsala, sherry, Madeira, balsamic vinegar, and lemon juice, the last being the test kitchen favorite and something that most cooks always have on hand.

Chunky sauces pair well with stubby, molded pasta shapes that have crevices in which the sauce can nestle. Our favorite choice is campanelle, a frilly, flower-shaped pasta, although any shaped pasta will work fine. As with many pasta dishes, this one is improved by a handful of grated Parmesan cheese, a dash of black pepper, and chopped fresh parsley.

Pasta with Sautéed Mushrooms

SERVES 2

Other pasta shapes can be substituted for the campanelle; however, their cup measurements may vary (see page 51). To make the dish vegetarian, substitute vegetable broth for the chicken broth.

- 1 **tablespoon olive oil**
- 1 **tablespoon unsalted butter**
- 3 **shallots, minced (about ½ cup)**

PASTA WITH SAUTÉED MUSHROOMS

4 ounces shiitake mushrooms, stemmed
   and sliced ¼ inch thick
6 ounces cremini mushrooms, sliced ¼ inch thick
   Salt
2 garlic cloves, minced
½ teaspoon dried thyme
⅔ cup low-sodium chicken broth (see note)
¼ cup heavy cream
½ pound campanelle (about 3 cups; see note)
1 ounce Parmesan cheese, grated (about ½ cup)
1 tablespoon chopped fresh parsley
1½ teaspoons fresh lemon juice
   Pepper

1. Heat the oil and butter over medium heat in a 10- inch skillet until the butter is melted. Add the shallots and cook until softened, 2 to 3 minutes. Increase the heat to medium-high, stir in the shiitake mushrooms, and cook for 1 minute. Stir in the cremini mushrooms and ¼ teaspoon salt, and cook until golden brown, about 6 minutes. Stir in the garlic and thyme, and cook until fragrant, about 30 seconds. Transfer the mushrooms to a bowl and cover to keep warm.

2. Stir the broth into the skillet and bring to a boil, scraping up any browned bits. Stir in the cream, bring to a simmer, and cook until the sauce has thickened slightly and reduced to about ⅔ cup, about 4 minutes.

3. Meanwhile, bring 4 quarts water to a boil in a large pot. Add the pasta and 1 tablespoon salt, and cook, stirring often, until al dente. Reserve ½ cup of the cooking water, then drain the pasta and return it to the pot.

4. Add the cooked mushrooms, sauce, Parmesan, parsley, and lemon juice to the pasta and toss to combine, adjusting the sauce consistency with the reserved cooking water as desired. Season with salt and pepper to taste and serve.

VARIATION

Pasta with Sautéed Mushrooms, Peas, and Camembert

Follow the recipe for Pasta with Sautéed Mushrooms, omitting the thyme and adding ½ cup thawed frozen peas to the skillet with the broth in step 2. Substitute 3 ounces Camembert, cut into ½-inch pieces (do not remove the rind), for the Parmesan, and 1 tablespoon minced fresh chives for the parsley.

SPAGHETTI WITH LEMON

SPAGHETTI AL LIMONE IS A GREAT EXAMPLE of simple Italian cooking at its best—a few basic ingredients are combined to create a boldly flavored, satisfying meal—and so it seemed like an ideal recipe to scale down for two. In researching various recipes for this dish, we found the ingredients varied only slightly. Lemon juice, lemon zest, pasta, and Parmesan cheese were essentials, and extra-virgin olive oil, butter, heavy cream, and basil were the variables.

To get a sense of what this dish should be, we tested three basic recipes—the first using extra-virgin olive oil, the second using butter, and the third using a combination of heavy cream and butter. The version with just butter tasted a bit bland (although tasters did enjoy the butter flavor), and the version made with butter and cream was much too heavy, overpowering the bright lemon flavor. The pasta also absorbed the cream quickly and reminded us of an Alfredo sauce. Tasters unanimously declared extra-virgin olive oil the winner—it complemented the lemon flavor beautifully. An added benefit of using oil was that the sauce did not need to be cooked; instead, the oil and lemon juice form a simple vinaigrette that can be tossed with the warm pasta just before serving.

But what is the ideal ratio of lemon to olive oil? In our first few tests, we used equal amounts of lemon juice and oil, but the tart citrus flavor was much too strong and left tasters puckering their lips. Reducing the amount of lemon juice in small increments, we found that 2½ tablespoons of lemon juice to ¼ cup of extra-virgin olive oil provided the best balance. One teaspoon of lemon zest boosted the lemon flavor without adding acidity.

Even with the lemon juice, zest, and olive oil amounts figured out, some tasters still felt that the sauce was a little unbalanced. Our first instinct was to add some pasta cooking water to see if it would mellow the flavor. This worked fine at keeping the sauce fluid over the pasta, but it did little for the flavor. Remembering that we liked the flavor of butter in our original tests, we wondered if a little butter might enrich the lemon flavor. We added a pat of butter to the warm pasta and it was just what we were looking for—the butter took the edge off the lemon and rounded out the flavor of the sauce.

The Parmesan cheese we simply stirred in with the olive oil and lemon juice; it thickened the sauce slightly and contributed a warm, nutty flavor that tasters appreciated. They also liked a sprinkling of basil. We then wondered if garlic had a place in our dish—we had seen it in a couple of the recipes we researched and thought we should give it a try. Wanting to stick with our working recipe, which required no cooking of the sauce, we decided to make a paste from the garlic by adding a little salt—a technique, often used when adding garlic to a vinaigrette, that helps mellow its pungent flavor slightly. The addition of just one clove prepared in this manner went a long way. Tasters loved the flavor it imparted; it gave depth to the lemon flavor without competing with it. We now had a dish that is easy enough to prepare for a quick but elegant weeknight meal.

Spaghetti with Lemon and Basil
SERVES 2

To measure spaghetti without a scale, bundle it into a tight, round bunch and measure the diameter with a ruler; ½ pound of spaghetti should measure 1¼ inches. The flavor of this dish depends on high-quality extra-virgin olive oil, fresh-squeezed lemon juice, and fresh basil.

- ½ **pound spaghetti (see note)**
- **Salt**
- ¼ **cup extra-virgin olive oil (see note)**
- 2½ **tablespoons fresh lemon juice plus**
  1 teaspoon grated lemon zest
- 1 **garlic clove, minced to a paste (see photo)**
- 1 **ounce Parmesan cheese, grated (about ½ cup)**
- 1 **tablespoon unsalted butter, softened**
- 2 **tablespoons shredded fresh basil (see page 52)**
- **Pepper**

1. Bring 4 quarts water to a boil in a large pot. Add the pasta and 1 tablespoon salt, and cook, stirring often, until al dente. Reserve ½ cup of the cooking water, then drain the pasta and return it to the pot.

2. Whisk the olive oil, lemon juice, lemon zest, garlic, and ¼ teaspoon salt together in a bowl, then stir in the Parmesan cheese until thick and creamy.

3. Add the olive oil mixture, butter, and basil to the pasta, and toss to combine, adjusting the sauce consistency with the reserved cooking water as desired. Season with salt and pepper to taste and serve.

MINCING GARLIC TO A PASTE

After mincing the garlic as you normally would, sprinkle it with a pinch of salt, then drag the side of a chef's knife over the mixture to make a fine paste. Continue to mince and drag the knife as necessary until the paste is smooth.

VARIATION
Spaghetti with Lemon, Basil, and Shrimp
To measure spaghetti without a scale, bundle it into a tight, round bunch and measure the diameter with a ruler; ⅓ pound of spaghetti should measure about 1 inch.

Follow the recipe for Spaghetti with Lemon and Basil, reducing the amount of spaghetti to ⅓ pound and reducing the amount of extra-virgin olive oil to 3 tablespoons. Before cooking the pasta, cook 8 ounces extra-large shrimp (21 to 25 per pound), completely peeled and deveined, in the boiling water until pink, curled, and cooked through, about 1 minute. Using a slotted spoon, transfer the shrimp to a bowl, season with salt and pepper to taste, and cover to keep warm while cooking the pasta. Add the cooked shrimp to the pasta with the olive oil mixture in step 3.

LASAGNA

LASAGNA IS AN IDEAL MAIN COURSE when serving a group—most recipes naturally make enough to feed masses. And it's a crowd-pleaser: What's not to love about a dish layered with tender noodles, meaty sauce, and gooey cheese that's baked until golden and bubbling? It's also time-consuming to prepare—boiling the noodles, slow-cooking the sauce, and layering the ingredients can take the better part of a day. But we didn't think this hearty and satisfying favorite should be off-limits when cooking for less than a crowd. Our goal was to produce a streamlined version for two people, and we knew that scaling back the components in just the right ratio would be key.

From prior testing, we'd found we preferred no-boil lasagna noodles to regular dried. No-boil noodles are simply more convenient and they taste better, too. We'd also found that the secret of no-boil noodles is to leave your tomato sauce a little on the watery side. The noodles can then absorb liquid without drying out the dish overall. After several tests with baking dishes of varying sizes, we learned that a 9 by 5-inch loaf pan (or a loaf pan of similar size) was the ideal baking dish for a casserole that will serve two generously, and that a single layer of no-boil lasagna noodles fit perfectly.

We wanted a meat sauce as rich and thick as traditional meat sauce, but we didn't want to simmer our sauce all day to achieve that rich flavor. We turned to meat loaf mix, a mix of equal parts ground beef, pork, and veal sold in one package at most supermarkets. This eliminated the need to buy multiple packages of ground meat and prevented us from having to settle for a less complex sauce by choosing just one. But although meat loaf mix gave us a full-flavored sauce, the texture wasn't right and was still a little thin. We aimed for something richer, creamier, and more cohesive, so our thoughts turned to Bolognese, the classic meat sauce enriched with dairy. Borrowing the notion of combining meat and dairy, we reduced a little cream with the meat before adding the tomatoes. Two tablespoons of cream was all it took for just a half pound of meat: The ground meat soaked up the sweet cream and the final product was rich and flavorful.

Because no-boil noodles rely primarily on the liquid in the sauce to rehydrate and soften, we had to get the moisture content just right. If the sauce was too thick, the noodles would be dry and crunchy; too loose, and they would be limp and lifeless. One 14.5-ounce can of diced tomatoes yielded too thin a sauce, although tasters liked the chunks of tomatoes. Next we drained the diced tomatoes, and to give the sauce some body we added a small can of tomato sauce. The combination yielded a thick, saucy sauce, with soft but substantial chunks of tomatoes. Tasters thought that the lasagna was coming out a bit too dry, so we reserved ¼ cup of the juice from the diced tomatoes and added it back to the sauce to keep it moist.

Cheese was the last component. It was a given that we would sprinkle each layer of the lasagna with mozzarella—the classic lasagna addition—and ricotta added its characteristic creamy richness. Grated Parmesan added a nice little kick to the mild, milky ricotta. An egg helped

to thicken and bind this mixture, and some chopped basil added flavor and freshness. Tucked neatly between the layers of lasagna, this ricotta mixture was easy to prepare and just what we wanted.

In our tests, we found that covering the lasagna with foil from the outset of baking prevented any loss of moisture and helped soften the noodles properly. Removing the foil for the last 10 minutes of baking ensured that the top layer of cheese turned golden brown.

Lasagna

SERVES 2

If you cannot find meat loaf mix, substitute equal parts 80 percent lean ground beef and sweet Italian sausage, casings removed. Do not substitute fat-free ricotta here. See page 61 for a recipe to use up some of the leftover ricotta cheese.

SAUCE

- 1 tablespoon olive oil
- 1 small onion, minced (about ½ cup)
   Salt
- 2 garlic cloves, minced
- 8 ounces meat loaf mix (see note)
- 2 tablespoons heavy cream
- 1 (14.5-ounce) can diced tomatoes, drained,
   ¼ cup juice reserved
- 1 (8-ounce) can tomato sauce
   Pepper

NOTES FROM THE TEST KITCHEN

OUR FAVORITE NO-BOIL NOODLES
Over the past few years, no-boil (also called oven-ready) lasagna noodles have become a permanent fixture on supermarket shelves. Much like "instant rice," no-boil noodles are precooked at the factory. The extruded noodles are run through a water bath and then dehydrated mechanically. During baking, the moisture from the sauce softens, or rehydrates, the noodles, especially when the pan is covered as the lasagna bakes.

For both our lasagna and manicotti recipes, we prefer **Barilla** no-boil noodles for their delicate texture, which resembles that of fresh pasta.

LASAGNA

FILLING, NOODLES, AND CHEESE

    4 ounces whole-milk or part-skim ricotta cheese
        (about ½ cup) (see note)
    1 ounce Parmesan cheese, grated (about ½ cup),
        plus 2 tablespoons
    3 tablespoons chopped fresh basil
    1 large egg, lightly beaten
    ⅛ teaspoon salt
    ⅛ teaspoon pepper
    4 no-boil lasagna noodles
    4 ounces whole-milk mozzarella cheese, shredded
        (about 1 cup)

1. Adjust an oven rack to the middle position and heat the oven to 400 degrees.

2. FOR THE SAUCE: Heat the oil in a large saucepan over medium heat until shimmering. Add the onion and ⅛ teaspoon salt, and cook until softened, 3 to 5 minutes. Stir in the garlic and cook until fragrant, about 30 seconds. Stir in the meat loaf mix and cook, breaking the meat into small pieces, until it is no longer pink, about 2 minutes.

3. Stir in the cream, bring to a simmer, and cook until the liquid evaporates, about 2 minutes. Stir in the drained tomatoes, reserved juice, and tomato sauce. Bring to a simmer and cook until the flavors are blended, about 2 minutes. Season with salt and pepper to taste.

4. FOR THE FILLING, NOODLES, AND CHEESE: Combine the ricotta, ½ cup of the Parmesan, basil, egg, salt, and pepper in a bowl.

5. Spread ½ cup of the sauce over the bottom of a 9 by 5-inch loaf pan, avoiding large chunks of meat. Place 1 of the noodles on top of the sauce and spread one-third of the ricotta mixture over the noodle. Sprinkle evenly with ¼ cup of the mozzarella, and spoon ½ cup of the sauce evenly over the top.

6. Starting with a noodle, repeat the layering process twice more. Place the remaining noodle on top, cover with the remaining 1 cup sauce, and sprinkle with the remaining ¼ cup mozzarella and remaining 2 tablespoons Parmesan.

7. Cover the dish tightly with foil that has been sprayed with vegetable oil spray (or use nonstick foil). Bake until the sauce bubbles lightly around the edges, 25 to 30 minutes. Remove the foil and continue to bake until hot throughout and the cheese is browned in spots, about 10 minutes longer. Let cool for 20 minutes before serving.

USE IT UP: RICOTTA CHEESE

Ricotta Spread
MAKES ABOUT ¾ CUP

Serve with toasted baguette slices, as a dip with bell peppers or fennel, dolloped on pizza, or tossed with pasta.

  4–6 ounces whole-milk or part-skim ricotta cheese
        (about ¾ cup)
    1 tablespoon extra-virgin olive oil
    1 tablespoon chopped fresh basil
  1½ teaspoons fresh lemon juice plus
        1 teaspoon grated lemon zest
    ½ garlic clove, minced to a paste (see page 58)
        Salt and pepper

Stir the ricotta, oil, basil, lemon juice, lemon zest, and garlic together in a bowl. Season with salt and pepper to taste before serving.

SPAGHETTI AND MEATBALLS

MAKING SPAGHETTI AND MEATBALLS is a labor of love— preparing and shaping the meatballs, as well as slowly simmering a tomato sauce, can be an all-day affair. And if you're going to spend that much time preparing a meal, you might as well make enough to serve a crowd. We wanted to streamline this time-intensive recipe so that it was worth making for just two people, without sacrificing flavor. Our goal was to create meatballs that were moist and light, as well as a quick tomato sauce that had the depth and complexity of a slow-cooked one.

We focused on the meatballs first. Meatballs start with ground meat but require additional ingredients to keep them moist and lighten their texture. Meatballs also require binders to keep them from falling apart in the tomato sauce. A traditional source of moisture in meatballs is egg. We tested meatballs made with and without egg and quickly determined that the egg was a welcome addition, giving us a more tender meatball.

The list of possible binders included dried bread crumbs, fresh bread crumbs, ground crackers, and bread soaked in milk. We found that bread and cracker crumbs soaked up any available moisture, making the meatballs tough and dry when cooked to well done. In comparison, the meatballs made with bread soaked in milk were moist, creamy, and rich.

We liked the milk but wondered if we could do better. We tried adding yogurt but had to thin it with milk in order to mix it with the bread. These meatballs were creamy and flavorful, but now the meatballs had a slight tanginess. We decided to stick with the richness imparted by whole milk.

With the dairy now part of our working recipe, we found the meatball mixture a tad sticky and hard to handle. By eliminating the egg white (the yolk has all the fat and emulsifiers that contribute smoothness), we eliminated the stickiness.

It was finally time to experiment with the crucial ingredient: the meat. Meatballs are often made of some combination of ground beef, pork, and often veal, but when cooking for two people, it is fussy to have to buy two or three types of ground meat. Using meat loaf mix (where the ground beef, pork, and veal are already combined) allowed us to get good texture and flavor without being stuck with a lot of leftover meat.

With our ingredients in order, it was time to test cooking methods. We tried roasting, broiling, and the traditional pan-frying. Roasting yielded dry, crumbly meatballs; broiling was extremely messy and also tended to produce dry meatballs. Pan-frying produced meatballs with a rich, dark crust and moist texture. We found that if we used a small 8-inch skillet we could get away with using less oil and still cook the meatballs in one batch.

We wondered if we could save cleanup time and build more flavor into the tomato sauce by making it in the same pan used to fry the meatballs. We emptied out the vegetable oil used to fry the meatballs, then added a little fresh olive oil (olive oil is important to the flavor of the sauce) before adding garlic and tomatoes. Not only did this method prove convenient, but it also gave the sauce depth, as the browned bits that had formed when the meatballs were fried helped flavor the sauce, eliminating the need to simmer it for hours.

Meatballs need a thick, smooth sauce; chunky sauces didn't meld with the meatballs and made them soggy. Crushed tomatoes had the right consistency, but as we discovered when developing our recipe for Pasta with Creamy Tomato Sauce (page 52), crushed tomatoes come only in large 28-ounce cans—impractical when cooking for two people. Pureeing a 14.5-ounce can of diced tomatoes in the food processor gave us the right texture and the right amount of sauce.

We now had a simple-to-prepare, yet hearty and satisfying, spaghetti and meatballs that didn't require all day in the kitchen—or result in a full week's worth of leftovers.

Spaghetti and Meatballs

SERVES 2

To measure spaghetti without a scale, bundle it into a tight, round bunch and measure the diameter with a ruler; ½ pound of spaghetti should measure 1¼ inches. If you can't find meat loaf mix, substitute equal parts 80 percent lean ground beef and sweet Italian sausage with the casings removed.

MEATBALLS

- 1 slice high-quality white sandwich bread, crusts removed, torn into pieces
- 3 tablespoons whole milk
- 8 ounces meat loaf mix (see note)
- 2 tablespoons grated Parmesan cheese
- 1 tablespoon chopped fresh basil
- 1 large egg yolk
- 1 garlic clove, minced
- ½ teaspoon salt
- ¼ teaspoon pepper
- ½ cup vegetable oil

SAUCE AND SPAGHETTI

- 1 (14.5-ounce) can diced tomatoes
- 1 tablespoon olive oil
- 1 garlic clove, minced
  Salt and pepper
- ½ pound spaghetti (see note)
- 1 tablespoon shredded fresh basil
  Grated Parmesan cheese, for serving

1. FOR THE MEATBALLS: Mash the bread pieces and milk to a smooth paste in a large bowl with a fork. Add the meat loaf mix, Parmesan, basil, egg yolk, garlic, salt, and pepper, and mix with your hands until uniform. Form the mixture into eight 1½-inch balls.

2. Heat the oil in an 8-inch skillet over medium-high heat until shimmering. Add the meatballs and cook until well browned on all sides, about 8 minutes, turning as needed. Transfer the meatballs to a paper towel–lined plate. Discard the oil in the skillet, leaving behind any browned bits.

3. FOR THE SAUCE AND SPAGHETTI: Process the tomatoes, with their juice, in a food processor until smooth, about 10 seconds. Add the oil and garlic to the skillet, and cook over medium heat until fragrant, about 30 seconds. Stir in the processed tomatoes, scraping up the browned bits, bring to a simmer, and cook until the sauce thickens slightly, 5 to 8 minutes.

4. Add the meatballs, cover, and simmer, turning the meatballs occasionally, until heated through, about 5 minutes. Season with salt and pepper to taste.

5. Meanwhile, bring 4 quarts water to a boil in a large pot. Add the pasta and 1 tablespoon salt, and cook until al dente. Reserve ½ cup of the cooking water, then drain the pasta and return it to the pot.

6. Spoon some of the sauce (without meatballs) over the spaghetti and toss to coat, adjusting the sauce consistency with the reserved cooking water as desired. Divide the pasta between two serving bowls, and top with the meatballs and remaining sauce. Sprinkle with the basil and serve with the Parmesan.

NOTES FROM THE TEST KITCHEN

THE BEST GRATER FOR PARMESAN
When we need to grate a hefty amount of hard cheese, like Parmesan, our first choice is not the ubiquitous box grater, but rather a rasp grater, a long, flat grater. Shaped like a ruler but with lots and lots of tiny, sharp raised teeth, it makes grating large amounts of hard cheese nearly effortless. Our favorite is the **Microplane Grater,** $12.95, which has a solid handle that provides great leverage for grating. It also makes quick work of ginger and citrus zest.

OUR FAVORITE SUPERMARKET PARMESAN
Can domestic Parmesan really stand up to imported Parmigiano-Reggiano? Simply put, no, it cannot. Our tasters effortlessly picked out the imports in our lineup of eight supermarket cheeses. The two genuine Parmigiano-Reggianos, sold by Boar's Head and Il Villaggio, were the clear favorites, and tasters deemed **Boar's Head Parmigiano-Reggiano** "best in show." The domestic cheeses, all made in Wisconsin, presented a wide range of flavors and textures from quite good to rubbery, salty, and bland.

BAKED MANICOTTI

WELL-MADE VERSIONS OF THIS ITALIAN-AMERICAN classic—pasta tubes stuffed with rich ricotta filling and blanketed with tomato sauce—can be eminently satisfying. So what's not to love? Putting it all together. For such a straightforward collection of ingredients (after all, manicotti is just a compilation of pasta, cheese, and tomato sauce), the preparation is surprisingly fussy. Blanching, shocking, draining, and stuffing slippery pasta tubes require more patience (and time) than we usually have. When cooking for two people, all this effort hardly seems worth it. Could we find a simpler, better method for making baked manicotti for two people?

We decided to start with a "quick" recipe that we found on the back of a manicotti box. It called for stuffing uncooked pasta tubes with ricotta, covering them with a thin tomato sauce, then baking. Filling raw pasta tubes with cheese was marginally easier than stuffing limp parboiled noodles, but it wasn't without missteps: A few shattered along the way. Still, we followed the recipe through, watering down a jar of tomato sauce with a cup of boiling water and pouring it over the manicotti. After 30 minutes in the oven, this manicotti was inedible; some of the pasta shells remained uncooked, and the pink, watered-down sauce tasted, well, like water.

Frustrated, we decided to first zero in on the noodles. What about using no-boil lasagna noodles? We softened the noodles in boiling water, turning them into pliable sheets of pasta, then spread them with the cheese filling. This method worked like a charm. After a quick soak, these noodles could be filled and rolled in minutes.

Now we had to figure out what to put the noodles in. Most baked manicotti recipes fill a 13 by 9-inch dish, making plenty for a group. Even a smaller 8 by 8-inch baking dish would serve four people. We tried filling half of an 8 by 8-inch baking dish and leaving the other side empty, but the noodles sagged and collapsed in the oven, oozing filling. They clearly needed to be snug. We then grabbed a loaf pan, which was also the best pick for our Lasagna (page 59). The stuffed manicotti, laid widthwise, fit perfectly and made two good-sized portions.

Next we addressed the filling. It was a given that ricotta would serve as the base for the filling—part-skim and whole-milk ricotta both worked very well, but fat-free ricotta tasted dry and chalky. In addition to ricotta, shredded low-moisture mozzarella and Parmesan are generally added to the filling, and we decided to stick with tradition. Adding an egg and tweaking the balance of cheeses (specifically, adding a generous amount of mozzarella) proved key to warding off a runny filling.

RICOTTA CHEESE

Originally crafted from the whey by-product of Romano cheese making, ricotta cheese has garnered fame as a white, cushiony filling for baked pasta dishes. Nowadays, there are many other uses for ricotta; for example, we use it to make pesto (see page 144). Our favorite ricotta cheese is **Calabro,** which boasts a certain freshness that many commercial brands lack. It's made from fresh curds—drawn from nothing other than Vermont farm whole milk, skim milk, a starter, and a sprinkle of salt. Granted, its shelf life spans only a matter of days, but one spoonful should be enough to guarantee its quick disappearance from your fridge, even if it comes in a 16-ounce or larger container. If you can't find Calabro, read labels and look for another fresh ricotta without gums or stabilizers.

MAKING MANICOTTI

1. Soak no-boil lasagna noodles in boiling water for 5 minutes until pliable, using the tip of a paring knife to separate the noodles and prevent them from sticking together.

2. Using a spoon, spread about ¼ cup of the filling evenly over the bottom three-quarters of each noodle, leaving the top quarter of the noodles exposed.

3. Starting at the bottom, roll each noodle up around the filling, and lay in the prepared loaf pan, seam-side down.

We wanted a simple, brightly flavored tomato sauce for our pasta, so we made one with olive oil, garlic, and diced canned tomatoes pureed in a food processor to give the sauce body quickly. We also gave the sauce a flavor boost with fresh basil leaves and a dash of red pepper flakes.

A slow-cooked tomato sauce didn't fit into our streamlining goal, so we simmered the sauce until just thickened before assembling and baking the manicotti. When tasters commented that the final manicotti was dry, we wondered if both simmering and baking the sauce was overkill for this scaled-down quantity. Happy to cut out a step, we made the manicotti again, this time putting the sauce into the oven raw. Thinking of our waterlogged earlier tests, the thinness of the unbaked sauce concerned us, but in the oven the extra moisture was absorbed by the manicotti, keeping it moist and tender. The sauce reduced enough that it didn't taste raw, but it still had bright and fresh tomato flavor.

To finish, we added a light sprinkling of Parmesan and baked the manicotti uncovered for the last 10 minutes to brown the cheese. This, at last, was a scaled-down manicotti that won our complete affection—great-tasting and easy to prepare.

Baked Manicotti

SERVES 2

Do not substitute fat-free ricotta cheese here. We prefer to use Barilla no-boil lasagna noodles in this dish because their thin, delicate texture makes them easier to roll into uniform manicotti. See page 61 for a recipe to use up some of the leftover ricotta cheese.

SAUCE

- 1 (14.5-ounce) can diced tomatoes
- 1 tablespoon extra-virgin olive oil
- 2 garlic cloves, minced
- ¼ teaspoon salt
- ⅛ teaspoon red pepper flakes (optional)
- 1 tablespoon chopped fresh basil

FILLING AND PASTA

- 8 ounces whole-milk or part-skim ricotta cheese (about 1 cup) (see note)
- 3 ounces whole-milk mozzarella cheese, shredded (about ¾ cup)
- 2 ounces Parmesan cheese, grated (about 1 cup)
- 1 large egg, lightly beaten

BAKED MANICOTTI

1 tablespoon chopped fresh basil
¼ teaspoon salt
⅛ teaspoon pepper
6 no-boil lasagna noodles (see note)

1. Adjust an oven rack to the middle position and heat the oven to 400 degrees.

2. FOR THE SAUCE: Process the tomatoes, with their juice, olive oil, garlic, salt, and pepper flakes (if using) together in a food processor until smooth, about 10 seconds. Transfer to a bowl and stir in the basil.

3. FOR THE FILLING AND PASTA: Combine the ricotta, mozzarella, ½ cup of the Parmesan, egg, basil, salt, and pepper in a bowl.

4. Fill a large bowl halfway with boiling water. Following the photos on page 64, slip the noodles into the water, one at a time, and let them soak until pliable, about 5 minutes, separating them with the tip of a knife to prevent sticking. Remove the noodles from the water and place in a single layer on clean kitchen towels.

5. Spread ½ cup of the sauce over the bottom of a 9 by 5-inch loaf pan. Use a spoon to spread about ¼ cup of the cheese mixture evenly over the bottom three-quarters of each noodle (with the short side facing you), leaving the top quarter of noodle exposed. Starting at the bottom, roll each noodle up around the filling, and lay in the prepared loaf pan, seam-side down. Spoon the remaining sauce evenly over the top, covering the pasta completely. Sprinkle with the remaining ½ cup Parmesan.

6. Cover the dish with foil and bake until bubbling, about 25 minutes. Remove the foil and continue to bake until the cheese is lightly browned, about 10 minutes. Let cool for 15 minutes before serving.

SESAME NOODLES WITH SHREDDED CHICKEN

YOU MAY THINK OF SESAME NOODLES as merely a humble bowl of cold noodles, but don't be fooled—just one bite and you're hooked on these noodles with shreds of tender chicken, all tossed with fresh sesame sauce. And then you've got a real problem: Once you get the hankering, good versions of this dish can be hard to find. The cold noodles have a habit of turning gummy, the chicken often dries out, and the sauce is notorious for turning bland and pasty. We wanted a recipe that not only could quell a serious craving but could do it fast and make an amount appropriate for two diners.

Fresh Chinese noodles have a slightly chewier texture and cleaner flavor than dried noodles, making them an ideal backdrop for a flavorful sauce. Though tasters liked fresh Chinese noodles best, we determined that dried noodles could be used as a substitute if you can't find the fresh ones. Tasters liked the sturdy texture of spaghetti here. Regardless of what type of noodle we used, however, the trouble was that after being cooked and chilled, they jelled into a rubbery skein. After trying a number of ways to avoid this, we found it necessary to rinse the noodles under cold tap water directly after cooking. This not only cooled the hot noodles immediately but also washed away much of their sticky starch. To further forestall any clumping, we tossed the rinsed noodles with a little oil.

Boneless, skinless chicken breasts are quick to cook and easy to shred; the real question was how to cook them. The microwave seemed easy in theory, but we found the rate of cooking difficult to monitor—30 seconds meant the difference between overdone and underdone. Many recipes suggested poaching the chicken in water or broth, but this chicken had a washed-out flavor. Nor was roasting the answer; it caused the outer meat to dry out before the interior was fully cooked. Cooking the chicken under the broiler, however, worked perfectly. The chicken cooked through in minutes, retaining much of its moisture and flavor. We found that when combined with the noodles, one breast easily served two people.

Most authentic sesame noodle recipes use Asian sesame paste (not to be confused with Middle Eastern tahini), but it can be hard to find. Noodles made with peanut butter were nearly as good, and it's a pantry staple cooks are likely to have on hand. Tasters preferred chunky peanut butter over smooth, describing its flavor as fresh and nutty. We had been making the sauce in a blender and realized that the chunky bits of peanuts were being freshly ground into the sauce, producing a cleaner, stronger flavor. We found the flavors of both fresh garlic and ginger necessary, along with soy sauce, rice vinegar, hot sauce, and brown sugar. We also ground some sesame seeds into the sauce for sesame flavor. To keep the sauce from being too thick or pasty, we thinned it out with water.

The addition of red bell pepper strips and cucumber slices provided some crunch as well as color. To give the dish additional layers of flavor, we tossed the rinsed pasta with toasted sesame oil instead of a neutral oil and garnished the noodles with toasted sesame seeds. At last we had a bowl of sesame noodles and chicken we could savor.

Sesame Noodles with Shredded Chicken

SERVES 2

Conventional chunky peanut butter works best in this recipe because it tends to be sweeter than natural or old-fashioned versions. Fresh Chinese noodles will cook more quickly than dried spaghetti; fresh noodles will take about 4 minutes, whereas spaghetti will take about 10 minutes. To measure spaghetti without a scale, bundle it into a tight, round bunch and measure the diameter with a ruler; ⅓ pound of spaghetti should measure about 1 inch. See pages 17 and 21, respectively, for recipes to use up the leftover red bell pepper and cucumber.

SAUCE

2½ tablespoons soy sauce

1½ tablespoons sesame seeds, toasted (see page 226)

2 tablespoons chunky peanut butter (see note)

1 tablespoon rice vinegar

1 tablespoon light brown sugar

1½ teaspoons grated or minced fresh ginger

1 garlic clove, minced

½ teaspoon hot sauce

Hot water

CHICKEN AND NOODLES

1 (8-ounce) boneless, skinless chicken breast, trimmed

8–9 ounces fresh Chinese noodles or ⅓ pound dried spaghetti (see note)

1 tablespoon salt

1 tablespoon toasted sesame oil

½ red bell pepper, cored, seeded, and sliced into ¼-inch-wide strips

½ cucumber, peeled, halved lengthwise, and seeded (see page 20), sliced ¼ inch thick

1 carrot, peeled and grated on the large holes of a box grater

2 scallions, sliced thin on the bias

1 tablespoon chopped fresh cilantro (optional)

1 tablespoon sesame seeds, toasted (see page 226)

1. FOR THE SAUCE: Blend the soy sauce, sesame seeds, peanut butter, vinegar, brown sugar, ginger, garlic, and hot sauce together in a blender until smooth, about 30 seconds. With the machine running, add hot water, 1 tablespoon at a time, until the sauce has the consistency of heavy cream (you should need about 2 tablespoons).

2. FOR THE CHICKEN AND NOODLES: Adjust an oven rack to be about 6 inches from the broiler element and heat the broiler. Set a slotted broiler pan top over a broiler pan bottom, spray the top with vegetable oil spray, and lay the chicken on the top.

3. Broil the chicken until lightly golden on both sides and the thickest part registers 160 to 165 degrees on an instant-read thermometer, 10 to 12 minutes, flipping the chicken halfway through. Transfer the chicken to a carving board, tent with foil, and let rest for 5 minutes. Shred the chicken into bite-sized pieces using 2 forks, following the photo on page 13.

4. Meanwhile, bring 4 quarts water to a boil in a large pot. Add the noodles and the salt, and cook, stirring often, until tender. Drain the noodles and rinse under cold running water until cold.

5. Transfer the noodles to a large bowl and toss with the sesame oil. Add the sauce, shredded chicken, bell pepper, cucumber, carrot, scallions, and cilantro (if using), and toss to combine. Sprinkle with the sesame seeds and serve.

NOTES FROM THE TEST KITCHEN

FRESH CHINESE NOODLES

Many varieties of fresh Chinese noodles are available in local supermarkets, though the selection is larger in an Asian market. Some noodles are cut thin (left), and others are cut slightly wider (right). Their texture is a bit more starchy and chewy than that of dried noodles, and their flavor is cleaner (less wheaty) than Italian pasta, making them an excellent match with potent, highly seasoned sauces. You can substitute dried Italian pasta, such as linguine or spaghetti, but we think these fresh noodles—often called Chinese noodles or Asian-style noodles—are worth tracking down.

Fresh Chinese noodles cook quickly, usually in no more than three to four minutes in boiling water. Adding salt to the water is sometimes, but not always, necessary—many Chinese noodle sauces are rich in soy sauce, which is high in sodium.

THIN

WIDE

CRUNCHY BAKED PORK CHOPS

CHAPTER 3

EVERYDAY MAIN DISHES

CHICKEN AND VEGETABLE BAKES

BAKED CHICKEN BREASTS ARE A CLASSIC standby for weeknight suppers, but they're usually met with little excitement at the dinner table. Diners often assume they'll be lifting their forks to a pedestrian dish of overcooked, dry, and just plain bland poultry. We were certain that simple baked chicken breasts could be an inspiring main course and set out to develop a recipe for two that would include an imaginative mix of vegetables and a zesty sauce.

We began our kitchen tests by choosing the type of chicken. Bone-in, skin-on breasts are a good choice because the bones and skin protect the meat from drying out in the oven, resulting in moist and tender chicken. Also, they're a natural pick when cooking for two because the butcher can package them individually if asked. Now we had to figure out the flavors of our dish and how to get them into the chicken breasts.

We turned to marinating, hoping to incorporate some of the marinade into a flavorful sauce at the end. The only problem, however, is that most marinades contain some sort of acidic component—such as lemon juice, vinegar, or yogurt—that breaks down the proteins in the meat, making for mealy, mushy chicken, even when marinated for a short length of time. To work around this problem, we created an acid-free marinade, but boosted the flavor of the finished dish by adding lemon juice to some reserved marinade and then, at the last minute, pouring this mixture over the baked chicken.

This technique worked wonders—the chicken was moist, tender, and flavorful, and the lemon juice that was incorporated in the reserved marinade and drizzled over the cooked chicken added a sharp, fresh dimension. Since we planned to add a few vegetables to our baked chicken, we made a garlic, shallot, and herb marinade with bright but neutral flavors.

Moving on to the vegetables, we chose those that would require minimal prep or could be thrown right into the baking dish with the chicken. Cherry tomatoes seemed like an obvious choice. Cut in half, they broke down too much in the oven, so we left them whole; 1 cup, or ½ pint, was just the right amount. They softened beautifully and released flavorful juices into the pan, but remained a separate element in the dish. Wanting to add a few Mediterranean notes to complement the tomatoes, we included fennel for its sweet anise flavor and whole pitted kalamata olives for their brininess. To ensure that the fennel cooked at the same rate as the chicken and tomatoes, we sliced it thin.

Tasters were happy with this trio of vegetables but wanted just a bit more flavor. Instead of spending extra time chopping more shallots, garlic, and herbs, we simply tossed the vegetables with a tablespoon of the reserved marinade. After baking the vegetables and breasts together in the oven, we found that the marinade mingled with the juices from the tomatoes and chicken to form a tasty sauce. Fresh basil, sprinkled on just before serving, was the perfect finishing touch and embellished the Mediterranean flavors nicely.

Up until now, we had cooked our chicken and vegetables in a moderate 350-degree oven, but after a little more testing, we found that cranking the oven up to 450 degrees produced nicely browned skin without compromising the juicy, tender texture of the meat. An 8-inch-square baking dish was just the right size to hold two chicken breasts and the vegetables; larger baking dishes caused the vegetables to scorch and the juices to evaporate too quickly.

USE IT UP: CHERRY TOMATOES

Quick Tomato Salsa
MAKES ABOUT 1 CUP

If you have any fresh chile peppers, feel free to substitute 1 tablespoon, minced, for the cayenne pepper. Serve this salsa with tortilla chips or our Chicken Fajitas (page 11) or Grilled Chicken Fajitas (page 200).

- 6 ounces cherry tomatoes (about 1 cup), chopped coarse
- 2 tablespoons chopped fresh cilantro
- 1 tablespoon extra-virgin olive oil
- 1 small shallot, minced (1 tablespoon)
- 1 teaspoon fresh lime juice
- Pinch cayenne pepper (see note)
- Salt and pepper
- Sugar

Combine all of the ingredients in a bowl, and season with salt, pepper, and sugar to taste. Let the salsa sit for 15 minutes until the flavors meld before serving.

Simple Chicken Bake with Fennel, Tomatoes, and Olives

SERVES 2

You can substitute boneless, skinless breasts here if desired; marinate the boneless chicken as directed, but reduce the baking time by 10 to 15 minutes. The marinade takes the place of the brine in this recipe, so there's no need to brine the chicken. See page 70 for a recipe to use up the leftover cherry tomatoes.

MARINADE AND CHICKEN

- ⅓ cup extra-virgin olive oil
- 1 shallot, minced (about 3 tablespoons)
- 2 tablespoons water
- 2 tablespoons chopped fresh basil
- 4 garlic cloves, minced
- ½ teaspoon salt
- ⅛ teaspoon pepper
- 2 (12-ounce) bone-in, skin-on split chicken breasts, trimmed (see page 7) (see note)

VEGETABLES

- 1 fennel bulb (about ¾ pound), stalks removed, halved, cored, and sliced thin (see photos)
- 6 ounces cherry tomatoes (about 1 cup)
- ¼ cup pitted kalamata olives (see photo)
- ¼ teaspoon salt
- ⅛ teaspoon pepper
- 1 tablespoon fresh lemon juice
- 2 tablespoons chopped fresh basil

1. **FOR THE MARINADE AND CHICKEN:** Whisk together all of the ingredients, except the chicken, in a bowl until well combined. Measure out and reserve ¼ cup of the marinade. Pour the remaining marinade into a large zipper-lock bag, add the chicken, seal the bag tightly, and toss to coat. Marinate the chicken in the refrigerator for at least 1 hour, or up to 24 hours. (If marinating the chicken for more than 1 hour, refrigerate the ¼ cup reserved marinade as well; return it to room temperature before using.)

2. **FOR THE VEGETABLES:** Adjust an oven rack to the middle position and heat the oven to 450 degrees. In a large bowl, combine 1 tablespoon of the reserved marinade with the fennel, tomatoes, olives, salt, and

NOTES FROM THE TEST KITCHEN

PITTING OLIVES

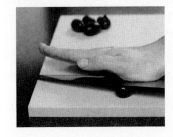

If your olives aren't pitted, here's a quick way to pit them. Place the olive on a cutting board and hold the flat edge of a knife over the olive. Press the blade firmly with your hand to loosen the pit, then remove the pit with your fingers.

PREPARING FENNEL

1. Cut off the stems and feathery fronds. (The fronds can be minced and used for a garnish, if desired.)

2. Trim a very thin slice from the base and remove any tough or blemished outer layers from the bulb.

3. Cut the bulb in half through the base. Use a small, sharp knife to remove the pyramid-shaped core.

4. Slice each fennel half into thin strips.

pepper and toss to coat. Transfer the vegetables to an 8-inch square baking dish.

3. Remove the chicken breasts from the marinade and lay them, skin-side up, on top of the vegetables; discard any marinade left in the bag. Bake until the thickest part of the breasts registers 160 to 165 degrees on an instant-read thermometer, 35 to 45 minutes. Meanwhile, stir the lemon juice into the remaining 3 tablespoons reserved marinade.

4. Transfer the chicken and vegetables to a serving platter along with the juices from the baking dish. Pour the lemon-marinade mixture over the chicken and let rest for 5 minutes. Sprinkle with the basil before serving.

VARIATION

Simple Chicken Bake with Fennel, Orange, and Oil-Cured Olives

Follow the recipe for Simple Chicken Bake with Fennel, Tomatoes, and Olives, substituting ¼ cup chopped fresh cilantro for the basil (in the marinade and for finishing the dish), 1 orange, peeled, segmented, and cut into ½-inch pieces, for the tomatoes, ¼ cup pitted oil-cured olives for the kalamata olives, and 1 tablespoon fresh lime juice for the lemon juice.

CHICKEN TIKKA MASALA

INDIAN CUISINE HAS GROWN EXPONENTIALLY in popularity in the last decade, and one of our favorite Indian dishes to spice up dinnertime is chicken tikka masala. At its best, chicken tikka masala consists of tender chunks of chicken marinated in yogurt and spices, which are then simmered in a rich, creamy tomato sauce. But all too often, the chicken is either mushy or dry and the sauce unbearably rich and overspiced. The good news is that these problems are not impossible to overcome, and we set our sights on creating a foolproof recipe for chicken tikka masala that we could tailor for two.

We wanted a four-season dish, so we chose the broiler (not the grill) as our cooking medium, replacing the tandoor oven typically used in India, and got rid of the fussy step of skewering raw, slippery chicken pieces. We had the most success retaining moisture by cooking boneless, skinless chicken breasts whole, then cutting them into pieces only after they were broiled.

In our tests, the larger breasts didn't dry out as quickly as the smaller cut pieces did under the searing heat of the broiler. But, even using whole breasts, the chicken still wasn't juicy enough.

To add moisture to the chicken breasts, we turned to the yogurt marinade. The marinade is meant to tenderize the meat and infuse it with the essence of spices and aromatics. But, as we learned with our Chicken and Vegetable Bakes (page 70), when chicken is left in an acidic marinade too long, the meat starts to break down and become mushy. The lactic acid in the yogurt was having this very effect on our chicken breasts. We had to find a different way to incorporate the yogurt. Still left with the problem of moderately dry chicken, we considered salting, a technique we have used for steaks, roasts, chicken parts, and whole turkeys, which initially draws moisture out of protein; then the reverse happens and the salt and moisture flow back in. We decided to salt the chicken, then dip it in yogurt—all we needed was ½ cup for our two breasts—just before cooking it. This move, we thought, would solve our dry chicken problem.

We rubbed the chicken with a simple mixture of salt and everyday spices and waited 30 minutes, which gave us time to prepare the masala sauce; then we dunked the chicken in yogurt and broiled it. The result was the best tikka yet—it was nicely seasoned and tender but not soft. In just half an hour's time, the salt rub had done its job of flavoring the chicken and keeping it moist, and the yogurt mixture acted as a protective barrier, shielding the lean meat from the powerful heat of the broiler. For more authentic flavor, we replaced the spices with a commercial garam masala—since it was already prepared, we wouldn't have to worry about mixing miniscule amounts of masala spices. To encourage gentle charring on the chicken, we added a tablespoon of oil to the yogurt. We also took advantage of the yogurt's thickness, mixing in minced garlic and freshly grated ginger for more flavor.

Having perfected the chicken, we shifted our focus to the sauce. *Masala* means "hot spice," and the ingredients in a masala sauce depend largely on the whims of the cook, but tomatoes and cream usually form the base. The hard part would be figuring out the right sauce proportions for our scaled-down chicken tikka.

We started our sauce with a mixture of sautéed aromatics—an onion, a bit of grated ginger, a garlic clove, and one small chile—and more garam masala. Then we added crushed tomatoes, which we favored over diced canned or fresh tomatoes because of their smoother consistency. The problem was that crushed tomatoes only come in a 28-ounce can, which is way too much tomato for chicken tikka for two. To avoid having half a can of tomatoes left, we made our own crushed tomatoes by processing a 14.5-ounce can of whole tomatoes in the food processor. A tablespoon of tomato paste added some depth and a pleasant shade of red to the dish. In place of the standard heavy cream used in chicken tikka, we decided to use yogurt—this way, we'd cut down on our shopping *and* make double use of an ingredient already on our grocery list. When the sauce had finished simmering, we simply stirred in ⅓ cup to add a creamy consistency.

When we stirred the juicy and lightly charred chicken pieces into the fragrant tomato sauce, we knew we had nailed it. Spooned over basmati rice and sprinkled with cilantro, this chicken tikka was foolproof—and delicious.

OUR FAVORITE GARAM MASALA

This spice blend is a key ingredient in our Chicken Tikka Masala and Shrimp Tikka Masala, but making it from scratch can add a great deal of time to recipe preparation. In search of a good-tasting commercial garam masala, we tested a handful of top brands. Tasters' favorite was **McCormick Gourmet Collection Garam Masala** for its ability to both blend into dishes and round out their acidic and sweet notes. Tasters also liked the subtle warmth of cardamom, cinnamon, and cloves. Widely available in supermarkets, McCormick won praise from tasters for adding a mellow, well-balanced aroma to most dishes.

STORING FRESH GINGER

We include fresh ginger in both the yogurt marinade and the sauce of our Chicken Tikka Masala, but we use modest amounts, definitely not the entire knob that we would have purchased at the store. Although this is an incredibly affordable ingredient, we didn't want to just pitch the remaining unused portion. To determine the best way to store fresh ginger, we cut several knobs and stored them in different ways—unwrapped in a dark pantry, on the counter exposed to sunlight, and in the refrigerator or freezer in a variety of unwrapped or foil- or plastic-wrapped permutations.

After two weeks, all of the samples had dried out, with the frozen ginger faring the worst—after a brief thaw, it was porous and mushy. The room-temperature ginger had shriveled and started to sprout. The wrapped, refrigerated ginger was moldy where condensation had trapped in the wrapper. The one ray of light was the unwrapped, refrigerated ginger, which had a relatively fresh appearance, with no mold. So the next time you have a leftover knob of ginger, ditch the plastic wrap and foil, and just toss it into the refrigerator unwrapped.

Chicken Tikka Masala

SERVES 2

This dish tastes best when prepared with whole-milk yogurt, but low-fat yogurt can be substituted; do not use fat-free yogurt. The sauce can be made and refrigerated up to 4 days in advance; gently reheat the sauce before adding the hot chicken. Serve with basmati rice.

CHICKEN

- ½ teaspoon garam masala
- ⅛ teaspoon cayenne pepper
- ½ teaspoon salt
- 2 (6 to 8-ounce) boneless, skinless chicken breasts, trimmed
- ½ cup plain yogurt (see note)
- 1 tablespoon vegetable oil
- 2 garlic cloves, minced
- 2 teaspoons grated or minced fresh ginger

SAUCE

- 1 (14.5-ounce) can whole tomatoes
- 2 tablespoons vegetable oil
- 1 small onion, minced (about ½ cup)
- 1 garlic clove, minced
- 1 teaspoon grated or minced fresh ginger
- 1 small serrano chile, stemmed, seeded, and minced
- 1½ teaspoons tomato paste
- 1½ teaspoons garam masala
- 1 teaspoon sugar
- Salt
- ⅓ cup plain yogurt (see note)
- 2 tablespoons chopped fresh cilantro

1. FOR THE CHICKEN: Combine the garam masala, cayenne, and salt in a bowl. Pat the chicken dry with paper towels, then coat the chicken thoroughly with the

CHICKEN TIKKA MASALA

spices, pressing to help them adhere. Place the chicken on a plate, cover, and refrigerate for 30 to 60 minutes. Whisk the yogurt, oil, garlic, and ginger together in a medium bowl, cover, and refrigerate until needed.

2. FOR THE SAUCE: Process the tomatoes with their juice in a food processor until pureed, about 15 seconds. Heat the oil in large saucepan over medium heat until shimmering. Add the onion and cook until softened and lightly browned, 5 to 7 minutes. Stir in the garlic, ginger, chile, tomato paste, and garam masala and cook until fragrant, about 30 seconds.

3. Stir in the processed tomatoes, sugar, and ¼ teaspoon salt, and bring to a boil. Reduce the heat to low, cover, and simmer, stirring occasionally, for 15 minutes. Off the heat, stir in the yogurt and cover to keep warm.

4. Meanwhile, adjust an oven rack to be 6 inches from the broiler element, and heat the broiler. Line a rimmed baking sheet with foil and top with a wire rack. Using tongs, dip the chicken into the yogurt mixture so that it is thickly coated and arrange on the prepared wire rack; discard any excess yogurt mixture. Broil the chicken until the exterior is lightly charred in spots and the thickest part of the breasts registers 160 to 165 degrees on an instant-read thermometer, 10 to 18 minutes, flipping the chicken halfway through cooking.

5. Let the chicken rest for 5 minutes, then cut into 1-inch chunks. Stir the chicken pieces into the warm sauce (do not simmer the chicken in the sauce). Stir in the cilantro, season with salt to taste, and serve.

VARIATION

Shrimp Tikka Masala

To make this dish easier to eat, we suggest peeling the shrimp completely, including the tail shells.

Follow the recipe for Chicken Tikka Masala, substituting 12 ounces extra-large shrimp (21 to 25 per pound), peeled and deveined, for the chicken. Season the shrimp with the spices as directed in step 1 (do not refrigerate) and coat with the yogurt mixture as directed in step 4, then spread out on a baking sheet and broil until cooked through and lightly browned, about 4 minutes (do not flip the shrimp during cooking). Stir the shrimp into the sauce and serve as directed.

CHICKEN MOLE

TO MIX UP MEXICAN NIGHT and give our taco shells and tortilla wrappers a rest, we make chicken mole. *Mole*, from the Aztec word for "sauce," is a rich blend of chiles, nuts, spices, fruit, and chocolate and is considered the national dish of Mexico—either paired with poultry, or ladled over enchiladas, rice, or potatoes. An authentic mole has complex layers of flavor, but these exotic flavors come with a price: an extensive and varied list of ingredients and a notoriously long and complicated cooking method. We wanted a streamlined recipe for a smaller batch of chicken mole that we could incorporate into our weeknight repertoire.

We began our testing with the sauce. Dried chiles are a key ingredient in mole, and most authentic mole recipes call for several different types of chiles (such as mulato, guajillo, pasilla, ancho, and chipotle). Hoping to keep the process (and the shopping) simple since we were cooking just for two, we tried substituting chili powder and canned chipotle chile in adobo sauce for the more exotic dried chiles. The chili powder provided a full yet mild base of chile flavor, and the chipotle added the necessary heat and smokiness.

Next, we moved on to the nut and seed components of the mole. Most recipes called for some combination of toasted almonds, pumpkin seeds, peanuts, and sesame seeds. We tested them all and, in the end, liked the rich, creamy flavors of toasted almonds and sesame seeds. However, grinding our own almonds—just for a tablespoon—was a bit of a hassle. So we came up with a clever substitute: peanut butter. We were pleased to find that it gave our sauce a great nutty flavor and a luxurious, velvety texture.

Our mole had begun to come together, but we noticed that it was still missing some complexity. We added chocolate—the best-known ingredient in mole—for depth and richness. Adding a few spices, including cinnamon and cloves, along with some raisins, helped the flavor take another leap forward. To further round out and deepen the flavors of the sauce, we added a chopped fresh tomato. We usually favor canned tomatoes in the test kitchen, but here we opted for a single fresh tomato because we needed much less than the contents of a 14.5-ounce can.

Until now we had been using water as the liquid base for the sauce, but we experimented with chicken broth and discovered that our sauce tasted richer and better. We found that we needed more broth than expected (1¼ cups) to yield enough sauce for two with the right consistency (not too thick).

NOTES FROM THE TEST KITCHEN

THE 30-MINUTE BRINE

Poultry and pork are quite lean, and in some preparations, they can cook up quite dry. The salt in a brine changes the structure of the muscle proteins and allows them to hold on to more moisture when exposed to heat. Tasters had no trouble in a sample test picking out brined pork chops versus chops left untreated.

Making the brine super-concentrated—dissolving salt in cold water using the amounts given below—gets the job done in just 30 minutes, the time it will take you to prepare the other elements of the meal. The 1-quart brines fit, along with the meat, in a medium container or gallon-sized zipper-lock bag; but for 2 quarts of water, you'll need to use a larger container.

There is one exception to brining: If you've purchased kosher poultry, frozen injected turkey, or enhanced pork chops injected with a salt solution, don't brine them. These treatments will keep the chicken, turkey, and chops moist, and brining will make the meat way too salty.

POULTRY OR MEAT	COLD WATER	SALT
Pork chops	1 quart	2 tablespoons
Bone-in, skin-on chicken breasts	1 quart	¼ cup
Game hens	1 quart	¼ cup
Boneless turkey breast halves	2 quarts	½ cup

THE BEST GARLIC PRESSES

A sticky, stinky job, hand-mincing garlic is a chore many cooks avoid by pressing the cloves through a garlic press. Our favorite garlic press is **Kuhn Rikon's Easy-Squeeze Garlic Press** (left), $20. Though its plastic material seems less sturdy than other metal models, this garlic press performed best— its longer handle and shorter distance between the pivot point and the plunger help make pressing less work. The deeply curving plastic handles are also easier to squeeze together than straight handles. Another favorite is the **Trudeau Garlic Press** (right)—with solid construction, it is sturdy and easy to use and is our best buy at a reasonable $11.99.

Finally, we took a close look at the cooking method and came up with a strategy to combine the individual elements of our mole. Rather than sautéing only the basic aromatics of onion and garlic, we found it beneficial to sauté the chili powder, chile, chocolate, and spices as well, which helped to develop and deepen their flavors. Also, using the right size pan helped— since we were making our sauce in a smaller quantity just for two, we found we could use a 10-inch skillet (instead of a big 12-inch pan) and reduce the heat to medium-low to prevent the sauce from burning. After just 10 minutes of simmering, the rich, spicy flavors had come together. We were after a smooth texture, so we pureed the mixture into a velvety sauce.

As the construction of our mole finally came to an end, we turned our attention to incorporating the chicken into the dish. We chose bone-in, skin-on chicken breasts, placed the chicken in an 8-inch baking dish, and topped it liberally with our sauce. The chicken came out moist and flavorful, but tasters overwhelmingly commented that the skin was flabby. We wanted to stick with bone-in breasts, since the bones prevented the meat from drying out, so we simply removed the skin before cooking. To prevent the meat from burning, we flipped the breasts midway through cooking.

After about 40 minutes at 400 degrees, they were perfectly done—tender, juicy, and richly flavored in a smooth and spicy mole sauce.

Chicken Mole

SERVES 2

If using kosher chicken, do not brine. If brining the chicken, do not season with salt in step 4. Take care not to burn the spice and chocolate mixture in step 2; add a small splash of water or broth to the skillet if it begins to scorch. The sauce can be made and refrigerated up to 4 days in advance; loosen it with water as needed before using.

- 1 tablespoon vegetable oil
- 1 small onion, minced (about ½ cup)
- 1 tablespoon chili powder
- 1 teaspoon minced canned chipotle chile in adobo sauce
- ¼ teaspoon ground cinnamon

Pinch ground cloves

½ ounce bittersweet, semisweet, or Mexican chocolate, chopped coarse

1 garlic clove, minced

1¼ cups low-sodium chicken broth

1 tomato, cored, seeded, and chopped medium

2 tablespoons raisins

1 tablespoon peanut butter

1 tablespoon sesame seeds, toasted (see page 226), plus extra for garnish

Salt and pepper

Sugar

2 (12-ounce) bone-in split chicken breasts, skin removed, trimmed (see page 7), brined if desired (see note; see page 76)

1. Adjust an oven rack to the middle position and heat the oven to 400 degrees. Heat the oil in a 10-inch skillet over medium heat until shimmering. Add the onion and cook until softened, 3 to 5 minutes.

2. Reduce the heat to medium-low, stir in the chili powder, chile, cinnamon, cloves, and chocolate, and cook, stirring constantly, until the spices are fragrant and the chocolate is melted and bubbly, about 1 minute. Stir in the garlic and cook until fragrant, about 30 seconds. Stir in the broth, tomato, raisins, peanut butter, and sesame seeds. Bring to a simmer and cook, stirring occasionally, until the sauce is slightly thickened and measures about 1¾ cups, 10 to 15 minutes.

3. Transfer the sauce to a blender and process until smooth, about 30 seconds. Season with salt, pepper, and sugar to taste.

4. Pat the chicken dry with paper towels, and season with salt and pepper. Arrange the chicken in an 8-inch square baking dish, skinned-side down, and pour the pureed sauce over the top, turning the chicken to coat evenly. Bake for 20 minutes. Flip the chicken skinned-side up, and continue to bake until the thickest part of the breasts registers 160 to 165 degrees on an instant-read thermometer, 15 to 25 minutes longer.

5. Remove the chicken from the oven, tent the dish loosely with foil, and let rest for 5 to 10 minutes. Transfer the chicken to individual serving plates, spoon the sauce over the top, sprinkle with the extra sesame seeds, and serve.

SWEET AND SPICY THICK-CUT PORK CHOPS

BIG, THICK PORK CHOPS are a great weeknight main course, and when covered with a sweet, sticky glaze, they are elevated to both hearty and heavenly. Glazed chops are especially well suited to weeknight cookery, since only one pan is required to cook both the protein and the sauce. But one big caveat is timing: The glaze ingredients can burn if added too soon, and the pork can quickly turn from succulent and moist to dry and leathery. We thought the glaze could help keep our chops moist, but with only two chops on the menu, would we be making enough glaze to prevent dryness and add flavor? We headed into the test kitchen to find out.

Initially, we tested various methods for cooking the chops. Most of the recipes we tried yielded tough chops that were overcooked; starting the chops over high heat (to create a flavorful browned crust) was the problem. Yes, the crust was nice and brown, but by the time the center of these thick chops finally came up to the desired temperature, much of the meat was dried out and tough. In the past, we've solved this problem by brining our chops so they retained their juice when cooked. But we were concerned that if we took this step, the pork chops would leach brining liquid into the glaze, causing the finished dish and sauce to be unbearably salty. We'd have to save the brine for another time.

Looking at our options, we recalled the peculiar method of cooking thin pork chops by starting them in a cold skillet and then turning the heat to medium-low. Would this work with thick-cut chops? We were pleasantly surprised when it did. After 10 minutes, the first side was nicely browned. Minutes later, our chops were juicy and tender. We then removed the chops from the pan and built enough glaze to keep the chops tender. A quarter-cup each of apple juice and brown sugar gave us a good base, and cider vinegar enhanced the flavor. For more kick, we enlivened the glaze with a little Dijon mustard and hot sauce.

Both the chops and the glaze tasted good, and we had ample glaze, but their flavors weren't integrated—the glaze was more like a separate sauce. To bring the flavors together, we tried adding the glaze ingredients to the pan after the first 10 minutes, when we flipped the chops, the theory being that this would keep the exterior of the chops moist as they finished cooking in the liquid. The problem was that with just two chops in a large skillet, the glaze burned. We moved to a smaller pan to minimize the surface area and eliminate charring. We also covered the pan while the chops cooked, so the meat stayed juicy and the glaze didn't become too thick or char.

Once the chops reached 140 degrees, we let them rest on a plate for five minutes and simmered the glaze until it had a nice thick consistency. We plated our two well-cooked pork chops and smiled to ourselves—these thick-cut chops were moist, juicy, and perfectly complemented by our sweet and tangy glaze.

Sweet and Spicy Thick-Cut Pork Chops

SERVES 2

If your chops are thinner than 1½ inches, they will cook through much more quickly.

- ¼ **cup apple juice**
- ¼ **cup packed dark brown sugar**
- 2 **tablespoons cider vinegar**
- 2 **garlic cloves, minced**
- 2 **teaspoons Dijon mustard**
- 2 **teaspoons hot sauce**
- ⅛ **teaspoon cornstarch**
- 2 **(12 to 14-ounce) bone-in rib or center-cut pork chops, about 1½ inches thick, sides slit (see page 24)**
- 1 **teaspoon vegetable oil**
  Salt and pepper
- ¼ **teaspoon granulated sugar**

1. Whisk the juice, brown sugar, vinegar, garlic, mustard, hot sauce, and cornstarch together in a bowl. Pat the chops dry with paper towels, rub them with the oil, season with salt and pepper, and sprinkle the granulated sugar over one side of each chop.

2. Place the chops, sugared-side down, in a 10-inch non-stick skillet. Place the skillet over medium-low heat and cook until the chops are lightly browned, 10 to 12 minutes. Flip the chops and add the juice mixture. Cover and cook until the centers of the chops register 140 to 145 degrees on an instant-read thermometer, 8 to 10 minutes.

3. Transfer the chops to a plate and let rest until the centers register 150 degrees on an instant-read thermometer. Meanwhile, increase the heat to medium-high and continue to simmer the sauce until it is thick and syrupy, about 5 minutes. Off the heat, return the chops to the skillet and coat them evenly with the glaze. Serve.

CRUNCHY BAKED PORK CHOPS

WHEN DONE RIGHT, baked breaded pork chops are the ultimate comfort food: tender cutlets surrounded by a crunchy coating that crackles apart with each bite. But all too often, baked chops miss the mark. Using preseasoned crumbs from the supermarket for the breading makes for a bland-tasting chop with a thin, sandy crust, and homemade bread crumbs result in a soggy, patchy crust that won't stick to the meat. Our goal was clear: to cook two juicy, flavorful chops with a crisp, substantial crust that would stay on the meat from fork to mouth.

Our first task was choosing the best cut of meat. Though bone-in chops retain moisture better, we decided on a boneless cut for this dish, so we wouldn't have to bread the bone and there would be no distraction from the crunchy crust. We chose center-cut boneless loin chops, which are easy to find in the supermarket and would cook evenly. When it came to size, pork chops that were between ¾ and 1 inch thick were our tasters' top choice, providing the perfect ratio of meat to crust.

The test kitchen's standard breading method (dusting with flour, dipping in beaten egg, and rolling in toasted bread crumbs) was a sufficient placeholder as we figured out the best cooking technique. Simply baking the breaded chops on a baking sheet, the most obvious method and one used in many recipes, made the bottoms soggy. Placing the chops on a wire rack set over the baking sheet so the air could circulate definitely helped. Upping the oven temperature from 350 to 425 degrees helped even more. The coating crisped up more readily, and the excess moisture evaporated by the time the pork reached the requisite 140-degree serving temperature.

Now that we'd figured out the right way to cook our chops, we could concentrate on the type of breading and how much we would need to coat two chops. Tasters deemed panko too fine-textured and bland. Crushed Melba toast was crunchier but didn't stick together. Ultimately, tasters preferred the fresh flavor and slight sweetness of crumbs made from white sandwich bread. Two slices of bread formed the perfect amount of crumbs to liberally coat two pork chops.

For flavor and to help the fresh crumbs brown, we tossed them with a little salt, pepper, and oil before toasting them on a baking sheet in the oven. They were still a bit bland, so in a subsequent test, we stirred some minced garlic and shallot into the crumbs before toasting them and tossed them with grated Parmesan cheese and herbs after they cooled. Chops coated with these fresh bread crumbs tasted great, except for one thing—the coating peeled off in patches, creating a few unappetizing bald spots on our pork chops.

With crumbs as thick and coarse as these, we knew we'd need more than a typical egg wash to glue them to the pork. We recalled a recipe that used mustard instead of eggs to hold the crumbs to the chops. It was worth a shot, so we started by dousing the chops in flour to help the mustard adhere, then dipped our chops in mustard. A straight swap made the taste too intense, but keeping the eggs and adding a few tablespoons of Dijon mustard thickened the mixture nicely and brought just enough new flavor to the mix. Unfortunately, a few areas were still flaking off. How could we prevent our chops from shedding their great bready coating?

The solution was to whisk a little flour into the egg and mustard mixture. We were pleased to find that our adhering agent was now more of a spackle than a watery glue. After flouring the chops, we coated them evenly in the egg mixture, covered them in bread crumbs, and

baked them. They were much better, but there was a soft, puffy layer just under the crumbs. Replacing the whole eggs with egg whites, which have less fat but enough protein to lend sticking power, provided just the crisp, dry crust we were looking for. And even more impressive, the crumbs clung firmly to the meat even during some heavy knife-and-fork action. This pork finally had some real chops.

Crunchy Baked Pork Chops
SERVES 2

If the pork is "enhanced" (see page 80 for more information), do not brine. If brining the pork, omit the salt when seasoning the chops in step 3. Once breaded, the chops can be frozen for up to 1 week; bake the frozen chops as directed (do not thaw), increasing the baking time to 35 to 40 minutes.

- 2 slices high-quality white sandwich bread, torn into 1-inch pieces
- 1 small shallot, minced (about 1 tablespoon)
- 2 garlic cloves, minced
- 1 tablespoon vegetable oil
- Salt and pepper
- 1 tablespoon grated Parmesan cheese
- 1 tablespoon chopped fresh parsley
- Pinch dried thyme
- 7 tablespoons unbleached all-purpose flour
- 2 large egg whites
- 4 teaspoons Dijon mustard
- 2 (6 to 8-ounce) boneless center-cut pork chops, ¾ to 1 inch thick, sides slit (see page 24), brined if desired (see note; see page 76)
- Lemon wedges, for serving

page 80; page 24; page 76

1. Adjust an oven rack to the middle position and heat the oven to 350 degrees. Pulse the bread in a food processor to coarse crumbs, about 8 pulses. Toss the crumbs with the shallot, garlic, oil, ⅛ teaspoon salt, and ⅛ teaspoon pepper, then spread them out on a rimmed baking sheet. Bake the crumbs, stirring occasionally, until deep golden brown and dry, about 15 minutes. Let the crumbs cool to room temperature, then toss with the Parmesan, parsley, and thyme.

2. Place ¼ cup of the flour in a shallow dish. In a second shallow dish, whisk the egg whites and mustard together until combined, then whisk in the remaining

---

USE IT UP: EGG YOLKS

Aïoli
MAKES ABOUT 1 CUP

This aïoli makes a nice condiment for our Crunchy Baked Pork Chops and Pan-Fried Crab Cakes (page 92). It also works as a spread on sandwiches. The aïoli can be refrigerated in an airtight container for up to 3 days.

page 92

- 2 large egg yolks
- 4 teaspoons fresh lemon juice
- 1 garlic clove, minced
- ⅛ teaspoon sugar
- Salt and pepper
- ¾ cup olive oil

Process the yolks, lemon juice, garlic, sugar, ¼ teaspoon salt, and ⅛ teaspoon pepper together in a food processor until combined, about 10 seconds. With the machine running, gradually add the oil through the feed tube in a slow, steady stream, about 30 seconds. Scrape down the sides of the bowl with a rubber spatula and process for 5 seconds longer. Season with salt and pepper to taste.

3 tablespoons flour until almost smooth, with just a few pea-sized lumps. Spread the prepared bread crumbs in a third shallow dish.

3. Increase the oven temperature to 425 degrees. Spray a wire rack with vegetable oil spray and place over a rimmed baking sheet. Pat the chops dry with paper towels, and season with salt and pepper.

4. Dredge the pork chops in the flour and shake off the excess. Following the photos, coat the chops with the egg mixture, allowing the excess to drip off. Coat all sides of the chops with a thick layer of bread crumbs, pressing to help them adhere. Lay the breaded chops on the prepared wire rack.

5. Bake the chops until the centers register 140 to 145 degrees on an instant-read thermometer, 15 to 20 minutes. Remove the chops from the oven, and let rest on the rack until the centers register 150 degrees on an instant-read thermometer, about 5 minutes. Serve with the lemon wedges.

VARIATION

Crunchy Baked Pork Chops with Prosciutto and Asiago Cheese

Follow the recipe for Crunchy Baked Pork Chops, omitting the salt in the bread crumbs and when seasoning the chops. Before breading the pork chops, place a ⅛-inch-thick slice Asiago cheese on top of each chop, then wrap the chops with a thin slice prosciutto, pressing on the prosciutto and cheese to help them adhere. Coat and bake the chops as directed, handling the chops gently to prevent the cheese and prosciutto from falling off.

OLD-FASHIONED BURGERS

SIXTY YEARS AGO, BURGERS AT THE DRIVE-IN were synonymous with freshly ground high-quality beef. Today they mean tasteless mass-produced patties. Could we bring back the genuine article?

We started by testing preground chuck from the supermarket to see if it would be a viable option for the meat. The answer was a resounding no—the resulting patties were dense, rubbery, and dry, with little beef flavor and no crisp exterior. To improve our burgers, we'd need freshly ground meat. But with the lack of good butchers nowadays, we were going to have to grind it ourselves.

With flavor, juiciness, and convenience at the grocery store in mind, we made burgers with over a dozen different cuts of meat. We settled on a combination of sirloin steak tips (also called flap meat), the winner for beefiness, and well-marbled beef short ribs, which added the perfect amount of fat without diminishing the beefy flavor. When it came to shopping, these cuts were great choices for scaling this recipe to serve two—one 5-ounce steak

OLD-FASHIONED BURGERS

CHOOSING THE RIGHT SIZE SKILLET

With a skillet in hand, you can cook just about anything. In this book, we call for 8-inch, 10-inch, and 12-inch skillets (see pages 15 and 53 for our recommended nonstick and traditional skillets). In general, we find that a large 12-inch skillet is the most versatile size to have, as it can hold a large quantity of food. We reach for this size when we need a greater surface area to brown food in a single, even layer, as with our Pan-Seared Shrimp with Chipotle Sauce (page 85) and stir-fries. But when cooking for two, an 8-inch or 10-inch skillet often works better, as with our Old-Fashioned Burgers and Pan-Fried Crab Cakes (page 92), because a smaller skillet provides ample room for the food. Also, a larger pan would scorch because the surface is exposed and uncovered. And, a smaller skillet can be a better choice when cooking in liquid or sauce; in a large pan the sauce would not cover the food. One last note: It's important to use the pan specified for in the recipe—if you use a pan that is too big, both the food and the bottom of the pan will burn. And if you use a pan that is too small, food will be packed too tight and steam.

GETTING THE PERFECT GRIND

Underprocessed meat will lead to gristly bits in our Old-Fashioned Hamburgers and patties that don't hold together. Overprocessed meat becomes rubbery as it cooks. Perfectly ground meat is fine enough to ensure tenderness but coarse enough that the patty will stay loose.

UNDERPROCESSED   **OVERPROCESSED**

GROUND TO PERFECTION

THE BEST HAMBURGER BUNS

In a tasting of supermarket hamburger buns, we were surprised by the differences in flavor and texture. Sunbeam and Wonder were so airy that they all but deflated if grasped too indelicately; heartier brands stood up well to ketchup, mustard, and other wet condiments. But the deal breaker was size: Several products measured less than 3½ inches across—a tight fit for most patties. Our favorites, **Pepperidge Farm Premium Bakery Rolls** (not the smaller "Classic" variety), have a generous 4½-inch diameter, hearty texture, and "wheaty" taste.

tip and one 3-ounce boneless short rib yielded just the right amount of meat to make two burgers.

We had the beefy flavor and juiciness right, but the patties still had a certain rubberiness. After looking through our food science books, we discovered the culprit: collagen. As collagen proteins get heated, they start to squeeze the meat, making it dense and rubbery. After a certain point, the collagen unravels, and the meat turns from tough to tender, but this process takes hours of cooking—far longer than the minutes our burger would spend on the griddle.

To keep our burgers tender, we had to keep them as loosely packed as possible and handle them as little as possible, to minimize the shrinking and tightening of the collagen proteins. To do this, we ground our meat, letting it fall directly from the grinding tube onto a baking sheet. Then, without lifting the meat, we separated it into two piles and gently pressed each one into a patty. Even as they were cooking in the pan, we could tell that these patties were going to be different. Their juice bubbled up through the meat's porous surface and dripped back down, basting the burgers as they cooked. Biting into one revealed meat so tender it virtually fell apart.

There was just one problem: Most home cooks don't own a meat grinder. We decided to give the food processor a shot. Right away, long, stringy bits of fat and meat got caught up in the blade, mashing the meat together and reviving the collagen. Our solution was to cut the meat into chunks and chill them in the freezer first, so they would provide some resistance in the food processor. This worked well—the chunks were chopped, not overprocessed and pulverized. After less than five minutes in a hot skillet, they were perfectly done and still juicy.

As for the sauce, we were in the mood for the tangy and sweet Thousand Island–style dressing that often accompanies this type of burger, so we whipped up a modest amount of sauce. For the requisite layer of cheese, American was our tasters' favorite for the way it completely enrobed the burger when melted, although cheddar and Swiss cheese had their proponents. A few thin slices of onion were preferred in lieu of "the works"—they allowed the flavor of the beef to take center stage unchallenged.

With a tender, juicy patty and toppings sandwiched by a soft toasted bun, we had finally perfected our small-batch burgers.

Old-Fashioned Burgers

SERVES 2

Sirloin steak tips are labeled "flap meat" by some butchers, so be sure you're buying the right meat; flank steak can be substituted if necessary. If you cannot find boneless beef short ribs, buy a bone-in beef rib and simply trim the fat and cut the meat off the bone yourself. Handling the ground meat minimally when shaping the burgers is crucial to their tender texture.

BURGERS

- 5 ounces sirloin steak tips, cut into 1-inch chunks (see note)
- 3 ounces boneless beef short ribs, cut into 1-inch chunks (see note)
- Salt and pepper
- 1 tablespoon unsalted butter
- 2 soft hamburger buns
- ½ teaspoon vegetable oil
- 2 slices American cheese
- Thinly sliced onion, for serving

SAUCE

- 1 tablespoon mayonnaise
- 1½ teaspoons ketchup
- ¼ teaspoon sweet pickle relish
- ¼ teaspoon sugar
- ¼ teaspoon white vinegar
- ⅛ teaspoon pepper

1. FOR THE BURGERS: Place the steak tip and short rib pieces on a baking sheet in a single layer (do not let the pieces touch). Freeze the meat until very firm and starting to harden around the edges but still pliable, 15 to 25 minutes.

2. FOR THE SAUCE: Meanwhile, whisk all of the ingredients together in a bowl, cover, and refrigerate until needed.

3. Place the frozen meat in a food processor and pulse until the meat is coarsely ground, 10 to 15 pulses, stopping to redistribute the meat around the blade as necessary to ensure an even grind. Transfer the ground meat to a baking sheet by simply overturning the bowl; do not touch the meat directly. Gently spread the meat out on the baking sheet and inspect it carefully, discarding any long strands of gristle or large chunks of hard meat or fat.

4. Carefully separate the ground meat into 2 equal mounds. Without picking the meat up, use your fingers to gently shape each mound into a loose patty about ½ inch thick and 4 inches in diameter, leaving the edges and surface ragged. Season the top of each patty with salt and pepper. Using a spatula, flip the patties, and season the other side. Refrigerate the patties while toasting the buns, or for up to 6 hours.

5. Melt the butter in a 10-inch skillet over medium heat. Add the buns, cut-side down, and toast until light golden brown, about 2 minutes. Set the buns aside and wipe out the skillet with paper towels.

6. Add the oil to the skillet and return to high heat until just smoking. Lay the burgers in the skillet using a spatula and cook without moving them for 3 minutes. Flip the burgers and cook for 1 minute. Top each patty with a slice of cheese and continue to cook until the cheese is melted, about 1 minute longer.

7. Lay the burgers on the bun bottoms and top with the onion. Spread the burger sauce on the top buns, lay the buns on the burgers, and serve.

PAN-SEARED SHRIMP

RECIPES USING SHRIMP ARE GREAT when you're cooking for two. You can buy just what you need from your local fish market, or you can keep a bag of frozen shrimp in your freezer for a last-minute dinner. For this recipe, we were aiming to perfect our cooking method for pan-seared shrimp and jazz the shrimp up a little with some Mexican flavors. Shrimp make a great main course for two because they cook fast, making it easy to put dinner on the table in record time.

Getting started, we knew that if we got our searing method down pat, we would be rewarded with shrimp that were well caramelized on the outside and moist and tender on the inside. When executed properly, searing helps to preserve the shrimp's plumpness and trademark briny sweetness. We decided to use peeled and deveined shrimp because unpeeled shrimp don't pick up as much of the delicious caramelized flavor that pan-searing provides. Also, peeled shrimp are easier to work with and eat, and this was meant to be a relatively easy main course; we didn't want to spend any extra time peeling shrimp if we didn't have to.

HOW TO BUY SHRIMP

Virtually all of the shrimp sold today in supermarkets have been previously frozen, either in large blocks of ice or by a method called "individually quick frozen," IQF for short. Supermarkets simply defrost the shrimp before displaying them on ice at the fish counter, where they look as though they are freshly plucked from the sea. As a general rule, we highly recommend purchasing bags of still-frozen, shell-on IQF shrimp and defrosting them as needed at home, since there is no telling how long "fresh" shrimp may have been kept on ice at the market. IQF shrimp also have a better flavor and texture than shrimp frozen in blocks. IQF shrimp are available both with and without their shells, but we find the shell-on shrimp to be firmer and sweeter. Also, shrimp should be the only ingredient listed on the bag (preservatives add an unpleasant texture).

PREPARING AVOCADOS

1. After slicing the avocado in half around the pit, lodge the edge of the knife blade into the pit and twist to remove. Use a large wooden spoon to pry the pit safely off the knife.

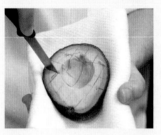

2. Use a dish towel to hold the avocado steady. Make ½-inch crosshatch incisions in the flesh of each avocado half with a knife, cutting down to but not through the skin.

3. Separate the diced flesh from the skin with a soup spoon inserted between the skin and the flesh, gently scooping out the avocado cubes.

IT'S NOT EASY KEEPING GREEN

It's hard keeping half an avocado green—avocados tend to turn brown shortly after being sliced and exposed to air. Here's a nifty trick to retain the color in avocado halves. Rub 1 tablespoon of olive oil on all of the exposed areas of avocado flesh. Then pour the extra oil onto a plate and place the avocado half cut-side down in the center of the oil puddle, creating a "seal." Now simply store it in the refrigerator.

To cook the shrimp, we reached for our 12-inch skillet; its large surface area kept the shrimp from overcrowding in the pan and steaming—a surefire way to prevent caramelization. And this recipe turned out to be well suited to cooking for two: ¾ pound of shrimp fit perfectly in the large skillet. Any more shrimp, and we would need to cook them in two batches.

To achieve the perfect sear, oil was the ideal cooking medium, favored over both a dry pan, which made the shrimp leathery and metallic-tasting, and butter, which tended to burn. To enhance and deepen the essential caramelization of the shrimp, we seasoned them with a little sugar in addition to salt and pepper. This promoted browning and accentuated the shrimp's natural sweetness. We pulled the shrimp from the pan when they were just underdone because we would add them back to the pan with the sauce to warm through, and the last thing we wanted was for our shrimp to be overdone and rubbery with that additional minute of cooking.

For our sauce, we began with small amounts of the usual suspects—a chopped fresh tomato, an onion, garlic, one jalapeño, lime juice, and minced cilantro. Made in the same pan as the cooked shrimp to pick up residual flavors, the mixture was cooked until the tomato broke down slightly and released its water. Unfortunately, this sauce was too loose, and tasters complained of the raw texture of the onion. Tasters also agreed that the dish needed a more assertive flavor, something to give it bite.

Our first step in revisiting the sauce was to reduce the amount of excess liquid, which we accomplished by seeding the tomato. To fix the unpleasing raw texture of the onions, we switched to soft-textured scallions, using the whites in the salsa and saving the green tops for garnish. To add a hot smokiness, we replaced the fresh jalapeño with chipotle chiles in adobo. Now we had a more potent flavor with a spicy punch. Also, instead of cooking down the tomatoes, we simply warmed the sauce through in the hot pan before adding the shrimp to finish cooking.

Once the shrimp had cooked through, which took about a minute, we transferred the whole dish to a platter and garnished it with the reserved scallion greens and freshly diced avocado. Our shrimp were now perfectly caramelized, with a flavor slightly amplified by a squeeze of lime.

Pan-Seared Shrimp with Chipotle Sauce

SERVES 2

If your shrimp are smaller than 21 to 25 per pound, the cooking times will be even shorter. Serve with plain white rice. For more heat, add the greater amount of chipotle chile.

- 1   tomato, cored, seeded, and cut into ½-inch pieces
- 2   scallions, white and green parts separated, each sliced thin
- 2   tablespoons minced fresh cilantro
- 2   garlic cloves, minced
- ½–1   teaspoon minced canned chipotle chile in adobo sauce (see note)
     Salt and pepper
- 12   ounces extra-large shrimp (21 to 25 per pound), peeled and deveined (see page 35)
     Pinch sugar
- 4   teaspoons vegetable oil

USE IT UP: AVOCADO

Creamy Avocado-Herb Dressing

MAKES ABOUT 1 CUP

Use this dressing on a salad of hearty greens. It can also be drizzled over simply prepared white fish. The dressing can be refrigerated in an airtight container for up to 2 days.

- ¼   cup chopped fresh tarragon, parsley, cilantro, or basil
- ¼   cup water
- 4   teaspoons white wine vinegar
- 1   small shallot, minced (about 1 tablespoon)
- 1   small garlic clove, minced
- ½   avocado, pitted, peeled, and chopped (see page 84)
- ¼   cup extra-virgin olive oil
     Salt and pepper
     Sugar

Blend the tarragon, water, vinegar, shallot, garlic, and avocado together in a blender until mostly smooth, about 1 minute. With the blender running, slowly add the oil in a steady stream until incorporated, about 10 seconds. Season with salt, pepper, and sugar to taste and serve.

- 2   teaspoons fresh lime juice
- ½   ripe avocado, halved, pitted, and diced (see page 84)
     Lime wedges, for serving

1. Combine the tomato, scallion whites, cilantro, garlic, chipotle, ¼ teaspoon salt, and a pinch of pepper in a bowl. In a separate bowl, toss the shrimp with the sugar, ⅛ teaspoon salt, and ⅛ teaspoon pepper.

2. Heat 1 tablespoon of the oil in a 12-inch skillet over high heat until just smoking. Add the shrimp in a single layer and cook, without moving, until spotty brown on one side, about 1 minute. Transfer the shrimp to a bowl (they will be underdone).

3. Add the remaining teaspoon oil to the skillet and return to high heat until just smoking. Add the tomato mixture and lime juice, and cook until the tomato softens slightly, about 1 minute. Return the shrimp to the skillet and continue to cook until they are cooked through and hot, about 1 minute.

4. Transfer the shrimp and sauce to a serving platter, sprinkle with the scallion greens and avocado, and serve immediately with the lime wedges.

OVEN-ROASTED SALMON

SALMON IS A POPULAR FISH, easy to shop for and prepare for a weeknight main course for two. Roasting salmon in the oven is a good way to preserve its buttery, succulent texture while also producing a flavorful, caramelized crust. We set out to perfect this method to cook two moist, rich salmon fillets for dinner.

We knew that roasting at a high temperature (from 400 to 475 degrees) could create browning on the exterior of the fish, but by the time that point is reached, the fish is well done. Slow-roasting at a gentle temperature, between 250 and 300 degrees, seemed like a better place to start. We bought two uniform pieces of salmon to ensure even cooking and we placed them in a 275-degree oven for about 20 minutes. This method resulted in moist, near-translucent flesh, but the fish was mushy, and there was no contrast in texture. Turning up the temperature would definitely create a more golden exterior, but it would also sacrifice some of the tender interior.

OVEN-ROASTED SALMON WITH TANGERINE AND GINGER RELISH

We thought that combining high and low heat, as we do with roasted chicken to get crisp skin and juicy meat, would help. After a bit of experimentation, we settled on a starting temperature of 500 degrees, which we reduced to 275 degrees immediately upon placing the fish in the oven. The initial blast of high heat firmed the exterior of the salmon and helped render some of the excess fat that had made the slower-roasted fish mushy. We also preheated the baking sheet, which necessitated cooking the fish with its skin on, so the fillets could be placed skin-side down in the pan to protect the flesh.

The fish tasted a bit fatty, but making several slits through the skin before moving it to the oven allowed most of the fat residing directly beneath the skin to render off onto the baking sheet. The fish then gently cooked while the oven temperature slowly dropped, and it was ready in just 10 minutes. This worked beautifully: We now had salmon with a little firmness on the outside and a lot of moist, succulent meat on the inside.

NOTES FROM THE TEST KITCHEN

PREPARING SALMON FOR ROASTING

 Make four or five shallow slashes along the skin side of each piece of fish, being careful not to cut into the flesh. This allows some of the fat to render off during cooking.

BUYING AND STORING FISH

Buying top-quality fish is just as important as cooking it right. We recommend buying your fish from a trusted source (preferably one with high volume to help ensure freshness). The store, and the fish in it, should smell like the sea, not fishy or sour, and all of the fish should be on ice or properly refrigerated. Be sure to examine the fish before you buy it— the flesh should look bright, shiny, and firm, not dull or mushy. Whole fish should have moist, taut skin, clear eyes, and bright red gills. When possible, have your fishmonger slice steaks and fillets to order rather than buying precut pieces that may have been sitting around.

To keep the fish fresh, keep it cold, especially if you have a long ride home; just ask your fishmonger for a plastic bag of ice to lay the fish on. At home, store the fish in the coldest part of your refrigerator (in a sealed bag over a bowl of ice is best). And try to cook your fish the day you buy it.

We wanted to add some flavor to our oven-roasted salmon. Quick salsas and easy, no-cook relishes were the answer; they stayed in line with our goal of a simple weeknight dinner for two. After trying dozens of combinations, we found those with an acidic element worked best to balance the richness of the fish. Tasters liked a tomato-basil relish, a spicy cucumber version, and a tangy tangerine and ginger pairing. In addition to bright flavor, each relish provided a further contrast in texture to complement the salmon's silkiness.

Oven-Roasted Salmon

SERVES 2

It is important to keep the skin on during cooking, but you can remove it afterward if desired.

- 2 **(6-ounce) skin-on salmon fillets, about 1½ inches thick**
- 1 **teaspoon olive oil**
  Salt and pepper
- 1 **recipe relish (recipes follow)**

1. Adjust an oven rack to the lowest position, place a rimmed baking sheet on the rack, and heat the oven to 500 degrees. Following the photo, use a sharp knife to make 4 or 5 shallow slashes about an inch apart along the skin side of each piece, being careful not to cut into the flesh.

2. Pat the salmon dry with paper towels. Rub the fillets evenly with the oil, and season liberally with salt and pepper. Reduce the oven temperature to 275 degrees and remove the baking sheet. Carefully place the salmon, skin-side down, on the baking sheet.

3. Roast the salmon until the thickest parts still look translucent when cut into with a paring knife and register 125 degrees on an instant-read thermometer, 9 to 13 minutes. Serve with the relish.

Fresh Tomato Relish

MAKES ABOUT 1 CUP

Other fresh herbs, such as mint, parsley, or tarragon, can be substituted for the basil.

- 1 **tomato, cored, seeded, and cut into ¼-inch pieces**
- 1 **tablespoon chopped fresh basil (see note)**
- 2 **teaspoons minced shallot**
- 2 **teaspoons extra-virgin olive oil**

1 small garlic clove, minced

½ teaspoon red wine vinegar

Salt and pepper

Combine all of the ingredients in a bowl and season with salt and pepper to taste.

Spicy Cucumber Relish
MAKES ABOUT 1 CUP

A small jalapeño can be substituted for the serrano. See page 21 for a recipe to use up the leftover cucumber.

½ cucumber, peeled, halved lengthwise, and seeded (see page 20), cut into ¼-inch dice (about 1 cup)

1 tablespoon chopped fresh mint

1 small shallot, minced (about 1 tablespoon)

½ serrano chile, stemmed, seeded, and minced (about 2 teaspoons) (see note)

2 teaspoons fresh lime juice, plus extra for serving

1 teaspoon extra-virgin olive oil

Salt

Combine all of the ingredients in a bowl, season with salt, and let sit at room temperature to blend the flavors, about 15 minutes. Season with extra lime juice to taste before serving.

Tangerine and Ginger Relish
MAKES ABOUT ¾ CUP

A large orange can be substituted for the tangerines.

2 tangerines, peeled, segmented, and cut into ½-inch pieces (see note)

1 scallion, sliced thin

1 teaspoon minced or grated fresh ginger

1 teaspoon fresh lemon juice

1 teaspoon extra-virgin olive oil

Salt and pepper

Place the tangerines in a fine-mesh strainer set over a medium bowl and let drain for 15 minutes, reserving 2 teaspoons of the drained juice. Whisk the reserved tangerine juice, scallion, ginger, lemon juice, and oil together, then stir in the tangerines and season with salt and pepper to taste.

STEAMED MUSSELS

THIS FRENCH BISTRO CLASSIC known as *moules à la marinière* contains just a few simple ingredients—mussels, shallots, parsley, wine, and butter, all cooked together—but the effect is astonishing. The mussels are tender and briny, and the rich broth is perfect for sopping up with chunks of a rustic baguette. With such a brief ingredient list, this would be an easy entrée for two.

Ready to find out if this classic French dish was really as simple as it sounded, we started with the mussels, which require very little prep. Most mussels are now farmed either on ropes or along seabeds. (You may also see "wild" mussels at the market; these mussels are caught by dredging along the seafloor. In our tests, we found them extremely muddy and not worth the bother.) Rope-cultured mussels can be as much as twice the cost of wild or bottom-cultured mussels, but we found them to be free of grit in our testing, and since mussels are generally inexpensive (no more than a few dollars a pound), we think clean mussels are worth the extra money. When selecting mussels, we also make sure to look for ones that are tightly closed; open or gaping mussels may be dying or dead and should not be eaten.

With our mussels in hand—scrubbed clean and debearded (see page 89)—we turned to the steaming liquid, which is typically white wine. Because we don't like to leave any stone unturned, we thought we'd see how straight fish stock would fare. The stock turned out to be bland in comparison to the bright acidity of the wine, which is necessary to offset the briny taste of the mussels. We found it was possible to steam 2 pounds of mussels (1 pound per person made a reasonable dinner serving) in less than ⅓ cup of liquid, but we like to have extra broth for dunking bread or for saucing rice. We settled on using ⅔ cup of white wine to cook 2 pounds of mussels. We also made some refinements to the cooking broth. A generous dose of garlic (two cloves) and a shallot, both sautéed in butter, further emboldened the broth's flavors.

Our mussels had steamed open, and we removed them from the pot. During cooking, the mussels released their own liquid and flavor into the wine mixture, so now we added an ingredient for richness. We tested the usual suspects: butter, cream, sour cream, and *crème fraîche*. The butter was essential; 1 tablespoon was the perfect amount, balancing the acid and enriching the mussel liquor. The sour cream and crème fraîche were eliminated immediately because the tanginess altered the flavor of the broth too much. Heavy cream alone deadened the flavors of this broth, but when it was added with the butter, the balance was just right. A mere 2 tablespoons of cream was all it took to round out the flavors. Finally, we added parsley and reunited the finished broth with the mussels.

In just 15 minutes flat, our mussels were full of rich and briny flavor and left almost nil dirty dishes behind, save for the serving vessel. Now all we needed was some crusty bread to dip in the broth.

Steamed Mussels in White Wine with Parsley

SERVES 2

Any type of mussel will work here; littlenecks or cherrystone clams can also be substituted (large clams will require 9 to 10 minutes of steaming time). Serve with crusty bread, garlic toasts, or rice.

- 2 **tablespoons unsalted butter**
- 1 **shallot, minced (about 3 tablespoons)**
- 2 **garlic cloves, minced**
- ⅔ **cup dry white wine**
- 1 **bay leaf**
- 2 **pounds mussels (see note), scrubbed and debearded if necessary (see photo)**
- 2 **tablespoons heavy cream**
- 3 **tablespoons minced fresh parsley**
  Salt and pepper

1. Melt 1 tablespoon of the butter in a large Dutch oven over medium heat. Add the shallot and cook until softened, about 2 minutes. Stir in the garlic and cook until fragrant, about 30 seconds. Stir in the wine and bay leaf and simmer until the flavors have blended, about 2 minutes.

2. Increase the heat to high and add the mussels. Cover and cook, stirring occasionally, until the mussels open, 3 to 7 minutes.

3. Using a slotted spoon, transfer the opened mussels to a large serving bowl, leaving the liquid in the pot; discard any mussels that have not opened. Remove and discard the bay leaf.

4. Stir the remaining tablespoon butter and cream into the broth and simmer over medium-high heat until the butter is melted and the liquid is slightly thickened, about 1 minute. Stir in the parsley and season with salt and pepper to taste. Pour the sauce over the mussels and serve immediately.

NOTES FROM THE TEST KITCHEN

DEBEARDING MUSSELS

Mussels contain a small, weedy beard that is easy to remove. Trap the beard between the side of a small paring knife and your thumb and pull it. Note that this should be done just before cooking the mussels.

SELECTING AND STORING MUSSELS

When selecting mussels, look for ones that are tightly closed or snap shut when tapped; gaping, open, or cracked mussels may be dying or dead and should not be eaten. Mussels should be stored in a bowl in the refrigerator and used within a day or two. Do not store them in a sealed container, as this will cause them to die. Before cooking, they may need to be scrubbed as well as debearded.

THE BEST PARING KNIFE

A short, nimble paring knife can accomplish all of the small, close jobs that a chef's knife can't, such as coring tomatoes, cutting citrus segments, slivering garlic, and aiding in the removal of mussel beards. In our tests, we found that the way a paring knife feels in your hand makes a big difference. Also, the blade should be somewhat flexible for easy maneuvering into tight spots (such as tomato cores) and for handling curves when peeling and paring. Our preferred paring knife is the **Victorinox Forschner Fibrox Paring Knife,** $12.95, which has a slightly flexible blade that holds a sharp edge for days.

DON'T REFRIGERATE THAT LEFTOVER BAGUETTE

So you've used half a baguette to sop up extra broth with your mussels—what do you do with the rest? Don't put it in the fridge. Storing bread in the refrigerator may seem like a good idea to extend its shelf life, but actually, it shortens it! Believe it or not, the cool temperatures of the fridge speed up the staling process (also known as retrogradation), and a loaf of refrigerated bread will go stale more quickly than a loaf stored in a zipper-lock bag on the counter. For long-term bread storage, we found that freezing is the way to go: Simply wrap the bread tightly with foil, then place it in a zipper-lock bag and freeze for up to 1 month. To serve, place the frozen foil-wrapped loaf directly on the hot rack of a 450-degree oven until warm and crisp, 10 to 30 minutes (depending on the size of the loaf).

Steamed Mussels with Tomato and Basil

Follow the recipe for Steamed Mussels in White Wine with Parsley, substituting 3 tablespoons chopped fresh basil for the parsley and adding 1 finely diced tomato with the basil in step 4.

Steamed Mussels in Coconut Milk with Cilantro

The Asian flavors of this variation offer a new take on steamed mussels.

Follow the recipe for Steamed Mussels in White Wine with Parsley, adding 1 sliced jalapeño chile to the pot with the shallot in step 1. Substitute ¾ cup unsweetened coconut milk for the wine, and 3 tablespoons chopped fresh cilantro for the parsley. Add 1 teaspoon fresh lime juice, 1 teaspoon brown sugar, and 1 teaspoon fish sauce along with the cilantro in step 4.

USE IT UP: COCONUT MILK

Coconut Rice Pudding
SERVES 2

Any type of milk, or even half-and-half, will work in this recipe.

- 1 cup water
- ½ cup medium-grain rice
- ⅛ teaspoon salt
- 1 cup unsweetened coconut milk
- 1½ cups milk (see note)
- ⅓ cup sugar
- ½ teaspoon vanilla extract
- ¼ teaspoon ground cinnamon

1. Bring the water to a boil in a small saucepan. Stir in the rice and salt, cover, and simmer over low heat, stirring occasionally, until the water is almost fully absorbed, 10 to 15 minutes.

2. Stir in the coconut milk, milk, sugar, vanilla, and cinnamon and continue to simmer, stirring frequently, until a spoon is able to stand up in the pudding, 45 to 55 minutes. Serve warm or chilled.

PAN-FRIED CRAB CAKES

UNLESS YOU LIVE NEAR THE CHESAPEAKE BAY or the coast of Maine, crab cakes are more likely an occasional indulgence or a treat reserved for dining out. But when you need to feed only two, they seem like a dish that can be included in your repertoire of weeknight recipes, since 8 ounces of crabmeat will make two healthy, satisfying crab cakes. That said, all too often the crab cakes we've sampled suffer from too much bread crumb or vegetable filler. By making them ourselves, we could cut back on the unnecessary ingredients and focus on the main ingredient: sweet crabmeat.

To find the best crabmeat, we tested the various options, and the differences are stark. Canned crabmeat is horrible; like canned tuna, it bears little resemblance to the fresh product. Frozen crabmeat is stringy and wet, and imitation crabmeat is, as the name implies, not even crabmeat. There is no substitute for fresh blue crabmeat, preferably crabmeat labeled "jumbo lump," which indicates the highest grade and large—not shredded—pieces.

Once we figured out what type of crab to use, our next task was to find the right binder. None of the usual suspects worked. Crushed saltines were a pain to smash into small enough bits, crumbled potato chips added too much richness, and store-bought bread crumbs tasted stale. We finally settled on fresh bread crumbs. They have no overwhelming flavor and are easy enough to make and mix in. The trickiest part is knowing when to stop; crab cakes need just enough binder to hold them together but not so much that the filler overwhelms the seafood, as is the case with many restaurant crab cakes. We started out with 1 cup of crumbs but ended up reducing it to just ½ cup for our final recipe.

The other ingredients are fairly basic in crab cake recipes. Good, sturdy commercial mayonnaise keeps the crabmeat moist and makes the crab, crumbs, and seasonings meld together both before and during cooking. Many recipes use an egg to bind the ingredients together, but we found the egg made our crab cakes rubbery. Classic recipes call for spiking crab cakes with everything from hot sauce to Worcestershire sauce, but our tasters preferred a blend of tradition and trendiness

PAN-FRIED CRAB CAKES

with Old Bay seasoning, lemon zest, minced scallion, and a few teaspoons of chopped fresh herbs.

With all of our ingredients together, we now carefully mixed our cakes with a rubber spatula, folding the ingredients together rather than stirring them in. This motion is important because it helps keep the chunky consistency of the crabmeat intact.

Next, we tried different cooking methods. After baking, deep-frying, broiling, and pan-frying, we settled on pan-frying in a nonstick skillet over medium-high heat. This method is fast and also gives the cook complete control over how brown and how crisp the cakes get. Plus, since we were cooking only two cakes, we could rely on our more manageable medium-sized 10-inch skillet instead of the larger 12-inch skillet.

We first tried frying the crab cakes in butter, but the butter burned too easily. Cut with vegetable oil, the butter was still too heavy. The ideal medium turned out to be vegetable oil, which created a crisp crust that didn't get in the way of the sweet crab flavor.

We were pleased with our basic recipe on most fronts, but we still had trouble keeping the cakes together as they cooked. We had an "aha!" moment when we tried chilling the shaped cakes before cooking—as little as half an hour in the refrigerator made an ocean of difference. The cold firmed up the cakes so that they fried into perfect plump rounds without falling apart.

At last, we had two perfect crab cakes, with minimal filler. Several tasters commented that they'd like a sauce to accompany the cakes, so we reserved some of the mayonnaise base to pair with our crab cakes. The sauce and a few squirts of lemon juice were just enough to call out the natural crab taste and give us that fresh-off-the-pier feeling.

NOTES FROM THE TEST KITCHEN

SITTIN' ON THE DOCK OF THE (OLD) BAY
Old Bay seasoning is a spice mix that's essential for crab boils, crab cakes, and many other seafood dishes, including some shrimp dishes. Created in the 1930s, this spice mix is a regional favorite in Maryland and Virginia along the coast. The predominant flavors in Old Bay are celery, mustard, and paprika. We like to use Old Bay to season steamed or boiled crustaceans and bivalves, in coatings for fried chicken and seafood, and in gumbos and seafood stews.

Pan-Fried Crab Cakes
SERVES 2

When shaping the crab cakes, be gentle and pack the cakes lightly so that they will be tender.

- 6 tablespoons mayonnaise
- 2 scallions, minced
- 1 tablespoon minced fresh parsley
  Salt and pepper
- 2 teaspoons fresh lemon juice and 2 teaspoons grated lemon zest from 1 lemon
- ¾ teaspoon Old Bay seasoning
- 8 ounces jumbo lump crabmeat, picked over to remove cartilage and shells
- 1 slice high-quality white sandwich bread, torn into pieces
- ¼ cup unbleached all-purpose flour
- 2 tablespoons vegetable oil
  Lemon wedges, for serving

1. Combine the mayonnaise, scallions, parsley, ⅛ teaspoon salt, and ⅛ teaspoon pepper in a bowl. Transfer ¼ cup of the mixture to a small bowl, stir in the lemon juice, and set aside for serving. Stir the lemon zest and Old Bay into the remaining mayonnaise mixture and gently fold in the crabmeat, being careful not to break up the lumps of crab.

2. Pulse the bread in a food processor to coarse crumbs, about 4 pulses. Sprinkle ½ cup of the bread crumbs over the crab mixture and gently fold until just incorporated; discard any extra bread crumbs.

3. Divide and shape the crab mixture into two flat, round cakes, about 1½ inches thick and 3 inches in diameter, handling them as little as possible. Transfer the crab cakes to a plate lined with parchment paper, cover, and refrigerate for at least 30 minutes, or up to 24 hours.

4. Place the flour in a shallow dish. Lightly dredge the crab cakes in the flour. Heat the oil in a 10-inch nonstick skillet over medium-high heat until shimmering. Gently lay the crab cakes in the skillet and cook until crisp and browned, 8 to 10 minutes, flipping them halfway through. Transfer the crab cakes to a paper towel–lined plate to drain briefly, then serve with the reserved sauce and lemon wedges.

STUFFED EGGPLANT

THE SMOOTH, SHINY EGGPLANT is a wonderful but underutilized fruit (that's right, it's not actually a vegetable). Even here in the test kitchen, we're guilty of not coming up with new ways to cook eggplant, instead relegating it to its traditional role in eggplant parmesan or ratatouille. But recently, we decided to branch out and create our own version of another popular Middle Eastern dish—stuffed eggplant. This dish, we thought, would be a great vegetarian entrée, filled with the lively punch of onions, garlic, warm spices, and fruity olive oil—an excellent alternative to meaty chops and steaks. Unfortunately, many recipes we came across featured oil-saturated eggplant and bland, watery fillings. We wanted a stuffed eggplant recipe with creamy, earthy eggplant and a hearty, flavorful filling. And, being that eggplants are already pre-portioned, we figured they were a natural for our recipe roster.

We began our testing with the long, slender Japanese or Asian eggplants, but we quickly found that they did not have enough flesh, which made stuffing them difficult. Large, or globe, eggplants, on the other hand, had too much flesh and took too long to cook. But the smaller variety of eggplant (sometimes labeled Italian) worked great. These were ideal for stuffing, and one 10-ounce eggplant was the perfect size for serving each person. The flesh of this eggplant cooked up creamy, with an earthy flavor that wasn't at all bitter—a trait often associated with eggplant.

With the type of eggplant resolved, we had to figure out the best cooking method. We started by roasting the eggplants whole, as in many recipes, but this caused the skins to break, which prevented the eggplants from holding the filling. In addition, tasters wanted more intense eggplant flavor. As a solution, we borrowed a technique we have used for stuffed zucchini. We cut the eggplants in half, brushed them with olive oil, and seasoned them with salt and pepper. Then we preheated a baking sheet, arranged the eggplants cut-side down on the sheet, and covered them with foil to trap the steam. After less than an hour in a 400-degree oven, the eggplants emerged golden brown and tender, with skins intact. Pleased with the results, we turned our attention to the filling.

We needed a filling that made enough for four eggplant halves, and one that could be easily prepared while the eggplant was in the oven. To start, we tried using a simple combination of onion, which we browned slightly, garlic, and grated Pecorino Romano cheese. Tasters liked the

PREPARING EGGPLANT FOR STUFFING

Using two forks, gently push the flesh to the sides of each eggplant half to make room for the filling.

KEEPING NUTS FRESH

Because of their high fat content, nuts can go rancid very quickly. A cool, dark pantry might seem like the perfect place to store your walnuts and pecans, but the only place to really guarantee their freshness is the refrigerator. Keep all nuts in the freezer, where they will stay fresh for at least six months.

flavor but wanted something more substantial, a filling that would hold its own against the meaty eggplant.

Bread cubes and bread crumbs both contributed a mushy texture to the filling, so we abandoned this path and turned to vegetables instead. Green bell peppers added a bitter flavor; the combination of diced tomatoes and toasted pine nuts, however, was a perfect fit. The tomatoes added bulk without making the filling mushy or adding too much moisture and brought a nice sweetness. The nuts, aside from contributing richness and flavor, also added a pleasant, lightly crunchy texture to the filling.

Now we just had to round out the flavors. We seasoned the filling with oregano, cinnamon, and a little cayenne for heat. After stirring in some red wine vinegar to brighten the overall flavor of the dish and balance the sweetness of the onions, we were ready to stuff the eggplants.

This part was easy—we simply opened up the center of each eggplant by pushing the flesh to the sides using two forks. We then mounded a generous amount (about ¼ cup) of filling into each opening and sprinkled extra grated cheese over the top of each eggplant half. In many recipes the stuffed eggplants are then steamed or braised in olive oil, but we found that after just five minutes back in the 400-degree oven, both the eggplant and the filling were heated through.

A sprinkling of fresh parsley for color and freshness was all it took to finish things off. Now we had a new way to cook eggplant that tasted so good, we might forgo our meaty entrées altogether.

Stuffed Eggplant

SERVES 2

Once stuffed, the eggplants can be refrigerated for up to 24 hours; bake as directed, increasing the baking time to 8 to 12 minutes in step 5. Serve with Tzatziki Sauce (page 27) if desired. This dish can be served hot or at room temperature.

- 2 (10-ounce) Italian eggplants, halved lengthwise
- 2 tablespoons olive oil
  Salt and pepper
- 1 small onion, minced (about ½ cup)
- 4 garlic cloves, minced
- ¼ teaspoon dried oregano
- ¼ teaspoon ground cinnamon
  Pinch cayenne pepper
- 2 plum tomatoes, cored, seeded, and chopped medium
- 1 ounce Pecorino Romano cheese, grated (about ½ cup)
- 2 tablespoons pine nuts, toasted (see page 226)
- 1 tablespoon red wine vinegar
- 2 tablespoons minced fresh parsley

1. Adjust the oven racks to the upper-middle and lowest positions, place a rimmed baking sheet on the lower rack, and heat the oven to 400 degrees.

2. Brush the cut sides of the eggplant with 1 tablespoon of the oil and season with salt and pepper. Lay the eggplant cut-side down on the hot baking sheet and carefully cover with foil. Roast until the eggplant is golden brown and tender, 45 to 55 minutes. Carefully transfer the eggplant to a paper towel–lined baking sheet and let drain.

3. Meanwhile, heat the remaining tablespoon oil in a 10-inch skillet over medium heat until shimmering. Add the onion and ¼ teaspoon salt and cook until softened and browned, 5 to 7 minutes. Stir in the garlic, oregano, cinnamon, and cayenne and cook until fragrant, about 30 seconds. Stir in the tomatoes, ¼ cup of the Pecorino, pine nuts, and vinegar and cook until warmed through, about 1 minute. Season with salt and pepper to taste and set aside.

4. Return the roasted eggplant, cut-side up, to the rimmed baking sheet. Following the photo on page 93, use two forks to gently push the flesh to the sides of each eggplant half to make room for the filling. Mound about ¼ cup of the filling into each eggplant.

5. Sprinkle with the remaining ¼ cup Pecorino and continue to bake on the upper-middle rack until the cheese is melted, 5 to 10 minutes. Sprinkle with the parsley and serve.

CRISPY TOFU

FRESH BEAN CURD, OR TOFU, is a great choice for a vegetarian entrée for two—it comes in a 14-ounce block, which is just the right amount to serve a couple. Tofu is a natural candidate for the effortless cooking method of pan-frying; the crispy coating makes a good foil for the creamy, mild tofu interior. A lively sweet and spicy sauce matches especially well with naturally mild tofu. With our final dish in mind, we set out to create our own version of this satisfying vegetarian main course.

We started our testing with the tofu. We coated and pan-fried extra-firm, firm, medium-firm, and soft tofus and tasted them side by side. Tasters preferred the medium-firm and soft tofu for their creamy texture. Because we were using a softer tofu, we didn't need to press the tofu to expel excess moisture (as we've had to do with extra-firm tofu in stir-fry recipes) because we didn't want the tofu to lose its shape. Instead, we simply cut the tofu into planks and then placed them on paper towels to drain. Once the drained tofu was encased in a coating, a little excess water only helped the tofu stay moist.

Next we tested the coating and, again, turned to our past stir-fries. We'd had good luck in the past with a pure cornstarch coating, which helps the sauce adhere to the tofu. We started our testing there; the cornstarch yielded a thin, crispy coating that barely browned but held up well in the pan. Unfortunately, there wasn't much to write home about with this tofu. Since the tofu wouldn't be tossed in the sauce, but instead served alongside it, we felt we could be a bit more adventurous.

In our library of Chinese cookbooks, we had stumbled across a couple of recipes where cornmeal is added to the coating. We decided to give it a try and started with ½ cup of cornmeal mixed with ½ cup of cornstarch, then pan-fried our tofu. But tasters complained of a gritty texture; this test was too heavy on the cornmeal. We cut back to ¼ cup of cornmeal with ¾ cup of cornstarch, which proved just the right combination. After just a couple of minutes over medium-high heat, this tofu had a crispy, golden coating with a creamy interior.

Up to this point, we'd been cutting the tofu blocks into planks about 1 inch thick, but tasters started to complain that there wasn't enough coating. Cutting each plank in half to make "fingers" quickly solved the problem. Now we had a greater coating-to-tofu ratio that everyone thought had the right balance of crispy and creamy.

Finally, we turned our attention to the sauce. We wanted a sweet and spicy sauce, just enough for two diners, and opted for a Chinese-style sweet chili sauce. In most recipes we found, five simple ingredients were simmered together in a saucepan until thickened: sugar, water, chili sauce, cornstarch, and rice vinegar. We started with ¼ cup of sugar, water, and rice vinegar, and 2 teaspoons each of chili sauce and cornstarch (for thickening). It was a good start, but tasters complained that it was too sweet and not hot enough. By cutting the amount of sugar to 3 tablespoons and increasing the amount of chili paste to 1 tablespoon, we kept almost the same volume and perfected the balance of sweet and spicy.

Now we just had to stack up our crispy tofu on a plate, dip it in the sauce, and start eating. Our vegetarian entrée for two was perfect—quick and easy with bright flavors.

NOTES FROM THE TEST KITCHEN

ASIAN CHILI-GARLIC SAUCE
Sriracha is the generic name for this Southeast Asian hot sauce from Thailand. It is named after the seaside town Si Racha, where it was first produced in small batches as a local product. It is made from sun-ripened chile peppers, vinegar, garlic, sugar, and salt and has a consistency like slightly chunky ketchup. We use Asian chili-garlic sauce to bump up the flavor in stir-fries and sauces.

ALL ABOUT TOFU
Popular across Asia, tofu is made from the curds of soy milk. In the United States, it is typically sold in blocks packed in water. You can find tofu in a variety of textures, such as silken, soft, medium-firm, firm, and extra-firm. We prefer the latter two for stir-frying because the tofu holds its shape well while being moved around a hot pan. In recipes where a crunchy crust on a creamy interior is desired, such as our Crispy Tofu with Sweet Chili Sauce, medium-firm or soft tofu is best.

Like dairy products, tofu is perishable and should be kept well chilled. We prefer to use it within a few days of opening. If you want to keep an opened package of tofu fresh for several days, cover the tofu with fresh water and refrigerate it in an airtight container, changing the water daily. Any hint of sourness means the tofu is past its prime.

Crispy Tofu with Sweet Chili Sauce
SERVES 2

We prefer the softer, creamier texture of medium-firm or soft tofu here, but firm or extra-firm tofu will also work (they will taste drier). Be sure to handle the tofu gently or else it may break apart. Serve with white rice if desired.

SAUCE

- 3 tablespoons sugar
- ¼ cup water
- ¼ cup rice vinegar
- 2 teaspoons cornstarch
- 1 tablespoon Asian chili-garlic sauce

TOFU

- 1 (14-ounce) block medium-firm or soft tofu (see note), sliced crosswise into 1-inch-thick slabs, each slab sliced into two 1-inch-wide fingers
- ¾ cup cornstarch
- ¼ cup yellow cornmeal
- Salt and pepper
- ¾ cup vegetable oil

1. FOR THE SAUCE: Whisk all of the ingredients together in a small saucepan and cook over medium-high heat, whisking constantly, until hot and thickened, about 4 minutes. Cover and set aside to keep warm.

2. FOR THE TOFU: Meanwhile, spread the tofu out on several layers of paper towels and let sit to drain slightly for 20 minutes.

3. Place a wire rack over a rimmed baking sheet and set aside. Toss the cornstarch and cornmeal together in a shallow dish. Season the tofu with salt and pepper. Working with a few pieces at a time, coat the tofu thoroughly with the cornstarch mixture, pressing to help it adhere, then transfer to the wire rack.

4. Line a plate with paper towels. Heat the oil in a 12-inch nonstick skillet over medium-high heat until shimmering. Carefully lay the tofu in the skillet and cook until crisp and lightly golden on all sides, about 4 minutes, turning the tofu as needed.

5. Using a spatula, gently transfer the tofu to the paper towel–lined plate, letting any excess oil drip back into the pan. Season with salt to taste and serve with the warm sauce.

INDIVIDUAL BEEF WELLINGTONS WITH MADEIRA SAUCE

FANCY DINNERS

ROAST RACK OF LAMB

LIKE OTHER SIMPLE BUT SATISFYING DISHES, such as roast chicken, rack of lamb can be easy to prepare. Unlike other simple dishes, lamb is more intimidating; many home cooks have little experience preparing it, and it's a fairly expensive cut of meat. You get only one shot to get it right, and it's a pricey shot at that.

When done right, the meat should be juicy and rosy, the outside should be intensely browned to boost the flavor, and the fat should be well enough rendered to provide a crisp outer shell. Since rack of lamb is the epitome of an elegant dinner—and one rack is just right for two people—we wanted to perfect this uncomplicated dish. Roasting produces perfectly pink and juicy meat, so we chose this method and would use the juice left in the pan to make a complementary sauce to highlight the rich flavors of the meat.

We started by exploring our cooking methods. Good exterior caramelization is essential to the flavor of any roasted meat, so we tried cooking the rack of lamb two ways: straight into the oven with no prior browning, and browning it first, then moving it to the oven. We had hoped that cooking the lamb from start to finish in the oven would win out—we liked the ease of simply sliding the rack into the oven and leaving it to cook. With our racks trimmed and frenched, meaning the rib bones had been thoroughly cleaned of their layers of fat, we tested both ways. Unfortunately, even when roasted at a high temperature on a preheated baking sheet, the rack of lamb cooked solely in the oven just didn't develop the crust we were looking for. It was obvious that pan-searing the rack first would be necessary.

To achieve a good crust, we browned the lamb in a skillet meat-side down, then stood the rack on its end for further browning. After about five minutes, we were ready for the oven. We tried roasting multiple racks at varying oven temperatures—350, 425, and 475 degrees—and ended up taking the middle road (425 degrees). After 15 minutes in the oven, the lamb had a crispy crust and a tender, juicy interior—our stovetop-to-oven technique worked perfectly.

Satisfied with our roasting technique, we were ready to focus on making a small amount of sauce. Aware that the finished lamb would cool off quickly, we started the sauce while the lamb was in the oven. We poured off all but a teaspoon of the rendered lamb fat from the pan and added one minced shallot, one minced garlic clove, and a sprig of rosemary, which always pairs nicely with lamb. Looking to incorporate a sophisticated and adult tone into our sauce, we stirred in some whiskey to deglaze the pan and mesh with the scraped-up browned bits from the bottom of the pan. We chose to use Scotch whiskey for its smokiness and delicate sweetness. It took a few tries to hit the right amount—¼ cup—that would evaporate enough to form the base of the sauce. Once it had mostly evaporated, we added a bit of chicken broth, reduced the mixture, and whisked in a pat of butter. The sauce clearly needed some thickening. A teaspoon of flour was too much; ½ teaspoon did the trick. Now we needed just a touch more flavor.

To fortify the whiskey flavor, we added another tablespoon of whiskey when we took the pan off the heat. Finally, to brighten the sauce, we finished it with chopped parsley and a squeeze of fresh lemon juice. The improved sauce was just the right amount to spoon over and cling to our roasted rack of lamb.

Roast Rack of Lamb with Whiskey Sauce
SERVES 2

We prefer the milder taste and bigger size of domestic lamb, but you may substitute imported lamb from New Zealand or Australia (see page 99). We like the smoky flavor imparted by Scotch whiskey, but Irish or American whiskey can be substituted. We prefer rack of lamb cooked to medium-rare, but if you prefer it more or less done, see our guidelines in "Testing Meat for Doneness" on page 208.

LAMB
- 1 (1¼ to 1½-pound) rack of lamb, 8 or 9 ribs, frenched and trimmed (see page 99)
    Salt and pepper
- 1 teaspoon vegetable oil

WHISKEY SAUCE
- 1 shallot, minced (about 3 tablespoons)
- 1 sprig fresh rosemary
- 1 garlic clove, minced

½ teaspoon unbleached all-purpose flour

5 tablespoons Scotch whiskey

¾ cup low-sodium chicken broth

1 tablespoon chopped fresh parsley

1 tablespoon unsalted butter

½ teaspoon fresh lemon juice

Salt and pepper

1. FOR THE LAMB: Adjust an oven rack to the lower-middle position, place a rimmed baking sheet on the rack, and heat the oven to 425 degrees.

2. Pat the lamb dry with paper towels and season with salt and pepper. Heat the oil in a 10-inch skillet over medium-high heat until just smoking. Carefully lay the lamb in the skillet, meat-side down, and cook until well browned, 3 to 4 minutes. Reduce the heat to medium and, using tongs, hold the rack upright in the skillet to brown the bottom, 2 to 3 minutes longer.

3. Transfer the lamb, meat-side up, to the hot baking sheet in the oven, setting the skillet aside for the sauce. Roast the lamb until the center registers 125 degrees on an instant-read thermometer (for medium-rare), 12 to 15 minutes. Transfer the lamb to a carving board, tent loosely with foil, and let rest for 5 minutes.

4. FOR THE WHISKEY SAUCE: Meanwhile, pour off all but 1 teaspoon of the fat left in the skillet and return to medium heat until shimmering. Add the shallot and rosemary and cook until softened, 2 to 3 minutes. Stir in the garlic and cook until fragrant, about 30 seconds. Stir in the flour until incorporated, about 30 seconds.

5. Off the heat, slowly stir in ¼ cup of the whiskey, scraping up any browned bits, and let sit until the bubbling subsides, about 1 minute. Carefully return the skillet to medium heat and simmer until the whiskey has almost completely evaporated, 2 to 3 minutes. Stir in the broth and continue to simmer, stirring occasionally, until the sauce has thickened slightly and reduced to about ⅓ cup, 3 to 5 minutes.

6. Off the heat, discard the rosemary sprig and whisk in the remaining tablespoon whiskey, parsley, butter, lemon juice, and any accumulated lamb juice. Season the sauce with salt and pepper to taste. Cut the lamb racks into individual chops by slicing between the ribs, and serve with the sauce.

STORING BUTTER

When cooking for two, chances are that unless you're baking, it will take you a while to run through a pound of butter. And when stored in the refrigerator, butter (even when wrapped) can pick up odors and turn rancid within just a few weeks. To avoid bad butter, keep it in the freezer and transfer it, one stick at a time, to the fridge.

BUYING LAMB

When you're buying lamb, the biggest determinant of flavor is origin. Domestic lamb is distinguished by its larger size and milder flavor, and lamb imported from Australia and New Zealand features a far gamier taste. The reason for this difference in taste boils down to diet—and the chemistry of lamb fat. Imported lamb has been pasture-fed on mixed grasses, whereas lambs raised in the United States begin on a diet of grass but finish with grain. This change of diet has a direct impact on the composition of the animal's fat, reducing the concentration of certain fats that give lamb its characteristic "lamb-y" flavor—and ultimately leading to sweeter-tasting meat.

DOMESTIC

FROM DOWN UNDER

PREPARING RACK OF LAMB

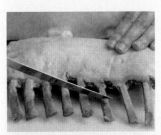

1. Using a boning knife, scrape the ribs clean of any scraps of meat or fat.

2. Trim off the outer layer of fat, the flap of meat underneath it, and the fat underneath that flap.

INDIVIDUAL BEEF WELLINGTONS

SOMETIMES THE CLASSIC DISHES from another era are worth reviving, and beef Wellington is one that's on the top of our list. It was de rigueur for fine hotel restaurants to have it on their menus in the 1950s, but today you rarely see it. Perhaps that's because of the daunting amount of prep work it takes to make it. But what could be more appealing than a substantial piece of tenderloin swathed in fine pâté and *duxelles* (a heady mix of mushrooms, shallots, herbs, and butter) and bundled up in a cloak of puff pastry? Sure, this is a big aging dinosaur of a dish, but its interplay of flavors and star presentation make it a peerless choice for a special-occasion dinner. We find beef Wellington so appealing that we sought to create our own scaled-down version of this famed restaurant classic.

First we had to figure out the cut and amount of beef to use. Traditionally, beef Wellington is made with a large tenderloin—usually 2 to 4 pounds. Tenderloin is an expensive but tender cut of beef, so we had no qualms about keeping it in the ingredient list. But when it came to the amount, we couldn't use as large a cut for two dinners. So we tried two different approaches: a small tenderloin roast (a center cut of the larger beef tenderloin) that could serve two, and two separate tenderloin steaks of about 8 ounces each. We prepared each cut according to the traditional method, searing the meat first, then coating it with pâté and cooked mushrooms before baking it in puff pastry.

Side-by-side testing revealed technical problems with both versions. The large roast was much easier to wrap with puff pastry, just as a larger gift box is easier to wrap than a smaller one, but it was quite messy and unattractive when we had to slice and serve it. The individual tenderloin steaks were easy to serve, able to go straight from the oven to the table, but posed challenges when it came to coordinating the cooking times of the steaks and the puff pastry. We were left with either perfectly cooked, flaky pastry paired with overcooked meat, or perfectly cooked, medium-rare meat enveloped by pale, slightly raw pastry. Pleased with the restaurant-worthy appearance of two individual beef Wellingtons, and confident that we could perfect the cooking time, we decided to pursue a recipe made with two steaks.

Employing a full roster of solutions to fix the problem of the beef and pastry being done at different times, we experimented with searing times for the steaks, wrapping techniques, oven temperatures, and oven rack positions, but we were still not obtaining the results we wanted—tenderloin steaks cooked to a perfect medium-rare with a light, flaky, golden brown crust. And although we liked the idea of creating two miniature replicas of beef Wellington, we concluded that this approach would just not work.

That's when it occurred to us that we should stop trying to cook the steaks wrapped in pastry and take a more modern, streamlined approach: Cook the steak and pastry separately, then serve them together. We cooked puff pastry squares (just a bit bigger than each steak) until light and flaky, and the steaks until medium-rare, then assembled the two elements. Success! Not only did we obtain the flavors and textures we wanted, but we also cut out over an hour of prep time. We were now on the path to creating individual beef Wellingtons that had all the familiar flavors without the familiar failures.

With our new twist on the cooking method uncovered, we wondered if we could also update and improve upon the pâté and mushrooms. Making pâté from scratch was not on the agenda—spending at least an hour to make just enough to cover two steaks was ludicrous. Besides, nearly every supermarket has a decent selection of at least one or two types (usually found in the cheese department). Unfortunately, supermarkets don't always carry the traditional goose liver pâté, so we went with a smooth duck liver pâté, which worked fine. Chunky or country-style pâté would have added too much contrasting texture.

As for the mushrooms, we ditched the antiquated, time-intensive method of preparing them—pulsing them until fine, slowly sautéing them with shallots, butter, and Madeira, and refrigerating them so they wouldn't heat either the steak or the puff pastry (as it did when prepared the traditional way). For efficiency's sake, we put together a quick pan sauce with sautéed sliced mushrooms, a shallot, a full cup of Madeira, and the drippings from the seared tenderloin steaks. Although we had made a modest amount of sauce, we were able to retain all of the original ingredients while adding a few new ones—parsley, Dijon mustard, and lemon juice.

At long last, we were ready to assemble the individual components. First, we cut one puff pastry square in half and set the bottom on a plate. Then we placed a steak, which we had already coated with pâté, on top and spooned mushroom sauce over it. Our crowning touch was setting the remaining pastry half on top. We prepared the second one, then dug in. The pastry was crispy, the meat perfectly pink, and the sauce rich and bold. We had done it—this updated entrée was faster but still impressive, combining a modern look with classic flavors.

NOTES FROM THE TEST KITCHEN

WORKING WITH PUFF PASTRY

Making your own puff pastry can be quite an undertaking. Thankfully, there's a reliable alternative. **Pepperidge Farm Puff Pastry Sheets** are available in virtually every supermarket, and they work very well for lots of recipes. Each 1-pound package contains two approximately 9-inch square sheets. Because the dough is frozen, however, it must be defrosted before you can use it; otherwise, it can crack and break apart. Thawing the dough in the refrigerator overnight is the best method, but it takes some forethought. Countertop defrosting works fine, too, but don't rush it. Depending on the temperature of your kitchen, it may take between 30 and 60 minutes. The dough should unfold easily once thawed, but still feel firm. If the seams crack, rejoin them by rolling them smooth with a rolling pin. And if the dough warms and softens, place it in the freezer until firm.

ASSEMBLING INDIVIDUAL BEEF WELLINGTONS

1. Bake the pastry squares as directed, then slice the squares in half with a serrated knife.

2. Place the pastry bottoms on individual serving plates and top with the steaks. Spoon the sauce over the steaks and top with the remaining pastry.

Individual Beef Wellingtons with Madeira Sauce

SERVES 2

This recipe uses half of a standard 9-inch square sheet of puff pastry. Be sure to let the pastry thaw on the counter before cutting it in half and cutting the squares; if the dough starts to separate at the seams before you cut it, simply rejoin the seams by rolling them smooth with a rolling pin. See page 102 for a recipe to use up the leftover pastry, or you can refreeze or refrigerate it for up to 2 days. We prefer these steaks cooked to medium-rare, but if you prefer them more or less done, see our guidelines in "Testing Meat for Doneness" on page 208. Serve immediately or else the pastry will turn soggy.

PASTRY AND BEEF

½ **(9-inch square) sheet frozen puff pastry, thawed, cut in half widthwise to make two 4½-inch squares (see note)**

2 **(7 to 8-ounce) center-cut beef tenderloin steaks, 1½ inches thick**
    Salt and pepper

2 **teaspoons vegetable oil**

2 **tablespoons smooth chicken or duck liver pâté, at room temperature**

MADEIRA SAUCE

1 **teaspoon vegetable oil**

8 **ounces white mushrooms, sliced thin**

1 **shallot, minced (about 3 tablespoons)**

1 **cup Madeira**

1 **tablespoon chopped fresh parsley**

1 **tablespoon minced fresh thyme**

1 **tablespoon Dijon mustard**

1 **tablespoon unsalted butter**

1 **teaspoon fresh lemon juice**
    Salt and pepper

1. FOR THE PASTRY AND BEEF: Adjust the oven racks to the upper-middle and lower-middle positions, place a rimmed baking sheet on the lower rack, and heat the oven to 425 degrees. Line another rimmed baking sheet with parchment paper. Place the pastry squares on the prepared baking sheet and refrigerate until needed.

Cheese Straws
MAKES ABOUT 8 STRAWS

These crunchy cheese straws make a great appetizer and are also nice paired with a salad.

½   (9-inch square) sheet frozen puff pastry, thawed on the counter for 10 minutes
1   ounce Parmesan or Asiago cheese, grated (about ½ cup)
    Salt and pepper

Adjust an oven rack to the upper-middle position and heat the oven to 425 degrees. Lay the pastry on a sheet of parchment paper and sprinkle with half of the cheese, a pinch of salt, and a pinch of pepper. Cover with another sheet of parchment paper and press the cheese into the dough with a rolling pin. Carefully flip the dough and repeat on the second side with the remaining cheese, a pinch of salt, and a pinch of pepper. Remove the parchment and cut the dough into ¾-inch-wide strips. Gently twist each strip of dough, transfer to a baking sheet lined with parchment paper, and bake until puffed and golden, 8 to 13 minutes. Let cool for 5 minutes before serving.

2. Pat the steaks dry with paper towels and season with salt and pepper. Heat the oil in a 10-inch skillet over medium-high heat until just smoking. Carefully lay the steaks in the skillet and sear until well browned on both sides, 4 to 6 minutes, flipping the steaks halfway through cooking.

3. Transfer the steaks to the hot baking sheet on the lower oven rack, setting the skillet aside for the sauce. Place the refrigerated baking sheet of pastry on the upper oven rack. Cook the tenderloin steaks and pastry until the centers of the steaks register 125 degrees on an instant-read thermometer (for medium-rare) and the pastry is puffed and golden, 10 to 15 minutes.

4. Transfer the steaks to a carving board, spread the pâté evenly over the top of each, tent loosely with foil, and let rest for 5 minutes. Remove the pastry from the oven and let cool on the baking sheet.

5. FOR THE MADEIRA SAUCE: Meanwhile, add the oil to the skillet and heat over medium heat until shimmering. Add the mushrooms and shallot, and cook until the mushrooms release their liquid and begin to brown, 5 to 7 minutes; transfer to a bowl.

6. Return the skillet to medium heat, stir in the Madeira, scraping up any browned bits, and simmer until it has thickened slightly and reduced to about ⅓ cup, 3 to 5 minutes. Off the heat, stir in the cooked mushroom mixture, parsley, thyme, mustard, butter, lemon juice, and any accumulated beef juice. Season with salt and pepper to taste, and cover to keep warm.

7. Following the photos on page 101, split the pastry squares in half with a serrated knife. Place the bottom half of each pastry on an individual serving plate and lay a tenderloin steak on top. Spoon the Madeira sauce over the steaks, top with the remaining pastry, and serve immediately.

HERB-ROASTED PRIME RIB

PRIME RIB IS AN EXPENSIVE CUT of meat and, for most people, is usually just a once-a-year indulgence around the holidays. It's also an extremely large roast, serving as many as 20 people. Even if you're willing to spend the money on prime rib, you're not going to buy it for just two people; a day or two of leftovers is fine, but eating the same thing for a week—even if it's prime rib—doesn't really hold much appeal. Still, just because there are only two of you doesn't mean you shouldn't be able to enjoy a meltingly tender, perfectly cooked piece of beef any time of year. We wanted to find a cut of beef small enough to serve two people that would be as close as possible (in flavor and texture) to prime rib. And since we would be preparing a relatively small amount of meat, we hoped to have enough room left in the pan to make a complete meal by adding some potatoes to the mix.

We had two options for the meat: bone-in rib steak or boneless rib-eye steak. Both are essentially slices of prime rib (they're cut from the rib roast) and, if cut about 1½ inches thick, are the perfect size for two. Because prime rib is a bone-in roast, we decided that bone-in

HERB-ROASTED PRIME RIB WITH POTATOES

rib steak would be the better choice. To flavor our steak, we assembled a simple herb crust consisting of thyme, rosemary, olive oil, salt, and pepper.

We wanted to cook the potatoes in the skillet along with the prime rib, as we hoped the rich juice from the meat would help flavor the potatoes. We started by slicing the potatoes in half, placing them cut-side down in the skillet, and then placing the prime rib on top.

Some recipes for prime rib call for a hot oven initially (around 450 degrees) to help brown the exterior, then the temperature is lowered so the roast can slowly reach medium-rare, ensuring a rosy, juicy interior. For our first run, we oven-seared the rib steak, then, once it was well browned, spread the herb crust over the top and reduced the oven temperature to 250 degrees. But what works for a large prime rib did not work for our smaller rib steaks: The meat was overcooked, the potatoes were undercooked, and the herb crust tasted raw and undeveloped. Could we find one temperature that would allow the prime rib to cook evenly, yet still give us the rosy interior of a larger prime rib?

Taking a cue from our Pan-Roasted Chicken and Vegetables (page 6), we decided to microwave the potatoes prior to adding them to the skillet to jump-start the cooking process. Spreading our herb crust on from the start this time, we tested a range of oven temperatures. At 250 degrees, the prime rib not only took close to an hour to cook, but the potatoes were pale and unappealing, and tasters decided that the results weren't worth the extended cooking time. At 450 degrees, the potatoes were nicely browned and crisp, but the meat was overcooked, with a tough gray band around the interior. The optimal temperature turned out to be 350 degrees. At this temperature, the oven was hot enough to cook the meat in a reasonable amount of time without sacrificing juiciness, and the potatoes, though not as dark as those cooked at 450 degrees, had ample color and a crisp exterior.

In an effort to crisp the herb crust, we tried broiling the prime rib for the last few minutes of cooking. To keep the meat from overcooking, we pulled it from the oven at 110 degrees, turned on the broiler, and placed the skillet on a rack about 6 inches from the broiler element. About 6 minutes was all that was needed to crisp the crust and bring the prime rib to a perfect medium-rare.

At this point we reexamined our herb crust. Tasters were dissatisfied by the way the crust had begun to slide off the meat during cooking, so it was clear that we needed a binder. We tried eggs, but they imparted an imposing flavor that was out of place on our prime rib. The bite of Dijon mustard was a perfect fit with the fresh herbs; however, it did little to keep the crust together. Adding a little flour kept the herb crust firmly in place.

We now had a perfect dinner for two with multiple layers of flavor: a beefy prime rib, fragrant herb crust, and crispy potatoes rich with drippings from the prime rib.

Herb-Roasted Prime Rib with Potatoes
SERVES 2

We prefer to use small red potatoes (1 to 2 inches in diameter) in this recipe; however, larger red potatoes, cut into 1-inch pieces, can be substituted. If you prefer your steak more done, simply increase the roasting time in step 4, moving the steak to the broiler when it is about 30 degrees shy of your desired doneness; see our guidelines in "Testing Meat for Doneness" on page 208.

12 ounces small red potatoes (about 4), halved
    (see note)
4½ teaspoons olive oil
    Salt and pepper
1   (1½-pound) bone-in rib steak, 1½ inches thick
4½ teaspoons minced fresh thyme
4½ teaspoons minced fresh rosemary
1   tablespoon Dijon mustard
1½ teaspoons unbleached all-purpose flour
½   teaspoon sugar

1. Adjust one oven rack to the lowest position and a second rack to be 6 inches from the broiler element, and heat the oven to 350 degrees.

2. Toss the potatoes with 1½ teaspoons of the oil, ⅛ teaspoon salt, and a pinch of pepper in a microwave-safe bowl. Microwave on high, uncovered, until the potatoes soften but still hold their shape, about 6 minutes, gently stirring once during cooking.

3. Meanwhile, pat the steak dry with paper towels and season with salt and pepper. Combine the remaining 1 tablespoon oil, thyme, rosemary, mustard, flour, and sugar to make a paste, then spread it evenly over one side of the steak.

4. Arrange the microwaved potatoes, cut-side down, over the bottom of a 10-inch ovensafe nonstick skillet, and place the steak, herb paste–side up, on top. Transfer the skillet to the lower oven rack and roast until the thickest part of the steak registers 110 degrees on an instant-read thermometer, about 30 minutes.

5. Heat the broiler. Using potholders (the skillet handle will be hot), transfer the skillet to the rack 6 inches beneath the broiler element, and broil until the center of the steak registers 125 degrees on an instant-read thermometer (for medium-rare), about 6 minutes.

6. Being careful of the hot skillet handle, remove the skillet from the oven. Transfer the steak to a carving board, leaving the potatoes in the hot skillet, and let rest, uncovered, for 15 minutes. Carve the meat off the bone, cut it into ¼-inch-thick slices, and serve with the potatoes.

NOTES FROM THE TEST KITCHEN

THE BEST INSTANT-READ THERMOMETERS

When cooking meat, we highly recommend using an instant-read thermometer to accurately gauge its temperature. Our favorite model is the **ThermoWorks Super-Fast Thermapen** (left), a true workhorse that quickly provides accurate readings across the board. But at $89, it isn't cheap. Recently, cheaper instant-read thermometers have come on the market, and we wondered if any of them could approach the performance of the Thermapen. We purchased eight models and put them through their paces in the test kitchen. None of the cheaper models could match the speed, temperature range, or accuracy of the Thermapen, but we were pleased with the performance of the **CDN ProAccurate Quick Tip Digital Cooking Thermometer DTQ450** (right), $14.95. Although not as fast as the Thermapen, it performed admirably enough to earn our endorsement.

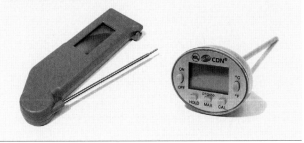

HERBED ROAST PORK TENDERLOIN

PORK TENDERLOIN IS THE PERFECT CUT when you're serving just two, but we wanted to come up with a recipe that would allow us to dress it up a little. Having created a recipe for an herb-stuffed pork tenderloin where two tenderloins are butterflied, spread with a layer of herbs, and then rolled into one big roast, we wondered if we could downsize it to serve two. The problem, of course, was that we would be working with a single tenderloin.

In the earlier incarnation of this recipe, we utilized the common butcher shop technique of butterflying two pork tenderloins, rolling them together, and tying them to form one big roast. This technique was a great success because we no longer had to sear the two roasts separately on the stovetop—they both browned well enough when they were tied together and roasted in the oven on a baking sheet. This technique cut our overall cooking time and produced a single, well-browned roast that cooked evenly in the oven. But now we would be using just one tenderloin. We attempted the same cooking method with a single butterflied pork tenderloin that we had layered with herb spread in the middle. Unfortunately, this move was a bust—the roast was much smaller now and finished cooking before the exterior had a chance to brown.

Looking back through the recipe's history, we surmised that since we were cooking a single roast, browning it in a skillet and then transferring it to the oven was the only reliable way to create a good crust without overcooking the interior of the tenderloin. After just one test, we knew this step could not be overlooked if we were to perfectly roast our pork tenderloin for two. By quickly searing the pork tenderloin in a hot skillet and then transferring the pan to a 400-degree oven, we were now getting the browning we wanted. But we still had to incorporate the herb stuffing somehow.

Instead of sandwiching the herbs between two split tenderloins, we decided to layer them in our single tenderloin. We simply split the tenderloin down the middle and added a layer of herbs mixed with butter. Unfortunately, even when the two flaps were tied tightly together, the spread leaked out of the tenderloin during

THE BEST WHOLE-GRAIN DIJON MUSTARD

Dijon mustard is made around the world—not just in France. Although it always starts with black or brown mustard seeds (rather than white or pale yellow), there is some variation among recipes, especially in the degree to which the raw seeds are milled. Smooth Dijon consists of very finely milled seeds, and grainy mustards often contain completely unmilled seeds. We use grainy Dijon to add bright flavor and help bind the filling in our Herbed Roast Pork Tenderloin. In our tasting of 11 leading brands of grainy Dijon, **Grey Poupon Country Dijon** (made in Pennsylvania) came out on top for its "pleasantly grainy" texture and spiciness.

PREPARING HERBED ROAST PORK TENDERLOIN

1. Butterfly the tenderloin by slicing it lengthwise down the middle, nearly all the way through, leaving about ¼ inch of meat on the bottom.

2. Open up the roast like a book and press it flat with your hands. Cover the meat with plastic wrap and lightly pound it to an even ½-inch thickness.

3. Spread the butter mixture evenly over the meat, leaving a ½-inch border at the edges. Starting at the short end, roll the meat up around the butter into a tidy roast.

4. Tie the roast securely with kitchen twine at 1-inch intervals.

the cooking process. Realizing we'd need a practically airtight seal to keep our herb butter in, we hit on the notion of pounding the tenderloin after butterflying it, then spreading the herbs evenly over the top of the meat. We then rolled up the flattened pork and tied it tightly with twine before searing and cooking it. This worked like a charm! The herbs were still inside the pork when it came out of the oven.

Turning our attention to the herb stuffing, we noticed that our finished tenderloin was nicely browned but needed more kick than our simple paste of parsley and butter could provide. We tried several herbs alone and in combination, finally settling on a blend of fragrant thyme and sage, which offered a fresh flavor that wasn't over-powering. With the addition of mustard, garlic, lemon juice, and lemon zest, our spread was now bolder.

Our herbed tenderloin for two was roasted just right—browned on the outside and juicy and tender inside—and the herb butter added richness to the lean pork. The presentation was impeccable, too; when sliced, this tenderloin revealed a perfect spiral of herbs.

Herbed Roast Pork Tenderloin
SERVES 2

Pork tenderloins can vary greatly in weight; try to find one that weighs between 12 and 16 ounces.

- 2 tablespoons unsalted butter, softened
- 4 teaspoons whole-grain Dijon mustard
- 3 garlic cloves, minced
- 1 tablespoon minced fresh thyme
- 2 teaspoons chopped fresh sage
- 1 teaspoon grated lemon zest plus 1 teaspoon fresh lemon juice
  Salt and pepper
- 1 (12 to 16-ounce) pork tenderloin, trimmed
- 2 teaspoons vegetable oil

1. Adjust an oven rack to the lower-middle position and heat the oven to 400 degrees. Mash the butter, mustard, garlic, thyme, sage, lemon zest and juice, ⅛ teaspoon salt, and ⅛ teaspoon pepper together in a bowl. Measure out and reserve 1 tablespoon of the butter mixture for serving.

2. Pat the tenderloin dry with paper towels and, following the photos on page 106, butterfly and pound the meat to an even ½-inch thickness. Spread the remaining butter mixture evenly over the meat, leaving a ½-inch border at the edges. Starting at the short end, roll the meat up around the butter into a tidy roast, and tie securely with kitchen twine at 1-inch intervals.

3. Heat the oil in a 10-inch ovenproof skillet over medium-high heat until just smoking. Brown the roast on all sides, 5 to 7 minutes, reducing the heat if the pan begins to scorch. Transfer the skillet to the oven and roast the pork until the center registers 140 to 145 degrees on an instant-read thermometer, 14 to 18 minutes, flipping the pork halfway through cooking.

4. Transfer the pork to a carving board and spread the reserved tablespoon butter mixture over the top. Tent the pork loosely with foil and let rest until the center registers 150 degrees on an instant-read thermometer, about 10 minutes. Remove the kitchen twine, slice the pork, and serve.

ROAST CORNISH GAME HENS WITH COUSCOUS STUFFING

EVEN THOUGH CORNISH GAME HENS are cheap enough (about five bucks each in our grocery store), are perfect for two diners (each person gets a bird), and cook quickly enough for a weeknight supper (less than 30 minutes unstuffed), most people think of them as festive fare. Although they do make a stunning presentation, cooking them to perfection is not an easy task, as problems abound: The white meat and dark meat cook at different rates, browning can be difficult (these small birds cook very quickly), and stuffing them requires increased cooking times that can cause the meat to become dry. Despite these challenges, we were determined to develop a recipe for roast Cornish game hens that would be perfect for an elegant dinner for two.

Our first move was to ditch the roasting pan in favor of a wire rack set over a rimmed baking sheet. A roasting pan might be the go-to equipment for other birds, but it would completely ruin this recipe—the high sides shield the small birds from oven heat, and the reduced airflow prevents essential browning. Next, we spaced the birds as far apart as possible. Just as chicken pieces won't brown if overcrowded in a skillet, Cornish hens won't brown if arranged too close together on the rack. We also determined that rotating the birds during cooking was crucial for moist and juicy breast meat. Because Cornish hens are in the oven for such a relatively short time, we settled on one turn, from breast-side down to breast-side up, instead of multiple turns.

After roasting several birds at temperatures ranging from 350 degrees to 500 degrees, as well as roasting one at a high temperature to start and then finishing low, and another starting low and finishing high, we found that all oven temperatures had their problems. We finally settled on a roasting temperature of 400 degrees, cranking the oven up to 450 degrees for the last few minutes of cooking. This hotter roasting temperature was high enough to encourage browning, but low enough to keep the oven from smoking dramatically.

Even after being roasted at a relatively high 400 degrees with a 450-degree finish, these birds hadn't spent enough time in the oven to develop the nice brown color we wanted. We turned to a glaze to fix the color problem and tested a few options: straight soy sauce, a balsamic vinegar and brown sugar mixture, and jam thinned with a little soy sauce. We applied the glaze right before the birds were turned and again after the oven temperature was increased to 450 degrees. Because the high oven heat caramelized the sugar in these glazes, all of the birds colored more beautifully than any of our unglazed birds. But the balsamic vinegar and brown sugar mixture finished as our favorite, giving the hens a pleasant spotty brown, barbecued look.

Next, we had to figure out how to roast these birds stuffed without overcooking them (the stuffing can take longer than the hens to come up to a safe temperature). Microwaving the stuffing before spooning it into the birds' cavities gave us a head start on raising its temperature quickly and meant we didn't have to prolong the cooking time.

Last up: finessing the stuffing. Up to this point, we'd been working with a slightly exotic couscous stuffing— ¼ cup uncooked couscous was all we needed to fill the small birds' cavities—cooked with chicken broth and enlivened with parsley and lemon juice. To contribute to the elegant tone of our dinner, we added 2 tablespoons each of currants and pistachios. Now we filled the cavities

ROAST CORNISH GAME HENS WITH COUSCOUS STUFFING

with ½ cup of stuffing each and simply tied each hen's legs together to secure both the legs and the stuffing.

After an hour in the oven, our birds were golden, crispy, and ready for the table. And with each person getting his or her own bird (and stuffing), there was no need for carving ahead of time or fighting over the dark meat.

Roast Cornish Game Hens with Couscous Stuffing

SERVES 2

If using kosher game hens, do not brine. If brining the hens (see page 76), do not season with salt in step 3. Toasted slivered almonds can be substituted for the pistachio nuts.

STUFFING

- 1 teaspoon extra-virgin olive oil
- 1 shallot, minced (about 3 tablespoons)
- ⅛ teaspoon ground cinnamon
  Pinch ground ginger
- ¼ cup couscous
- 3 tablespoons low-sodium chicken broth
- 2 tablespoons shelled pistachio nuts (see note), toasted (see page 226) and chopped coarse
- 2 tablespoons currants
- 1 tablespoon chopped fresh parsley
- 1 tablespoon fresh lemon juice
  Salt and pepper

GAME HENS

- 2 (1¼ to 1½-pound) Cornish game hens, giblets removed, brined if desired (see note; see page 76), and wings tucked
  Salt and pepper
- ⅓ cup packed brown sugar
- ¼ cup balsamic vinegar
- ¼ teaspoon salt

1. FOR THE STUFFING: Heat the oil in a small saucepan over medium heat until shimmering. Add the shallot, cinnamon, and ginger, and cook until softened and fragrant, 2 to 3 minutes. Stir in the couscous and cook until lightly toasted, 1 to 2 minutes.

2. Stir in the broth and bring to a brief simmer. Remove the saucepan from the heat, cover, and let stand

NOTES FROM THE TEST KITCHEN

PREPARING A CORNISH GAME HEN

After filling the cavity of the hen with the hot stuffing, tie the ends of the legs together securely with kitchen twine.

THE BEST BALSAMIC VINEGAR

Traditional balsamic vinegar takes a minimum of 12 years to make and costs an astonishing $60 per ounce. We were happy to discover that for use in salad dressings or for cooking, you don't need to spend a fortune for this ingredient—a supermarket balsamic works just fine. Tasters thought **Lucini Gran Riserva Balsamico** most closely resembled a traditional balsamic vinegar with its balance of sweet and tart and its viscosity. And at $2 an ounce, it won't break the bank.

BUYING CORNISH GAME HENS

You may not have many choices at the supermarket when it comes to buying Cornish game hens, but if you do, it pays to shop carefully. We tasted four widely available brands. **Bell and Evans,** all-natural and soybean-fed, easily took top honors with our tasters, earning praise for its "juicy" meat, "crisp" skin, and "clean flavors." Tyson came in second, followed by Foster Farms, a West Coast natural brand. Perdue, our last-place game hen, received negative comments and is not recommended.

DEFROSTING CORNISH GAME HENS

If the only game hens available at the supermarket are frozen, don't fret—they can still be on tonight's menu. The quickest way to defrost Cornish hens without a significant loss of quality is to submerge them (unwrapped) in cold tap water, changing the water every 15 minutes. After one hour, poke the thickest part of the breast with a thin skewer to check if the meat is fully thawed. If the interior still feels frozen, change the water and check again at 10-minute intervals. Two giblet-free 1½-pound hens will take between one and one and a half hours to fully defrost. Extend the thawing time by half an hour if the hens come with giblets in the cavity. (Or, you can take the time to thaw the hens overnight in the refrigerator, which can take 24 to 36 hours.)

for 5 minutes. Fluff the couscous with a fork and transfer to a medium microwave-safe bowl. Stir in the pistachios, currants, parsley, and lemon juice, and season with salt and pepper to taste. (The stuffing can be covered and refrigerated for up to 24 hours.)

3. FOR THE GAME HENS: Line a rimmed baking sheet with foil and top with a wire rack. Adjust an oven rack to the middle position and heat the oven to 400 degrees. Pat the hens dry with paper towels and season with salt and pepper.

4. Cover the stuffing and microwave on high until very hot, about 2 minutes. Spoon ½ cup of the hot stuffing into the cavity of each hen, then tie each hen's legs together with kitchen twine, following the photo on page 109. Lay the hens, breast-side down, on the prepared wire rack. Roast the hens until the backs are golden brown, about 25 minutes.

5. Meanwhile, simmer the sugar, vinegar, and salt together in a small saucepan over medium heat until the glaze has thickened slightly and reduced to about ⅓ cup, 1 to 2 minutes. Measure out and reserve 2 tablespoons of the glaze for serving. Cover the remaining glaze to keep warm.

6. Remove the hens from the oven and brush with one-third of the remaining glaze. Flip the hens, breast-side up, and brush with half of the remaining glaze. Continue to roast until the stuffed cavities register 150 degrees on an instant-read thermometer, 15 to 20 minutes longer.

7. Increase the oven temperature to 450 degrees. Brush each hen with the remaining glaze, and continue to roast until the hens are spotty brown and the stuffed cavities register 160 to 165 degrees on an instant-read thermometer, 5 to 10 minutes longer. Remove the hens from the oven, transfer to a carving board, and brush with the glaze reserved for serving. Let the hens rest for 5 minutes before serving.

PAN-ROASTED DUCK BREASTS WITH DRIED CHERRY SAUCE

WE'RE IN FAVOR OF SIMPLE DISHES that look impressive, and nothing equals roasted duck, especially the breasts, which flaunt moist meat and crispy skin. There are two ways to cook duck breasts: as part of a whole roasted duck or as boneless fillets. The breast meat is considerably more tender than the leg meat, so the whole duck must

usually be slow-roasted for two to three hours until the fat has rendered from the skin and the meat is tender. But roasting an entire duck—for three hours, no less—isn't exactly practical for two people. So, for a special dinner of pink, tender meat covered by a well-rendered, thin layer of fat and crispy golden skin, we decided to pan-roast our duck breasts.

Even though we'd settled on our method, we knew the thick layer of skin and fat could make things tricky. The skin on a duck breast adds flavor and a pleasantly crisp texture when prepared correctly, but our initial tests proved that cooking a piece of meat with so much fat can be challenging. We experimented with heat level first and put the meat into the sauté pan at varying temperatures, skin-side down for half the time, then flipping the meat to finish. The duck breasts cooked over high heat turned a deep mahogany brown quickly, but they didn't render enough fat before we had to flip them to avoid burning the skin. The duck finished cooking in a matter of minutes, and tasters were not impressed with the resulting flabby skin. The duck breasts cooked at medium heat fared much better, and the fat rendered further before the skin turned a desirable golden color, but after we flipped the breasts, the meat overcooked quickly and the skin was still too flabby. We finally came close to success when we cooked the breasts over medium-low heat; they weren't perfect, but at least we were close.

With the heat set at medium-low, we put into practice a tip we had encountered elsewhere: scoring the duck skin to allow extra fat to melt away. Thanks to this quick step, the skin now cooked up crisper and with little chewiness. Allowing the duck breasts to cook just a couple of minutes longer on the skin side, we discovered that the meat was still perfectly cooked and the skin even crisper than before. The skin acted as a sort of insulator for the meat, letting the breast cook until the fat properly rendered and browned. Once the breasts were flipped, it took only three minutes to cook the duck to medium-rare, resulting in meat that was sweet, tender, and moist.

While the duck breasts rested on a carving board, we set out to create a simple pan sauce that we could whip together quickly. Our sauce was built around dried cherries, which are a common pairing for duck. Because the cherries are so sweet, we used red wine to temper their sweetness with acidity and finished the sauce with lemon juice and butter. With two well-cooked duck breasts and one simple sauce, we were looking at one perfectly fancy meal for two.

Pan-Roasted Duck Breasts with Dried Cherry Sauce

SERVES 2

We prefer duck breasts cooked to medium-rare, but if you prefer them more done, see our guidelines in "Testing Meat for Doneness" on page 208.

DUCK

2 **(6-ounce) boneless duck breast halves, skin scored (see photo)**

Salt and pepper

CHERRY SAUCE

1 **shallot, minced (about 3 tablespoons)**

¼ **cup dry red wine**

2 **tablespoons dried cherries**

¾ **cup low-sodium chicken broth**

1 **tablespoon unsalted butter**

1 **teaspoon fresh lemon juice**

Salt and pepper

1. FOR THE DUCK: Pat the duck breasts dry with paper towels and season with salt and pepper. Heat a 10-inch skillet over medium heat until hot, about 3 minutes. Carefully lay the duck breasts in the skillet, skin-side down, lower the heat to medium-low, and cook, adjusting the heat as needed for the fat to maintain a constant but gentle simmer, until most of the fat has rendered and the skin is deep golden and crisp, 15 to 20 minutes.

2. Flip the duck breasts and continue to cook until the thickest part registers 125 degrees on an instant-read thermometer (for medium-rare), 2 to 5 minutes. Transfer the duck to a carving board, tent loosely with foil, and let rest while making the sauce (the duck temperature will rise to 130 degrees before serving).

3. FOR THE CHERRY SAUCE: Pour off all but 1 teaspoon of the fat left in the skillet and return to medium heat until shimmering. Add the shallot and cook until softened, 2 to 3 minutes. Stir in the wine and cherries, scraping up any browned bits, and simmer, until the wine has almost completely evaporated, 2 to 3 minutes.

4. Stir in the broth and simmer, stirring occasionally, until the sauce has thickened slightly and reduced to about ⅓ cup, 3 to 5 minutes. Off the heat, stir in the butter and lemon juice, and season with salt and pepper to taste. Serve the duck breasts with the sauce.

SCORING DUCK BREASTS

To render the most fat and yield the crispiest duck skin, score the skin at approximately ¼-inch intervals with a sharp knife in a diagonal pattern, being careful not to cut into the meat.

CHICKEN KIEV

CHICKEN KIEV WAS A SUPERSTAR DECADES AGO. Nowadays, it tends to be a sad, soggy mess of flavorless chicken breast with a greasy, leaky center—definitely not appealing or sophisticated. We recently revisited this Cold War classic and brought it back up to par. Our renewed chicken Kiev is crispy and packed with herbed butter. But it also serves four. Could we keep the flavors of our Kiev (and in our Kiev) while scaling it down for two diners? That's what we wanted to find out.

We started by looking at the essential parts of chicken Kiev: the chicken, the butter, and the coating. Traditionally, chilled butter is stuffed inside a boneless chicken breast, and the whole thing is rolled in a coating, then fried until crisp. As was clear from the flawed recipes we had tried, getting the butter to survive cooking without leaking was key, so we started there. Some recipes called for cutting a slit in the thickest part of the breast and inserting a disk of butter. This method was easy, but it became apparent that providing any outlet for the butter to escape was risky.

We knew from our prior testing that we had to encase the butter completely to prevent any leakage and found that butterflying the breast and pounding the chicken thin before placing a chilled disk of butter on top was our best solution. There was now so much raw chicken available to encase the butter that it couldn't escape. Using a rolling and folding technique, we placed a small rectangle of butter just above the tapered end of the pounded chicken breast and proceeded as if wrapping a burrito: rolling the tapered end completely over the butter, folding in the sides, then continuing to roll until we had a tight bundle.

Next up was the coating. Nothing less than making our own bread crumbs and toasting them would do. To keep their flavor and lightness and prevent a corn dog–like exterior, we had already nixed deep-frying the chicken bundles in favor of baking them in the oven. (Pan-frying was out because it led to unraveled Kievs.) But how much of our own bread crumbs would we need? Working our way down from five slices of bread, which created a wasteful surplus, we found that three slices provided just the right amount of crumbs. To get the bread crumbs to adhere, we first dredged the Kievs in flour (a modest ½ cup did the job) and dipped them in egg before coating them with the toasted bread crumbs and baking them at 350 degrees. Forty minutes later, we had a perfectly crisp crust with a filling (straight butter as a placeholder) that didn't stray.

Now we had to find the right proportions and flavoring for our butter filling. In traditional recipes, chicken Kiev is stuffed with parsley-chive butter, but we upped the flavor ante by replacing the chives with a touch of tarragon and one minced shallot. To get the right amount of butter, we cut the stick of butter used for four chicken Kievs in half; each Kiev was now stuffed with 2 tablespoons—not too much and not too little. A squeeze of lemon juice gave the rich butter some much needed acidity, and a teaspoon of Dijon mustard, whisked into the egg wash we used to coat the chicken, provided another layer of flavor.

Our Chicken Kiev now had all the right flavors in balance, along with tender, moist meat and a crisp, golden brown crust.

Chicken Kiev

SERVES 2

The breaded, unbaked chicken can be covered and refrigerated for up to 24 hours, or wrapped tightly and frozen for up to 1 month. If refrigerated, bake as directed, or if frozen (do not thaw), increase the baking time to 50 to 55 minutes.

HERB BUTTER

- 4 tablespoons (½ stick) unsalted butter, softened
- 1 small shallot, minced (about 1 tablespoon)
- 1 tablespoon chopped fresh parsley
- 2 teaspoons fresh lemon juice
- ½ teaspoon chopped fresh tarragon or ⅛ teaspoon dried

  Salt and pepper

CHICKEN

- 3 slices high-quality white sandwich bread, torn into pieces
- 1 tablespoon vegetable oil

  Salt and pepper
- 2 (7 to 8-ounce) boneless, skinless chicken breasts, trimmed
- ½ cup unbleached all-purpose flour
- 2 large eggs, lightly beaten
- 1 teaspoon Dijon mustard

1. FOR THE HERB BUTTER: Mash the butter, shallot, parsley, lemon juice, tarragon, ⅛ teaspoon salt, and a pinch of pepper together in a bowl. Following the photo on page 114, shape the butter mixture into a 2 by 3-inch rectangle on plastic wrap, wrap it tightly, and refrigerate until firm, about 30 minutes.

2. FOR THE CHICKEN: Adjust an oven rack to the lower-middle position and heat the oven to 300 degrees. Pulse the bread in a food processor to coarse crumbs, about 16 pulses. Transfer the crumbs to a bowl and stir in the oil, ⅛ teaspoon salt, and ⅛ teaspoon pepper. Spread the crumbs out on a rimmed baking sheet and bake, stirring occasionally, until golden brown and dry, about 25 minutes. Let cool to room temperature.

3. Following the photos on page 114, butterfly and pound each chicken breast into a large ¼-inch-thick cutlet and season with salt and pepper. Unwrap the butter and cut it into two 1 by 3-inch pieces. With the cut side of the chicken facing up, place 1 piece of the butter near the tapered end of each cutlet. Roll the tapered edge of each cutlet over the butter, then fold in the sides and continue rolling the chicken around the butter to form a tidy package, pressing on the seam to seal. Lay the chicken on a plate and refrigerate for about 1 hour to help seal the edges.

4. Adjust an oven rack to the middle position and heat the oven to 350 degrees. Set a wire rack over a rimmed baking sheet. Combine the flour, ⅛ teaspoon salt, and a pinch of pepper in a shallow dish. In a second shallow dish, whisk the eggs and mustard together. In a third shallow dish, combine the cooled bread crumbs, ¼ teaspoon salt, and ⅛ teaspoon pepper.

CHICKEN KIEV

SHAPING THE BUTTER FOR CHICKEN KIEV

Shape the butter mixture into a 2 by 3-inch rectangle on plastic wrap, then wrap tightly and refrigerate until firm, about 30 minutes.

MAKING CHICKEN KIEV

1. Butterfly the chicken breast by starting on the thinnest side and slicing lengthwise almost in half; do not cut the chicken all the way through.

2. Open up the chicken like a book, cover with plastic wrap, and pound lightly to an even ¼-inch thickness.

3. Cut the chilled butter into two 1 by 3-inch pieces, and place one piece near the tapered end of each cutlet.

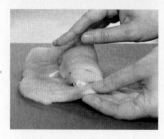

4. Roll the tapered end of the chicken over the butter, then fold in the sides and continue rolling the chicken around the butter to form a tidy package, pressing on the seam to seal.

5. Dredge the chicken in the flour, shaking off the excess. Using tongs, coat the chicken with the egg mixture, allowing the excess to drip off. Coat all sides of the chicken with a thick layer of bread crumbs, pressing to help them adhere. Transfer the breaded chicken to the prepared wire rack.

6. Bake the chicken until the centers register 160 degrees on an instant-read thermometer, 40 to 45 minutes. Let the chicken rest on the wire rack for 5 minutes before serving.

BROILED SCALLOPS WITH CREAMY MUSHROOM SAUCE

ONE OF THE TEST KITCHEN'S FAVORITE scallop dishes is our French-inspired Broiled Scallops with Creamy Mushroom Sauce, known as *Coquilles St. Jacques Bonne Femme* in France. In this simple dish, sea scallops are coated with a mushroom and cream sauce and then broiled in a casserole dish until the tops are just lightly browned. With few ingredients and minimal preparation, this uncomplicated dish, we were certain, had the potential to be a great meal for two.

We started by selecting sea scallops, which are the largest variety of scallops (usually at least an inch in diameter) and are available year-round throughout the country. (Small, cork-shaped bay scallops are very expensive and hard to find.) Sea scallops were clearly the best option; their availability made them much more affordable, their larger size was better suited for the intense heat of the broiler, and a modest eight scallops was plenty for two people.

With our scallops selected, we took a look at the cream sauce. Classic recipes for mushroom sauces relied on outdated cooking methods that contained fussy steps, such as using whipped cream or egg yolks to thicken the sauce, to achieve results that were mediocre and inconsistent from batch to batch. Even our own recipe utilized ½ cup of whipped cream to add some body to the final sauce. In an effort to streamline the cooking technique, we decided to nix this step in our scaled-down recipe (¼ cup of whipped cream was a minimal amount as it was), while keeping the main ingredients—heavy cream, white wine, and mushrooms—in place.

We began by cutting the total amount of mushrooms used in half, to ½ pound, and sautéing them in a skillet until they released their moisture and began to brown. We then simmered the mushrooms with 1 cup (down from 2 cups in the original) of heavy cream and wine until the liquid had reduced. This sauce had good mushroom flavor but was a bit bland. To strengthen the flavor of the sauce, we added a small amount of fresh thyme, a minced shallot, a heavy splash of chicken broth, and lemon juice. Now we had a mushroom sauce that tasted great and was much easier to make than its predecessors.

As we moved our attention to cooking the scallops, one thing was clear: To preserve their creamy and delicate texture, we'd have to cook them until there was just a hint of translucence in the very center, meaning the scallops were hot all the way through but not overcooked in the middle. Many recipes we found called for parcooking the scallops before spooning the sauce over them to brown. However, by the time the sauce had thickened and finished browning in the oven, the parcooked scallops were overcooked and rubbery. Skipping the parcooking step, we tried simply spooning the warm sauce over the raw scallops and cooked the entire dish under the broiler. After a few minutes, the scallops were perfectly cooked and had a light brown crown on top. But as tasters gathered around, they were dismayed to see that although the scallops were nicely browned, the sauce underneath was quite watery and runny—no doubt a result of the shortened time under the broiler and the absence of whipped cream, which would give our sauce some body.

To thicken the sauce, we first played with the proportions of cream, wine, and chicken broth to create a sauce that did not require further reduction under the broiler, but the sauce began to lose its flavor and richness. Thinking about standard thickening ingredients, we wondered if adding flour could help the situation. It did—1 teaspoon of flour, added to the sautéed mushrooms, was all we needed to stabilize the sauce and prevent it from falling apart under the broiler.

Now when we broiled our scallops, they were accompanied by a sauce that clung to their sides rather than sliding off. Finally, our tender, sweet sea scallops were cozily nestled in a rich, creamy sauce studded with slivers of cooked mushroom.

NOTES FROM THE TEST KITCHEN

PREPARING SCALLOPS

The small crescent-shaped muscle that is sometimes attached to the scallop will be incredibly tough when cooked. Use your fingers to peel it away from the side of each scallop before cooking.

BUYING SCALLOPS

When buying sea scallops, look first at their color. Scallops are naturally ivory or pinkish tan; processing (dipping them in a phosphate and water mixture to extend shelf life) turns them bright white. Processed scallops are slippery and swollen and are usually sitting in a milky white liquid at the store. You should look for unprocessed scallops (also called dry scallops), which are sticky and flabby; they will taste fresher than processed scallops and will develop a nice crust when browned because they are not pumped full of water.

Broiled Scallops with Creamy Mushroom Sauce

SERVES 2

For this recipe, we prefer using large sea scallops. Depending on the size of your scallops and the strength of your broiler, the cooking time may vary slightly.

- 1 **tablespoon unsalted butter**
- 8 **ounces white mushrooms, sliced thin**
- 1 **shallot, minced (about 3 tablespoons)**
- 1 **teaspoon unbleached all-purpose flour**
- ½ **cup dry white wine**
- 1 **cup heavy cream**
- ¼ **cup low-sodium chicken broth**
- ½ **teaspoon minced fresh thyme**
- **Salt**
- ½ **teaspoon fresh lemon juice**
- **Pepper**
- 12 **ounces large sea scallops (about 8 scallops), muscle removed (see photo) (see note)**

1. Adjust an oven rack to be 6 inches from the broiler element and heat the broiler. Melt the butter in a 10-inch skillet over medium heat. Add the mushrooms and shallot, and cook until the mushrooms release their liquid and begin to brown, 5 to 7 minutes.

2. Stir in the flour until incorporated, about 30 seconds. Stir in the wine, scraping up any browned bits, and simmer until it is almost completely evaporated, 3 to 5 minutes. Stir in the cream, broth, thyme, and ¼ teaspoon salt, and continue to simmer, stirring occasionally, until the mixture has thickened and reduced to about 1 cup, 12 to 15 minutes. Off the heat, stir in the lemon juice and season with pepper to taste.

3. Pat the scallops dry with paper towels, season with salt and pepper, and arrange in a single layer in a 2-quart broiler-safe baking dish. Spoon the sauce and mushrooms over the scallops and broil until the sauce is nicely browned and the scallops are cooked through, 3 to 4 minutes. Serve immediately.

PAELLA

DESPITE ITS REPUTATION as a Spanish restaurant staple, paella hasn't always been categorized as a lavish meal. Developed just outside Valencia, Spain, as a means of cooking large quantities of rice, traditional paella was anything but fancy. Cooked in flat-bottomed pans over a wood fire and flavored with local, easy-to-find ingredients such as snails, rabbit, and green beans, this utilitarian dish was a far cry from today's paella.

Nowadays, paella is a production with a daunting ingredient list of anything from artichokes to green beans to pork, chicken, and lobster. Clearly, narrowing down our ingredients and creating a simpler, smaller recipe would be a challenge.

To keep our ingredient list manageable, we quickly ruled out certain items—lobster (too much work, when it wouldn't even be the star of the dish), diced pork (sausage was a natural substitute), and rabbit and snails (too unconventional). We were left with traditional chorizo, chicken, and shrimp (which were preferred over other types of shellfish, including scallops and calamari).

We began by browning the chicken in a skillet, having already swapped out the paella pan for the more common household pan. Many recipes call for bone-in, skin-on chicken pieces, but to save time we opted for boneless, skinless thighs, which are richer in flavor and less prone to drying out than breasts. Two thighs provided enough meat, considering that we would include chorizo and shrimp in our paella as well. We seared both sides of the chicken thighs in a skillet and removed them from the pan before they were cooked through, so they would be tender and juicy when added back to finish cooking. Then we sautéed sliced chorizo with half a sliced pepper, shallot, and saffron—all ingredients that added flavor to the leftover fat in the pan, which we could use to coat and flavor the rice.

Turning to the rice, we knew short- or medium-grain was the best pick; long-grain rice would be too light and fluffy. We preferred Valencia rice for its creamy but distinct grains, with Italian Arborio rice following as a close second. To feed two people, ¾ cup of uncooked rice was just the right amount. We sautéed the rice with the garlic long enough to become fragrant and be coated with the flavorful base, then returned the chicken thighs to the pan. Now it was time to add the cooking liquid. Water alone made for a bland dish, so we fell back on chicken broth, as chicken was already featured prominently in our dish. After multiple tests, we settled on just over 1 cup of liquid as the right amount to cook our rice. We added the chicken back to the skillet and let the contents simmer and the flavors blend.

After 15 minutes, the rice was nearly done, so we added the quick-cooking shrimp, along with some thawed frozen peas. Peas are a requisite ingredient in paella, and they add a bright splash of green to the dish. At this point, we could easily have called it a day, with flavorful and tender rice, chicken, and chorizo ready to be dished out, but several tasters demanded *soccarat,* the crusty brown layer of rice that develops on the bottom of a perfectly cooked batch of paella.

Curious to see if we could get this to work in our skillet, we waited until the dish was completely cooked, then removed the lid and turned the heat up. After only five minutes, a spoon inserted into the depths of the rice revealed nicely caramelized grains. Before we let anyone dig in, we allowed the paella to rest, covered, so the rice could continue to firm up and absorb excess moisture. After adding a garnish of parsley and lemon, we were done. Our finished paella had all the flavor and sparkle of this Spanish dish minus the absurdly long ingredient list.

Paella

SERVES 2

If you can't find chorizo sausage, use andouille or lin-guiça. Soccarat, the traditional crusty brown layer of rice that develops on the bottom of a perfectly cooked batch of paella, is optional in step 5, but it adds a nice roasted flavor to the paella. See page 17 for a recipe to use up the leftover red bell pepper.

- 8 ounces extra-large shrimp (21 to 25 per pound), peeled and deveined (see page 35)
   Salt and pepper
- 8 ounces boneless, skinless chicken thighs (about 2 thighs), trimmed
- 1 tablespoon extra-virgin olive oil
- 4 ounces chorizo (see note), halved lengthwise and cut crosswise into ¼-inch pieces
- ½ red bell pepper, stemmed, seeded, and cut into ½-inch-wide strips
- 1 shallot, minced (about 3 tablespoons)
   Pinch saffron threads, crumbled
- ¾ cup Valencia or Arborio rice
- 3 garlic cloves, minced
- 1¼ cups low-sodium chicken broth
- ¼ cup frozen peas (about 1 ounce), thawed
- 1 tablespoon chopped fresh parsley
   Lemon wedges, for serving

1. Pat the shrimp dry with paper towels, season with salt and pepper, and refrigerate until needed.

2. Pat the chicken dry with paper towels and season with salt and pepper. Heat the oil in a 10-inch skillet over medium-high heat until just smoking. Brown the chicken well on both sides, about 5 minutes, flipping it halfway through cooking. Transfer the chicken to a plate and set aside.

3. Return the skillet to medium heat, add the chorizo, bell pepper, shallot, saffron, and ½ teaspoon salt and cook until the chorizo and pepper are well browned, about 4 minutes. Stir in the rice and garlic and cook until fragrant, about 30 seconds.

4. Stir in the broth, scraping up any browned bits. Return the chicken to the pan and bring to a simmer. Reduce the heat to medium-low, cover, and cook until the thickest part of the thighs registers 170 to

NOTES FROM THE TEST KITCHEN

THE BEST PAELLA RICE
Since paella is basically a rice dish, it's vital to use the right kind of rice. Long-grain rice is great in dishes that need fluffy, light rice (think pilaf), but it's not right in paella. Only certain kinds of short-grain and medium-grain rice retain distinct, individual grains while having the creamy-chewy texture vital for this dish. After testing several kinds of rice for our paella, we determined that Arborio and Valencia rice were the best varieties for this preparation. Italian Arborio rice has large, long grains that cook up creamy and tender in our Paella. Spanish Valencia rice has grains that are short and round, which tasters also liked. They praised its balance of textures— separate and chewy, but with a bit of creaminess.

BUYING SAFFRON
When shopping for saffron, what should you look for? We've seen threads that were incredibly red and other threads that also contained some yellow or orange. We held a small tasting of broths infused with different saffron samples, and the threads with considerable spots of yellow and orange did in fact yield the weakest-colored and flattest-tasting broths. The reddest threads yielded intensely flavorful, heady, perfumed broths. So, when shopping, go for red—the reddest threads, that is, with no spots of yellow or orange. Or, to save money, a good-quality powdered saffron purchased from a reputable source would be just as flavorful and fragrant as even the highest-quality threads.

175 degrees on an instant-read thermometer and most of the liquid is absorbed, about 15 minutes.

5. Scatter the shrimp over the rice and continue to cook, covered, until the rice is tender and the shrimp are cooked through, about 5 minutes longer. If soccarat is desired (see note), set the skillet, uncovered, over medium-high heat and continue to cook until the bottom layer of rice is golden and crisp, about 5 minutes, rotating the skillet halfway through cooking to ensure even browning.

6. Off the heat, sprinkle the peas and parsley over the rice, cover, and let warm through, about 2 minutes. Season with salt and pepper to taste and serve with lemon wedges.

FRESH FETTUCCINE WITH LOBSTER

IF A CASTE SYSTEM EVER EXISTED in the food world, lobsters would be right at the top, next to other culinary stars such as truffles and foie gras. Unfortunately, as a result of the preparation involved, lobsters are generally reserved for that rare lobster bake in the summer, when the chef is cooking a whole fleet of crustaceans. Wanting to prove that lobster, although still requiring some effort, was a worthwhile option for a special-occasion dinner for two, we set out to create a recipe for the common pairing of lobster and pasta (pasta would be the easy portion of the menu) in a creamy sauce.

We started by examining other recipes for pasta with creamy lobster sauce and the ways they incorporated lobster flavor into the finished dish. A few recipes called for sautéing raw lobster pieces with aromatics and then adding cream before reducing the sauce. Others required making a lobster broth, which was then added to cream and reduced. In some other recipes, precooked lobster meat was added to reduced cream that had been flavored with aromatics and strained. But none of these methods produced the right amount of lobster flavor in the finished dish. Sautéing raw lobster pieces was out—it was hard enough removing the meat after the lobster was cooked—and making our own broth provided merely a hint of flavor in the finished dish. Comfortable with the ease of steaming a whole lobster and adding the cooked meat to a reduced cream sauce, we decided to move forward in that direction.

Unfortunately, we discovered in our first test that adding cooked lobster meat from the tail and claws to a strained sauce of heavy cream, white wine, tomato paste, shallots, and thyme did not result in as much pure lobster flavor in the sauce as we had hoped. We tried cooking the sauce further, after adding the lobster meat, to infuse it with lobster flavor. But this only resulted in overcooked, rubbery meat.

Looking at our pile of lobster shells, we realized that the lobster legs were not being used at all and were going to waste. Suddenly a light bulb flickered on—the legs could easily be taken off the body before cooking and added to the cream sauce to impart additional flavor. Taking a cue from traditional stock recipes, which are made with bones, we sautéed the legs with a shallot, thyme, and tomato paste before adding the cream and

simmering the sauce, allowing the flavors to blend and deepen. Clam juice and reserved lobster juice added even more briny sea flavors. Now when we added the cooked lobster meat, we had a rich sauce full of lobster flavor and tender, moist lobster pieces.

All that was left to do now was find a pasta that would help showcase our sauce. We settled on fettuccine, the usual partner for cream sauces because of its thin, flat shape that holds on to sauce exceptionally well. As this was already an elegant lobster dinner, we decided to look into prepackaged fresh fettuccine from the supermarket refrigerator case. Fresh pasta costs a bit more money than dried pasta, but for this dinner, it was well worth it. Before committing to the fresh fettuccine, we tried both fresh and dried pasta with our sauce and lobster, and tasters far preferred the tender texture of the fresh fettuccine.

Surveying our bowl of fettuccine in a decadent, creamy sauce studded with red and pink lobster bits, we knew we had created something special.

Fresh Fettuccine with Lobster
SERVES 2

Be sure to use fresh pasta for this dish; supermarkets sell 8- and 9-ounce containers of fresh pasta in the refrigerator section. We prefer hard-shell lobsters, but a soft-shell lobster would work here; the cooking time for a soft-shell lobster will be on the lower end of the range given. Freezing the live lobster for about 15 minutes before preparing it will help to sedate it; do not over-freeze the lobster or it will ruin the texture of the meat. You may not need to use the entire bottle of clam juice in step 3.

- 1 (1½-pound) live lobster, frozen for 15 minutes (see note)
- 1 (8-ounce) bottle clam juice (see note)
- 1 tablespoon vegetable oil
- 1 teaspoon tomato paste
- 1 shallot, sliced thin
- 1 sprig fresh thyme
- ½ cup dry white wine
- 1½ cups heavy cream
- 8-9 ounces fresh fettuccine (see note)
- Salt and pepper
- 1 tablespoon chopped fresh parsley

1. Fit a large Dutch oven with a steamer basket, fill the pot with water until it just touches the bottom of the basket, and bring to a boil over high heat. Following the photos, hold the lobster firmly on a cutting board and, with a knife, split the head completely in half. Twist off the legs, cut them in half crosswise, and refrigerate until needed for the sauce.

2. Add the lobster to the pot, cover, and steam until bright red and fully cooked, 13 to 15 minutes. Check the pot periodically to make sure the water has not boiled dry, adding more water as needed.

3. Transfer the cooked lobster to a bowl and let it cool slightly. Holding the lobster over the bowl to catch all the juice, remove the tail and claw appendages by twisting them off the body. Drain the body of any extra juice and discard. Pour the lobster juice into a liquid measuring cup and add enough clam juice to measure 1 cup. Remove the lobster meat from the tail, arms, and claws, and cut into bite-sized pieces. (The cooked lobster meat, reserved lobster juice, and raw lobster legs can be refrigerated for up to 1 day before continuing.)

4. Heat the oil in a 10-inch skillet over medium heat until shimmering. Add the uncooked lobster legs, tomato paste, shallot, and thyme and cook until the shallot is softened, 2 to 3 minutes. Stir in the wine, scraping up any browned bits, and simmer until the wine has almost completely evaporated, 4 to 5 minutes. Stir in the cream and lobster juice, and continue to simmer, stirring occasionally, until the liquid has thickened and measures about 1 cup, 20 to 25 minutes.

5. Meanwhile, bring 4 quarts water to a boil in a large pot. Add the pasta and 1 tablespoon salt, and cook, stirring often, until al dente. Reserve ½ cup of the cooking water, then drain the pasta and return it to the pot.

6. Strain the sauce through a fine-mesh strainer, discarding the solids. Return the sauce to the skillet, add the reserved lobster meat, and warm through over low heat. Season with salt and pepper to taste. Add the lobster sauce to the cooked pasta and toss to combine, adjusting the sauce consistency with the reserved cooking water as desired. Stir in the parsley and serve immediately.

HARD-SHELL VERSUS SOFT-SHELL LOBSTERS
During the year, lobsters go through a molting stage to grow into a larger shell. If caught during this stage, the lobsters are called soft-shell—if squeezed, their soft sides will yield to pressure, whereas a hard-shell lobster will feel hard. Soft-shell lobsters have less meat and are considered less flavorful; they also cook faster than hard-shelled ones do.

PREPARING A LOBSTER

1. After freezing the lobster to sedate it, insert the tip of a chef's knife into the body near the head where the shell forms a "T," with the blade of the chef's knife facing the head. Move the blade down, splitting the head in half.

2. Before cooking the lobster, twist off the legs, cut them in half crosswise, and reserve separately for the sauce.

3. After the lobster is cooked and cooled, hold it over a large bowl, and remove the tail and claw appendages by twisting them off the body, reserving any lobster juice. Discard the lobster body.

4. After cutting the tail down the middle, pull the meat out with a fork.

5. Twist the claw from the connecting joint. Use lobster crackers or a mallet to break open the connecting joint and claw and remove the meat from both with a cocktail fork if necessary. If possible, remove the meat in a single piece.

RICOTTA GNOCCHI

WHEN IT COMES TO GNOCCHI, the type most familiar in the United States is made with potato. But in our research, we found a potatoless version—ricotta gnocchi, which hails from Florence. Described as pillowy and tender, this dish intrigued us, and we were eager to develop our own version. And since gnocchi is a hand-shaped pasta that doesn't require any special equipment, we figured it would be a fairly simple yet elegant dish for just two people.

Reviewing a wide swath of recipes revealed that, like many other Italian dishes, this Florentine specialty doesn't require a long list of ingredients—just ricotta, eggs, flour, Parmesan cheese, salt, pepper, and sometimes herbs or spinach. The technique is quite simple, too. The dough is simply rolled into ropes, cut into small pieces, and boiled. Even the two Italian names for ricotta gnocchi sound forgiving: *malfatti* (badly made), referring to their sometimes less-than-model-perfect appearance, and *gnudi* (naked), because they resemble ravioli without their pasta jackets.

We knew the success of this dish would hinge on its most prominent ingredient: ricotta cheese. Tasters preferred whole-milk ricotta to the leaner, less flavorful part-skim variety. Most recipes called for a whole pound, so we simply cut this amount in half. We began by forming a basic dough, combining the ricotta with an egg, 1 cup of flour, ¼ cup of Parmesan cheese, and some salt and pepper. Instead of the pillowy bundles we'd been hoping for, we got leaden, floury blobs lacking in cheese flavor. More Parmesan helped ramp up the cheese flavor, and more ricotta (we upped the amount to 10 ounces) contributed moistness, but to lighten the texture we needed to use less flour. However, when we cut back on the flour, the dough was too sticky and unworkable.

When a fellow test cook commented on the wateriness of supermarket ricotta (in Italy, ricotta is creamy and dry, but American supermarket brands are curdy and wet), we saw an opportunity. In the test kitchen, we often thicken yogurt by draining it in the refrigerator. What if we drained the ricotta? Sure enough, the result was a slightly drier dough that had more structure. Now we could work on cutting back the amount of flour.

Taking baby steps, we reduced the amount of flour to ¾ cup, which made the gnocchi slightly less gummy. At ½ cup, they were even better, but still not perfect. Any less flour, though, and the dough became a batter that was overly sticky.

We then remembered a recipe found in our research that we'd tried and dismissed for its use of an unexpected ingredient: fresh bread crumbs. Could this simple addition—one that's often coupled with milk or egg to add tenderness to meat loaf—absorb more of the moisture in the dough and allow us to add less flour? These gnocchi were a little better, but not enough to justify the extra effort. But we weren't ready to give up. What if we toasted the crumbs? For our next test, we made a dough with just ¼ cup of flour and ⅓ cup of homemade dried bread crumbs. The resulting gnocchi held together and had the perfect combination of tenderness and structure. (Hoping for a shortcut, we tried substituting store-bought bread crumbs, but they gave the gnocchi a stale taste.)

But there was one element still missing from this balancing act—proper technique. We wondered if chilling the dough would help. We tested various chilling times

 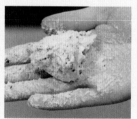

and found that just 15 minutes in the refrigerator helped the dough stiffen and become more workable. Rolling it out afterward by hand wasn't difficult, provided we did so gently and worked with a little bit at a time.

The gnocchi were ready to be simmered. By the time they floated to the surface, they needed just two more minutes in the water before being scooped out. One last step remained: tossing the tender little dumplings in a simple sauce of browned butter, minced shallots, and sage. When we set the platter of gnocchi in front of tasters, it took all of five minutes for the last piece to disappear. We guess they weren't so "badly made" after all.

Ricotta Gnocchi with Browned Butter and Sage Sauce

SERVES 2

We prefer to use whole-milk ricotta here, although part-skim ricotta will also work; do not use fat-free ricotta. When rolling out the gnocchi, use just enough flour to keep the dough from sticking to your hands and the counter; using too much flour will make the gnocchi tough. After being cut and spread out on the parchment-lined baking sheet, the gnocchi can be covered and refrigerated for up to 24 hours before cooking. See page 61 for a recipe to use up some or all of the leftover ricotta cheese.

GNOCCHI

- 10 ounces whole-milk ricotta cheese (about 1¼ cups) (see note)
- 1 slice high-quality white sandwich bread, crusts removed, torn into pieces
- ⅓ cup grated Parmesan cheese
- 1 large egg, lightly beaten
- ¼ cup chopped fresh parsley
  Salt
- ¼ teaspoon pepper
- ¼ cup unbleached all-purpose flour, plus extra for the counter

SAUCE

- 3 tablespoons unsalted butter
- ⅛ teaspoon salt
- 1 tablespoon minced shallot
- 1½ teaspoons chopped fresh sage
- 1 teaspoon fresh lemon juice

1. FOR THE GNOCCHI: Line a fine-mesh strainer set over a deep bowl with 3 paper coffee filters or a triple layer of paper towels. Place the ricotta in the lined strainer, cover, and refrigerate for 1 hour.

2. Adjust an oven rack to the middle position and heat the oven to 300 degrees. Pulse the bread in a food processor to fine crumbs, about 10 pulses. Spread the crumbs on a rimmed baking sheet and bake, stirring occasionally, until dry and lightly golden, about 10 minutes; let cool. (You should have about ⅓ cup crumbs.)

3. Transfer the drained ricotta to the food processor and pulse until the curds break down to a fine, grainy consistency, about 8 pulses. Transfer the processed ricotta to a large bowl and stir in the Parmesan, egg, parsley, ½ teaspoon salt, and pepper until combined. Sprinkle the flour and bread crumbs over the mixture, and stir until well combined. Refrigerate the dough for 15 minutes. Check the texture of the dough (see page 120) and add extra flour, 1 tablespoon at a time, if the dough is too wet.

4. Line a rimmed baking sheet with parchment paper. Lightly dust the counter with flour. With floured hands, roll a lemon-sized piece of dough into a ¾-inch-thick rope. Cut the rope into ¾-inch-long pieces and transfer to the prepared baking sheet. Repeat with the remaining dough, dusting the counter with extra flour as needed.

5. FOR THE SAUCE: Melt the butter with the salt in a 12-inch skillet over medium-high heat, swirling occasionally, until the butter is browned and releases a nutty aroma, about 1½ minutes. Off the heat, stir in the shallot and sage until fragrant, about 1 minute. Stir in the lemon juice and cover to keep warm.

6. Bring 4 quarts water to a boil in a large pot. Add 1 tablespoon salt. Reduce the heat so that the water is simmering, gently drop half of the gnocchi into the water, and cook until they float to the surface. Continue to cook the gnocchi, adjusting the heat as needed to maintain a gentle simmer, until they are cooked through, about 2 minutes longer. Scoop the gnocchi from the water with a slotted spoon, allowing the excess water to drain back into the pot, and transfer to the covered skillet with the sauce. Repeat with the remaining gnocchi.

7. Using a rubber spatula, gently toss the gnocchi with the sauce until uniformly coated and serve.

PASTA WITH LIGHTER ROASTED RED PEPPER PESTO

ON THE LIGHTER SIDE

SAUTÉED CHICKEN BREASTS

IF YOU'RE LOOKING TO LOWER THE AMOUNT OF FAT in your diet but still have a substantial and satisfying meal, boneless, skinless chicken breasts should be in your repertoire. Virtually fat-free and packed with protein, boneless chicken breasts also have the added bonus of being exceptionally easy to prepare. And, of course, they make a great main course for two, since you can easily divide a package, using half and freezing half for later. There are many ways to prepare boneless breasts, but sautéing is the best way to achieve a beautiful golden brown exterior. The major problem is that boneless, skinless breasts have a tendency to dry out because they're so lean, and sautéing can amplify the problem. We wanted to develop a foolproof technique for what should be a simple dish—tender, flavorful, and moist sautéed chicken breasts. We also wanted to develop a couple of boldly flavored pan sauces to jazz up our chicken without relying on butter or heavy cream.

We knew the type of pan we used would be crucial to a successful sauté. A large 12-inch skillet was much too big when cooking only two breasts—there was too much empty space in the pan, which made it susceptible to scorching. We tried an 8-inch skillet, but this pan was too small and the chicken was crowded. Crowding led to the creation of steam, which resulted in pale and unappetizing chicken. A 10-inch skillet was a much better choice, giving the chicken plenty of space to properly brown without leaving an excessive amount of skillet exposed. Also, we noted that a nonstick skillet did not work as well as a traditional skillet. Although this may seem counterintuitive for healthier cooking (because nonstick pans allow you to cook with less fat), we found that regardless of skillet type, a certain amount of fat is necessary for a good sauté. Without enough fat the crust turns out spotty—burnt in some spots and completely pale in others. And using a traditional skillet is necessary when making pan sauces; those flavorful browned bits left in the skillet are essential to the flavor of the sauce.

We preferred vegetable oil to olive oil here; not only does it have a higher smoke point, but unlike olive oil, the flavor of vegetable oil is neutral and pairs with anything. We found the optimum amount of vegetable oil for sautéing two chicken breasts to be 1 tablespoon.

We also experimented with various heat levels. When we sautéed the chicken over the highest heat, it browned too quickly while remaining underdone on the inside. On the other hand, cooking the chicken very slowly over low heat made the chicken chewy and didn't produce that all-important golden crust. Working between these two extremes, we determined that the optimal heat level was a combination of medium-high and medium. First, we achieved a golden crust on one side over medium-high heat, then flipped the chicken, turned the heat to medium, and continued to cook the chicken through. This way, the chicken achieved a gorgeous sautéed crust while its interior remained tender.

NOTES FROM THE TEST KITCHEN

SHALLOTS

Shallots are much smaller than most onions, making them ideal for scaled-down recipes. They also have a unique flavor that is milder and more delicate than that of onions—and when shallots and onions are cooked, the differences between them show up even more. In a quick-cooking pan sauce, a shallot's mild flavor melds much more smoothly with the other ingredients. A finely minced shallot also melts into the sauce until it's all but indiscernible. No matter how finely you mince an onion, it's not going to disappear into an otherwise silky sauce. An onion also needs much more cooking time for its flavor to mellow. A raw shallot also adds gentle heat to a vinaigrette or salsa, with a minimum of crunch. If you were to use a raw onion in the same recipe, the pungent onion crunch would seem out of place.

THE BEST MEAT POUNDER

To find a meat pounder that could produce thin cutlets of uniform thickness in the fewest number of strokes, we bought five models in a variety of shapes and weights. Our previous favorite, the middleweight **Norpro Meat Pounder**, $27.99, beat the new contenders by pounding out clean, even cutlets in a reasonable 35 strokes, with an offset handle that distributes its weight comfortably.

If you don't have a meat pounder, we have found that you can make do with a rubber mallet or a sturdy 8-inch skillet. These makeshift meat pounders may not be elegant or ergonomic, but they will suffice in a pinch.

Up to this point, we had been using unfloured breasts. We were curious whether flouring the breasts would be beneficial, and indeed it was. Flour promoted more even browning on the exterior of the chicken. More important, however, it seemed to protect both the crust and the interior of the chicken. It prevented the crust from turning tough and stringy, while keeping the interior moist.

We wanted to top off our perfectly sautéed chicken with pan sauces, and we uncovered a few tricks to keep these sauces low in fat without losing any flavor. Pan sauces are typically finished with some sort of fat—butter or cream—to add richness and help emulsify the sauce. For our first sauce, a white wine and herb pan sauce, we needed something to replace the butter; then for a creamy mustard and dill sauce, we would need to find a replacement for the cream. We tried many substitutes for both of these ingredients, including low-fat sour cream, buttermilk, yogurt, yogurt cheese, milk, and half-and-half. The winning substitutes turned out to be a whole milk–cornstarch slurry for the butter, and light cream cheese for the heavy cream. A sprinkling of fresh herbs and some potent aromatics contributed bold flavors to both of our sauces without adding calories.

Sautéed Chicken Breasts with White Wine and Herb Pan Sauce

SERVES 2

We prefer the flavor of whole milk in the sauce; however, 2 percent milk will also work. Do not use 1 percent or skim milk.

CHICKEN

¼ cup unbleached all-purpose flour
2 (6-ounce) boneless, skinless chicken breasts, trimmed and pounded ½ inch thick
   Salt and pepper
1 tablespoon vegetable oil

SAUCE

1 shallot, minced (about 3 tablespoons)
1 garlic clove, minced
¼ cup dry white wine or vermouth
¾ cup low-sodium chicken broth
1 tablespoon whole milk (see note)

½ teaspoon cornstarch
2 teaspoons chopped fresh parsley
2 teaspoons chopped fresh tarragon
   Salt and pepper

1. FOR THE CHICKEN: Place the flour in a shallow dish. Pat the chicken dry with paper towels and season with ¼ teaspoon salt and a pinch of pepper. Working with one breast at a time, dredge the chicken in the flour, shaking off the excess.

2. Meanwhile, heat the oil in a 10-inch skillet over medium-high heat until just smoking. Carefully lay the chicken breasts in the skillet and cook until well browned on the first side, 6 to 8 minutes. Flip the chicken breasts, reduce the heat to medium, and continue to cook until the thickest part of the breasts registers 160 to 165 degrees on an instant-read thermometer, 6 to 8 minutes longer. Transfer the chicken to a plate, tent loosely with foil, and let rest while preparing the sauce.

3. FOR THE SAUCE: Reduce the heat to medium-low, add the shallot to the skillet, and cook until softened, 2 to 3 minutes. Stir in the garlic and cook until fragrant, about 30 seconds. Stir in the wine, scraping up any browned bits. Stir in the broth, bring to a simmer, and cook until the mixture has reduced to ½ cup, about 5 minutes.

4. Pour any accumulated chicken juice into the simmering sauce. Whisk the milk and cornstarch together in a small bowl, then whisk into the simmering sauce. Continue to simmer the sauce until thickened, about 1 minute. Off the heat, stir in the parsley and tarragon, and season with salt and pepper to taste. Spoon the sauce over the chicken and serve.

PER SERVING: Cal 280; Fat 7 g; Sat fat 1 g; Chol 100 mg; Carb 7 g; Protein 41 g; Fiber 0 g; Sodium 620 mg

VARIATION

Sautéed Chicken Breasts with Creamy Whole-Grain Mustard and Dill Pan Sauce

Follow the recipe for Sautéed Chicken Breasts with White Wine and Herb Pan Sauce, substituting 1 tablespoon light cream cheese for the milk and cornstarch mixture, and 1 tablespoon whole-grain mustard and 2 teaspoons chopped fresh dill for the parsley and tarragon.

PER SERVING: Cal 300; Fat 8 g; Sat fat 2 g; Chol 100 mg; Carb 8 g; Protein 43 g; Fiber 0 g; Sodium 830 mg

LIGHTER CHICKEN PARMESAN

THE BEST PART OF CHICKEN PARMESAN—composed of breaded, fried chicken cutlets topped with tomato sauce, Parmesan cheese, and melted mozzarella—is the crisp, golden coating on the cutlets. Unfortunately, this terrific breaded coating is the result of frying the cutlets in a good amount of oil—a process that's not only calorie-laden but time-consuming as well. Sure, there are lots of recipes for low-fat or "un-fried" chicken Parmesan where the breaded cutlets are baked rather than fried, but none that we tried even came close to the flavor, color, or crispness of a traditional fried recipe. These cutlets literally paled by comparison, with their flavorless, washed-out crusts. We wondered if we could develop a better, lighter version, one actually worth eating. And since we knew we'd have to find an alternative to frying, we hoped that our lighter version would be a streamlined version as well, one that was worth making for just two people.

Setting the issue of the sauce and cheese aside, we started with how to cook the breaded cutlets. Obviously, deep-frying and pan-frying the cutlets were both out—these methods used too much oil. That left us with the oven, but simply breading the cutlets (using the classic breading of flour, then egg—in this case egg white—then bread crumbs) and baking them on a baking sheet didn't work: The breading never turned brown or crisp, the bottoms were soggy, the breading tasted stale, and the chicken was rubbery and dry—a real loser on all counts. We had our work cut out for us.

Homing in on the issue of oven temperature first, we found that baking the chicken breasts for 15 minutes at 475 degrees produced the most tender and juicy chicken. We tried coating the baking sheet with a thin film of oil and heating it in the oven before adding the breaded chicken to encourage browning, but the bread crumbs merely soaked up the oil and turned greasy. Baking the chicken on a wire rack set over a baking sheet quickly solved the soggy bottom issue, and spraying the tops with vegetable oil spray helped the breading on top of the cutlets crisp up nicely. We still, however, had issues with their bland flavor and pale color.

Then it hit us—what if we toasted the bread crumbs to a golden color before breading the cutlets? We toasted the bread crumbs in a skillet over medium heat until golden, then breaded the cutlets, sprayed the tops with vegetable oil, and baked them on the rack. These cutlets were a big improvement, with an even golden color and crisp fried texture. Adding 2 teaspoons of olive oil to the crumbs as they toasted gave them a nice "fried" flavor without turning them greasy or adding too many calories, and tossing the crumbs with some grated Parmesan cheese helped boost their flavor dramatically.

Testing the difference between store-bought dried bread crumbs, fresh bread crumbs, and panko (Japanese-style bread crumbs), the test kitchen universally disliked the "old," "ground cardboard" flavor of the store-bought dried bread crumbs. Both the fresh bread crumbs and the panko were well liked; however, tasters preferred the ultra-crisp texture of panko to that of the fresh bread crumbs.

Now that we had flavorful, crisp, golden, "oven-fried" chicken breasts, we tried placing them in a small baking dish with some tomato sauce (we made a fresh-tasting but quick one with diced tomatoes, garlic, tomato paste, red pepper flakes, and basil) and low-fat shredded mozzarella. Returning the dish to the oven so that the mozzarella could melt, we were disappointed at how quickly the crisp breading turned soggy. Any area of breading that touched the sauce, cheese, or the other cutlet lost its crispness. Looking for a better method, we decided to leave the cutlets right on the rack and spoon just a small portion of the sauce and mozzarella onto the center of each piece of chicken, leaving the edges clean.

NOTES FROM THE TEST KITCHEN

THE BEST PANKO
To see if there really is a difference between the brands of this light, Japanese-style bread crumb coating, we picked up four samples at the supermarket and tested them in our Lighter Chicken Parmesan. Each brand worked fine for this application, but they had slightly different textural qualities. Wel-Pac, Dynasty, and Kikkoman brands possessed a delicate crispness, but the oil-free **Ian's** (purchased from a large natural foods supermarket) provided a much more substantial crunch. In the end, if a super-crunchy—rather than delicate and crisp—texture is what you're aiming for, choose Ian's. Otherwise, brand doesn't really matter.

We returned the rack to the oven, and the clean edges and bottoms of the breaded cutlets remained crisp while the mozzarella cheese melted. Bingo! These oven-baked chicken Parmesan breasts not only knock fat and calories off the traditional fried recipe, but they really do taste just as good—without the mess.

Lighter Chicken Parmesan

SERVES 2

If you are tight on time, you can substitute 1 cup of your favorite plain tomato sauce for the sauce below. Panko is Japanese-style bread crumbs and can be found in the international aisle of the supermarket. Two cups of fresh bread crumbs can be substituted for the panko (they will shrink as they toast).

SAUCE

- 1 (14.5-ounce) can diced tomatoes
- 2 garlic cloves, minced
- 1 teaspoon tomato paste
- 1 teaspoon olive oil
  Salt
  Pinch red pepper flakes
- 2 teaspoons chopped fresh basil
  Pepper

CHICKEN

- 1 cup panko (see note)
- 2 teaspoons olive oil
- ¼ cup grated Parmesan cheese
- ¼ cup unbleached all-purpose flour
- ½ teaspoon garlic powder
  Salt and pepper
- 1 large egg white
- 1 teaspoon water
  Vegetable oil spray
- 2 (6-ounce) boneless, skinless chicken breasts, trimmed and pounded ½ inch thick
- 1 ounce low-fat mozzarella cheese, shredded (about ¼ cup)
- 2 teaspoons chopped fresh basil

1. FOR THE SAUCE: Pulse the tomatoes, with their juice, in a food processor until mostly smooth, about 10 pulses. Cook the garlic, tomato paste, oil, ¼ teaspoon salt, and pepper flakes in a small saucepan over medium heat until the tomato paste begins to brown and the garlic is fragrant, about 2 minutes. Stir in the pureed tomatoes, bring to a simmer, and cook until the sauce is thickened and has reduced to 1 cup, about 10 minutes. Off the heat, stir in the basil and season with salt and pepper to taste. Cover and set aside until needed.

2. FOR THE CHICKEN: Adjust an oven rack to the middle position and heat the oven to 475 degrees. Combine the panko and oil in a 10-inch skillet and toast over medium heat, stirring often, until golden, 5 to 7 minutes. Spread the bread crumbs in a shallow dish and cool slightly; when cool, stir in the Parmesan. In a second shallow dish, combine the flour, garlic powder, ½ teaspoon salt, and ¼ teaspoon pepper. In a third shallow dish, whisk the egg white and water together.

3. Line a rimmed baking sheet with foil, place a wire rack over it, and spray the rack with vegetable oil spray. Pat the chicken dry with paper towels, then season with ⅛ teaspoon salt and a pinch of pepper. Dredge the chicken in the flour mixture and shake off the excess. Using tongs, coat the chicken with the egg white mixture, allowing the excess to drip off. Coat all sides of the chicken with a thick layer of the bread crumb mixture, pressing to help it adhere. Lay the chicken on the wire rack.

4. Spray the tops of the chicken with vegetable oil spray. Bake until the chicken feels firm when pressed with a finger, about 15 minutes. Remove the chicken from the oven. Spoon 2 tablespoons of the sauce onto the center of each breast and top the sauce on each breast with 2 tablespoons of the mozzarella.

5. Return the chicken to the oven and continue to bake until the cheese has melted and the thickest part of the breasts registers 160 to 165 degrees on an instant-read thermometer, about 5 minutes. Sprinkle with the basil and serve with the remaining sauce.

PER SERVING: Cal 460; Fat 14 g; Sat fat 3.5 g; Chol 110 mg; Carb 28 g; Protein 52 g; Fiber 2 g; Sodium 1490 mg

CHICKEN EN PAPILLOTE

COOKING *EN PAPILLOTE* IS A CLASSIC FRENCH METHOD that involves baking food in a tightly sealed parchment paper packet. In effect, the food—often a protein—steams in its own juice, developing a delicate texture and an intense, clean flavor. Unlike many other classic French cooking methods, which usually feature butter and cream, cooking en papillote is naturally light and healthy. Since there is so much moisture and concentrated flavor sealed in the packet, little added fat is needed. And with the addition of vegetables, you get a well-rounded main course. Best of all, this dish takes little work outside of assembly; there's no stovetop cooking and little mess, making it an ideal fresh and healthy meal for two. Our goal was to develop an easy, more contemporary version of this French classic, with perfectly moist and tender pieces of chicken, well-seasoned vegetables, and flavorful juices.

Traditional French methods for cooking en papillote are somewhat arcane. Pieces of parchment must be trimmed to an exact size, and folding patterns reminiscent of origami are employed to ensure a tight seal. Admittedly, the results make for a dramatic presentation—the paper balloons and browns in the oven and is slit open at the table by the diner. But to keep things simple, we opted to use aluminum foil as a more convenient, modern upgrade. Although it lacks the dramatic presentation of the parchment, foil works just as effectively and doesn't require labor-intensive folding. The seams can simply be crimped together.

We quickly settled on using naturally lean boneless, skinless breasts—all they require is a quick trim and they are ready to go—and then turned our attention to the vegetables. Since it was obvious that the chicken and vegetables would have to cook at the same rate (because they are all contained in one packet), we knew there would be some limitations. Dense vegetables like potatoes were immediately out of the running because they would take far too long to cook through, and we knew that any other vegetables we chose would have to be thinly cut. We needed to find vegetables that were suitable for steaming, without becoming flavorless and mushy, as well as compatible with the cooking time of the chicken. After a lot of trial and error, we found that using two types of vegetables was best. Firmer vegetables provided a sturdy base for the chicken and protected it from the direct heat of the oven; tasters liked clean-tasting zucchini for one version and artichokes for another. We also found it essential to use a juicy vegetable to complement the sturdier ones, and tomatoes were just right. Placed on top of the chicken, the tomatoes exuded a lot of moisture and created the steam needed for cooking; as an added benefit, their flavorful juice also seeped into the chicken.

NOTES FROM THE TEST KITCHEN

MAKING FOIL PACKETS

1. Place the zucchini and seasoned chicken in the center of a 14 by 12-inch sheet of heavy-duty aluminum foil. Arrange the tomatoes on top.

2. Bring the longer sides of the foil up to meet over the chicken. Crimp the edges together in a ¼-inch fold, then fold over three more times. Fold the open edges at either end of the packets together in a ¼-inch fold, then fold over twice again to seal.

THE BEST CHEF'S KNIFE

We want a chef's knife that's versatile enough to handle almost any cutting task, whether it's mincing delicate herbs or cutting through meat and bones. We want a sharp blade that slices easily, without requiring a lot of force, and a comfortable handle that doesn't get slippery when greasy.

We tested nine chef's knives by butchering whole chickens, chopping butternut squash, chopping parsley, and dicing onions. We also evaluated their comfort and user-friendliness based on feedback from a variety of testers. We rated sharpness and edge retention by cutting ordinary sheets of paper before and after kitchen tests.

We found plenty to admire among the top-rated innovative knives, but we remain hard-pressed to pay a premium—sometimes as much as $175—for their innovations. The very affordable **Victorinox Forschner Fibrox 8-inch Chef's Knife,** $24.95, is our favorite—lightweight and agile, it also has a comfortable nonslip handle.

The overall flavor of these two dishes was still a bit lean and mild, so we looked for a way to add flavor and fullness to them. We found that we could easily liven them up by mixing a little olive oil with bold ingredients such as garlic, shallots, red pepper flakes, and fresh herbs, then tossing the vegetables with the mixture before placing them in the foil packets.

Chicken en Papillote with Zucchini and Tomatoes

SERVES 2

The packets can be assembled several hours ahead of time and refrigerated, but they should be baked just before serving. To prevent overcooking, open each packet promptly after baking.

2 (6-ounce) boneless, skinless chicken breasts, trimmed and pounded ½ inch thick
Salt and pepper
1 tablespoon extra-virgin olive oil
1 garlic clove, minced
1 teaspoon chopped fresh oregano
Pinch red pepper flakes
2 plum tomatoes, cored, seeded, and chopped medium
1 zucchini (about 8 ounces), sliced ¼ inch thick
2 tablespoons chopped fresh basil

1. Adjust an oven rack to the middle position and heat the oven to 450 degrees. Pat the chicken dry with paper towels and season with ⅛ teaspoon salt and a pinch of pepper.

2. Combine the oil, garlic, oregano, pepper flakes, ⅛ teaspoon salt, and ⅛ teaspoon pepper in a bowl. Toss half of the oil mixture with the tomatoes, and toss the remaining mixture separately with the zucchini.

3. Following the photos on page 128, cut two 14 by 12-inch rectangles of heavy-duty foil and lay them flat on the counter. Shingle half of the zucchini in the center of a piece of foil. Place a chicken breast on top of the zucchini, then top with half of the tomatoes. Tightly crimp the foil into a packet. Repeat with the other piece of foil and the remaining chicken and vegetables.

4. Set the packets on a rimmed baking sheet and bake until the thickest part of the breasts registers 160 to 165 degrees on an instant-read thermometer, about 25 minutes.

5. Carefully open the packets, allowing the steam to escape away from you, and let cool briefly. Smooth out the edges of the foil and, using a spatula, gently transfer the chicken, vegetables, and any accumulated juice to individual plates. Sprinkle with the basil and drizzle with extra olive oil if desired before serving.

PER SERVING: Cal 290; Fat 10 g; Sat fat 1.5 g; Chol 100 mg; Carb 9 g; Protein 42 g; Fiber 3 g; Sodium 270 mg

VARIATION

Chicken en Papillote with Artichokes, Lemon, and Tomatoes

Follow the recipe for Chicken en Papillote with Zucchini and Tomatoes, substituting 1 teaspoon minced fresh thyme for the oregano, 2 teaspoons grated lemon zest for the red pepper flakes, and 1 (9-ounce) box frozen artichoke hearts, thawed and patted dry with paper towels, for the zucchini. Add 1 thinly sliced shallot to the artichoke and olive oil mixture in step 2.

PER SERVING: Cal 330; Fat 10 g; Sat fat 1.5 g; Chol 100 mg; Carb 18 g; Protein 44 g; Fiber 9 g; Sodium 320 mg

CHICKEN BURGERS

WHETHER GRILLED, FRIED, OR BROILED, burgers are one of America's favorite foods. Unfortunately, a good hamburger is usually made with the fattiest meat you can find (about 34 grams of fat for a 5-ounce burger). To satisfy a burger craving, you can try lower-fat chicken burgers. But in our experience, these burgers often disappoint—they're typically dry, tasteless, and colorless. We set out to develop a chicken burger that would satisfy us whenever the craving for a burger struck.

Focusing first on the type of ground chicken, we found two types at the supermarket—one generically labeled "ground chicken," which turned out to be a mix of dark and white meat, and another labeled "ground breast meat" (all white meat). When we pitted them against each other in burgers, tasters far preferred the heartier flavor and juicier texture of the ground chicken blend over the bland, dry ground breast meat. Of course, the blend is slightly higher in fat and calories, but the added flavor was worth it, and these chicken burgers were still much less fatty than a traditional beef burger. We figured this was a good start, and with a little help, we knew we could make these burgers taste even better.

Compared to a typical beef burger, a chicken burger lacks serious heft and moistness. To compensate for ground chicken's relative leanness, we tried adding a combination of milk and bread (also called a panade) to the meat—the same mixture we use to lend moisture to meatballs. The resulting burgers tasted, well, like meatballs, and the patties had an unattractive pale color. We tried a whole host of other ingredients (mashed beans, rehydrated mushrooms, and minced tempeh among them), but they were no better. All of these ingredients either gave the burgers a strong flavor that overshadowed the chicken or failed to add any moistness to the patties. Then we stumbled onto fat-free ricotta. It was exactly what we were looking for. The ricotta gave the burgers a moist, chewy texture, and its mildness allowed the chicken flavor to stand out.

Flavoring the chicken patties was tricky. We tried every ingredient in the test kitchen that we thought would add a meaty flavor to the burgers, from teriyaki sauce and fermented black beans to olive paste. After eating a lot of bad (and some good) burgers, we found two ingredients that gave our chicken burgers optimal flavor: Worcestershire sauce and Dijon mustard. Whether by association (because these are condiments that typically complement beef) or pure chemistry, these sharp and tangy flavors made our chicken burger taste enough like a full-fat burger to satisfy our craving.

Because chicken must be cooked to well-done for safety reasons, figuring out how to maintain a juicy burger was difficult: If the heat was too high, the burgers burned before they were done; too low, and they were pale and virtually steamed (and very unappealing). We experimented with several different cooking methods,

including broiling and roasting, but nothing beat the simplicity of browning in a heavy-bottomed skillet. We found the best way to cook the chicken burgers without drying them out was to sear them over medium heat, then cook them, partially covered, over low heat until they reached an internal temperature of 160 to 165 degrees. This resulted in a burger that had a rich crust and remained moist inside (and required a minimal amount of fat to cook). This burger was now so good that if we closed our eyes we would swear we were eating a real, full-fat hamburger.

Chicken Burgers

SERVES 2

Stay away from packages of ground chicken labeled "ground breast meat" or "all white meat," and look for packages of generic "ground chicken," which are a blend of white and dark meat; an all–white meat burger will taste incredibly dry and bland. The ricotta cheese can burn easily, so keep a close watch on the burgers as they cook.

- 12 **ounces ground chicken (see note)**
- 2 **tablespoons fat-free ricotta cheese**
- 1 **teaspoon Worcestershire sauce**
- 1 **teaspoon Dijon mustard**
- ¼ **teaspoon salt**
- ¼ **teaspoon pepper**
- 2 **teaspoons vegetable oil**

1. In a large bowl, mix the chicken, ricotta, Worcestershire, mustard, salt, and pepper together with your hands until uniform. Divide the mixture into 2 portions, form each portion into a ball, then lightly flatten each ball with your fingertips into a 1-inch-thick patty.

2. Heat the oil in a 10-inch nonstick skillet over medium heat until just smoking. Lay the burgers in the skillet and cook until light brown and crusted on one side, 3 to 4 minutes. Flip the burgers and continue to cook until the second side is light brown, 3 to 4 minutes longer.

3. Reduce the heat to low, partially cover the skillet, and continue to cook the burgers until the thickest part registers 160 to 165 degrees on an instant-read thermometer, 8 to 10 minutes longer, flipping once more if necessary for even browning. Serve.

PER SERVING: Cal 260; Fat 16 g; Sat fat 4 g; Chol 115 mg; Carb 2 g; Protein 28 g; Fiber 0 g; Sodium 500 mg

---

NOTES FROM THE TEST KITCHEN

THE BEST DIJON MUSTARD
Dijon mustard is a staple here in the test kitchen, and we wanted to find out which nationally available brands were the best. We rounded up eight Dijon mustards and tasted them plain and in a simple vinaigrette. The result: Our tasters preferred the spicier mustards, and the most important factor was balance of flavor. Mustards that were too acidic or too salty or muddied with other flavors were downgraded. Our favorite Dijon mustard was **Grey Poupon Dijon Mustard,** which tasters described as having a "nice balance of sweet, tangy, and sharp."

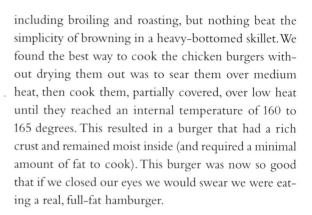

CHICKEN BURGERS

DINNER SALAD WITH CHICKEN

A MAIN-COURSE SALAD WITH CHICKEN should be a quick and easy way to get dinner for two on the table. And because it's a salad, many assume it's a safe bet when watching fat and calories. Think again. Dressing, toppings such as cheese, bacon, nuts, and croutons, how the chicken is prepared—well, it all adds up. We were pretty sure we could create a substantial dinner salad without all the high-fat toppings—we'd just have to carefully pick flavorful and satisfying vegetables—but the dressing was another story. Most store-bought light dressings have a strange off-taste, as they try to make up for the loss of flavor from the fat with artificial ingredients and flavorings. The result is a wildly out-of-balance dressing, without enough body to cling to the lettuce and vegetables. Could we create a light vinaigrette worth eating?

In our quest to develop a lower-fat vinaigrette, we came across a technique for making bold, fruit-flavored dressings: Fruit juice is simmered until it has reduced to a syrup, which is then mixed with the other vinaigrette ingredients. This method worked beautifully. Reducing the juice not only concentrates the fruit flavor, but it also gives the light dressing body tantamount to that of a full-fat version. The viscous nature of the finished vinaigrette causes the dressing to cling to pieces of lettuce, and the reduced juice takes on the role that oil usually plays. And by replacing most of the oil with this thick and syrupy reduced fruit juice, we were able to retain a rich, bright flavor.

For our first recipe we focused on orange juice. Reducing 1 cup to ¼ cup concentrated its flavor and upped the viscosity. Instead of vinegar, we used lime juice to balance the sweetness of the orange juice, and after some testing we settled on 5 teaspoons. Minced shallot added just the right amount of pungency (we found it important to use a small shallot for this relatively small amount of dressing), and a splash of honey balanced everything out. Although we were after a lighter vinaigrette, we still found it necessary to add a dash of extra-virgin olive oil to truly allow the flavors to meld.

With our vinaigrette squared away, we turned our attention to the bulk of the salad—the lettuce and vegetables. A wide variety of salad greens are available at the grocery store. One readily available and convenient option is mesclun mix. Composed of greens including arugula, mizuna, tatsoi, frisée, oak leaf lettuce, red chard, radicchio, and mustard greens, mesclun mix offers many flavors and textures in one convenient package. After comparing mesclun mix to other stand-alone lettuces such as Bibb, iceberg, red and green leaf, and romaine, tasters preferred mesclun mix. Because we were making this salad for only two people, we wanted to minimize the number of vegetables we used (and thus the amount of prep), so we'd have to pick vegetables with a strong presence. Spicy, peppery radishes added flavor and color, and fennel brought a welcome crunch. Briny kalamatas provided a pleasing textural contrast, and together these components made our salad truly satisfying.

Finally, we turned our attention to the chicken. We wanted the chicken in our salad to be fresh and moist, so leftover roast or grilled chicken was not an option. At the same time, we didn't want to make a big production out of preparing just two chicken breasts. We found our answer in a half sautéing and half poaching method using very little fat. We browned the breasts on just one side, which took about five minutes—and by using a nonstick skillet, we could get away with just 1 teaspoon of oil. Next we flipped the chicken, added water to the skillet, reduced the heat, and covered the skillet until the breasts were cooked through, which took only about five minutes more. This method yielded just what we were looking for: moist, well-seasoned chicken.

Tasters loved this salad so much that we developed a variation with a pomegranate-honey vinaigrette, pears, and thinly sliced red onion. Now we had two dinner salads that were everything we wanted them to be—quick, healthy, satisfying, and packed with flavor.

NOTES FROM THE TEST KITCHEN

OUR SECRET TO LIGHTER VINAIGRETTE

We tested a number of methods for making a lighter vinaigrette and discovered that substituting fruit juice for most of the oil worked well. But you can't just replace the oil with juice, or the dressing will be thin with a diluted flavor. The fruit juice needs to be cooked to a syrupy consistency, a technique known as reducing. This not only concentrates the fruit flavor, but it also gives the lighter dressing body similar to that of a full-fat version. And by using reduced fruit juice in the place of oil, we were able to work with flavors that are otherwise difficult to get into a dressing, such as orange and pomegranate.

Chicken Dinner Salad with Orange-Lime Vinaigrette

SERVES 2

Any type of orange juice will work here; however, the flavor of freshly squeezed juice really sparkles. You can use most any type of lettuce, but we particularly like mesclun mix.

DRESSING

1 cup orange juice (see note)

5 teaspoons fresh lime juice

1 tablespoon extra-virgin olive oil

1 small shallot, minced (about 1 tablespoon)

2 teaspoons honey

¼ teaspoon salt

¼ teaspoon pepper

CHICKEN AND SALAD

2 (6-ounce) boneless, skinless chicken breasts, trimmed and pounded ½ inch thick

¼ teaspoon salt

¼ teaspoon pepper

1 teaspoon vegetable oil

½ cup water

4 ounces salad greens (about 4 cups) (see note)

4 red radishes, sliced thin

1 small fennel bulb, halved, cored, and sliced thin (see page 71)

2 tablespoons kalamata olives, pitted and halved

1. FOR THE DRESSING: Briskly simmer the orange juice in a small saucepan over medium heat until it has thickened and reduced to about ¼ cup, 12 to 15 minutes. Transfer to a small bowl and refrigerate until cool, about 15 minutes. When cool, whisk in the lime juice, oil, shallot, honey, salt, and pepper. (The dressing can be refrigerated for up to 1 week; return to room temperature and whisk to recombine before using.)

2. FOR THE CHICKEN AND SALAD: Meanwhile, pat the chicken dry with paper towels and season with the salt and pepper. Heat the oil in a 10-inch nonstick skillet over medium-high heat until just smoking. Add the chicken and cook until browned on one side, about 3 minutes.

3. Flip the chicken, add the water, and cover. Reduce the heat to medium and continue to cook until the thickest part of the breasts registers 160 to 165 degrees

on an instant-read thermometer, 5 to 7 minutes longer. Transfer to a carving board and tent loosely with foil while assembling the salad.

4. In a large bowl toss the salad greens, radishes, fennel, and olives together with 2 tablespoons of the dressing. Divide the salad between two plates. Slice the chicken ¼ inch thick and arrange on top of the salads. Serve, passing the remaining dressing separately.

PER SERVING: Cal 440; Fat 16 g; Sat fat 2.5 g; Chol 100 mg; Carb 33 g; Protein 43 g; Fiber 5 g; Sodium 1080 mg

VARIATION

Chicken Dinner Salad with Pomegranate-Honey Vinaigrette

We prefer the clean flavor of plain pomegranate juice here; however, pomegranate juice blends will also work fine.

Follow the recipe for Chicken Dinner Salad with Orange-Lime Vinaigrette, substituting 1 cup pomegranate juice for the orange juice and 5 teaspoons red wine vinegar for the lime juice in the dressing. Omit the radishes, fennel, and olives and add 1 pear, peeled, cored, and thinly sliced, and ½ thinly sliced red onion to the salad.

PER SERVING: Cal 440; Fat 11 g; Sat fat 1.5 g; Chol 100 mg; Carb 45 g; Protein 42 g; Fiber 5 g; Sodium 720 mg

TURKEY CHILI

MANY LIGHTER TURKEY CHILI RECIPES yield a pot of raw-tasting spices and dry meat. Our goal was to develop a no-fuss chili that would rival its beef counterpart—rich, meaty, and thick, with just the right amount of spices. Our other challenge would be developing a recipe to serve two; chili is typically made for a crowd, so we knew scaling it down would require a careful balancing act.

Most recipes begin with sautéing onions and garlic; we followed suit. Tasters also liked the addition of red bell pepper. After this first step, things became less clear. The most pressing concerns were the spices and the turkey (how much and what fat percentage). There were also the cooking liquid (what kind, if any) and the proportions of tomatoes and beans to consider.

A single tablespoon of chili powder was just right. Though this seems like a modest amount for chili (even for just two servings), we found that if we used any more it simply overpowered the other layers of flavor in our chili. Cumin, coriander, red pepper flakes, and oregano rounded out our spices, but something was missing. Although we didn't want a chili with killer heat, we did want real warmth and depth of flavor, so we added just a touch of cayenne. In many recipes the spices are added after the turkey has been browned, but we have found that ground spices generally need to have direct contact with the hot cooking oil, so they have a chance to develop their flavors, or "bloom," and our chili was no exception. In fact, subsequent testing revealed that the spices should be added at the outset—along with the aromatics—to develop their flavors fully.

Twelve ounces of turkey was the right amount for two servings, and ¾ cup of canned beans provided a good meat-to-bean ratio. Ground turkey that was 99 percent fat-free meat cooked up dry and stringy and contributed nothing in terms of flavor to the chili. Although 93 percent lean ground turkey adds a bit more fat, we found it absolutely essential; it added excellent flavor to the chili, and the meat remained moist and juicy.

Tasters did complain, however, that the chili was visually unappealing. Since the meat is stirred into the pot with the cooked vegetables and then simmered for an hour, it breaks down dramatically—the chili looked more like a fine meat sauce, such as Bolognese, than thick meat chili. We tried adding the meat at a later stage, which helped visually, but the chili then lacked a cohesive flavor. By adding half of the meat to the cooked vegetables in the beginning and the other half after the chili had simmered for 30 minutes, we were able to create the perfect balance of flavor, at the same time keeping some of the meat in larger pieces.

As for the type of liquid to add to our chili, we tried batches made with water (too watery), wine (too acidic), chicken broth (too chicken-y and dull), and no liquid at all except for that in the tomatoes (by far the best). This gave us the perfect amount of flavor, and the chili was rich and rounded.

Tomatoes were definitely going into the pot, but we had yet to decide on the type and amount. We first tried a 14.5-ounce can of diced tomatoes. Tasters liked the tomato chunks, but the chili needed more body. We paired the diced tomatoes with an 8-ounce can of tomato sauce, and without exception, tasters preferred the thick consistency of this combination of tomato products.

In most recipes the beans are added toward the end of cooking, the idea being to let them heat through without causing them to fall apart. But this method often results in very bland beans floating in a sea of highly flavorful chili. After testing several options, we found it best to add the beans with the tomatoes. The more time the beans spent in the pot, the better they tasted. In the end, we preferred dark red kidney beans because they keep their shape better than light red kidney beans, the other common choice.

One hour of gentle simmering was sufficient to meld the flavors. Our chili, basically complete, required little more than lime wedges, passed separately at the table, which both brightened the flavor of the chili and accentuated the heat of the spices.

USE IT UP: KIDNEY BEANS

Kidney Bean Salad
SERVES 2

This fresh side dish is a great accompaniment to Crunchy Baked Pork Chops (page 79) or Pan-Fried Crab Cakes (page 92).

- ¾ cup drained and rinsed canned dark red kidney beans
- 1 small carrot, peeled and sliced thin on the bias
- 1 celery rib, sliced thin on the bias
- 1 small shallot, sliced thin
- 1 tablespoon white wine vinegar
- 1 tablespoon extra-virgin olive oil
  Salt
- 1 tablespoon chopped fresh parsley (optional)
  Pepper

Toss the beans, vegetables, vinegar, oil, ¼ teaspoon salt, and parsley (if using) together in a bowl, and let marinate for 30 minutes. Season with salt and pepper to taste and serve.

PER SERVING: Cal 170; Fat 7 g; Sat fat 1 g; Chol 0 mg; Carb 20 g; Protein 7 g; Fiber 6 g; Sodium 580 mg

Turkey Chili
SERVES 2

Serve with lime wedges, chopped fresh cilantro, sliced scallions, minced onion, diced avocado, shredded cheddar or Monterey Jack cheese, or sour cream. See pages 17 and 134 for recipes to use up the leftover red bell pepper and leftover kidney beans, respectively.

<table>
<tr><td>2</td><td>teaspoons vegetable oil</td></tr>
<tr><td>1</td><td>small onion, minced (about ½ cup)</td></tr>
<tr><td>½</td><td>red bell pepper, stemmed, seeded, and cut into ½-inch pieces</td></tr>
<tr><td>2</td><td>garlic cloves, minced</td></tr>
<tr><td>1</td><td>tablespoon chili powder</td></tr>
<tr><td>1</td><td>teaspoon ground cumin</td></tr>
<tr><td>¾</td><td>teaspoon ground coriander</td></tr>
<tr><td>¼</td><td>teaspoon red pepper flakes</td></tr>
<tr><td>¼</td><td>teaspoon dried oregano</td></tr>
<tr><td></td><td>Salt</td></tr>
<tr><td>⅛</td><td>teaspoon cayenne pepper</td></tr>
<tr><td>12</td><td>ounces 93 percent lean ground turkey</td></tr>
<tr><td>¾</td><td>cup drained and rinsed canned dark red kidney beans</td></tr>
<tr><td>1</td><td>(14.5-ounce) can diced tomatoes</td></tr>
<tr><td>1</td><td>(8-ounce) can tomato sauce</td></tr>
</table>

1. Heat the oil in a medium saucepan over medium heat until shimmering. Add the onion, bell pepper, garlic, chili powder, cumin, coriander, pepper flakes, oregano, ¼ teaspoon salt, and cayenne, and cook, stirring often, until the onion begins to soften and the spices are fragrant, 3 to 5 minutes.

2. Stir in half of the ground turkey and cook, breaking up the meat into small pieces, until no longer pink, 3 to 5 minutes.

3. Stir in the beans, diced tomatoes with their juice, and tomato sauce, and bring to a boil. Cover, reduce the heat to low, and simmer, stirring occasionally, for 30 minutes.

4. Uncover and add the remaining ground turkey, pinched in teaspoon-sized pieces following the photo. Continue to simmer, uncovered, stirring occasionally, until the turkey is tender and the chili is dark, rich, and slightly thickened, about 30 minutes longer. (If at any time the chili begins to stick to the bottom of the pot, stir in ¼ cup water.) Season with salt to taste, and serve.

PER SERVING: Cal 450; Fat 16 g; Sat fat 3.5 g; Chol 95 mg; Carb 37 g; Protein 44 g; Fiber 8 g; Sodium 1790 mg

---

NOTES FROM THE TEST KITCHEN

THE SECRET TO CRUMBLED TURKEY

Pack the meat together into a ball, then pinch off teaspoon-sized pieces of meat and stir them into the chili. This technique makes the ground turkey appear crumbled, like ground beef, rather than stringy.

THE BEST CHILI POWDER

There are numerous applications for chili powder, but its most common use is in chili. We gathered as many brands as possible to find the one that made the best chili. To focus on the flavor of the chili powder, we made a bare-bones version of our chili and rated each chili powder for aroma, depth of flavor, and level of spiciness. Tasters concluded that **Spice Islands Chili Powder** was the clear winner, with a perfect balance of chili flavor and spiciness.

THE BEST CANNED DICED TOMATOES

Ten months out of the year, the quality of canned tomatoes easily surpasses that of any fresh tomatoes you may be able to find. Picked at the peak of ripeness and canned immediately, they are sweet, flavorful, and convenient. We tasted several brands of canned diced tomatoes and discovered that not every brand was up to snuff. Some suffered from excessive sweetness or saltiness, while others had issues with texture, such as unappealing mushiness.

We suggest looking for canned tomatoes that are packed in juice rather than puree, which is heavier and pulpier than juice and contributes an unpleasant cooked flavor to the tomatoes. Our favorite brand is **Muir Glen Organic Diced Tomatoes,** which has a favorable balance of sweetness and saltiness. It also boasts a vibrant, fresh-from-the-garden flavor.

SPICE-RUBBED PORK TENDERLOIN

PORK TENDERLOIN IS NATURALLY LEAN, requires little in the way of prep, and cooks quickly. One pork tenderloin is also just the right size for two people, making it an ideal easy, healthy weeknight choice. But because pork tenderloin is so incredibly lean, it is quick to dry out and can be a little too mild in flavor. We hoped to solve both of these problems and create a flavorful and juicy pork tenderloin without relying on high-fat ingredients to do so.

Working with a 12-ounce tenderloin, we figured that oven temperature was one key to success. We started out with a moderate oven (375 degrees) and worked our way up (475 degrees) and down (250 degrees) the temperature scale. Unfortunately, none of these temperatures was a winner. Cooler ovens produced evenly cooked tenderloins, but they had a pallid, spongy appearance. The tenderloin fared little better in a moderate oven. Confident that a blast of intense heat would give us the seared, crusted exterior we were looking for, we placed the tenderloin inside a hot oven, closed the door, and waited expectantly. We got color, but it was spotty at best. Even worse, this boneless tenderloin had managed to become as dry as a bone, exactly what we were hoping to avoid. Having been let down by the oven, we thought we would try the stovetop. We tried sautéing the tenderloin and were heartened by the brilliant crust that formed on the exterior of the pork. But when we cut into the meat, it was nearly raw.

A marriage of pan-searing and roasting has worked well for us in the past (it's the best way to cook bone-in chicken breasts), and we thought this two-step technique might be just the solution we needed. We heated up a little oil in our skillet, browned the tenderloin on all sides, then slid the pan into a 425-degree oven to finish cooking. The tenderloin came out of the oven deeply colored and evenly cooked, but the meat was still on the dry side. Tests subsequently revealed that it was best to take the pork out of the oven when the internal temperature was 140 degrees. After a 10-minute rest, the temperature climbed to 150, and the meat remained juicy.

Although the golden crust now contributed flavor, we wanted more. Our first thought was brining or marinating, but we wanted a method that delivered big flavor quickly, so we turned to a dry rub. We tried dry rubs with various combinations of salt and spices. Our favorite was a simple mixture of cocoa powder, chili powder, and salt. Many recipes for spice rubs call for toasting the spices, but we found this step unnecessary.

The intense heat of the skillet does the toasting for you. Taking a bite of the warm-spiced pork, we thought that a refreshing fruit relish would be an ideal low-fat accompaniment, adding flavor, moisture, and textural interest. While the tenderloin was in the oven, we had ample time to make the relish, a combination of mango, shallot, jalapeño, lime juice, and cilantro. In less than 30 minutes we had a light and lean juicy pork tenderloin and a brightly flavored relish just big enough to serve two.

Spice-Rubbed Pork Tenderloin with Mango Relish

SERVES 2

Frozen mango can be substituted for the fresh; if using frozen mango, you may need to chop the pieces more finely. The cocoa and chili powders will make the exterior of the pork look almost blackened. See page 136 for a recipe to use up the leftover mango.

  1 **(12-ounce) pork tenderloin, trimmed**
  2 **teaspoons chili powder**
  ½ **teaspoon natural cocoa powder**
     Salt
  1 **teaspoon vegetable oil**
  ½ **medium mango (about 5 ounces), cut into ½-inch pieces (about 1 cup) (see note and photos)**
  2 **tablespoons chopped fresh cilantro**
  1 **tablespoon fresh lime juice**
  1 **small shallot, minced (about 1 tablespoon)**
  1 **teaspoon minced jalapeño chile, seeds and ribs removed**

1. Adjust an oven rack to the middle position and heat the oven to 425 degrees. Pat the pork dry with paper towels. Combine the chili powder, cocoa, and ¼ teaspoon salt, then rub the spice mixture evenly over the pork.

2. Heat the oil in a 12-inch ovensafe nonstick skillet over medium-high heat until just smoking. Brown the tenderloin on all sides, about 6 minutes, reducing the heat if the spices begin to burn. Transfer the skillet to the oven and roast the tenderloin until the thickest part registers 140 degrees on an instant-read thermometer, 12 to 15 minutes.

NOTES FROM THE TEST KITCHEN

CUTTING MANGO FOR RELISH

1. Cut a thin slice from one end of the mango so that it sits flat on the cutting board.

2. Resting the mango on the trimmed bottom, cut off the skin in thin strips from top to bottom, using a sharp paring, serrated, or chef's knife.

3. Cut down along each side of the flat pit to remove the flesh.

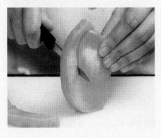

4. Trim around the pit to remove any remaining flesh. The mango flesh can now be chopped into ½-inch pieces.

3. Using potholders (the skillet handle will be hot), remove the skillet from the oven. Transfer the tenderloin to a carving board, tent loosely with foil, and let rest until the very center registers 150 degrees, about 10 minutes.

4. Meanwhile, combine the mango, cilantro, lime juice, shallot, jalapeño, and ⅛ teaspoon salt in a bowl. Cut the pork into ¼-inch-thick slices and serve with the mango relish.

PER SERVING: **Cal** 300; **Fat** 8 g; **Sat fat** 2 g; **Chol** 110 mg; **Carb** 20 g; **Protein** 36 g; **Fiber** 2 g; **Sodium** 550 mg

LIGHTER MEAT LOAF

THERE ARE FEW DISHES MORE HOMEY and satisfying than meat loaf. Like most comfort meals, however, meat loaf is packed with fat and calories—about 43 grams of fat and 740 calories in one serving! Hardly surprising, since its core ingredients include ground beef, eggs, milk, and bread (or crackers). Most low-fat recipes use leaner meats like chicken or turkey, but we were curious if we could make a lighter all-beef meat loaf.

We rounded up a slew of light recipes, most of which included terrifying (for meat loaf) ingredients such as rolled oats, egg substitutes, and frozen hash browns, and

NOTES FROM THE TEST KITCHEN

A BETTER WAY TO COOK MEAT LOAF

1. Set a wire rack on a rimmed baking sheet and top with a 6 by 4-inch rectangle of aluminum foil. Using a skewer, poke holes in the foil about ½ inch apart; this will allow the fat to drain away during baking.

2. Shape the mixture into an evenly thick loaf on top of the foil; the loaf should cover the foil completely.

THE BEST HOT SAUCE

Considering that most hot sauces are made from a basic combination of red peppers, vinegar, and salt, does brand even matter? We rounded up eight supermarket samples to find out. We sampled them simply sprinkled atop a portion of steamed white rice and in a Buffalo sauce for chicken wings. Across the board, tasters deemed one sauce a knockout: **Frank's RedHot** won points for its "bright" and "tangy" notes and potent heat. Other brands, such as Tabasco, had a searing heat that masked any other flavor in the sauce, and most found the thin, watery body to be unappealing. We'll still use Tabasco for adding heat to recipes, but when it's flavor we're after, we'll reach for Frank's.

reluctantly headed into the kitchen to see if any had promise. The wretched flavors and grainy, chewy textures of these failed recipes didn't make us any friends in the test kitchen that day. An improvised recipe using lean ground beef, skim milk, egg whites, and reduced-calorie bread wasn't any better. Was this recipe destined for failure?

We started with the cooking method. Most recipes specify cooking meat loaf in a loaf pan, but the test kitchen prefers to use a foil-covered wire rack—a technique that's particularly useful when cooking for two, since our meat loaf would be too small for a loaf pan anyway. The rack keeps the meat from steaming, thus allowing a better crust to form, and the foil makes it easier to move the meat loaf when it's done. Poking some holes in the foil helps the fat drain off, ridding the meat loaf of some of its fat calories.

We knew that we couldn't use 80 percent lean ground beef here—it is just too fatty. Meat loaf made with 85 percent lean ground beef tasted good, but it was still higher in fat and calories than we would have liked. Working with 90 or 93 percent lean ground beef reduced the fat grams substantially, but tasters felt the meat loaf had a dry texture. We decided to keep the leaner 93 percent beef and look for other ingredients to add moisture back into the meat loaf.

The test kitchen's standard meat loaf uses saltines for structure, but their presence was too apparent when combined with the relatively small amount of meat we were using—they just dried out the loaf's texture even more. Instead, we returned to the more traditional ingredient: bread. Using an egg white as a binder helped hold the loaf together, and we ditched the traditional addition of milk in favor of water, which added moisture without having a dulling effect on the other flavors. We often use soy sauce to help emphasize meaty flavor in beef dishes, and it worked like a charm here, providing welcome flavor and moisture. Garlic, thyme, parsley, and a hit of tomato paste rounded out the flavors.

Our meat loaf was better, but still too dry. Recalling previous recipes in which we cut the ground beef with "meaty" mushrooms, we wondered if mushrooms would work here. They did. Sautéing the mushrooms first was necessary to rid them of excess moisture, and a quick spin in the food processor broke them down so that they practically disappeared into the meat loaf.

Since we had reduced the fat and calories so much

already, we didn't have to sacrifice the ketchup and brown sugar glaze, which caramelized after a few minutes under the broiler—giving the meat loaf its characteristic deep red, sweet-and-sour finish.

Lighter Meat Loaf

SERVES 2

The test kitchen's favorite brand of hot sauce is Frank's RedHot.

MEAT LOAF

- 1 teaspoon vegetable oil
- 1 small onion, minced (about ½ cup)
  Salt
- 5 ounces cremini or white mushrooms, sliced thin
- 2 garlic cloves, minced
- ½ teaspoon minced fresh thyme or ⅛ teaspoon dried
- ½ teaspoon tomato paste
- 2 tablespoons water
- ½ slice high-quality white sandwich bread, torn into pieces
- 10 ounces 93 percent lean ground beef
- 1 large egg white
- 1 tablespoon chopped fresh parsley
- 1½ teaspoons soy sauce
- 1½ teaspoons Dijon mustard
- ¼ teaspoon pepper

GLAZE

- 3 tablespoons ketchup
- 1½ tablespoons cider vinegar
- 1 tablespoon light brown sugar
- ½ teaspoon hot sauce (see note)

1. FOR THE MEAT LOAF: Adjust an oven rack to the middle position and heat the oven to 375 degrees. Following the photos on page 138, set a wire rack on a rimmed baking sheet and lay a 6 by 4-inch piece of aluminum foil in the center of the rack. Using a skewer, poke holes in the foil at ½-inch intervals.

2. Heat the oil in a 10-inch nonstick skillet over medium heat until shimmering. Add the onion and ¼ teaspoon salt, and cook until softened, 5 to 7 minutes. Stir in the mushrooms and cook until they release their liquid, about 5 minutes. Increase the heat to medium-high and cook until the liquid has evaporated, about 3 minutes. Stir in the garlic, thyme, and tomato paste,

and cook until fragrant, about 30 seconds. Stir in the water and cook until thickened, about 30 seconds. Set aside to cool slightly, about 5 minutes.

3. Process the cooled vegetable mixture and bread together in a food processor until smooth, about 10 seconds. Add the beef and pulse to combine, about 5 pulses. In a large bowl, whisk together the egg white, parsley, soy sauce, mustard, pepper, and ⅛ teaspoon salt. Add the processed beef mixture and mix with your hands until uniform.

4. Press the mixture into a compact mass, then turn it out onto the prepared foil rectangle. Using your hands, press the mixture into an evenly thick loaf that is the same size as the foil. Bake until the center of the meat loaf registers 160 degrees on an instant-read thermometer, 35 to 40 minutes. Remove the meat loaf from the oven, adjust an oven rack to be 8 inches from the broiler element, and heat the broiler.

5. FOR THE GLAZE: Simmer all of the ingredients together in a small saucepan over medium heat until thick and syrupy, about 3 minutes. Spread the glaze over the meat loaf and broil until the glaze begins to bubble, about 3 minutes. Let the meat loaf rest for 10 minutes before serving.

PER SERVING: Cal 350; Fat 13 g; Sat fat 4.5 g; Chol 90 mg; Carb 24 g; Protein 35 g; Fiber 2 g; Sodium 1100 mg

STEAMED SOLE

IT'S NO SECRET THAT FISH IS NATURALLY HEALTHY fare. Generally low in fat and calories, fish is also an excellent way to incorporate high-quality protein into your diet. And steaming is perhaps the ultimate healthy, low-fat cooking technique for fish. The problem is that most anything steamed has a reputation as diet fare—boring, washed out, and void of any flavor. We wanted to set the record straight and create a recipe for steamed fish that would impress anyone, whether counting calories or not.

While researching recipes for steamed fish, we came upon a recipe for steamed sole bundles, which consisted of sole fillets wrapped around thinly sliced vegetables. This seemed like a perfect light dinner for two—the vegetables give you a built-in side dish—but after giving it a whirl in the test kitchen, we thought it fell far below expectations. The vegetables were practically raw, and the fish was overcooked and flavorless. Undeterred, we set about fixing these problems.

The first issue to address was the size of the sole fillets, which tend to range from 3 ounces (small) to over 6 ounces (large). In our testing we found that small fillets were easier to roll, especially once filled with the vegetables. Since we would be using small fillets, we allowed two bundles per person.

Next, we turned our attention to the vegetable filling. We wanted our sole bundles not only to taste good, but also to be visually appealing. After sifting through myriad vegetable combinations, we settled on asparagus, carrot, and red onion. We trimmed the vegetables to the width of the sole fillets, then rolled the fish around the vegetables, creating a tidy bundle, and into the steamer they went. About five minutes later the fish emerged from the steamer fully cooked, but cradling still-raw vegetables. It was obvious that the vegetables would need a jump start before joining the sole. Since we were already utilizing a steamer basket to cook the sole, it made sense to parcook the vegetables in the steamer as well. Five minutes was all it took to achieve crisp-tender vegetables, and a quick rinse under cold running water prevented them from cooking further.

After resolving the vegetable issues, we addressed the flavor of the fish. Tasters felt that this dish required more than just salt and pepper—sole has virtually no fat, so naturally the fish was tasting a little lean. We lightly rubbed the fillets with olive oil and, in addition to salt and pepper, sprinkled them with fresh tarragon and minced shallot. Although this was an improvement, the flavors didn't seem to adhere to the fish bundles. A fellow test cook suggested that instead of olive oil we try a compound butter. This sounded promising, but we were hesitant to add too much fat, so we limited the butter to 1 tablespoon and boosted the flavor with lemon juice and zest as well as a clove of garlic (in addition to the tarragon and shallot that we had used in our previous test). The flavor and moistness of this fish were a significant improvement.

Throughout testing, we had been having trouble with the fish tearing as we tried to remove it from the steamer basket after cooking. Lining the steamer basket with parchment paper inhibited the steam, and the fish cooked unevenly. Our solution was to use lemon slices as a sort of pedestal for the sole bundles. This worked like a charm, and it had the added benefit of imparting a pleasant lemon essence to the fish. Tasters liked this

fortified lemon flavor so much that we sandwiched the fish with yet another lemon slice. Topped with a sprinkling of fresh tarragon, these steamed fish bundles offered more flavor than recipes with three times the fat.

Steamed Sole and Vegetable Bundles with Tarragon
SERVES 2

Small flounder or haddock fillets can be substituted for the sole. The fish bundles can be filled and rolled through step 3, then covered and refrigerated for up to 4 hours before steaming. If your asparagus spears are very thick, simply halve them lengthwise before using.

½ bunch thin asparagus (about 8 ounces), tough ends trimmed (see page 224), cut into 2-inch lengths (see note)
1 carrot, peeled and cut into 2-inch matchsticks
½ red onion, sliced thin
1 tablespoon unsalted butter, softened
1 tablespoon chopped fresh tarragon
1 small shallot, minced (about 1 tablespoon)
1 garlic clove, minced
¼ teaspoon grated lemon zest plus ½ teaspoon fresh lemon juice
Salt and pepper
4 (3-ounce) skinless sole fillets (see note)
8 (¼-inch-thick) slices lemon

1. Fit a large Dutch oven with a steamer basket. Fill the pot with water until it just touches the bottom of the basket and bring to a boil. Add the asparagus, carrot, and onion to the basket, cover, and steam until just tender, about 5 minutes. Remove the steamer basket and vegetables from the pot, rinse the vegetables until cool, then pat dry. Cover the pot to keep the steaming liquid warm.

2. Meanwhile, mix together the butter, 2 teaspoons of the tarragon, shallot, garlic, lemon zest, lemon juice, ⅛ teaspoon salt, and a pinch of pepper.

3. Pat the fish dry with paper towels, then season with ⅛ teaspoon salt and a pinch of pepper. Following the photos on page 142, spread 1 teaspoon of the tarragon butter over each fillet. Divide the vegetables among the 4 fillets, laying them across the wider end of each piece of fish. Roll the fish up around the vegetables into tidy bundles.

STEAMED SOLE AND VEGETABLE BUNDLES WITH TARRAGON

MAKING FISH BUNDLES

1. Spread 1 teaspoon of the tarragon butter over each fillet.

2. Gather the vegetables into a neat pile and lay them across the wider end of the fish.

3. Roll the fillet up snugly around the vegetables, forming a bundle.

4. Place the bundles on the lemon slices, seam-side down, to keep them from opening during steaming.

THE BEST DUTCH OVEN

So what should you consider when selecting a Dutch oven? Look for one that is roughly twice as wide as it is tall, with a minimum capacity of 6 quarts, though 7 is even better. The bottom should be thick to prevent food from scorching, and the lid should fit tightly to prevent excessive moisture loss. Looking for a less expensive alternative to our favorites made by All-Clad and Le Creuset, we tested Dutch ovens in the under-$100 range. The **Tramontina 6.5-Quart Cast Iron Dutch Oven** is comparable in size to the All-Clad and Le Creuset ovens and performs nearly as well. Better yet, at $40, it costs a fraction of the price of either.

4. Line the steamer basket with 4 of the lemon slices and gently lower it into the Dutch oven. Lay 1 of the fish bundles, seam-side down, on top of each slice. Sprinkle the fish with the remaining 1 teaspoon tarragon and lay the remaining 4 lemon slices on top of the bundles.

5. Bring the water in the Dutch oven to a boil. Cover and steam the fish until it flakes apart when gently prodded with a paring knife, 5 to 7 minutes. Using a spatula, gently transfer the fish bundles to individual plates (2 bundles per person), discarding the lemon slices and steaming liquid, and serve.

PER SERVING: **Cal** 270; **Fat** 8 g; **Sat fat** 4.5 g; **Chol** 95 mg; **Carb** 13 g; **Protein** 35 g; **Fiber** 4 g; **Sodium** 450 mg

LIGHTER NEW ENGLAND CLAM CHOWDER

MANY HEALTH-CONSCIOUS COOKBOOKS avoid clam chowder, for obvious reasons—the fat from butter, bacon or salt pork, and heavy cream. Recipes for clam chowder also tend to yield a fair amount, so if you're cooking for two you're stuck with a lot of leftovers for a rich indulgence you want to eat only once. Could we scale down and lighten up clam chowder at the same time? And could we do so without compromising its rich flavor?

Before we could begin to make a lighter clam chowder, we first needed to understand how full-fat clam chowders are built. A typical recipe follows this general outline: Several slices of bacon are crisped, onions are sautéed in the drippings, and flour is stirred in to make a thick roux. Clam juice and potatoes go into the pot, and the chowder is eventually finished with the clams and a cup of heavy cream.

We rounded up a handful of low-fat recipes and got busy cooking. Since we wanted this recipe to be accessible to everyone, we decided to use canned clams. In several recipes the bacon was replaced with turkey bacon, but those chowders lacked depth and complexity; those that swapped out the cream for low-fat sour cream or cream cheese were too sour. Clearly, some fat was necessary; our goal was to figure out what was absolutely essential for the chowder's characteristic flavor and texture.

Eventually we realized that we couldn't eliminate the bacon altogether. We could, however, reduce the amount to just one slice if we chopped it fine so its smoky, meaty flavor was dispersed into every spoonful.

After we sautéed the onion in the drippings (tasters also liked the additions of garlic, thyme, and a little white wine), it was evident that there was a problem with using so little bacon: It didn't render enough fat upon which to build a sturdy roux to thicken the chowder.

To help thicken the chowder, we tried pureeing half of the potatoes (we needed 4 ounces of red potatoes for two people); this gave every drop of chowder good flavor, but tasters complained about a lack of potato chunks left in the broth. Looking for other thickeners, we tried whisking in a slurry of flour and broth (too raw) and even cooked and pureed white rice (too distinct). Rifling through the pantry, we landed on a box of instant potato flakes. Remembering the flavor from the chowder we had made with pureed potatoes, we had high hopes for potato flakes. Tasters loved the flavor of the soup but didn't think the flakes were fully dissolved. Microwaving the flakes with some bottled clam juice ensured that they dissolved fully in the chowder, and a little cornstarch gave the soup a silky finish.

Our chowder was now flavorful and thick, but without cream it was lacking the velvety consistency of full-fat versions. Simply using less heavy cream (or light cream or milk) left the soup feeling light and thin. Half-and-half was still too fatty, but what about fat-free half-and-half? We were shocked that just ½ cup of this product gave our reduced-fat clam chowder the rich texture and flavor of full-fat cream—with just a fraction of the fat and calories. This creamy, briny, lighter chowder was so good, we would have no hesitation pitting it against full-fat versions.

Lighter New England Clam Chowder

SERVES 2

Both instant potato flakes and potato buds will work here, but avoid potato granules, which have a slightly metallic taste. Do not boil the soup after adding the half-and-half in step 4, or it will curdle.

- 1 slice bacon, minced
- 1 small onion, minced (about ½ cup)
- 2 garlic cloves, minced
- ½ teaspoon minced fresh thyme or ⅛ teaspoon dried
- 4 ounces red potatoes (about 2 small), scrubbed and cut into ½-inch pieces
- 3 tablespoons dry white wine
- 1 bay leaf

- 2 (6.5-ounce) cans chopped clams, drained, juice reserved
- ⅓ cup instant potato flakes (see note)
- 1½ teaspoons cornstarch
- ½ cup bottled clam juice
- ½ cup fat-free half-and-half
- 2 teaspoons chopped fresh parsley
   Salt and pepper

1. Cook the bacon in a medium saucepan over medium heat until the fat has rendered and the bacon begins to crisp, about 3 minutes. Stir in the onion and cook until softened, 5 to 7 minutes.

2. Stir in the garlic and thyme, and cook until fragrant, about 30 seconds. Stir in the potatoes, wine, bay leaf, and reserved canned clam juice, bring to a simmer, cover, reduce the heat to low, and cook until the potatoes are tender, 10 to 12 minutes.

3. Whisk the potato flakes, cornstarch, and bottled clam juice together in a small bowl. Microwave the mixture until it is thickened and smooth, about 1 minute. Stir the mixture into the pot, bring to a simmer, and cook until thickened slightly, about 3 minutes.

4. Stir in the half-and-half, parsley, and chopped clams and cook until heated through, about 2 minutes (do not boil). Discard the bay leaf, season with salt and pepper to taste, and serve.

PER SERVING: Cal 290; Fat 7 g; Sat fat 2 g; Chol 40 mg; Carb 32 g; Protein 18 g; Fiber 2 g; Sodium 1080 mg

PASTA WITH LIGHTER PESTO

TRADITIONAL PESTO IS MADE WITH BASIL, garlic, nuts, cheese, and a generous amount of olive oil—it's definitely not light fare. In fact, most pestos (both basil pesto and the myriad variations you see around today) have about 270 calories and 28 grams of fat per serving. But because pesto packs quite a flavor punch with just a few simple ingredients and is quick to put together, it makes an ideal weeknight meal for two when tossed with pasta. We hoped to reduce its calorie and fat counts to make a truly light pesto that was just as flavorful and quick as a traditional one.

In our quest to develop a flavorful pesto that would not be prohibitively fat-laden, we knew the first thing we'd need to tackle was the olive oil. Most pestos rely on at least ½ cup of oil to emulsify and blend the sauce. We knew that we would need to change the character of the pesto somewhat in order to drastically reduce the amount of oil, but our hope was that we could still keep its trademark flavors intact. Thinking that ricotta cheese, when pureed with the other ingredients, would make a creamy sauce, we tried multiple batches, lowering the amount of olive oil each time. The combination of ¼ cup of part-skim ricotta and 1 tablespoon of olive oil gave us a creamy texture as well as a sweet but subtle dairy flavor.

Garlic is a hallmark ingredient in pesto, and we figured we would need to simply halve the amount called for in a typical recipe, which is about three cloves. But when we used just a clove or two, tasters could barely detect any garlic flavor. When we used any more garlic, however, tasters found its flavor overpowering; garlic should complement the star ingredient in pesto—the basil—without overpowering it. Oil tames the harshness of garlic in a regular pesto, and since our lightened pesto contained far less oil than the standard pesto, it made sense that the garlic flavor was much too strong. We then tried toasting the garlic to tame the flavor, which worked wonders, and we found we could now use the full three cloves. This pesto was much improved, but still a bit lackluster. Adding a small minced shallot gave the garlic just the boost it needed. (The flavor of shallots is milder and more delicate than that of onions, making them a good choice for a sauce that isn't cooked.)

Next, we knew we had to eliminate another high-fat culprit in pesto—the nuts. Nuts add bulk as well as flavor, so we would have to find a way to compensate for both losses. As with the garlic, we found that our recipe for two needed just as much basil as a typical recipe for four would use—2 cups. This generous amount gave our lightened pesto a much needed flavor boost as well as body, and a relatively modest ¼ cup of Parmesan cheese contributed a welcome nutty richness to our nut-free pesto.

Because basil is at its best in the summer, we experimented with other flavor combinations to come up with some variations we could make any time of year. One pairs hearty, sweet roasted red peppers with thyme and parsley; the other features earthy mushrooms and herbs.

Our lightened pestos don't look or taste like original pesto, but they make a very tasty stand-in—and with just a fraction of the fat and calories per serving, they make a quick and light meal for two.

Pasta with Lighter Creamy Basil Pesto
SERVES 2

Do not substitute fat-free ricotta for the part-skim, or the pesto will be dry and a bit gummy. Do not include the stems or buds of the basil because they taste bitter. Any shape of pasta can be used here, but we like short, sturdy pasta such as penne, fusilli, and campanelle with this pesto. See page 61 for a recipe to use up the leftover ricotta.

- 3 garlic cloves, unpeeled
- 2 cups fresh basil (1 to 2 bunches), stems and buds discarded
- ¼ cup grated Parmesan cheese
- ¼ cup part-skim ricotta cheese (see note)
- 1 tablespoon extra-virgin olive oil
- 1 small shallot, minced (about 1 tablespoon)
    Salt and pepper
- ½ pound pasta (see note and page 51)

1. Toast the garlic in a small skillet over medium heat, shaking the pan often, until the skins are spotty brown, about 7 minutes. Let the garlic cool, then peel and mince.

2. Process the garlic, basil, Parmesan, ricotta, oil, shallot, and ¼ teaspoon salt together in a food processor until smooth, about 30 seconds. Transfer the mixture to a bowl and season with salt and pepper to taste. (The pesto can be covered with plastic wrap pressed flush against its surface and refrigerated for up to 3 days.)

3. Meanwhile, bring 4 quarts water to a boil in a large pot. Add the pasta and 1 tablespoon salt, and cook, stirring often, until al dente. Reserve ½ cup of the cooking water, then drain the pasta and return it to the pot.

4. Add the pesto to the cooked pasta and toss to combine, adjusting the sauce consistency with the reserved cooking water as desired. Season with salt and pepper to taste and serve.

PER SERVING: Cal 350; Fat 14 g; Sat fat 4.5 g; Chol 20 mg; Carb 38 g; Protein 16 g; Fiber 4 g; Sodium 700 mg

Pasta with Lighter Mushroom Pesto

Do not substitute fat-free ricotta for the part-skim, or the pesto will be dry and a bit gummy. Any shape of pasta can be used here, but we like short, sturdy pasta such as penne, fusilli, and campanelle with this pesto. See page 61 for a recipe to use up the leftover ricotta.

- 1 tablespoon extra-virgin olive oil
- 5 ounces white mushrooms, sliced thin
- ¼ ounce dried porcini mushrooms, rehydrated and minced, 2 tablespoons of the rehydrating liquid strained and reserved
- 1 small shallot, minced (about 1 tablespoon)
  Salt
- 3 garlic cloves, minced
- 1½ teaspoons minced fresh thyme
- ¼ cup grated Parmesan cheese
- ¼ cup part-skim ricotta cheese (see note)
- 2 tablespoons chopped fresh parsley
  Pepper
- ½ pound pasta (see note and page 51)

1. Heat 1 teaspoon of the oil in a 12-inch nonstick skillet over medium-low heat until shimmering. Add the white mushrooms, porcini mushrooms, shallot, and ¼ teaspoon salt, cover, and cook over medium-low heat until the mushrooms release their juice, about 7 minutes.

2. Stir in the garlic and thyme, increase the heat to medium-high, and cook, uncovered, until the mushroom juice has evaporated and the mushrooms are golden brown, 3 to 5 minutes. Off the heat, stir in the reserved porcini rehydrating liquid, scraping up any browned bits.

3. Process the mushroom mixture, Parmesan, ricotta, parsley, and remaining 2 teaspoons oil in a food processor until smooth, about 30 seconds. Transfer the mixture to a bowl and season with salt and pepper to taste. (The pesto can be covered with plastic wrap pressed flush against its surface and refrigerated for up to 3 days.)

4. Meanwhile, bring 4 quarts water to a boil in a large pot. Add the pasta and 1 tablespoon salt, and cook, stirring often, until al dente. Reserve ½ cup of the cooking water, then drain the pasta and return it to the pot.

5. Add the pesto to the cooked pasta and toss to combine, adjusting the sauce consistency with the reserved cooking water as desired. Season with salt and pepper to taste and serve.

PER SERVING: Cal 360; Fat 14 g; Sat fat 4.5 g; Chol 25 mg; Carb 40 g; Protein 15 g; Fiber 3 g; Sodium 710 mg

Pasta with Lighter Roasted Red Pepper Pesto

Do not substitute fat-free ricotta for the part-skim, or the pesto will be dry and a bit gummy. Any shape of pasta can be used here, but we like short, sturdy pasta such as penne, fusilli, and campanelle with this pesto. See page 61 for a recipe to use up the leftover ricotta.

- 3 garlic cloves, unpeeled
- ¾ cup jarred roasted red peppers (about 5 ounces), patted dry and coarsely chopped
- ¼ cup grated Parmesan cheese
- ¼ cup part-skim ricotta cheese (see note)
- 2 tablespoons chopped fresh parsley
- 1 tablespoon extra-virgin olive oil
- 1 small shallot, minced (about 1 tablespoon)
- 1½ teaspoons minced fresh thyme
  Salt and pepper
- ½ pound pasta (see note and page 51)

1. Toast the garlic in a small skillet over medium heat, shaking the pan often, until the skins are spotty brown, about 7 minutes. Let the garlic cool, then peel and mince.

2. Process the garlic, peppers, Parmesan, ricotta, parsley, oil, shallot, thyme, and ¼ teaspoon salt together in a food processor until smooth, about 30 seconds. Transfer the mixture to a bowl and season with salt and pepper to taste. (The pesto can be covered with plastic wrap pressed flush against its surface and refrigerated for up to 3 days.)

3. Meanwhile, bring 4 quarts water to a boil in a large pot. Add the pasta and 1 tablespoon salt, and cook, stirring often, until al dente. Reserve ½ cup of the cooking water, then drain the pasta and return it to the pot.

4. Add the pesto to the cooked pasta and toss to combine, adjusting the sauce consistency with the reserved cooking water as desired. Season with salt and pepper to taste and serve.

PER SERVING: Cal 360; Fat 14 g; Sat fat 4.5 g; Chol 25 mg; Carb 41 g; Protein 15 g; Fiber 2 g; Sodium 880 mg

PASTA WITH GARDEN VEGETABLE SAUCE

PASTA WITH GARDEN VEGETABLE SAUCE

WHEN THE END OF SUMMER ROLLS AROUND and backyard gardens and farmers markets are overflowing with bumper crops of ripe vegetables and fresh herbs, pasta with garden vegetable sauce is an ideal way to reap the benefits of this bounty, and what could be healthier? We were looking for a fresh and light-tasting dish that mimicked the brightness of a hearty tomato sauce, but with a variety of vegetables taking center stage. The trick was to sort out how to cook the vegetables and then find a way to allow them to meld with the pasta without resorting to fatty ingredients like oil, meat, or cheese.

Many of the recipes we tried turned out soggy vegetables (especially true with summer squashes) with heavy tomato sauces that obscured not only the flavors but also the brilliant colors of the vegetables. We wanted perfectly cooked pasta with a light, clean-tasting sauce. We wanted the vegetables to be crisp, not mushy, with vibrant colors and a substantial texture. And although we were developing a recipe to serve just two, we wanted to use several vegetables, so we knew we'd have to select carefully—picking vegetables that not only complemented each other but were just the right size as well, so we weren't left with a refrigerator full of partially used vegetables.

To begin, we gathered a mixture of some of our favorite vegetables: zucchini, carrots, cherry tomatoes, onions, and bell peppers. We quickly sautéed them until just softened, then transferred them to a large bowl and tossed them with pasta and fresh basil. The results were tasty, but the dish had the appearance and flavor of something more akin to a warm pasta salad than pasta with an abundant vegetable sauce. It just wasn't saucy enough, and the flavors were too homogeneous.

Next we decided to try adding the vegetables to the skillet in batches, rather than all at once, hoping this would allow them to retain their individual flavors. First, we sautéed the zucchini until browned, then we added the cherry tomatoes and cooked them until they were just softened. We then removed those vegetables from the skillet and added the firmer vegetables: onion, carrot, and bell pepper. We covered the skillet and cooked the vegetables until they softened.

Now that we had a flavorful base with distinct layers of flavor, we needed to extend it into a sauce. We turned

USE IT UP: ZUCCHINI

Zucchini and Chickpea Salad

SERVES 2

This salad pairs well with roasted chicken or pork.

- ½ zucchini (about 4 ounces)
- 1 (15-ounce) can chickpeas, rinsed
- 1 tablespoon extra-virgin olive oil
- 1 shallot, sliced thin
- 1 tablespoon grated Parmesan cheese
- 1 tablespoon capers, rinsed
- 1 tablespoon chopped fresh parsley (optional)
- 1 garlic clove, minced
- 1 teaspoon fresh lemon juice
- Pinch red pepper flakes
- Salt and pepper

Shred the zucchini on the large holes of a box grater, rotating as needed to avoid shredding the seeds and core; discard the seeds and core. Toss the zucchini with the remaining ingredients and season with salt and pepper to taste. Serve.

PER SERVING: Cal 280; Fat 11 g; Sat fat 1.5 g; Chol 5 mg; Carb 35 g; Protein 13 g; Fiber 9 g; Sodium 430 mg

to tomato paste, hoping it would add plenty of tomato flavor without overwhelming the other components the way canned tomatoes had—even a relatively small 14.5-ounce can of diced tomatoes was too much for a two-serving recipe. We added 1½ tablespoons to the skillet with the vegetables and cooked it until the paste browned. Garlic and red pepper flakes were then added to the skillet and sautéed until fragrant. We then added liquid to loosen the sauce; tasters liked the richness of chicken broth.

This sauce was great served with our pasta, but tasters felt that it was lacking a little something. Chopped parsley added a nice burst of bright green color, but not much in the way of flavor. We then tried tossing in some arugula, which wilted perfectly when tossed with the hot pasta. Its peppery and slightly bitter taste elevated our pasta to a new level. To pull it all together, we finished the dish by adding a mere teaspoon of extra-virgin olive oil and salt and pepper, then gave it a good toss.

Pasta with Garden Vegetable Sauce

SERVES 2

We like this recipe made with low-sodium chicken broth, but to make it vegetarian, you can substitute low-sodium vegetable broth. Yellow summer squash can be substituted for the zucchini. We like rotini here, but you can substitute other small, curly-shaped pasta; however, the cup measurements may vary (see page 51). See page 147 for a recipe to use up the leftover zucchini, and page 70 for a recipe to use up the leftover cherry tomatoes.

    1   tablespoon extra-virgin olive oil
    ½   zucchini (about 4 ounces), halved lengthwise and
        sliced ¼ inch thick (see note)
    ½   cup cherry tomatoes (about 3 ounces), halved
    1   carrot, peeled and grated on the large holes
        of a box grater
    1   small onion, sliced thin
    ½   medium red bell pepper, stemmed, seeded, and cut
        into ¼-inch pieces
        Salt
    1½ tablespoons tomato paste
    2   garlic cloves, minced
        Pinch red pepper flakes
    ¾   cup low-sodium chicken broth (see note)
    ¼   pound rotini pasta (about 1½ cups) (see note)
    1½ cups baby arugula (about 1½ ounces)
    2   tablespoons chopped fresh basil
        Pepper
        Grated Parmesan cheese, for serving (optional)

1. Heat 1 teaspoon of the oil in a 10-inch nonstick skillet over medium-high heat until shimmering. Add the zucchini and cook, stirring often, until well browned, about 3 minutes. Add the cherry tomatoes, toss to combine, and cook until slightly wilted, about 1 minute. Transfer to a large bowl.

2. Add 1 teaspoon more oil to the skillet and heat over medium heat until shimmering. Add the carrot, onion, bell pepper, and ⅛ teaspoon salt, cover, and cook until the vegetables have softened, 5 to 7 minutes. Stir in the tomato paste and continue to cook until it begins to brown, about 1 minute. Stir in the garlic and pepper flakes, and cook until fragrant, about 30 seconds. Stir in the broth, scraping up any browned bits. Bring to a simmer and cook until slightly thickened, about 1 minute; cover and set aside.

3. Meanwhile, bring 4 quarts water to a boil in a large pot. Add the pasta and 1 tablespoon salt, and cook, stirring often, until al dente. Reserve ½ cup of the cooking water, then drain the pasta and return it to the pot.

4. Add the sautéed zucchini-tomato mixture, broth mixture, arugula, basil, and remaining 1 teaspoon oil to the cooked pasta, and gently toss to combine. Cover and let sit off the heat until the vegetables are hot, about 1 minute. Season with salt and pepper to taste and adjust the sauce consistency with the reserved cooking water as desired. Serve, passing grated Parmesan separately (if using).

PER SERVING: Cal 220; Fat 8 g; Sat fat 1 g; Chol 0 mg; Carb 33 g; Protein 7 g; Fiber 5 g; Sodium 460 mg

NOTES FROM THE TEST KITCHEN

THE BEST BOX GRATER
A sharp box grater is indispensable for many tasks, from uniformly grating blocks of cheddar to shredding potatoes, carrots, and other vegetables. Our favorite is the **OXO Good Grips Box Grater,** $14.99. This razor-sharp box grater requires little effort or pressure to get results. It also comes with a handy container marked with cup measurements that snaps onto the bottom for easy storage and cleanup.

PASTA SALAD

PASTA SALAD SEEMS LIKE IT SHOULD BE A QUICK and easy meal, but really good pasta salad is hard to come by. Usually the pasta is so mushy it falls apart, and the vegetables are tired and sad. Worse yet, the flavor of the vegetables is bland and washed out, dulled by overcooking and the addition of a greasy dressing. We wanted a pasta salad for two that combined perfectly cooked pasta with flavorful vegetables and a bright, lively vinaigrette.

To make our pasta salad a healthy one, we knew we'd have to get rid of some of the oil in the dressing, but first we needed to decide what type of vinegar to use. Balsamic vinegar, white wine vinegar, lemon juice, and red wine vinegar seemed like the best choices to test in our vinaigrettes. The balsamic gave a lackluster performance; tasters disliked it for its sweetness, lack of bite, and the beige color it added to the pasta. White wine vinegar and lemon juice were just too acidic and lacked dimension. Red wine vinegar stole the show with its pleasing sharpness, and tasters agreed that it had a cohesive effect in the salad—it brought all the flavors together.

Many recipes for pasta salad call for up to ½ cup of oil. Since our recipe would be scaled down for two anyway, it was obvious we could cut back on the oil, but just how little could we get away with? After scaling it back to ¼ cup, we made several vinaigrettes, removing 1 tablespoon of oil at a time. We were pleasantly surprised to find that just 1 tablespoon of olive oil was all our pasta salad needed, even when combined with 1½ tablespoons of vinegar—a much different ratio from what we would normally use for a vinaigrette, but we discovered that pasta salad can handle the extra acidity. A little garlic, Dijon, and red pepper flakes rounded out the flavors of our vinaigrette.

Wanting our pasta salad to pack a nutritional punch, we decided not to reduce the amount of vegetables called for in an average pasta salad, even though we were otherwise downsizing our recipe. Cherry tomatoes were a good choice, as they have a perky tomato flavor, even out of season. And lightly cooked fresh green beans had a subtle vegetal sweetness that we liked. Minced shallot was a welcome addition, and shredded carrot not only added its sweet earthiness, but its small size and rough texture helped our vinaigrette cling to all the components of the salad.

However, tasters complained that the vegetables tasted bland and didn't really meld with the rest of the salad. To correct this, we tried tossing the vegetables with the vinaigrette first and letting them stand for 30 minutes to marinate. This didn't work as well as we'd hoped—the veggies still weren't soaking up any of the vinaigrette. Pressing on, we tried tossing the tomatoes, green beans, shallot, and carrot with a smidgen of salt and 1 tablespoon of the vinegar slated to go into the vinaigrette. This was just what the vegetables needed. And when tossed with the pasta and vinaigrette, the vegetables became a lively, cohesive component of the salad.

At this point, we had a master recipe that we really liked, but it still needed further flavors to really stand out. For herbs, we chose basil and parsley to perk things up (although other herbs work well, too). And tasters raved about the subtle, nutty richness and piquancy of Parmesan. For a variation we decided to pair peppery arugula with bold sun-dried tomatoes and provolone. With a couple of turns of the pepper mill, we had created a perfect, light—and easy—pasta salad.

Pasta Salad with Summer Vegetables
SERVES 2

Other short, bite-sized pasta such as fusilli, farfalle, or orecchiette can be substituted for the penne in this salad; however, their cup measurements may vary (see page 51). See page 70 for a recipe to use up the leftover cherry tomatoes.

3	ounces green beans, trimmed and cut into 2-inch lengths (about ½ cup) (see page 150)
	Salt
½	cup cherry tomatoes (about 3 ounces), halved
1	carrot, peeled and grated on the large holes of a box grater
1	small shallot, minced (about 1 tablespoon)
4½	teaspoons red wine vinegar
¼	pound penne pasta (about 1¼ cups) (see note)
2	tablespoons chopped fresh basil
1	teaspoon chopped fresh parsley
1	tablespoon extra-virgin olive oil
1	teaspoon Dijon mustard
1	garlic clove, minced
	Pinch red pepper flakes
¼	cup grated Parmesan cheese
	Pepper

1. Bring 4 quarts water to a boil in a large pot, and fill a medium bowl with ice water. Add the green beans and 1 tablespoon salt to the boiling water, and cook until the green beans are tender, about 3 minutes.

2. Using a slotted spoon, transfer the green beans to the ice water and let the beans chill for 3 minutes. (Do not drain the boiling water from the pot.) Remove the beans from the ice water, pat them dry with paper towels, and transfer them to a large bowl. Add the tomatoes, carrot, shallot, 1 tablespoon of the vinegar, and ⅛ teaspoon salt to the beans and toss to combine.

3. Return the water to a boil, add the pasta, and cook, stirring often, until al dente. Drain the pasta and rinse under cold water until cool. Drain the pasta well and transfer it to the bowl with the vegetables. Add the basil and parsley and toss to combine.

4. Whisk the remaining 1½ teaspoons vinegar, oil, mustard, garlic, and pepper flakes together, then toss with the pasta and vegetables until combined. Stir in the Parmesan, season with salt and pepper to taste, and serve.

PER SERVING: **Cal** 250; **Fat** 12 g; **Sat fat** 3 g; **Chol** 10 mg; **Carb** 26 g; **Protein** 11 g; **Fiber** 4 g; **Sodium** 550 mg

VARIATION

Pasta Salad with Arugula and Sun-Dried Tomatoes

Be sure to use oil-cured sun-dried tomatoes here because they have a soft, supple texture necessary for the salad. Other short, bite-sized pasta such as fusilli, farfalle, or orecchiette can be substituted for the penne in this salad; however, their cup measurements may vary (see page 51).

2 tablespoons minced oil-cured sun-dried tomatoes, patted dry (see note)

1 small shallot, minced (about 1 tablespoon)

4½ teaspoons red wine vinegar

Salt

¼ pound penne (about 1¼ cups) (see note)

1 cup baby arugula (about 1 ounce)

1 tablespoon chopped fresh parsley

1 tablespoon extra-virgin olive oil

1 teaspoon Dijon mustard

1 garlic clove, minced

Pinch red pepper flakes

1 ounce provolone cheese, shredded (about ¼ cup)

Pepper

1. Toss the sun-dried tomatoes, shallot, 1 tablespoon of the vinegar, and ⅛ teaspoon salt together in a large bowl.

2. Meanwhile, bring 4 quarts water to a boil in a large pot. Add the pasta and 1 tablespoon salt, and cook, stirring often, until al dente. Drain the pasta and rinse under cold water until cool. Drain the pasta well and transfer it to the bowl with the vegetables. Add the arugula and parsley and toss to combine.

3. Whisk the remaining 1½ teaspoons vinegar, oil, mustard, garlic, and pepper flakes together, then toss with the pasta and vegetables until combined. Stir in the provolone, season with salt and pepper to taste, and serve.

PER SERVING: **Cal** 220; **Fat** 13 g; **Sat fat** 3.5 g; **Chol** 10 mg; **Carb** 20 g; **Protein** 7 g; **Fiber** 2 g; **Sodium** 410 mg

HEARTY ROOT VEGETABLE AND MUSHROOM STEW

GREAT VEGETABLE STEWS MARRY hearty vegetables with a richly flavored broth and herbs or spices that complement the vegetables. But all too often, they are little more than a jumble of soggy vegetables devoid of color and flavor. We were after a hearty vegetable stew, one that could be as soul-satisfying in the dead of winter as a beef stew, and inherently healthier. And considering that most vegetable stews call for an endless number of vegetables, we hoped to pare down that list to the essentials, carefully selecting a few vegetables that would contribute the most in terms of flavor and texture.

With this in mind, we began our first order of business: selecting the veggies. Hearty root vegetables, an integral part of many meat stews, would be key, both for their earthy flavor and for their thickening properties (root vegetables are quite starchy). We really liked the flavor of parsnips, turnips, and rutabaga, as well as carrots and potatoes. Although we found that any combination of root vegetables produced a flavorful, balanced stew, it was important to include potatoes, which balanced the sweetness of the other vegetables. Picking just two other root vegetables gave us enough variety without leaving us with a refrigerator full of half-used vegetables.

Next we looked for other vegetables to serve as a contrast to the starchy ones. We wanted a hearty stew, not a soup, so delicate spring vegetables like asparagus and zucchini were out. Mushrooms, with their meaty flavor and texture, were an ideal choice. We were happy to find that we didn't need to use a combination of fresh mushrooms—simple white mushrooms were just right.

Meat stews typically begin with browning the meat, and we began similarly, sautéing the mushrooms in oil (a mere 4 teaspoons was all it took). A little thyme and garlic deepened their flavor. Next we deglazed the pot (a large saucepan was sufficient for our scaled-down recipe) with white wine for flavor and acidity. After adding the broth to the pot, we tossed in the root vegetables and a bay leaf.

An hour of simmering was far too much time for our small stew—the vegetables completely disintegrated. After 30 minutes of simmering, the vegetables were tender and had released enough starch to thicken the sauce somewhat without falling apart, but the sauce had a disappointing canned flavor that was simply not rich enough. Up to this point, we had been using store-bought vegetable broth, but clearly it wasn't providing enough flavor on its own.

We made our stew again, sautéing a traditional mirepoix of minced celery, onion, and carrot along with some dried porcini, which added depth, before adding the fresh mushrooms. Additionally, we browned some tomato paste with the garlic and thyme before adding the liquid. Now we were getting somewhere. Tasters no longer found the stew to be canned-tasting and were impressed by its hearty flavor and thick texture, but they still found it a little light. Could we make our stew richer without adding unnecessary fat and calories?

We looked more closely at our existing ingredients to see if we could eke more flavor out of them. In meat stew, much of the flavor comes from fond, the browned bits that cling to the bottom of the pan when the meat is browned. In our vegetable stew, we were getting our fond from browning the mirepoix and mushrooms. We had sautéed them until they were just beginning to brown; but if browning was the key to flavor, how could we go wrong with more of a good thing? We extended the cooking time, sautéing the aromatics until they were well browned—a full 10 minutes. We then added the mushrooms and cooked them over medium-high heat until they released their liquid. Once their liquid had evaporated and the pot was dry, the mushrooms began browning. We were able to cook them until a dark brown fond coated the bottom of the pan, another full 10 minutes, without burning them.

This increased stovetop time for both the aromatics and the mushrooms turned out to be the key—the stew now had the deep, rich flavor that we had been looking for. With some lemon juice and parsley for brightness, our stew was finished and full of intense flavor.

Hearty Root Vegetable and Mushroom Stew

SERVES 2

We think this stew tastes best with a combination of root vegetables; we suggest picking two, such as carrots, parsnips, turnips, rutabaga, celery root, and parsley root.

    4   teaspoons olive oil
    1   small onion, minced (about ½ cup)
    1   celery rib, minced
    1   carrot, peeled and minced
    ¼   ounce dried porcini mushrooms, rinsed
        and minced
        Salt
   12   ounces white mushrooms, halved if small,
        quartered if large
    3   garlic cloves, minced
    2   teaspoons tomato paste
    1   teaspoon minced fresh thyme or ½ teaspoon dried
    ¼   cup dry white wine
   1½   cups low-sodium vegetable broth
   1¼   cups water
    6   ounces root vegetables, peeled and cut
        into 1-inch pieces (see note)
    6   ounces red potatoes (about 2 small),
        cut into 1-inch pieces
    1   bay leaf
    1   tablespoon chopped fresh parsley
    1   teaspoon fresh lemon juice
        Pepper

1. Heat 2 teaspoons of the oil in a large saucepan over medium heat until shimmering. Add the onion, celery, carrot, porcini mushrooms, and ½ teaspoon salt, and cook, stirring often, until the vegetables are well browned, about 10 minutes.

2. Add the remaining 2 teaspoons oil and white mushrooms, increase the heat to medium-high, and cook, stirring often, until their liquid is released and evaporates

KEEPING WINE FRESH

We've all had the unpleasant experience of wine that tastes sour the day after being opened. There is a way of extending its shelf life: Use a Vacu Vin Vacuum Wine Saver, which prevents wine from oxidizing and keeps it palatable for weeks. But if you don't own one of these gadgets, how long can you expect the wine to stay fit for cooking? Taking a bottle of red and a bottle of white, we cooked up pan sauces every day for a week, corking the bottle and storing it in the refrigerator after each daily batch. The white wine remained usable until the end of the week; the red fared less well, developing off-flavors after just four days. The culprit is a class of chemical compounds called phenols, which react to oxygen and turn the wine astringent and vinegary. Red wine has five times the level of phenols as white wine; if you need to keep red wine longer than two to three days, we suggest you buy half bottles or boxed wine (which contains an inner bag that deflates as the wine is used, preventing exposure to oxygen).

and a dark, thick fond forms on the bottom of the pot, 10 to 12 minutes.

3. Stir in the garlic, tomato paste, and thyme, and cook until fragrant, about 30 seconds. Stir in the wine, scraping up any browned bits. Stir in the broth, water, root vegetables, potatoes, and bay leaf, and bring to a simmer.

4. Reduce the heat to medium-low, partially cover the pan, and cook until the stew is thickened and the vegetables are tender, 30 to 35 minutes. Off the heat, remove the bay leaf and stir in the parsley and lemon juice. Season with salt and pepper to taste and serve.

PER SERVING: Cal 330; Fat 11 g; Sat fat 1.5 g; Chol 0 mg; Carb 47 g; Protein 9 g; Fiber 9 g; Sodium 1110 mg

PROVENÇAL VEGETABLE SOUP WITH PISTOU

DURING THE SUMMER MONTHS in the south of France, there is one soup that reigns supreme: *soupe au pistou*, a summer vegetable soup with a delicate broth that is intensified by a dollop of garlicky pistou—the French equivalent of Italy's pesto. The recipe for this soup reads like the offerings at a Provençal farmers market in August: basil, garlic, haricots verts (slim green beans), zucchini, and white beans. It's no wonder that soupe au pistou works so well—as they say, what grows together, goes together. This soup is naturally light and healthy (as long as you don't go overboard with the pistou), so our goal was to develop a recipe for two to guarantee the perfect balance of all the elements in this classic Provençal soup.

Every soup needs a base, a broth in which to simmer (in this case) the vegetables. To make a good summer soup, these tender vegetables would need the support of a broth that was rich and multidimensional, not characterized by any single, distinctive flavor. We started our testing by making a vegetable stock. Herbs, garlic, and vegetables such as onion, carrot, celery, tomato, and fennel were simmered in water, then strained out before fresh vegetables were added to create the soup. The resulting broth had the pleasant flavor of fresh vegetables, but once we swirled in the pistou, the delicate flavors became overwhelmed by the pistou's heady garlic, basil, and cheese.

These early steps quickly taught us something about the inherent nature of a vegetable soup that has a flavorful condiment like pistou stirred in—the pistou and vegetables are dominant, while the broth acts as a canvas to show them off. In other words, we needn't labor over a delicate broth whose flavor would be obscured by stronger flavors. So instead of homemade stock, we focused on testing store-bought vegetable broth. Although store-bought broth worked well, we achieved the best balance of flavors when we mixed it with an equal amount of water.

Now we could focus on the stars of this soup: summer vegetables. We hoped to eliminate the tedious work of prepping a multitude of vegetables, so we needed to select just the right ones. Leeks, green beans, and zucchini all made the cut quickly. Their tender flavors, different shapes, and varying shades of green made for a balanced summer lineup. We added carrots and garlic to give the soup an aromatic quality. Finally, a tomato (one was all we needed) added a modicum of acid as well as a dash of color. We seeded and diced the tomato to prevent any bitterness from spoiling the clean flavors of the soup.

Next we turned to traditional white beans to give the soup some heft. Typically, fresh white beans are used, but fresh beans can be difficult to find. Instead, we tested both canned and dried white beans (cannellini or navy beans). Both canned and dried were great in this dish, but the canned white beans won out for sheer convenience.

For this recipe, timing is everything. Ideally, all the vegetables need to finish cooking at once and the soup should be served immediately before any of them can overcook. To accomplish that we simply added first the elements that needed to cook the longest and staggered the addition of the rest based on their required cooking times.

Now it was time to tackle the pistou. Although it's traditionally made by mashing fresh basil, garlic, and olive oil together in a mortar and pestle, our first task was to update this technique for modern kitchens. Since we were cooking for two, the amount of pesto needed was too small to use a food processor—the blade barely touched the ingredients. Instead, we simply combined minced garlic, chopped basil, grated Parmesan, and a touch of olive oil in a small bowl. (Cheese is sometimes added to the finished soup, but we decided to simplify things and add it directly to the pistou.)

With our condiment prepared, we were ready to serve the soup. We ladled it into individual serving bowls, then topped each with a dollop of pistou to be stirred in as desired. Our soup, healthy and packed with nutrients, looked just like summer—and tasted like it, too.

Provençal Vegetable Soup with Pistou
SERVES 2

If you cannot find haricots verts (thin green beans), substitute regular green beans and cook them for an extra minute or two. See page 147 for a recipe to use up the leftover zucchini.

- 4   teaspoons olive oil
- 1   carrot, peeled and cut into ¼-inch dice
- ½   large leek (about 4 ounces), white and light green part only, halved lengthwise, sliced ½ inch thick and rinsed thoroughly
    Salt
- 3   garlic cloves, minced (about 3 teaspoons)
- 1½ cups low-sodium vegetable broth
- 1½ cups water
- 3   ounces haricots verts, trimmed and cut into ½-inch pieces (about ½ cup) (see note)
- ½   zucchini (about 4 ounces), quartered lengthwise and sliced ¼ inch thick
- ¾   cup drained and rinsed canned cannellini or navy beans
- 1   plum tomato, seeded and chopped medium
- 2   tablespoons chopped fresh basil
- 2   tablespoons grated Parmesan cheese
    Pepper

STORING BASIL
Since many of our recipes call for just a tablespoon or two of basil, we wondered how long we could keep leftover store-bought basil and what would be the best way to store it. Leaving basil out on the counter caused it to wilt within hours, so we were stuck with refrigerator storage, which is about 15 degrees colder than the recommended temperature for basil. We tested storing basil in unsealed zipper-lock bags (to prevent buildup of moisture, which can cause basil to turn black), both plain and wrapped in damp paper towels. After three days in the refrigerator, both samples were still green and perky. But after one week, only the towel-wrapped basil was still fresh-looking and fresh-tasting. Don't be tempted to rinse basil until just before you need to use it; when we performed the same tests after rinsing, the shelf life was decreased by half.

BUYING LEEKS
We try to buy leeks with the longest white stems, the most tender and usable part of a leek; the white parts can vary from 4 up to 8 inches, so it pays to be discriminating when selecting them. But don't be fooled by supermarkets that sell leeks that are already trimmed down to the lighter base part. This may seem like a good deal because you aren't paying for the upper leaves, which are discarded anyway, but the truth is that the actual purpose of this procedure is to trim away aging leaves and make tough, old leeks look fresher to the unwary consumer. The bottom line: Hand-select your leeks, and try to find a store that sells them untrimmed.

1. Heat 1 tablespoon of the oil in a large saucepan over medium heat until shimmering. Add the carrot, leek, and ¼ teaspoon salt, and cook, stirring occasionally, until softened, 5 to 7 minutes.

2. Stir in 2 teaspoons of the garlic and cook until fragrant, about 30 seconds. Stir in the broth and water and bring to a simmer. Stir in the haricots verts and simmer until bright green but still crunchy, about 3 minutes. Stir in the zucchini, beans, and tomato, and simmer until all the vegetables are tender, about 3 minutes longer.

3. Meanwhile, combine the remaining 1 teaspoon oil, remaining 1 teaspoon garlic, basil, and Parmesan in a small bowl, and season with pepper to taste. Season the soup with salt and pepper to taste. Ladle the soup into individual serving bowls and garnish each with a generous tablespoon of the basil mixture before serving.

PER SERVING: Cal 280; Fat 13 g; Sat fat 2.5 g; Chol 5 mg; Carb 33 g; Protein 11 g; Fiber 8 g; Sodium 1100 mg

SUN-DRIED TOMATO, POTATO, AND MOZZARELLA FRITTATA

CHAPTER 6

LAST–MINUTE SUPPERS FROM THE PANTRY

FRITTATAS

A FRITTATA IS A QUICK AND EASY SUPPER that can be infinitely varied just by changing the fillings. Still, even with the frittata's relatively easy preparation, it is certainly not foolproof. Tough, rubbery, dry frittatas are all too common, so we set out to create a recipe that would result in a perfect frittata every time—a frittata that was firm yet moist, with a pleasing balance of egg and filling and a nicely browned exterior.

Considering lessons we had learned in the past from egg recipes gone bad, we knew that a nonstick skillet was the right choice of vessel. A traditional skillet could be used to make our frittata, but the surface of the pan required extra oil to prevent the eggs from sticking, and this oil has a tendency to make the eggs greasy. With this in mind, we decided to test different sizes of nonstick skillets using six eggs—an appropriate amount for two diners. The frittatas made in a 12-inch skillet were too thin and ended up overcooked, and frittatas made in an 8-inch skillet took too long to cook, resulting in dry and tough edges. A 10-inch skillet produced the best results, enabling the eggs to finish cooking before the edges turned rubbery.

Now we needed the proper cooking method to go with our 10-inch skillet. Looking over the wide range of frittata recipes available, we noticed three basic cooking styles: cooking the frittata fully on the stovetop, cooking it fully in the oven, or starting it on the stovetop and then finishing it in the oven. A stovetop-only frittata, even after we varied both time and temperature, always ended up tough and overcooked. An oven-only frittata also produced poor results, remaining dry and uneven when we experimented with different temperatures and different lengths of time. We hoped that the one remaining method, a combination of stovetop and oven, would have the most promise.

We did a trial run, cooking the frittata almost fully on top of the stove, then sliding the skillet into the oven to finish. This frittata was already much better than those made solely on the stove or in the oven, but it still lacked a nicely browned top. Modifying our stovetop-to-oven method slightly, we tried finishing the frittata under the broiler. This was the best frittata yet—evenly cooked, lightly browned, and firm without being too dry—exactly what we had been seeking.

With our cooking method figured out, we concentrated on the fillings. We needed a frittata that was

hearty enough to serve for dinner (which meant the addition of meat and vegetables), but not overwhelming for two people (which meant not too much meat or vegetables). After testing several filling options, we settled on the satisfying combination of bacon, potato, and cheddar cheese. To achieve the right ratio of eggs to filling, we paired four slices of bacon, one potato, a minced shallot, and just ⅓ cup of cubed cheddar cheese—chosen over shredded for a nice change in texture—with our six eggs. We also added a touch of half-and-half to the eggs before pouring them into the skillet. Though not traditional for a frittata, it lent a nice touch of creaminess.

To avoid a frittata with undercooked ingredients, we knew that we would need to cut the potato and bacon into small pieces and precook them before adding the eggs to the pan. We began by rendering the bacon, then strained out the crisp bits to avoid burning them and utilized a tablespoon of the bacon fat to cook the potato and shallot. While the potato and shallot browned, we added the cheese and crisped bacon to the beaten eggs and half-and-half. Our frittata now set even faster, since we were adding the egg mixture to ingredients and a pan that were hot, not cold. After just minutes on the stovetop and a minute under the broiler, we now had a perfectly browned and hearty frittata for two.

Bacon, Potato, and Cheddar Frittata
SERVES 2

You will need a 10-inch oven-safe nonstick skillet to make this recipe. Because broilers can vary in intensity, watch the frittata carefully as it cooks.

- 6 **large eggs**
- 2 **tablespoons half-and-half**
  - **Salt and pepper**
- 4 **slices bacon, cut into ¼-inch pieces**
- 1 **Yukon Gold potato (about 8 ounces), peeled and cut into ½-inch pieces**
- 1 **shallot, minced (about 3 tablespoons)**
- 1½ **ounces cheddar cheese, cut into ¼-inch cubes (about ⅓ cup)**

1. Adjust an oven rack to be about 6 inches from the broiler element and heat the broiler. Whisk the eggs, half-and-half, ¼ teaspoon salt, and ⅛ teaspoon pepper together in a bowl for 30 seconds; set aside.

2. Cook the bacon in a 10-inch oven-safe nonstick skillet over medium-low heat until crisp, about 10 minutes. Using a slotted spoon, transfer the bacon to a paper towel–lined plate.

3. Pour off all but 1 tablespoon of the bacon fat from the skillet, then add the potato, ¼ teaspoon salt, and ⅛ teaspoon pepper. Cook over medium heat, stirring occasionally, until the potato pieces begin to brown and are almost tender, about 10 minutes. Add the shallot and continue to cook until the potato is golden brown and tender and the shallot is softened and lightly browned, 4 to 6 minutes longer.

4. Stir the reserved bacon and cheese into the eggs. Add the egg mixture to the skillet and cook, using a rubber spatula to stir and scrape the bottom of the skillet, until large curds form and the spatula begins to leave a wake but the eggs are still very wet, about 1 minute. Shake the skillet to distribute the eggs evenly and continue to cook without stirring to let the bottom set, about 30 seconds.

5. Slide the skillet under the broiler and cook until the surface is puffed and spotty brown, yet the center remains slightly wet and runny when cut into with a paring knife, 1 to 2 minutes.

6. Using potholders (the skillet handle will be hot), remove the skillet from the oven. Let sit until the eggs in the middle are just set, about 3 minutes. Use a rubber spatula to loosen the frittata from the skillet, then slide onto a cutting board, slice into wedges, and serve.

VARIATION

Sun-Dried Tomato, Potato, and Mozzarella Frittata
Dried basil (½ teaspoon) can be substituted for the fresh basil.

Follow the recipe for Bacon, Potato, and Cheddar Frittata, omitting the bacon and substituting 1 tablespoon vegetable oil for the bacon fat in step 3. Substitute mozzarella cheese for the cheddar cheese, and add ¼ cup oil-packed sun-dried tomatoes, drained, patted dry, and minced, and 2 tablespoons chopped fresh basil to the eggs in step 4.

SKILLET STRATAS

STRATA IN ITS MOST BASIC FORM consists of layered day-old bread, eggs, cheese, and milk. The result is a satisfying breakfast casserole that can feed a small crowd for breakfast or brunch. Typically, strata is prepared the night before serving so the bread can soak up the richness of the eggs and milk, then it's baked for an hour before serving. We had recently developed our own version of strata, which traded the casserole dish for a skillet and could be made on the spot out of basic ingredients. But our strata was big enough to feed eight, so we'd have to scale it down for our serves-two pantry dinner.

To convert this crowd-friendly dish to a smaller size, we began by tossing our large skillet out the window, replacing it with a small 8-inch skillet. In our prior testing, we had found that many recipes were simply too rich and squeezed in as many fillings as possible. This everything-but-the-kitchen-sink approach led to wet, sagging stratas—not the balance between bread and custard that is the hallmark of a perfect strata. To form a cohesive casserole rather than a bunch of stray ingredients cooked together in a skillet, we knew we had to get the proportions of custard, bread, and filling right.

The foundation of a strata is the bread. Working with the ingredient list of our earlier skillet strata, we knew basic sliced white sandwich bread was the best choice, thanks to its convenience and neutral flavor. This selection worked to our benefit, since we would need just a few slices for the strata and could use the leftover slices for sandwiches or in other recipes that called for bread crumbs. We left the crusts on and cut the bread into 1-inch squares, then toasted it in the skillet; toasting the bread prevented it from turning to mush by the end of cooking and gave the strata some structure. Two slices of bread, cut down from five in our original recipe, gave us a good base to start with.

We then turned our attention to the tender custard that binds the bread and other fillings together. Recipes commonly call for low-fat milk, whole milk, or half-and-half, though sometimes we saw heavy cream (usually in combination with another dairy liquid). We stuck with the straight whole milk from our earlier strata, cut just in half from 1½ cups to ¾ cup because we needed to retain some depth in the skillet. The milk provided a balanced but not overwhelming richness. Also, we kept the same ratio of eggs, cutting down from six to three; this combination of milk and eggs made a custard base that provided two good portions and balanced the amount of bread.

As for the flavoring of our strata, we stayed with the standard sautéed onion, a traditional strata inclusion, which beat out shallots and garlic in our tests. Though another common strata flavoring, white wine, showed promise because it lightened the flavor of the dish, it imparted a booziness that was out of place, so the wine was nixed. A half-cup of shredded cheddar cheese mixed into the eggs added sharpness, and dried thyme brought a nice herbal note.

Finally, we refined our process. After sautéing the onions and then adding the bread to toast in the skillet, we folded in the custard-cheese mixture off the heat and moved the skillet to the oven. Finishing up in the oven produced a delicate texture, similar to that of a soufflé, and we found that increasing the baking temperature from 350 degrees, fairly standard for stratas, to 425 degrees produced a more evenly cooked strata.

Now that our skillet strata was smaller, we couldn't wait for the usual visual cue of a browned top to tell us when it was done—because by that point the strata was overcooked. So we tried removing the strata from the oven when the top was just beginning to brown and the center and edges were barely puffed and still slightly loose when the pan was gently jiggled. We wondered if the strata was cooked through, but after a mere five-minute rest, not only was our strata cool enough to eat, but the center had finished cooking from the residual heat, reaching that perfectly set, supple strata texture.

Skillet Strata with Cheddar and Thyme
SERVES 2

Do not trim the crusts from the bread or the strata will be too dense and eggy. Using an 8-inch skillet is crucial to obtaining the proper thickness and texture in this dish.

- 3 **large eggs**
- ¾ **cup whole milk**
- ¼ **teaspoon dried thyme**
  Salt and pepper
- 2 **ounces cheddar cheese, shredded (about ½ cup)**
- 2 **tablespoons unsalted butter**
- 1 **small onion, minced (about ½ cup)**
- 2 **slices high-quality white sandwich bread, cut into 1-inch squares (see note)**

1. Adjust an oven rack to the middle position and heat the oven to 425 degrees. Whisk the eggs, milk, thyme, ¼ teaspoon salt, and ¼ teaspoon pepper together in a bowl, then stir in the cheese and set aside.

2. Melt the butter in an 8-inch oven-safe nonstick skillet over medium heat. Add the onion and cook, stirring occasionally, until softened and lightly browned, 5 to 7 minutes.

3. Add the bread and, using a rubber spatula, carefully fold it into the onions until evenly coated. Cook the bread, folding occasionally, until lightly toasted, about 3 minutes.

4. Off the heat, fold in the egg mixture until thickened slightly and well combined with the bread. Gently press down on the bread to help it soak up the egg mixture. Bake until the edges and center of the strata are puffed and the edges have pulled away slightly from the sides of the pan, 12 to 15 minutes. Using potholders (the skillet handle will be hot), remove the skillet from the oven. Let sit for 5 minutes before serving.

VARIATION

Skillet Strata with Sausage and Gruyère

Follow the recipe for Skillet Strata with Cheddar and Thyme, substituting Gruyère cheese for the cheddar cheese. Reduce the amount of butter to 1 tablespoon and add 4 ounces raw breakfast sausage, crumbled, to the skillet with the onion in step 2.

NOTES FROM THE TEST KITCHEN

OUR FAVORITE RUBBER SPATULAS

An essential tool when it comes to making stratas, frittatas, and any other egg dish is the rubber spatula. We evaluated 10 heatproof rubber (also called silicone) spatulas, all dishwasher-safe, running each through nine tests, including lifting omelets, scraping the bowl of a food processor, folding whipped egg whites into cake batter, making a pan sauce, and stirring risotto. We also simmered the spatulas in a pot of tomato-curry sauce for an hour to see if they would stain and absorb odors, and we ran them through the dishwasher twice to see if they would come through clean and odor-free. Finally, we asked a variety of test cooks to weigh in on the spatulas' comfort and performance.

Our favorites are the **Rubbermaid Professional 13½-Inch Heat Resistant Scraper,** $23.50 (top); and the **Tovolo Silicone Spatula** (bottom), which at $8.99 is our best buy. The Rubbermaid is a practical, no-nonsense spatula that aced every cooking test, with a great balance of flexibility and firmness in both the head and the handle. The Tovolo is a sleek spatula with nice curves. It passed every performance test, scraping, stirring, folding, and sautéing like a champ. It also withstood our attempts to stain and melt it. The Tovolo's good looks and nice price make it hard to resist, but, in the end, the larger overall size and sturdiness of the Rubbermaid won our highest accolades.

SPAGHETTI WITH FRIED EGGS

REQUIRING ONLY A FEW PANTRY STAPLES, spaghetti with fried eggs is a simple and satisfying weeknight supper. You simply toss some spaghetti with olive oil and a handful of freshly grated Parmesan, and top each portion with a softly fried egg that helps create a savory sauce once the yolk is broken. The preparation is so easy, who would need a recipe? Yet after a couple of tries, we realized we had a few things to learn. If the fried eggs sat for just a few extra minutes (waiting on the pasta), the yolks hardened and we were unable to achieve the rich, silky sauce that defines the dish. If the pasta sat too long (waiting on the eggs), it would stick together and form a solid mound that we could not serve. It seemed that success depended on two things: timing, and cooking the perfect fried egg. We turned our attention to the eggs first.

Our cooked eggs—two of them, of course—had to have whites that were firm and yolks that were slightly runny. To achieve these results, we found a nonstick skillet to be crucial—we could slide the eggs right out of the pan unbroken. Preheating the pan to just the right temperature before cooking the eggs was also key. If we used a pan that was too cool, the egg whites spread out and became rubbery and tough. When the pan was too hot, the whites would brown at the edges as soon as they hit the pan and end up tasting overcooked and metallic. When the pan was heated just right—for five minutes over low heat—the whites neither ran nor sputtered and bubbled; instead, they just sizzled and set up into perfectly thick, restrained ovals.

Another key aspect was placing the eggs in the pan at the same time. Because they took so little time to cook, if we added the eggs to the pan as we cracked them, one after the other, we ended up with unevenly cooked eggs. The easiest way to get the eggs into the pan at the same time was to crack them into a small bowl, then tip them into the hot skillet. Covering the skillet as the eggs cooked also helped by trapping the steam and allowing the tops of the eggs to cook evenly without being flipped over. We now had two

SPAGHETTI WITH FRIED EGGS

perfectly cooked eggs, but we wondered how to time their cooking with that of the pasta.

Ideally, the pasta and eggs would be done at the same time, but trying to time al dente pasta with perfectly cooked eggs—both of which have a short window for perfect doneness—was tricky. We would have to cook the eggs either just before or just after the spaghetti was finished cooking. After a few trials of cooking the eggs first, we realized that our perfectly cooked eggs began to deteriorate while they waited; when we moved the eggs from the skillet to a plate, they turned cold and rubbery within a minute, yet if we left them in the skillet, they overcooked from the residual heat. It was much easier, therefore, to fry the eggs just after the spaghetti was drained. To cut down on the time lag, we gave the skillet a head start by preheating it as the pasta finished cooking. To keep the pasta from sticking together or drying out while waiting on the eggs, we simply tossed it with a good dose of the pasta cooking water and olive oil and held it in the pasta cooking pot with the lid on.

Now we simply added a few finishing touches. Caramelizing two cloves of minced garlic with the oil helped boost the flavor, and a pinch of crushed red pepper flakes brought a spicy kick and another level of complexity. We were almost finished, but tasters requested a contrasting texture in this otherwise soft-textured dish of pasta and eggs, and toasted homemade bread crumbs seemed a natural fit. Tossing them into the pasta didn't work because they clumped together and became soggy very quickly. Instead, we found that sprinkling them on top of the pasta just before adding the eggs provided the perfect light crunch to this simple pantry dinner.

NOTES FROM THE TEST KITCHEN

SELECTING THE BEST GARLIC
Heads of garlic vary in quality and age throughout the year, and it can be hard to pick a flavorful head. Here's the test kitchen's advice: Go for the loose garlic, not the heads sold packaged in little cellophane-wrapped boxes that don't allow for close inspection. Look for heads with no spots of mold or signs of sprouting. Take a whiff; the garlic should not smell unusually fragrant or fermented—signs of spoilage, to be sure. Finally, squeeze the head in your hand. If you feel hollow skins where cloves used to reside or if the head feels at all spongy or rubbery, pass it up—a head of garlic should feel firm and solid.

Spaghetti with Fried Eggs
SERVES 2

Timing is key here; the pasta should be drained just before cooking the eggs. A preheated nonstick skillet is essential for ensuring properly cooked eggs that will release easily from the pan. For added contrast, 2 tablespoons minced fresh parsley or chives can be incorporated into the pasta in step 4.

- 2 slices high-quality white sandwich bread, torn into quarters
- 6 tablespoons extra-virgin olive oil
- Salt and pepper
- 2 garlic cloves, minced
- Pinch red pepper flakes
- ½ pound spaghetti
- ¼ cup grated Parmesan cheese, plus extra for serving
- 2 large eggs, cracked into a small bowl

1. Adjust an oven rack to the lower-middle position and heat the oven to 300 degrees. Pulse the bread in a food processor to coarse crumbs, about 10 pulses. Transfer the crumbs to a bowl and stir in 1 tablespoon of the oil, a pinch of salt, and a pinch of pepper. Spread the crumbs out on a rimmed baking sheet and bake, stirring occasionally, until golden brown and dry, about 25 minutes.

2. Cook 2 tablespoons more oil, garlic, pepper flakes, and ⅛ teaspoon salt in a 10-inch nonstick skillet over low heat, stirring constantly, until the garlic foams and is sticky and straw-colored, 8 to 10 minutes. Transfer the garlic mixture to a small bowl and set aside. Wipe out the skillet with a wad of paper towels and set aside.

3. Meanwhile, bring 4 quarts water to a boil in a large pot. Add the pasta and 1 tablespoon salt, and cook, stirring often, until al dente. A minute or two before draining the pasta, return the skillet to low heat for 5 minutes (for the eggs). Reserve ½ cup of the cooking water, then drain the pasta and return it to the pot.

4. Stir ¼ cup of the reserved cooking water, garlic mixture, 2 tablespoons more oil, the cheese, and ¼ teaspoon salt into the pasta. Cover and set aside to keep warm while cooking the eggs.

5. When the skillet is hot, add the remaining 1 tablespoon oil and swirl to coat the pan. Quickly add the eggs to the skillet and season with salt and pepper. Cover and cook until the whites are set but the yolks are still runny, 2 to 3 minutes. Uncover the eggs and remove from the heat.

6. Loosen the pasta with the remaining reserved cooking water as desired, then divide it between 2 individual serving bowls. Sprinkle each serving with the bread crumbs. Carefully slide 1 fried egg on top of the pasta in each bowl and serve, passing extra Parmesan separately.

PASTA WITH TUNA AND GARLIC

WHO HASN'T COME HOME FROM A LONG DAY at work, tired and hungry, to find the refrigerator bare, offering poor prospects for a good, quick dinner? In our own home pantries, it seems we always have at least a box of pasta and a can of tuna hanging out. Starting with pasta and tuna as our foundation, we set out to make a fast and reliable dish that would be so good we might crave it even when the fridge wasn't empty.

A side-by-side tasting of different types of tuna got us started. The lineup was composed of water-packed solid white tuna, its vegetable oil–packed counterpart, and tuna packed in olive oil, which, like the other tunas, is available on many supermarket shelves. The surprise winner was the water-packed tuna, preferred for its pleasant texture and light, clear flavor. A few dissenters favored the rich flavor of the tuna packed in olive oil, but everyone frowned on the off-flavor and mushy texture of the tuna packed in vegetable oil. Fortuitously, one 6-ounce can provided the right amount of meat for two diners.

Now we could consider a light sauce, which would be simply and easily prepared. Working with just 2 tablespoons of olive oil as the base, we flavored the oil by cooking it with capers, minced garlic, red pepper flakes, lemon juice, and zest until the garlic just began to sizzle. Next we added ¼ cup of dry white wine and reduced it until the pan was almost dry. At this point, the flavors of our light sauce were nice, but the bright citrus flavor from the lemon was lost because of the cooking. We decided to hold the lemon juice and zest until the end, to be added with the cooked pasta. Satisfied with our working sauce, which we would bulk up with the pasta cooking water later on, we wondered about when to add the tuna and found that adding it late in the game, like the lemon juice and zest, was

best. When sautéed from the start, the tuna dried out and became gritty, dragging down the texture of the whole dish. When the tuna was added to the sauce at the last minute and allowed to just heat through, it remained moist and tender. Draining the tuna well was important in preventing any metallic flavors from the canning liquid to enter our dish. We also found it useful to use our fingers to break apart the large chunks to a uniform texture, thereby ensuring an even distribution of the tuna. These techniques added just a minute to the preparation time but made significant improvements to the overall consistency of the final dish.

Because our sauce was relatively light, we needed to pair it with stubby, open, or tubular pasta shapes that could trap the sauce and tuna effectively; penne was the favorite among tasters, and fusilli followed close behind. Both shapes were appealing for their ability to hold on to the sauce, but they also received much approval for their common presence in most household pantries. Using ½ pound of pasta gave us ample portions for two.

After combining the cooked pasta with the tuna sauce and some reserved pasta cooking water, we mixed in the lemon juice and zest for brightness, along with a little extra olive oil for added richness. We also made the most of our multitasking skills, cooking the pasta while building the sauce. In under 30 minutes, we had a delicious pasta dinner from the pantry for two.

Pasta with Tuna and Garlic

SERVES 2

Other pasta shapes can be substituted for the penne; however, their cup measurements may vary (see page 51). For this recipe, we prefer water-packed solid white tuna for its light, clear flavor. If you like the stronger flavor of tuna packed in olive oil, we find it best to drain the tuna and use fresh oil to avoid imparting any metallic flavors to the pasta sauce. If desired, 2 tablespoons minced fresh parsley or chives can be incorporated with the pasta in step 3.

- ½ pound penne (about 2½ cups; see note)
- Salt
- 3 tablespoons extra-virgin olive oil
- 1 tablespoon capers, drained and rinsed
- 1 garlic clove, minced
- Pinch red pepper flakes
- ¼ cup dry white wine or vermouth
- 1 (6-ounce) can solid white tuna in water, drained well and broken into chunks (see note; see page 162)
- 1 teaspoon fresh lemon juice plus ½ teaspoon grated lemon zest
- Pepper

1. Bring 4 quarts water to a boil in a large pot. Add the pasta and 1 tablespoon salt, and cook, stirring often, until al dente. Reserve ½ cup of the cooking water, then drain the pasta and return it to the pot.

2. Meanwhile, cook 2 tablespoons of the oil, the capers, garlic, and pepper flakes in a 10-inch skillet over medium-low heat, stirring frequently, until sizzling, about 1 minute. Add the wine and simmer until almost dry, about 1 minute. Stir in the tuna and ¼ teaspoon salt and cook until the tuna is heated through, about 1 minute.

3. Add the tuna sauce to the cooked pasta and toss to combine, adjusting the sauce consistency with the reserved cooking water as desired. Stir in the remaining 1 tablespoon oil, the lemon juice, and zest. Season with salt and pepper to taste and serve.

PANTRY CORN CHOWDER

SURE, CORN CHOWDER MADE AT THE HEIGHT of summer with fresh corn is delicious, but it's also time-consuming and requires picking out perfect corn, then stripping multiple cobs of their kernels. Luckily, there's an easy way to make corn chowder in the dead of winter—with frozen corn. We thought this favorite American vegetable deserved some attention—even when it came cold and in a bag—and set out to create a simple chowder that would highlight corn's distinct sweetness and hearty nature. Normally, chowder would need to simmer for an hour and produce enough food to feed a family of 10; but our chowder would be streamlined and sped up, making for an easy weeknight solution to dinner for two.

The ingredients in most corn chowder recipes are relatively standard: corn and other vegetables (usually potatoes and onions at least); water or chicken broth enriched with half-and-half, cream, or milk; and some fat, be it butter, oil, or rendered fat from bacon. Working off this basic ingredient list, we decided to start building our recipe from the ground up.

After testing a few recipes, we learned that the flavor of the base (made up of the broth and dairy) was critical to a great chowder. The first contributor to that flavor was fat, and the first way to incorporate fat was using it to sauté our aromatics—onion, garlic, and herbs. Unfortunately, neither butter nor oil provided enough flavor to our finished chowder, so we turned to cooking a few slices of bacon and sautéing the aromatics in the rendered fat; this imparted a wonderfully rich undertone to our chowder. We toyed with leaving the crisp bacon slices in the pot—the chowder developed

PANTRY CORN CHOWDER

a truly delectable flavor when we did. But, sadly, the bacon itself morphed into fatty pieces that were tough and chewy. Our solution was to finely mince the bacon so that after rendering, it would almost dissolve into the chowder. It occurred to us that some minced bacon would make a great garnish, so we reserved a tablespoon of the cooked bacon to sprinkle over our bowls. For the aromatics, a minced onion, some garlic, and thyme helped to add sweetness and flavor to the chowder.

Now we could go on to consider the best way to infuse the chowder base with corn flavor. Traditional methods utilized a stock made from corncobs and fortified with corn milk—the juicy, creamy roots of the kernels left attached to corncobs after the kernels are cut off. Since we were working with a bag of frozen corn, this was not an option. To re-create this method in a speedy manner, we simmered the corn kernels in milk and chicken stock with a few potatoes. But this produced a runny chowder that lacked the desired richness and sweet corn flavor.

Looking for a way to impart more corn flavor, we tried making our own version of corn milk. Using our food processor, we processed half of the corn kernels with whole milk—heavy cream and half-and-half made this quick chowder too heavy—to produce a smooth, creamy mixture. When we added the corn slurry to our chowder base, along with the chicken stock, we quickly realized how much flavor we had been missing out on. We incorporated the remaining whole kernels after the mixture had simmered for about five minutes and were rewarded with a chowder that was rich in corn flavor and had the perfect thick consistency—minus the hour of simmering time.

At this point, our corn chowder tasted great, but it wasn't quite hearty enough—enter the potatoes. We decided chunks of potato would add a nice textural contrast to the whole corn kernels. We cut three red potatoes into ½-inch pieces (using one russet potato instead would work too) and stirred them into the pot with the corn slurry. Just as we thought, the small size of the potatoes ensured that they cooked through in just minutes. Now our quick corn chowder was perfect; it boasted rich corn flavor (no one would suspect these were frozen kernels) and had a hearty presence thanks to the potatoes and crispy bacon we had sprinkled on top. Our method for cooking this chowder was efficient—taking less than 30 minutes—without sacrificing any flavor.

Pantry Corn Chowder

SERVES 2

If you have forgotten to thaw the corn, you can quickly defrost it in a bowl in the microwave.

- 1 pound frozen corn, thawed (see note)
- ¾ cup whole milk
- 3 slices bacon, minced
- 1 small onion, minced (about ½ cup)
  Salt
- 2 garlic cloves, minced
- ⅛ teaspoon dried thyme
- 1 bay leaf
- 1¾ cups low-sodium chicken broth
- 8 ounces red potatoes (about 3 small)
  or 1 russet potato, cut into ½-inch pieces
  Pepper

1. Process half of the corn with the milk in a food processor until smooth; set aside.

2. Cook the bacon in a large saucepan over medium-low heat until beginning to brown, 5 to 7 minutes. Transfer 1 tablespoon of the bacon to a paper towel–lined plate and set aside. Add the onion and a pinch of salt

NOTES FROM THE TEST KITCHEN

THE BEST FOOD PROCESSOR

What should a food processor be able to do? For starters, it ought to chop, grate, and slice vegetables; grind dry ingredients; and cut fat into flour for pie pastry. If it can't whiz through these tasks, it's wasting precious counter space. Recently, we tested inexpensive food processors to find out which one performed best. Unfortunately, many brands failed basic tests: vegetables were torn into mangled slices, soup leaked from the work bowl, and attempts to make pizza dough resulted in seriously strained motors and an acrid, smoky smell. We realized it would be necessary to open our wallet and check out the more expensive options. After we put the high-priced machines through a battery of tests, it was obvious that more money does indeed buy a better food processor—though you don't need to buy the most expensive one. Our top pick is the **KitchenAid 12-cup Food Processor**, $199.95. It has a sturdy, sharp blade and a weighty motor that did not slow under a heavy load of dough. It performs almost every task as well as (or better than) its pricier competition.

and cook, stirring occasionally, until softened and lightly browned, 5 to 7 minutes. Stir in the garlic, thyme, and bay leaf, and cook until fragrant, about 30 seconds.

3. Add the pureed corn, broth, potatoes, and ¼ teaspoon salt, bring to a simmer, and cook until the potatoes are almost tender, about 5 minutes. Stir in the remaining corn; return to a simmer and cook until the corn is warmed through and the potatoes are tender, about 2 minutes. Off the heat, remove the bay leaf, season with salt and pepper to taste, sprinkle with the reserved bacon, and serve.

TUSCAN WHITE BEAN SOUP

WITH JUST A HANDFUL OF INGREDIENTS, Tuscan white bean soup highlights the straightforward simplicity that Italian cooking is known for. A testament to the less-is-more philosophy, this soup is composed of tender, creamy beans and a soup base perfumed with garlic and rosemary. Unfortunately, although this traditional dish requires a small list of ingredients, it also relies heavily on low-and-slow cooking to build its robust flavor and achieve the proper creaminess in the beans. Our original recipe for Tuscan white bean soup required simmering the beans for almost two hours to achieve the correct texture—and it was certainly worth every minute. But now we wanted to make a scaled-down version of the same dish in a fraction of the time, with staples that most kitchens already have on hand.

Creating a flavorful bean soup quickly would certainly be a challenge. All too often, we came across quick white bean soup recipes that were hollow replicas of their more time-consuming cousins, with bland, watery broths and undercooked beans. Removing the low-and-slow cooking was greatly affecting our end result—flavors were not given the opportunity to develop as deeply, and the starches in the beans were not cooking long enough to break down and turn creamy—causing us to reconsider how we would change the original recipe to achieve a soup that we were satisfied with. Instead of trying to simply change the cooking method to cut time while still keeping the original ingredients—a method many recipes attempted with little success—we decided instead to first look at our ingredient list and see what changes could be made there.

The key to a rich white bean soup, which we put into practice with our original recipe, was to simmer the beans slowly in a strongly flavored broth. We had done this by first rendering pork fat (traditionally pancetta) with other vegetables and aromatics and then adding water to create a rich, meaty broth in which to cook the beans. This approach, although traditional and very tasty, was not practical for two people trying to make a quick weeknight supper. We wanted to retain the flavorful broth, but it couldn't take forever to make. Beginning with rendered bacon—more of a staple than pancetta—we sautéed the basic bean soup aromatics of carrot, onion, garlic, and dried rosemary, then added chicken broth and a bit of water. After just a half-hour of simmering, we tested the results and were pleasantly surprised with the depth of flavor we had obtained.

We were confident in our soup base, but we knew that the beans were really the star of the soup. Concerned that we couldn't develop the flavor and texture of dried beans in a short amount of time, we recalled previous successes with adding canned beans to soups. Unfortunately, our success did not come easily; adding the beans for a lengthy simmering caused their skins to break and fall apart, and beans added at the end of simmering took on no flavor whatsoever. Seeing that

---

USE IT UP: FROZEN LEAF SPINACH

Herbed Spinach Dip
MAKES ABOUT 1 CUP
Serve with corn chips, tortilla chips, potato chips, or crudités.

- 5 ounces frozen leaf spinach, thawed and squeezed dry
- ½ cup mayonnaise
- 1 small shallot, minced (about 1 tablespoon)
- ½ teaspoon dried parsley
- ½ teaspoon dried dill
- ½ teaspoon white wine vinegar
- ¼ teaspoon salt
- ⅛ teaspoon pepper

Process all of the ingredients together in a food processor until smooth, about 1 minute. Transfer to a serving bowl, cover, and refrigerate before serving until the flavors have blended, at least 30 minutes or up to 2 days.

the beans needed to be warmed gently for at least five minutes to gain flavor, we tried adding them with the broth and water, then simmered the soup for a few minutes to thicken. This technique worked extremely well, enabling the beans to absorb as much flavor from the broth as possible without breaking, while ridding them of their canned flavor. As a last adjustment, we added frozen spinach along with the beans to help bring some extra heartiness to the dish.

Served with some grated Parmesan cheese and a wedge of crusty bread, this soup tasted like it had simmered for hours.

Tuscan White Bean Soup

SERVES 2

We prefer the texture of cannellini beans in this soup; however, small white beans can be substituted. Serve with grated Parmesan cheese and drizzle with extra-virgin olive oil. See page 166 for a recipe to use up the leftover frozen spinach.

- 2 slices bacon, minced
- 1 small onion, minced (about ½ cup)
- 1 carrot, peeled and chopped fine
- ¼ teaspoon dried rosemary, crushed
  Salt
- 1 garlic clove, minced
- 1¾ cups low-sodium chicken broth
- ¼ cup water
- 1 (15-ounce) can cannellini beans, drained and rinsed (see note)
- 5 ounces frozen leaf spinach, thawed and squeezed dry
  Pepper

1. Cook the bacon in a large saucepan over medium-low heat until beginning to brown, 5 to 7 minutes. Add the onion, carrot, rosemary, and a pinch of salt and cook, stirring occasionally, until the vegetables are softened and lightly browned, 5 to 7 minutes. Stir in the garlic and cook until fragrant, about 30 seconds.

2. Stir in the broth, water, beans, spinach, and ½ teaspoon salt. Bring to a simmer and cook until the mixture has thickened slightly, about 5 minutes. Season with salt and pepper to taste and serve.

PASTA E FAGIOLI

PASTA E FAGIOLI IS A HEARTY ITALIAN SOUP composed of pasta and beans. A popular restaurant standby, this peasant soup is favored for its rich flavor created with affordable and satisfying ingredients. Although the beans and pasta shapes used can vary, the broad outlines of the dish remain constant—a thick tomato base, loads of well-cooked beans and al dente pasta, and chunks of vegetables.

Most recipes we found for pasta e fagioli followed a procedure common in Italian soup making. The aromatics are first sautéed with rendered pancetta. Next, the tomatoes and broth go into the pot, followed by the beans, which are simmered until they become tender. Once the beans are tender, the pasta is added and cooked to al dente. Our goal was to make this soup an accessible dinner for two by cutting down the overall yield and simplifying the cooking method.

We began by rendering two slices of minced bacon, then sautéing onion, celery, carrot, and garlic in the rendered fat until they had softened. These vegetables are fairly traditional for aromatics, but tasters felt that the carrot added too much sweetness, so we omitted it. A 14.5-ounce can of diced tomatoes and 2 cups of chicken broth were added next to deglaze the pan. The tomatoes and the broth produced a respectable soup, but we knew we could improve it.

Since pasta e fagioli is known for its tomato base, we felt that simply adding the canned tomatoes was not doing enough to highlight their robust flavor. Instead, we allowed the tomatoes to cook down with the aromatics before adding the chicken broth, which helped to reduce the tomato juice and concentrate its flavor. Tasters also felt that the 2 cups of chicken broth were overpowering the tomatoes and causing our soup to taste more like a hearty chicken soup with tomatoes. We replaced half of the broth with water; this cut down on the chicken flavor and produced a winning soup base with rich tomato flavor.

Our recipe was coming together, but we had a few more points to consider. Pasta e fagioli usually involves cooking raw beans, but to save some time, we decided to use canned cannellini beans. Because canned beans often lack flavor, we wondered if adding the beans to the tomato mixture—before adding the broth—would help infuse them with the flavors of the bacon and vegetables. We prepared two batches of soup: one with the

PASTA E FAGIOLI

beans and broth added simultaneously, and one with beans added to the tomatoes and cooked for 5 minutes before the broth went into the pot. As we had hoped, simmering the beans in the thick tomato mixture infused them with more flavor.

Finally, we added pasta to our soup. Tests showed that smaller shapes were best in this soup. Larger shapes crowded out the other ingredients and soaked up too much liquid. Ditalini (small tubes) and macaroni (elbows) cooked fairly quickly and were favorites among our tasters.

Packed with delicious and robust flavors, our smaller batch of Pasta e Fagioli was easy to make and ready in just minutes.

Pasta e Fagioli

SERVES 2

For this recipe, we prefer using ditalini or macaroni, but any short, bite-size pasta will work. If desired, garnish with grated Parmesan cheese and minced fresh parsley, or drizzle with extra-virgin olive oil. See page 54 for a recipe to use up the leftover cannellini beans.

- 2 slices bacon, minced
- 1 small onion, minced (about ½ cup)
- 1 celery rib, chopped fine
   Salt
- 1 garlic clove, minced
- ¼ teaspoon dried oregano
   Pinch red pepper flakes
- 1 (14.5-ounce) can diced tomatoes
- ¾ cup drained and rinsed canned cannellini beans
- 1 cup low-sodium chicken broth
- 1 cup water
- 2 ounces short pasta, such as ditalini
   or macaroni (about ⅔ cup) (see note)
   Pepper

1. Cook the bacon in a large saucepan over medium-low heat until beginning to brown, 5 to 7 minutes. Add the onion, celery, and a pinch of salt, and cook, stirring occasionally, until the vegetables are softened and lightly browned, 5 to 7 minutes. Stir in the garlic, oregano, and pepper flakes and cook until fragrant, about 30 seconds.

2. Stir in the tomatoes with their juice, scraping up any browned bits from the bottom of the pan. Add the beans,

bring to a boil, then reduce the heat to low and simmer until slightly thickened, about 5 minutes. Add the broth, water, and ¼ teaspoon salt, increase the heat to high, and bring to a boil. Add the pasta and cook until al dente. Season with salt and pepper to taste and serve.

NOTES FROM THE TEST KITCHEN

THE BEST CANNED WHITE BEANS

It is hard to beat the full flavor and firm texture of dried beans cooked from scratch, but it's much easier and speedier—especially when you need only a small amount—to substitute canned beans. Our Tuscan White Bean Soup (page 167) and Pasta e Fagioli have enough flavor that the stronger flavor of the dried beans isn't missed, and the cooking time is so short that the softer canned beans do not have a chance to overcook and turn mushy.

But are all canned cannellini beans of equal caliber? We looked for multiple brands of nationally distributed cannellini beans to taste against one another and found so few that we decided to include both great Northern and navy beans in the tasting as well. From sweet to bland and chalky to mushy, the different brands ran the gamut in quality. Our favorite of the bunch was **Westbrae Organic Great Northern Beans** (left), which won accolades for their earthy flavor and creamy texture. In second place, tasters liked **Progresso Cannellini Beans** (right) for their "plump shape" and "sweet, slightly salty" flavor.

THE BEST LARGE SAUCEPAN

A large saucepan is an essential piece of cookware. When cooking for two, you can use this versatile pot for many tasks, including cooking a half pound of pasta and making soup. To find out if brand matters, we tested eight models, all between 3.3 and 4 quarts in size. We tested the pans for sauté speed, ability to heat evenly, and user-friendliness. The most important quality turned out to be slow, even heating. The best pans for slow and steady cooking either were very heavy or had relatively thick bottoms, while an aluminum core also ensured even heating and minimal scorching. We also liked pans with long handles. Our favorite was the **All-Clad Stainless 4-Quart Saucepan,** $184.95, which was the only pan to pass every test with flying colors. Testers liked the "solid," "restaurant-quality" feel and "perfectly proportioned" shape.

QUESADILLAS

CONSTRUCTED OF ODDS AND ENDS typically found in the refrigerator and prepared with minimal effort, the quesadilla is the epitome of a pantry meal. Unfortunately, most quesadillas tend to be nothing more than greasy Mexican pizzas—stale and soggy supermarket tortillas bulging with excess fillings and sliced into big, floppy triangles. This was not the dinner we were hoping for. We wanted to create a quesadilla that would fill the role of quick and casual but still filling dinner, with a crisp exterior and warm, tender interior, ready at a moment's notice from simple ingredients.

We began our testing by figuring out the best way to achieve the crisp crust. Starting with a basic filling of shredded cheddar cheese, we tested several techniques for cooking quesadillas, including a deep fry, a shallow fry, a lightly oiled skillet, and a completely dry one. Witnessing the spectrum of cooking styles, we quickly understood why many quesadillas fail. Quesadillas that were deep-fried and shallow-fried were typically accompanied by a pool of oil on the bottom of the serving plate, foreshadowing their greasy interior and soggy bottom layer. The lightly oiled and dry nonstick skillets produced better—though not perfect—results. The exterior of the tortillas was nicely browned and free from excess oil, but the interior had a raw, doughy texture, and the cheese was not entirely melted.

What we needed was a way to preheat the tortillas so that we could assemble the quesadillas while they were still warm. We could then crisp them up quickly without worrying that the filling would not be sufficiently heated. Some cookbooks suggest passing the tortillas over the flame of a gas burner to lightly char and soften them. This idea worked, but it excluded electric cooktops and demanded close attention to keep the tortillas from going up in flames. We got better results by simply toasting the tortillas in a hot, dry skillet. As the tortillas heated up, they released their own steam, causing the tortillas to puff up and their layers to separate. We then filled the tortillas and returned them to the skillet, and found that these quesadillas had a pleasing contrast in texture—their outer layers were thin and toasted, and their inner layers were warm and soft, with just a little bit of chew.

The dry skillet was working well for browning the tortillas, but we felt that a little oil in the hot skillet was needed to achieve the really crisp exterior that we were looking for. We knew we didn't need much, but when we added even a few drops of oil, they puddled in the middle of the nonstick skillet, resulting in uneven crispiness. A better approach, we found, was to brush the tortillas with oil before adding them to the skillet. We sprinkled the tortillas lightly with salt after brushing them with oil, and tasters agreed that this made them crisp and delicious.

Our quesadillas were shaping up, but they still suffered from a few design flaws. Our working recipe called for sandwiching cheese between two 12-inch flour tortillas. These were tricky to flip without spilling the uncooked shredded cheese, and they oozed melted cheese all over the cutting board once finished and divided for two people. To help retain the filling, we switched to two smaller, individual 10-inch tortillas and began folding them in half around the filling, fitting them into the skillet at the same time. These half-moon quesadillas were much sturdier and easier to eat, and, thanks to the folded edges, they kept their filling inside, where it belonged.

Looking to make the filling more substantial, we stuck with simple ingredients that home cooks tend to have on hand. We utilized a couple slices of bacon, which we minced and rendered until crispy; then we sautéed a minced shallot in the rendered fat for additional flavor. Tasters were pleased with this combination of soft shallot and crisp bacon bites, but some were left looking for a little spice. Minced pickled jalapeños were our answer for those looking for some heat (but they can be omitted for a milder version). We also created a bar-worthy variation of our pantry quesadillas in which a mixture of salsa, refried beans, and chipotle chiles is spread on the tortillas with the cheese.

No longer a greasy happy-hour spectacle, our quesadillas were now beaming with crisp, brown crusts and flavorful, gooey fillings.

Cheese and Bacon Quesadillas

SERVES 2

The skillet should be fairly hot, but it should never smoke; if it does, reduce the heat to low. Allow the quesadillas to cool before cutting and serving them, or else the hot cheese will ooze out. Serve with salsa, guacamole, and sour cream.

- 2 slices bacon, minced
- 1 shallot, minced (about 3 tablespoons)
  Salt
- 2 (10-inch) flour tortillas
- 6 ounces cheddar cheese, shredded (about 1½ cups)
- 4 teaspoons minced pickled jalapeño chiles
  (optional)
  Vegetable oil

1. Cook the bacon in a 12-inch nonstick skillet over medium-low heat until crisp, about 10 minutes. Using a slotted spoon, transfer the bacon to a paper towel–lined plate.

2. Pour off all but 1 tablespoon of the bacon fat from the skillet, then return to medium heat. Add the shallot and a pinch of salt and cook, stirring occasionally, until softened, about 2 minutes. Transfer the shallot to a small bowl and set aside. Wipe out the skillet with paper towels.

3. Return the skillet to medium-low heat and toast the tortillas, one at a time, until soft and slightly puffed on both sides, 2 to 3 minutes per tortilla, flipping them halfway through toasting. Slide the tortillas out onto a cutting board.

4. Spread the bacon, shallot, cheese, and jalapeños (if using) over half of each tortilla, leaving a ½-inch border around the edge. Fold the tortillas in half and press to flatten. Brush the tops generously with oil and sprinkle lightly with salt.

5. Following the photo on page 170, place both of the quesadillas in the skillet, oiled-sides down, and cook over medium-low heat until crisp and well browned, 1 to 2 minutes. Brush the tops with oil and sprinkle lightly with salt. Flip the quesadillas and continue to cook until the second sides are crisp and well browned, 1 to 2 minutes longer. Transfer the quesadillas to a cutting board and cool for 3 minutes. Cut each quesadilla in half and serve.

VARIATION

Bean and Cheese Quesadillas
Pace Chunky Salsa is the test kitchen's favorite, but any brand will do. For more information on our favorite canned refried beans, see page 192.

Combine ½ cup canned refried beans, 2 tablespoons salsa, 2 tablespoons chopped canned chipotle chiles in adobo sauce, and 1 teaspoon ground cumin in a bowl. Follow the recipe for Cheese and Bacon Quesadillas, omitting the bacon, shallot, and jalapeños and spreading the bean mixture over half of each tortilla with the cheese in step 4, leaving a ½-inch border around the edge.

SOUFFLÉS

WHEN HOME COOKS CONSIDER MAKING A SOUFFLÉ, they immediately think it will take hours to prepare and that it will require tiptoeing around the oven, hoping no loud or unplanned thumps will cause a sad collapse. But the truth is, soufflés are actually incredibly easy to put together and, when made properly, are unlikely to fall at even the heaviest of stomping. With our original savory

PROPERLY WHIPPED EGG WHITES

Soufflés rely on perfectly whipped whites for their lightness, so it's important to whip them right. Egg whites whipped to soft peaks (top), drooping slightly from the tip of the whisk or beater, will not have the structure to properly support the soufflé. Overwhipped egg whites (center), looking curdled and separated, will not incorporate well into the soufflé base and often result in flat soufflés. (If your whites are overwhipped, start over with new whites and a clean bowl.) Egg whites whipped to stiff peaks (bottom), standing up tall on their own on the tip of the whisk or beater, have the ideal structure to support a light-as-air soufflé.

PROBLEM:
Soft Peaks

PROBLEM:
Overwhipped Whites

PERFECT:
Stiff Peaks

ACHIEVING AN EVEN RISE

After pouring the soufflé mixture into the ramekins, trace a circle in the mixture with your finger, ½ inch from the edge of the dish. This breaks the surface tension and helps achieve a high, even rise.

cheese soufflé recipe in hand, we set out to develop a smaller version for two people that would make for a light yet substantial dinner, perfectly complemented by a salad of mixed greens. After all, a cheese soufflé is a perfect option for a dinner from the pantry; all we would need was butter, flour, milk, eggs, and cheese.

We had already done extensive testing on soufflé bases and favored the rich flavor and body imparted by a béchamel base, made with butter, flour, and milk, over that of a bouillie base, made with only flour and milk (the butter makes all the difference). Working with a béchamel-based soufflé recipe, we began to reformulate its ingredient list to make it appropriate for two people.

To start, we focused on the ratio of eggs yolks to egg whites. In our original recipe, we found that three whites to three yolks produced a light soufflé that was sure to impress; recipes with more egg whites than yolks resulted in foamy, flavorless soufflés, and those with more yolks than whites produced a dense, heavy soufflé. Reducing the number of eggs by just one—a move that did not seem drastic on paper but proved significant in the baking dish—produced a generously sized soufflé for two diners. We also reduced the amounts of flour, milk, and butter proportionately.

When it came to the cheese for our soufflé, we stuck with our favorites: Gruyère and Parmesan. We used a modest ¼ cup of Parmesan for coating the baking dish and sprinkling on top. As for the amount of Gruyère, we learned that if we added too much to the dish, the structure of the soufflé would be heavy and the soufflé would collapse. With 2½ ounces of cheese, cut down from 4 ounces in our original, the soufflé had plenty of flavor and still puffed beautifully.

The cheese and egg provided the soufflé with ample flavor, but we felt that we needed to provide some depth to the soufflé. Shallots had worked well in our previous recipe, and we found that one finely minced shallot added to the béchamel base provided just the right amount of pungency and complemented the dominant flavor of the cheese. In addition to the shallot, dry mustard added a hint of spiciness, and ground nutmeg helped to draw out the nuttiness of the Gruyère. With our base ready to go, we whipped our egg whites in a clean mixing bowl—a bowl with even the tiniest speck of oil or dirt can prevent the whites from rising well—with a small amount of cream of tartar, then folded the whites into the soufflé base.

Now we had one item left to examine: the baking dish. Our original recipe called for a round ceramic soufflé dish, but now that we were working with a scaled-down recipe, our smaller soufflé was looking sad and flat after baking, even though it had risen perfectly. Concerned that we were losing the striking visual aspect of a perfectly baked soufflé—straight, high sides that rise out of the dish—we began looking around the test kitchen for a better baking dish and spotted two 12-ounce ramekins. Following the technique we had used with the soufflé dish, we simply divided the mixture between the ramekins and ran one finger around the outer edge of the soufflé (about ½ inch from the ramekin wall) so it would rise. After just 20 minutes of baking time, we were rewarded with two dazzling soufflés in the same amount of time it took to make one.

Cheese Soufflé

SERVES 2

Cheddar, Swiss, or Gouda can be substituted for the Gruyère. Begin beating the egg whites as soon as you finish making the soufflé base—don't let the base cool too much. Do not open the oven door during the first 15 minutes of baking; as the soufflé nears the end of baking, you can check its progress by opening the oven door slightly. For this recipe we prefer using two 12-ounce ramekins to achieve the rise above the rim of the dishes. If you don't have two soufflé dishes, you can use a 9 by 5-inch glass loaf pan, but the soufflé will not rise above the rim.

 ¼ **cup grated Parmesan cheese**

 2 **tablespoons unsalted butter**

 1 **shallot, minced (about 3 tablespoons)**
    Salt

 2 **tablespoons unbleached all-purpose flour**

 ⅔ **cup whole milk**

 2½ **ounces Gruyère cheese (see note), shredded**
    (about ⅔ cup)
    Pinch dry mustard
    Pinch pepper
    Pinch ground nutmeg

 2 **large eggs, separated, at room temperature**

 ⅛ **teaspoon cream of tartar**

1. Adjust an oven rack to the middle position and heat the oven to 350 degrees. Grease two 12-ounce ceramic ramekins, then sprinkle each ramekin with 1 tablespoon of the Parmesan and shake to coat evenly; tap out any excess cheese.

2. Melt the butter in a medium saucepan over medium heat. Add the shallot and a pinch of salt and cook, stirring occasionally, until softened, about 2 minutes. Stir in the flour and cook until golden, about 1 minute. Slowly whisk in the milk, bring to a simmer, and cook, whisking constantly, until thickened and smooth, about 1 minute. Off the heat, whisk in the Gruyère, a pinch of salt, mustard, pepper, and nutmeg. Scrape the mixture into a medium bowl, then whisk in the egg yolks until incorporated (this is the soufflé base).

3. In a large bowl, whip the egg whites and cream of tartar together with an electric mixer on medium-low speed until foamy, about 1 minute. Increase the mixer speed to medium-high and continue to whip until the whites are glossy and form stiff peaks, 1 to 2 minutes.

4. Fold one-quarter of the whipped egg whites into the soufflé base until almost no white streaks remain. Fold in the remaining egg whites until just incorporated. Gently pour the mixture evenly into the prepared dishes, wiping any mixture from the rims with a wet paper towel. Following the photo on page 172, with your finger, trace a circle on the surface of the soufflé mixture about ½ inch in from the side of the dish (this will help the soufflé rise evenly). Sprinkle the tops with the remaining 2 tablespoons Parmesan.

5. Place the soufflés on a rimmed baking sheet and bake until their surfaces are deep brown, the centers jiggle slightly when shaken, and they have risen 2 to 2½ inches above the rims of the dishes, 20 to 22 minutes. Serve immediately.

VARIATION

Spinach Soufflé

Follow the recipe for Cheese Soufflé, stirring 2 ounces chopped frozen spinach, thawed and squeezed dry, and ⅛ teaspoon dried thyme into the soufflé base with the egg yolks in step 2.

FRENCH-STYLE POT ROAST

ONE BIG ROAST, THREE GREAT MEALS

PAN-ROASTED CHICKEN BREASTS

PERFECTLY ROASTED CHICKEN BREASTS with crisp, brown skin are always welcome on the dinner table. And they make leftovers that can easily be transformed into second meals. Our goal was simple: We wanted to determine the best way to pan-roast bone-in chicken breasts, then come up with interesting dishes for using the leftover meat in two more dinners for two people.

Pan-roasting is a technique typically used in restaurants; food is browned in a skillet on the stovetop and then placed in a hot oven to finish cooking. We often employ this technique to cook a whole cut-up chicken and thought we could adapt it to chicken breasts to get the moist, tender meat and crackling skin we were after. In addition, we wanted to build a pan sauce to serve with the chicken and bring some complementary flavors to the dish and some richness to the otherwise lean chicken breasts.

We figured that five chicken breasts would be perfect for our main recipe—two of the breasts (along with the pan sauce) would be served right away, leaving three extra breasts that could be used to make two dinners later in the week. To make sure they cooked at the same rate, we selected breasts of similar size. But if the pieces you purchase are of divergent sizes (as they often are when bought prepackaged), just be sure to monitor them closely during cooking and remove the smaller breasts from the heat earlier. We also found it necessary to trim away the extra skin and bones from the rib cage. Not only did this make the breasts more uniform so that they cooked more evenly, but it also enabled us to fit all five breasts in a 12-inch skillet.

Not surprisingly, we found that it was just as easy to cook five breasts as it was to cook two. We heated 1 tablespoon of vegetable oil in the skillet until it was smoking, then browned both sides of the chicken breasts before transferring them, still in the pan, to the oven. To ensure seriously crisp skin, we found it best to oven-roast the chicken skin-side down.

As for the oven temperature, we tried a range from 375 degrees up to 500 degrees. At 500 degrees, we noted profuse smoking and sometimes singed drippings, which imparted an acrid flavor to our pan sauce. But temperatures on the lower end meant prolonged cooking times.

A compromise worked best; at 450 degrees, the skin was handsomely browned and cracklingly crisp, and the chicken cooked quickly (in about 15 minutes).

Setting the cooked chicken aside to rest, we then used the caramelized drippings, or *fond*, left behind in the skillet to make a quick pan sauce. Traditionally, pan sauces are made by sautéing aromatics on top of the fond, then adding broth or wine and simmering the mixture until it has reduced and thickened. We approached our pan sauce this way, but sprinkled a little flour into the skillet before adding broth to help the sauce thicken a bit more quickly and give it some extra body. Also, by shortening the time and amount by which the broth was reduced, we prevented the sauce from tasting overly salty, which can happen when using overseasoned store-bought chicken broth (even low-sodium broth).

With our main recipe set, we turned to the secondary recipes. We found that three leftover breasts, roughly 20 ounces of cooked chicken meat, was the perfect amount to make two more dinners for two people. To start, we created a lively chicken and pasta dish by using two potent and quick-cooking ingredients: cherry tomatoes and olives. We made a chicken broth–based sauce flavored with garlic and red pepper flakes, then stirred in the chicken, tomatoes, and olives and cooked them just until they were hot. We then tossed the chicken mixture with pasta, and dinner was ready.

For another simple meal, we combined 10 ounces of cooked chicken with large croutons, salad greens, and a brothy dressing to make a warm chicken and bread salad similar to an Italian *panzanella*. Getting the crouton texture just right was the trick to this recipe—the bread cubes had to be toasted and crisp on the outside, but still soft in the middle. To do this, we made our own croutons using rustic bread and a 400-degree oven. Any type of greens will work here, but we like the sharp, somewhat spicy flavor of arugula, along with a few shavings of good Parmesan.

For yet a third meal option, we took the ubiquitous chicken salad, a popular ending for leftover chicken, and jazzed it up by making a hot sandwich wrap. As with making burritos, we filled and rolled large tortillas around shredded cheddar cheese and chicken salad that we had spiced up with hot sauce, then we seared the wraps in a hot, dry skillet to crisp the tortillas and melt the cheese for another easy and tasty meal.

Pan-Roasted Chicken Breasts with Lemon and Caper Sauce

SERVES 2

You can use the leftovers to make two of the
following recipes:

- Penne with Chicken, Cherry Tomatoes, and Olives (page 177)
- Crispy Chicken Salad Wraps (page 178)
- Warm Roast Chicken and Bread Salad
  with Arugula (page 179)

If using kosher chicken, do not brine. If brining the
chicken, do not season with salt in step 1. Season this dish
sparingly with salt because capers tend to be salty.

CHICKEN

- 5 **(12-ounce) bone-in, skin-on split chicken breasts,
  trimmed (see page 7) and brined if desired
  (see note; see page 76)**
- **Salt and pepper**
- 1 **tablespoon vegetable oil**

SAUCE

- 1 **teaspoon vegetable oil**
- 1 **shallot, minced (about 3 tablespoons)**
- 1 **teaspoon unbleached all-purpose flour**
- ¾ **cup low-sodium chicken broth**
- 1 **tablespoon unsalted butter**
- 1 **tablespoon capers, rinsed and chopped**
- 1 **tablespoon chopped fresh parsley**
- 2 **teaspoons fresh lemon juice**
- **Salt and pepper**

1. FOR THE CHICKEN: Adjust an oven rack to the lowest position and heat the oven to 450 degrees. Pat the
chicken dry with paper towels and season with salt and
pepper. Heat the oil in a 12-inch oven-safe skillet over
medium-high heat until just smoking. Carefully lay the
chicken breasts, skin-side down, in the skillet and cook
until well browned, 6 to 8 minutes. Flip the chicken
breasts and continue to brown lightly on the second side,
about 3 minutes.

2. Flip the chicken breasts skin-side down, transfer the
skillet to the oven, and roast until the thickest part of the
breasts registers 160 to 165 degrees on an instant-read
thermometer, 15 to 20 minutes.

3. Using potholders (the skillet handle will be hot),
remove the skillet from the oven. Transfer the chicken
breasts to a plate, tent loosely with foil, and let rest

NOTES FROM THE TEST KITCHEN

ALL ABOUT CAPERS
Capers are actually pickles made from the unopened flower
buds of a Mediterranean shrub. Capers are never used fresh
and are preserved in one of two ways: in a salt and water
brine, sometimes with added vinegar, or in salt. The brine
method is most common, and brined capers are available in
most supermarkets. Salt-preserved capers are harder to find.

Capers can vary in size, from tiny to raisin-sized. (Caper-
berries, quite large and usually complete with a stem, are
formed when the buds are allowed to open and set fruit.)
For cooking, small capers are best because they can be used
as is; larger capers are too potent to eat whole and should
be chopped. Because brined capers can be very salty or
vinegary, you should rinse them before cooking.

while making the sauce. *To make any two of the recipes on
pages 177–179, reserve 3 of the chicken breasts and refrigerate
in an airtight container for up to 3 days.*

4. FOR THE SAUCE: Being careful of the hot skillet
handle, add the oil to the skillet and return to medium
heat until shimmering. Add the shallot and cook until
softened, about 2 minutes. Stir in the flour and cook for
30 seconds. Stir in the broth, scraping up any browned
bits. Bring to a simmer and cook until the sauce has
reduced to ½ cup, 2 to 3 minutes.

5. Stir in any accumulated chicken juice, return to a
simmer, and cook for 30 seconds. Off the heat, whisk
in the butter, capers, parsley, and lemon juice. Season
with salt and pepper to taste. Pour ¼ cup of the sauce
over the chicken breasts and serve, passing the remaining
sauce separately.

Penne with Chicken, Cherry Tomatoes, and Olives

SERVES 2

The cooked chicken in this recipe is from Pan-Roasted
Chicken Breasts with Lemon and Caper Sauce on
page 177. Other pasta shapes can be substituted for the
penne; however, their cup measurements may vary (see
page 51). See page 70 for a recipe to use up the leftover
cherry tomatoes. Fresh basil or scallions can be substituted for the parsley.

- ½ **pound penne (about 2½ cups) (see note)**
- **Salt**
- 3 **tablespoons olive oil**

THE BEST EXTRA-SHARP CHEDDAR

There are so many varieties of cheddar—mild, medium, sharp, extra-sharp, and beyond—so how do you know what's what at the supermarket? When cheese plays a starring role in a dish, as in our Crispy Chicken Salad Wraps, we turn to extra-sharp cheddar, which must contain at least 50 percent milk-fat solids and no more than 39 percent moisture by weight. As the cheddar ages, new flavor compounds are created, and the cheese gets firmer in texture and more concentrated in flavor—and it gets sharper. But does more sharpness make for better cheddar? To find out which supermarket extra-sharp cheddar cheese our tasters liked best, we purchased eight varieties (plus Cabot Sharp Cheddar, the winner of our previous tasting of regular sharp cheddars) and tried them plain and in grilled cheese sandwiches. Our two top-rated cheeses, **Cabot Private Stock** (left) and **Cabot Extra Sharp** (right), are aged for at least 12 months, and tasters rated them the sharpest.

HOW TO ROLL A TIGHT WRAP

1. After sprinkling the cheese over the tortillas, mound the chicken salad 1½ inches from the bottom of each tortilla, leaving a 2-inch border at the ends.

2. Roll the bottom edge of the tortilla up over the filling to cover it completely. Using the tortilla for leverage, press the filling back onto itself into a tight, compact log.

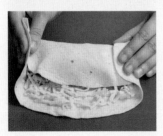

3. Fold the sides of the tortilla over the filling. Continue to roll the wrap into a tidy bundle. Place in the preheated skillet seam-side down. If the ends come unfolded, simply tuck them under the wrap.

---

3   garlic cloves, minced

    Pinch red pepper flakes

1   cup low-sodium chicken broth

10 ounces cooked chicken (see note), shredded (about 2 cups)

6   ounces cherry tomatoes (about 1 cup), halved

¼   cup pitted kalamata olives, chopped coarse

    Pepper

1   tablespoon fresh lemon juice

1   tablespoon chopped fresh parsley (see note)

    Grated Parmesan cheese, for serving

1. Bring 4 quarts water to a boil in a large pot. Add the pasta and 1 tablespoon salt, and cook, stirring often, until al dente. Reserve ½ cup of the cooking water, then drain the pasta and return it to the pot.

2. Meanwhile, cook 2 tablespoons of the oil, garlic, pepper flakes, and a pinch of salt together in a 10-inch skillet over medium heat until sizzling, about 2 minutes. Slowly stir in the broth and simmer until the sauce has reduced to ¾ cup, about 6 minutes. Stir in the chicken, tomatoes, and olives and cook until heated through, about 2 minutes. Season with salt and pepper to taste.

3. Add the chicken mixture, remaining 1 tablespoon oil, and lemon juice to the cooked pasta, and toss to combine, adjusting the sauce consistency with the reserved cooking water as desired. Stir in the parsley and serve with the Parmesan.

Crispy Chicken Salad Wraps

SERVES 2

The cooked chicken in this recipe is from Pan-Roasted Chicken Breasts with Lemon and Caper Sauce on page 177. To prevent the wraps from unrolling during cooking, be sure to start them seam-side down in step 3. Fresh cilantro can be substituted for the parsley. If you prefer a spicier dish, use the higher amount of hot sauce given.

¼   cup mayonnaise

3   tablespoons chopped fresh parsley (see note)

2   scallions, sliced thin

1   celery rib, chopped fine

½–1 teaspoon hot sauce (see note)

10   ounces cooked chicken (see note), shredded (about 2 cups)

Salt and pepper

3 ounces extra-sharp cheddar cheese, shredded (about ¾ cup)

2 (10-inch) flour tortillas

Vegetable oil spray

1. Whisk the mayonnaise, parsley, scallions, celery, and hot sauce together in a large bowl. Stir in the chicken and season with salt and pepper to taste.

2. Sprinkle the cheese evenly over the tortillas, leaving a ½-inch border around the edges. Following the photos on page 178, arrange the chicken salad 1½ inches from the bottom of each tortilla, leaving a 2-inch border at the ends, and roll up the tortillas like a burrito. Coat the outside of the wraps thoroughly with vegetable oil spray and season with salt and pepper.

3. Heat a 12-inch nonstick skillet over medium heat for 1 minute. Lay the wraps, seam-side down, in the pan and cook until golden brown and crisp on all sides, 3 to 5 minutes, turning as needed. Serve.

Warm Roast Chicken and Bread Salad with Arugula

SERVES 2

The cooked chicken in this recipe is from Pan-Roasted Chicken Breasts with Lemon and Caper Sauce on page 177. Baby spinach can be substituted for the arugula.

5 ounces French or Italian bread, cut or torn into 1-inch cubes (about 3½ cups)

¼ cup olive oil

Salt and pepper

1 shallot, minced (about 3 tablespoons)

2 garlic cloves, minced

½ teaspoon minced fresh thyme or ⅛ teaspoon dried

⅔ cup low-sodium chicken broth

10 ounces cooked chicken (see note), shredded (about 2 cups)

2 tablespoons red wine vinegar

4 ounces baby arugula (about 4 cups) (see note)

1 tomato, cored and chopped medium

1 tablespoon pine nuts, toasted (see page 226)

Shaved Parmesan cheese, for serving (see photo)

1. Adjust an oven rack to the middle position and heat the oven to 400 degrees. Toss the bread with 3 tablespoons of the oil, ⅛ teaspoon salt, and a pinch of pepper,

NOTES FROM THE TEST KITCHEN

MAKING PARMESAN SHAVINGS

Thin shavings of Parmesan can be used to garnish a variety of dishes. Simply run a sharp vegetable peeler along the length of a piece of cheese to make paper-thin curls.

and spread out on a rimmed baking sheet. Bake the bread cubes until light golden brown and still slightly soft in the center, 8 to 12 minutes.

2. Meanwhile, heat the remaining 1 tablespoon oil in a 10-inch skillet over medium heat until shimmering. Add the shallot and cook until softened, about 2 minutes. Stir in the garlic and thyme, and cook until fragrant, about 30 seconds. Slowly stir in the broth and simmer until thickened slightly, about 3 minutes. Stir in the chicken and vinegar, and cover to keep warm.

3. Transfer the warm bread cubes to a large bowl and gently fold in the arugula, tomato, and pine nuts. Pour the warm chicken mixture over the salad and toss to coat. Season with salt and pepper to taste. Sprinkle the Parmesan over the top of individual portions before serving.

PAN-ROASTED TURKEY BREAST WITH GRAVY

TURKEY MAKES A GREAT DINNER YEAR-ROUND, not just on Thanksgiving. But tackling the whole bird is a bit much for an everyday meal and not even remotely practical for two people, even when leftovers are welcome. Turkey breast, meanwhile, is an ideal, often overlooked alternative. For one thing, many people prefer the white meat of a breast to the dark meat of legs and thighs. Also, it's much easier to handle a breast than the whole bird, and the breast on its own still provides a substantial amount of meat. On the downside, turkey breast frequently ends up dry and flavorless. We knew we could do better and set out to develop an easy turkey breast recipe—with gravy—that would produce moist meat and could be made any night of the week. Then we would use the reasonable amount of extra turkey and gravy to make subsequent meals.

Unlike boneless chicken breasts, boneless turkey breasts are always sold with their skin intact, making pan-roasting the perfect approach for cooking them. By starting them off on the stovetop, we would be able to quickly achieve a crisp, golden skin, and finishing in the oven would ensure tender, juicy meat. And because the meat gets a jump start on the stovetop before heading into the hot oven, the whole process would be much quicker than traditional roasting.

At the supermarket, we had a choice between a whole bone-in and half boneless turkey breast. Although bone-in meat generally stays more moist, we were drawn to the smaller size of a boneless turkey breast because it would cook more quickly and be easier to slice and serve. We decided two breasts, at 2 pounds each, would give us just the right amount of meat for two main courses and two additional meals. Boneless turkey breast is usually sold in a few different preparations—natural (untreated), self-basting (injected with a brine solution), and kosher (salted and rinsed). We prefer the taste of natural turkey, which we most often brine ourselves, but any of the options would work here, with brining optional. (Kosher and self-basting birds should not be brined since they have already been salted.)

Getting started, we knew a uniform shape and thickness would guarantee even cooking, so we tucked the tapered end of each breast underneath and tied the breast with twine. After browning the tied breasts for about 10 minutes on the stovetop, we began experimenting with oven temperatures and found that a 325-degree oven produced the juiciest turkey meat.

Since pan-roasting a boneless turkey breast doesn't yield much in the way of drippings, we knew making a classic pan gravy was not an option. Instead, after browning the turkey breasts, we set them aside while we sautéed celery, onion, and carrot in the skillet. Then we set the turkey on top of the vegetables and put the whole pan in the oven. When the internal temperature of the turkey reached 160 degrees, we knew it was time to take it out of the oven. There were deep mahogany juices in the pan, and the vegetables had gone from a

light golden to a deep brown. It was the perfect foundation for our gravy. We set the turkey aside to rest and finished our sauce, browning flour in the skillet with the vegetables, fat, and juices. Then we slowly whisked in equal amounts of chicken broth and beef broth, a combination that tasters favored over a single broth for the complexity it brought to our gravy.

Tasters were impressed with the rich and meaty flavors of our strained gravy, but it still needed an extra boost. The trio of minced garlic, fresh thyme, and a bay leaf, added to the skillet before putting the turkey and vegetables in the oven, did the trick. The result was a deeply flavored gravy reminiscent of a Thanksgiving dinner, the perfect accompaniment to our moist turkey breast.

Now we were ready to focus on the leftovers. Everyone knows that leftover turkey can be incredibly tired

NOTES FROM THE TEST KITCHEN

ROLLING AND TYING A TURKEY BREAST

1. To prepare the turkey breast for pan-roasting, fold the tapered end underneath the rest of the breast.

2. Gently shape the breast into a compact roast by tucking the sides under with your hands.

3. Loosely tie the turkey breast lengthwise with kitchen twine to secure, then tie it firmly at 1½-inch intervals, crosswise, to make a tidy, even roast.

and dull, so we developed dishes with bold flavors, like a rich turkey chili and an Indian curry with complex flavors. In addition, we created a speedy skillet version of turkey pot pie. We had reserved enough turkey meat to make two of these options. And because we were using our flavorful gravy in these dishes, they all had an intense, long-cooked flavor in a short amount of time.

We started with the white chili—a fresher, lighter cousin of thick, beefy chili. For big chile flavor, we used Anaheim and jalapeño peppers, which we cooked with onion and a little cumin before adding the gravy and chicken broth. Some recipes for white chili call for beans, but tasters preferred the hearty texture and full flavor of canned hominy over that of the beans. To avoid rubbery turkey, we built the flavor in the pot, then stirred in the turkey and cooked it for just two minutes to heat it through. Finally, a hit of lime juice and some fresh cilantro added brightness and south-of-the-border feel.

Next, we worked on our curry recipe, which takes little time to prepare and delivers complex flavor. We built the sauce using onion, carrot, curry powder, and fresh ginger. We added some sweetness with raisins, which we cooked with the onions and carrots so they had a chance to plump and soften. Then it was time for the turkey gravy, and a cup of chicken broth to thin it out, to hit the pan. We simmered the mixture briefly before stirring in the turkey and some green beans. Last, a small amount of yogurt (added off the heat to prevent curdling) enriched the sauce and tempered its spicy flavors.

For our streamlined turkey pot pie, we zeroed in on a puff pastry topping instead of the typical pie dough. We found that cutting half a sheet of puff pastry into six rectangles and parbaking them while assembling the turkey filling on the stovetop in a skillet allowed us to speed this family favorite to the dinner table. We built the filling with the extra gravy, chicken broth, carrots, and fennel. Once the sauce was properly thickened, all that was left to do was stir in the turkey, top the pie with the pastry rectangles, and finish baking it in the oven. This may not look like your grandmother's pot pie, but it's definitely a great way to jazz up your turkey leftovers.

Pan-Roasted Turkey Breast with Gravy
SERVES 2

You can use the leftovers to make two of the following recipes:
- White Turkey Chili (page 182)
- Skillet Turkey Pot Pie with Fennel (page 182)
- Turkey Curry with Carrots and Green Beans (page 184)

If using kosher or self-basting turkey, do not brine. If brining the turkey, do not season with salt in step 1. Often, boneless turkey breast halves are sold in elastic netting; be sure to remove the netting before brining or cooking. You can substitute a single 4 to 4½-pound boneless turkey breast here, but you will need to increase the roasting time to about 1½ hours.

2	(2-pound) boneless turkey breast halves (see note), trimmed, tied (see page 180), and brined if desired (see note; see page 76)
	Salt and pepper
¼	cup vegetable oil
1	onion, chopped (about 1 cup)
1	carrot, peeled and chopped
1	celery rib, chopped
6	garlic cloves, minced
½	teaspoon dried thyme
1	bay leaf
¼	cup unbleached all-purpose flour
2	cups low-sodium chicken broth
2	cups low-sodium beef broth

1. Adjust an oven rack to the middle position and heat the oven to 325 degrees. Pat the turkey breasts dry with paper towels and season with salt and pepper. Heat 2 tablespoons of the oil in a 12-inch oven-safe skillet over medium-high heat until just smoking. Carefully lay the turkey breasts in the skillet and cook until well browned on all sides, about 10 minutes, turning as needed and reducing the heat if the pan begins to scorch. Transfer the turkey breasts to a plate.

2. Add the remaining 2 tablespoons oil to the skillet and return to medium heat until shimmering. Add the onion, carrot, and celery, and cook, stirring often, until the vegetables are softened and browned lightly, 6 to 8 minutes. Stir in the garlic, thyme, and bay leaf and cook until fragrant, about 30 seconds.

3. Lay the turkey breasts, skin-side up, on top of the vegetables. Transfer the skillet to the oven and roast until the thickest part of the breasts registers 160 to 165 degrees on an instant-read thermometer, 50 to 60 minutes.

4. Using potholders (the skillet handle will be hot), remove the skillet from the oven. Transfer the turkey breasts to a carving board, tent loosely with foil, and let rest while making the gravy.

5. Being careful of the hot skillet handle, return the skillet to medium-high heat. Add the flour and cook, stirring constantly, until well browned, about 5 minutes. Slowly whisk in the broths, scraping up any browned bits. Bring to a simmer and cook, stirring often, until the gravy has thickened and reduced to about 3 cups, 30 to 35 minutes.

6. Strain the gravy through a fine-mesh strainer and season with salt and pepper to taste. *To make any two of the recipes on pages 182–184, reserve 1¼ pounds of the turkey breasts and refrigerate in an airtight container for up to 3 days. Reserve 1 cup of the gravy and refrigerate in a separate airtight container for up to 3 days.* Remove the twine, cut the turkey breasts crosswise into ¼-inch-thick slices, and serve with the gravy.

White Turkey Chili
SERVES 2

The cooked turkey and gravy in this recipe are from Pan-Roasted Turkey Breast with Gravy on page 181. Both yellow hominy and white hominy will work in this chili; however, we prefer the deeper flavor of white hominy. If you like your chili spicy, include some of the jalapeño seeds.

    2 **Anaheim peppers, stemmed, seeded, and cut into large pieces**
    1 **small jalapeño pepper, stemmed, seeded, and cut into large pieces (see note)**
    1 **small onion, peeled and cut into large pieces**
    2 **garlic cloves, peeled**
    2 **tablespoons vegetable oil**
    1 **teaspoon ground cumin**
       Salt
 2½ **cups low-sodium chicken broth**
    ½ **cup gravy (see note)**
    1 **(15-ounce) can white hominy, rinsed (see note)**
   10 **ounces cooked turkey (see note), shredded (about 2 cups)**

    2 **tablespoons chopped fresh cilantro**
    1 **tablespoon fresh lime juice**
       Pepper

1. Pulse the peppers, onion, and garlic together in a food processor until roughly chopped, about 10 pulses.

2. Heat the oil in a medium saucepan over medium heat until shimmering. Add the processed vegetables, cumin, and ½ teaspoon salt and cook until the vegetables are beginning to brown, 6 to 8 minutes.

3. Stir in the broth, gravy, and hominy, scraping up any browned bits. Bring to a simmer and cook until the hominy is softened and the mixture has thickened slightly, 10 to 15 minutes.

4. Stir in the turkey and cook until heated through, about 2 minutes. Off the heat, stir in the cilantro and lime juice. Season with salt and pepper to taste and serve.

Skillet Turkey Pot Pie with Fennel
SERVES 2

The cooked turkey and gravy in this recipe are from Pan-Roasted Turkey Breast with Gravy on page 181. This recipe uses half of a standard 9-inch square sheet of puff pastry. Be sure to let the pastry thaw on the counter before cutting the rectangles; if the dough starts to separate at the seams before you cut it, simply rejoin the seams by rolling them smooth with a rolling pin. See page 102 for a recipe to use up the leftover puff pastry.

    ½ **(9-inch square) sheet frozen puff pastry (see note; see page 101), thawed, cut into 6 rectangles (see page 184)**
    2 **tablespoons unsalted butter**
    2 **carrots, peeled and sliced ¼ inch thick**

WHITE TURKEY CHILI

1 small onion, minced

1 small head fennel, halved, cored, and chopped medium (see page 71)

¼ teaspoon ground coriander

Salt

1 cup low-sodium chicken broth

½ cup gravy (see note)

10 ounces cooked turkey (see note), shredded (about 2 cups)

1 tablespoon chopped fresh parsley or tarragon

Pepper

1. Adjust an oven rack to the middle position and heat the oven to 425 degrees. Line a rimmed baking sheet with parchment paper. Place the pastry rectangles on the prepared baking sheet and bake until puffed and light golden brown, 5 to 10 minutes. Set aside until needed.

2. Meanwhile, melt the butter in a 10-inch oven-safe skillet over medium heat. Add the carrots, onion, fennel, coriander, and ½ teaspoon salt and cook until the vegetables are softened, 5 to 7 minutes. Add the broth and gravy. Bring to a simmer, cover, and cook until the sauce has thickened slightly, 5 to 10 minutes.

3. Off the heat, stir in the turkey and parsley. Season with salt and pepper to taste. Following the photo, arrange the pastry rectangles over the filling and bake until the filling is bubbling and the pastry is deep golden brown, about 15 minutes. Let cool for 10 minutes before serving.

Turkey Curry with Carrots and Green Beans
SERVES 2

The cooked turkey and gravy in this recipe are from Pan-Roasted Turkey Breast with Gravy on page 181. Don't substitute low-fat or nonfat yogurt here, or the sauce will be too thin and have an off-flavor. If desired, ½ cup frozen peas can be substituted for the green beans.

2 tablespoons vegetable oil

1 small onion, halved and sliced thin

1 carrot, peeled and sliced ¼ inch thick

2 tablespoons raisins

4 teaspoons curry powder

Salt

2 teaspoons grated or minced fresh ginger

1 cup low-sodium chicken broth

½ cup gravy (see note)

3 ounces green beans, cut into 2-inch lengths (about ½ cup) (see note)

10 ounces cooked turkey (see note), shredded (about 2 cups)

⅓ cup plain whole-milk yogurt (see note)

2 tablespoons chopped fresh cilantro

1. Heat the oil in a 12-inch skillet over medium heat until shimmering. Add the onion, carrot, raisins, curry powder, and ½ teaspoon salt and cook until the vegetables are softened, 5 to 7 minutes. Stir in the ginger and cook until fragrant, about 30 seconds.

2. Add the broth, gravy, and green beans. Bring to a simmer, cover, and cook until the green beans are tender and the mixture has thickened slightly, 8 to 10 minutes. Stir in the turkey and cook until heated through, about 2 minutes. Off the heat, stir in the yogurt and cilantro. Season with salt to taste and serve.

NOTES FROM THE TEST KITCHEN

PREPARING THE PASTRY FOR SKILLET TURKEY POT PIE

1. Using a pizza cutter or paring knife, cut the thawed puff pastry sheet in half.

2. Cut one half-sheet of pastry in half again to make two rectangles. Then cut each rectangle into three smaller rectangles for a total of six.

3. After parbaking the puff pastry rectangles, arrange them on top of the pot pie filling and return the skillet to the oven until the pastry is golden brown.

THE BEST CURRY POWDER

Though blends can vary dramatically, curry powders come in two basic styles—mild or sweet, and a hotter version called Madras. The former combines as many as 20 different ground spices, herbs, and seeds, and is what we prefer to use in our Turkey Curry with Carrots and Green Beans. After tasting six curry powders—mixed into rice pilaf and in a vegetable curry—we determined our favorite: **Penzeys Sweet Curry Powder.** We found it to be neither too sweet nor too hot, while still being balanced yet complex.

FRENCH-STYLE POT ROAST

A GOOD POT ROAST TURNS WHAT WOULD BE A DRY and chewy cut of meat into a tender, moist, and flavorful roast. And the classic French recipe of *boeuf à la mode*—"beef in the latest fashion"—brings basic pot roast to a new level. This elegant French dish relies on wine for flavor and a lightly thickened, silky sauce and sautéed mushrooms and onions for garnish. Since this recipe is time-consuming to make, we thought it was a prime candidate for our "big roast" roster. We could cook the pot roast on Sunday; then, during the week, the meat and flavorful sauce could be transformed into two more dinners.

We began by choosing the right cut of meat, one that would provide plenty of flavor due to its fat content. After a few preliminary tests, boneless chuck-eye roast won over our tasters. Traditionally, the meat is marinated in a mixture of red wine and carrots, onions, and celery for days to pick up the wine flavor, but we decided to ax this step in favor of long braising. Three hours of a straight wine and vegetable braise, we thought, would be sufficient.

In fact, after three hours of braising, some tasters actually complained that the wine flavor was too overpowering. So, we decided to employ a common trick used when cooking with wine—simmering and reducing it before using it as an ingredient. This both intensifies its flavor and softens it at the same time. We added a bottle of red wine to the pot after sautéing our aromatics (garlic, onion, and thyme) and let it cook for 15 minutes until thickened and reduced, then added chicken and beef broths and braised the meat for three hours. Tasters were much happier with this sauce—the wine tasted intense, complex, and fruity, but not overpowering.

Compared with regular pot roast braising liquid, which is flavorful but thin and brothy, the sauce that accompanies this pot roast is richer and more luxurious. Reducing the wine helped, but our sauce wasn't there just yet. In another test, we added four slices of bacon to the pot, then sautéed the aromatics in the bacon drippings—now our sauce was improving. To balance the wine and meat flavors, we added large chunks of carrots to the braising liquid later in the cooking process. Adding some flour to the sautéed onion and garlic helped with the overall consistency; then, a quick, final simmer at the end of cooking was all this sauce needed to thicken to the proper consistency.

Most of the vegetable flavor in this dish comes from the garnish of glazed pearl onions and mushrooms, which are traditionally cooked separately and added just before serving. To speed up the process, we used frozen (not fresh) pearl onions, which we cooked until tender before adding quartered mushrooms and letting the mixture brown.

Surrounded by the well-browned mushrooms and onions, and drizzled with our intense sauce, this pot roast was the best we'd ever tasted. Now we were ready to move on to our other recipes. With 10 ounces of pot roast, a cup of flavorful sauce, and ¾ cup of pearl onion and mushroom garnish (bonus!) reserved for the next meal, we couldn't help but think of a beef *ragù*. The pot roast, sauce, and garnish were packed with so much deep, rich, beefy flavor that it was easy to make a quick ragù that tasted like it had cooked for hours. We used the leftovers to form the base of the sauce, then added processed diced tomatoes, garlic, dried oregano, and tomato paste. A touch of heavy cream enriched the dish. After just 20 minutes of simmering, we had a full-fledged beef ragù, which we then tossed with rigatoni.

Next, we took a completely different route and developed a recipe for a hearty beef and barley stew. To skimp on the cooking time, we used instant barley, which takes just 15 minutes to cook compared to the hour or so for traditional barley. Carrots added welcome sweetness and fresh vegetal flavor, but tasters wanted a little more depth. Dried porcini mushrooms, along with the water in which we soaked them, provided what we were looking for, and they also fortified the mushroom flavor from the pot roast mushrooms. In less than 30 minutes, we had a stew that tasted like it had been simmering for hours.

Last, we turned to the traditional British use for a leftover stew or braise and made a shepherd's pie—hearty chunks of meat blanketed under a mashed-potato crust. Armed with our pot roast, sauce, and garnish, all we really had to do was round out the filling with some carrots, peas, and parsley. We microwaved the carrots to give them a head start on cooking, then stirred in the remaining ingredients and transferred the mixture to a loaf pan, the perfect size for two. For the potatoes, we simply simmered them on the stove, then mashed them with butter, milk, and a single egg yolk for structure. We spread the potatoes over the filling and baked the pie at 500 degrees until the potatoes had a brown crust and the filling was hot. This pie was so good we couldn't believe it was made from leftovers.

NOTES FROM THE TEST KITCHEN

ONE ROAST BECOMES TWO
The chuck-eye roast has great flavor, but we found that the interior fat is best trimmed before cooking. Simply pull the roast apart at the natural seam and trim away the large knobs of fat from each half.

TOO FATTY

GOOD TO GO

STORING MUSHROOMS
Because of their high moisture content, mushrooms are very perishable—they can go from plump to shriveled and slimy in no time at all. Over the years we've tested numerous storage methods to find the best approach. Packaged mushrooms should be stored in their original containers; these containers are designed to "breathe," maximizing the life of the mushrooms by balancing the retention of moisture and release of ethylene gas. If you open a sealed package of mushrooms but don't use all the contents, simply rewrap the remaining mushrooms in the box with plastic wrap. Loose mushrooms can be stored in a partially open zipper-lock bag, which maximizes air circulation without drying out the mushrooms. Leaving the bag slightly open allows for the release of the ethylene gas.

Don't wrap mushrooms in a paper bag—as directed by many sources—as it turns the fungi spongy and wrinkly. And don't cover mushrooms with a damp paper towel (another common technique), as it only speeds up their deterioration.

French-Style Pot Roast
SERVES 2

You can use the leftovers to make two of the following recipes:
- Rigatoni with Beef Ragù (page 187)
- Shepherd's Pie (page 189)
- Hearty Beef and Barley Stew (page 189)

A $7 to $10 bottle of medium-bodied red table wine, such as a Côtes du Rhône, which is made from a blend of grapes, will work well here. Serve this dish with boiled potatoes, buttered noodles, or rice.

STEW

- 1 (3½ to 4-pound) boneless chuck-eye roast, pulled apart into 2 pieces, trimmed
  Salt and pepper
- 1 tablespoon vegetable oil
- 4 slices bacon, cut into ¼-inch pieces
- 1 onion, chopped medium
- 3 garlic cloves, minced
- ½ teaspoon dried thyme
- 1 tablespoon unbleached all-purpose flour
- 1 (750-ml) bottle dry red wine (see note)
- ⅔ cup low-sodium chicken broth
- ⅔ cup low-sodium beef broth
- 2 bay leaves
- 2 carrots, peeled and sliced 1½ inches thick

GARNISH

- 2 cups frozen pearl onions (8 ounces)
- ½ cup water
- 3 tablespoons unsalted butter
- 1 teaspoon sugar
- ¼ teaspoon salt
- 10 ounces white mushrooms, stems trimmed, halved if small or quartered if large
- 1 tablespoon chopped fresh parsley

1. FOR THE STEW: Adjust an oven rack to the lower-middle position and heat the oven to 300 degrees. Pat the roasts dry with paper towels and season with salt and pepper. Tie three pieces of kitchen twine around each piece of meat to keep it from falling apart. Heat the oil in a large Dutch oven over medium-high heat until just smoking. Carefully lay the roasts in the pot and cook until well browned on all sides, about 10 minutes, turning as needed and reducing the heat if the pot begins to scorch. Transfer the roasts to a plate.

2. Pour off all of the fat left in the pot, add the bacon, and cook over medium-low heat until browned and crisp, about 10 minutes. Stir in the onion and ¼ teaspoon salt and cook until softened, 5 to 7 minutes. Stir in the garlic and thyme and cook until fragrant, about 30 seconds. Stir in the flour and cook until incorporated, about 1 minute. Slowly whisk in the wine, scraping up any browned bits, and simmer until thickened slightly and reduced to about 2½ cups, about 15 minutes.

3. Stir in the broths and bay leaves and bring to a simmer. Nestle the meat, along with any accumulated juice, into the pot and return to a simmer. Cover, transfer the pot to the oven, and cook for 2 hours, flipping the meat halfway through cooking. Stir in the carrots and continue to cook in the oven, covered, until the meat is very tender and a fork inserted into the center meets little resistance, 1 to 1½ hours longer, flipping the meat again halfway through cooking.

4. FOR THE GARNISH: Meanwhile, combine the frozen pearl onions, water, butter, sugar, and salt in a 12-inch nonstick skillet. Cover and cook over medium-high heat, stirring often, until the onions are fully thawed and tender, about 10 minutes. Uncover, increase the heat to medium-high, and cook until all the liquid evaporates, about 4 minutes. Stir in the mushrooms and continue to cook, stirring occasionally, until the vegetables are dark brown and well glazed, 10 to 15 minutes. Remove from the heat and set aside.

5. Remove the pot from the oven. Transfer the meat to a carving board and tent loosely with foil while finishing the sauce. Transfer the carrots to a bowl and set aside. Using a wide spoon, skim off any fat that rises to the surface of the sauce. Bring the sauce to a simmer over medium-high heat and cook until thickened and reduced to about 3 cups, 15 to 20 minutes. Season with salt and pepper to taste. *To make any two of the recipes on pages 187–189, reserve 1¼ pounds of the meat and refrigerate in an airtight container for up to 3 days. Reserve 2 cups of the sauce and 1½ cups of the garnish, and refrigerate in separate airtight containers for up to 3 days.*

6. Remove the twine, cut the meat against the grain into ¼-inch-thick slices, and transfer to a serving platter. Stir the carrots and garnish into the sauce and rewarm over medium-low heat. Spoon the sauce and vegetables over the meat, sprinkle with the parsley, and serve.

Rigatoni with Beef Ragù
SERVES 2

The cooked pot roast, pot roast sauce, and pot roast garnish in this recipe are from French-Style Pot Roast on page 186. If you don't have heavy cream on hand, substitute 3 tablespoons unsalted butter.

½   **pound rigatoni (about 3 cups)**
    Salt
1   **(14.5-ounce) can diced tomatoes**
1   **tablespoon olive oil**
3   **garlic cloves, minced**
2   **teaspoons tomato paste**
⅛   **teaspoon dried oregano**
1   **cup pot roast sauce (see note)**
¾   **cup pot roast garnish (see note)**
10 **ounces cooked pot roast (see note), shredded (about 2 cups)**
¼   **cup heavy cream (see note)**
    Pepper
1   **tablespoon chopped fresh parsley**
    Grated Parmesan cheese, for serving

1. Bring 4 quarts water to a boil in a large pot. Add the pasta and 1 tablespoon salt and cook, stirring often, until al dente. Reserve ½ cup of the cooking water, then drain the pasta and return it to the pot.

2. Meanwhile, process the tomatoes with their juice in a food processor until pureed, about 15 seconds. Combine the oil, garlic, tomato paste, and oregano in a large saucepan, and cook over medium heat until fragrant, about 1 minute.

3. Stir in the pureed tomatoes, pot roast sauce, and pot roast garnish and simmer until the sauce has thickened and the flavors have melded, about 15 minutes. Stir the pot roast and cream into the sauce and cook until heated through, about 2 minutes. Season with salt and pepper to taste.

4. Add the sauce and parsley to the cooked pasta and toss to combine, adjusting the sauce consistency with the reserved cooking water as desired. Serve with the Parmesan.

SHEPHERD'S PIE

Shepherd's Pie

SERVES 2

The cooked pot roast, pot roast sauce, and pot roast garnish in this recipe are from French-Style Pot Roast on page 186.

- 2 russet potatoes (about 8 ounces each), peeled and cut into 1-inch cubes
- 2 tablespoons unsalted butter, softened
- ¼ cup whole milk, warmed
- 1 large egg yolk
   Salt and pepper
- 2 carrots, peeled and sliced ¼ inch thick
- 2 tablespoons water
- 10 ounces cooked pot roast (see note), shredded (about 2 cups)
- 1 cup pot roast sauce (see note)
- ¾ cup pot roast garnish (see note)
- ½ cup frozen peas
- 1 tablespoon chopped fresh parsley
- 1 garlic clove, minced

1. Adjust an oven rack to the middle position and heat the oven to 500 degrees. Put the potatoes in a medium saucepan, cover with water, and simmer until tender and a fork inserted into the center meets little resistance, about 20 minutes.

2. Drain the potatoes well and return to the saucepan over low heat. Mash the potatoes thoroughly with a potato masher. Add the butter and stir until melted, then stir in the warm milk and egg yolk. Season with salt and pepper to taste and cover to keep warm while preparing the filling.

3. Meanwhile, combine the carrots and water in a large microwave-safe bowl, cover, and microwave on high until tender, 2 to 4 minutes. Stir in the pot roast, pot roast sauce, pot roast garnish, peas, parsley, and garlic. Season with salt and pepper to taste and transfer to a 9 by 5-inch loaf pan.

4. Spread the potato topping evenly over the filling to cover it completely. Bake until the top is golden brown, about 15 minutes. Let cool for 10 minutes before serving.

Hearty Beef and Barley Stew

SERVES 2

The cooked pot roast, pot roast sauce, and pot roast garnish in this recipe are from French-Style Pot Roast on page 186. Instant barley is sometimes labeled "quick barley."

- 1 tablespoon vegetable oil
- ¼ ounce dried porcini mushrooms, rehydrated in ½ cup water, then minced, rehydrating liquid strained and reserved
- 1 tablespoon tomato paste
- ⅛ teaspoon dried thyme
- 2¼ cups water
- 1 cup pot roast sauce (see note)
- ¾ cup pot roast garnish (see note)
- 2 carrots, peeled and sliced ¼ inch thick
- ½ cup instant barley (see note)
- 10 ounces cooked pot roast (see note), shredded (about 2 cups)
- 1 tablespoon chopped fresh parsley
   Salt and pepper

1. Combine the oil, mushrooms, tomato paste, and thyme in a large saucepan, and cook over medium heat until fragrant, about 1 minute. Stir in the reserved porcini liquid, water, pot roast sauce, pot roast garnish, carrots, and barley. Bring to a simmer, cover, and cook until the carrots and barley are tender, about 20 minutes.

2. Stir in the pot roast and cook until heated through, about 2 minutes. Stir in the parsley, season with salt and pepper to taste, and serve.

NOTES FROM THE TEST KITCHEN

THE BEST CUTTING BOARD

No kitchen is complete without a good cutting board. But with so many cutting boards on the market—and so many materials to choose from—it's hard to know what to look for. We tested 13 cutting boards, made of everything from bamboo to glass, to find out which ones held up best. After cutting on, washing, and dropping each board, we determined the winner to be the **Totally Bamboo Congo**, $39.99.

MEXICAN PULLED PORK (CARNITAS)

FOR PORK LOVERS, FEW THINGS CAN TOP the rich flavor and supple texture of barbecued pulled pork. But making it is an all-day affair. In the test kitchen, we recently developed a recipe for *carnitas* (Spanish for "little meats"), a Mexican version of shredded pork, which is cooked in a lot less time. These tender chunks of pork have a lightly crisped, caramelized exterior, subtly accented by earthy oregano and bright citrus. Usually, carnitas is made in a big batch and then used as a filling in everything from tacos to burritos and enchiladas—the very same idea behind this chapter.

Getting started, we selected a boneless Boston butt, the cut most carnitas recipes call for and the same cut used for barbecued pulled pork. This shoulder roast contains a good amount of fat, which translates to deep flavor, even when some is trimmed. A 4-pound roast provided the right amount of meat for three meals for two people.

Traditionally, carnitas is prepared by gently frying well-marbled chunks of pork in gallons of lard or oil. But we opted for a common, more manageable method: simmering the meat in a seasoned broth in the oven (essentially braising it) and then sautéing it in some of the rendered fat. Over the course of several tests, we went from 8 cups of liquid down to 2, the bare minimum for cooking our roast—we wanted to braise the meat, not boil it. When the pork was so tender it fell apart, we removed it from the pot and reduced the remaining liquid on the stovetop until it had the consistency of a thick, syrupy glaze, which we would use to give our meat flavor.

Because we needed to get the exterior of the pork to crisp, more cooking was a must. Instead of sautéing the pork in the glaze, we decided to toss it with the glaze and put it in the oven. We spread the coated meat on a rack set over a rimmed baking sheet, so excess fat could drip off the pork, and turned on the broiler. To ensure that neither glaze nor meat would burn, we placed the sheet on

NOTES FROM THE TEST KITCHEN

DON'T CUT THE FAT

Leaving a ⅛-inch layer of fat on the pork is critical to imparting the best flavor and texture to our Mexican Pulled Pork (Carnitas). Overtrimming the meat will lead to dry, bland pork.

TOO LEAN   **JUST RIGHT**

WARMING TORTILLAS

Warming tortillas over the open flame of a gas burner or in a skillet gives them a toasted flavor; however, an oven or microwave will also work. If your tortillas are dry, pat them with a little water first.

If using a gas stove, toast the tortillas, one at a time, directly on the cooking grate over a medium flame until slightly charred around the edges, about 30 seconds per side. If using a skillet, toast the tortillas, one at a time, over medium-high heat until softened and speckled with brown, 20 to 30 seconds per side. Wrap the warmed tortillas in foil or a kitchen towel to them keep warm and soft until serving time.

If using an oven, stack the tortillas in a foil packet and heat at 350 degrees until warm and soft, about 5 minutes. Keep them in the foil until serving time. To use a microwave, stack the tortillas on a plate, cover with microwave-safe plastic wrap, and heat on high until warm and soft, 1 to 2 minutes. Remove the plastic wrap and cover the tortillas with a kitchen towel or foil to keep them warm and soft.

THREE STEPS TO MEXICAN PULLED PORK

1. For fall-apart tender meat, oven-braise the pork at a low temperature in a covered Dutch oven for about two hours.

2. Remove the pork and reduce the braising liquid to a glaze thick enough for a spatula to leave a trail when pulled through it.

3. Toss the pork with the glaze and broil it on the lower-middle rack in the oven to yield well-browned meat with crisp edges.

the lower-middle rack, which we'd also used for braising. Minutes later, the pork emerged from the broiler beautifully caramelized, the shredded parts of the meat transformed into crisp wisps with wonderfully rich flavor.

Next, we worked to refine the flavors in the braising liquid, which gives the pork its character. Instead of garlic, we stuck with the mellow sweetness of onion. A mix of fresh lime and orange juices, and the juiced orange halves, imparted some brightness. Bay leaves and oregano gave the meat aromatic accents. Cumin, though not a typical ingredient in carnitas, brought an earthy dimension that complemented the other flavors.

After we tucked our Mexican braised pork into warm corn tortillas and topped it with minced onion, fresh cilantro, and a spritz of lime, its mouth-watering taste and texture kept tasters coming back for more; unfortunately, we had to save some of the meat for two more meals.

Keeping with the Mexican theme, we decided to make some quick enchiladas. For the filling, we stirred refried beans, green chiles, cheese, cilantro, and some enchilada sauce into the pork. We then wrapped up the filling in tortillas and arranged them in a baking dish. To keep the tortillas from drying out and cracking, we coated them with vegetable oil spray, poured more enchilada sauce over the top, and sprinkled on a little cheese. Into the oven they went. The enchiladas that emerged—45 minutes later—were great, but we wanted to shave some time off. By microwaving the filling before rolling it up, we were able to reduce the oven time to just 10 minutes, long enough to melt the cheese.

For our next recipe, we developed an Italian-style stew with white beans. We simply sautéed onion and carrot, then added garlic, thyme, and a bay leaf for depth. Dry white wine, water, and chicken broth provided our liquid base, and tomato added color and sweetness; as we often do when cooking for two, we chose a single fresh tomato rather than using a partial can.

When we added the pork and simmered it in the stew, it became rubbery. Instead, we simmered the liquid until the flavors had blended, then we added the pork and cooked it just until it was hot. Now the only thing missing was some crusty bread—so we made big, rustic, garlicky croutons to sprinkle over the top. We tossed cubed bread with garlic, olive oil, salt, and pepper and toasted it in the oven.

Next, we changed gears and developed a ramen noodle dish with the remaining braised pork. We picked up a couple of packs of instant ramen noodle soups and ditched the sodium-heavy seasoning packets in favor of our own flavorful hot-and-sour broth (made quickly and easily with garlic, ginger, Asian chili-garlic sauce, and cider vinegar). We simmered the noodles in the broth so that they soaked up the liquid and became tender. To turn our dish into a hearty meal, we chose to partner the braised pork with shiitake mushrooms and spinach.

Our Mexican Pulled Pork—juicy and flavorful on its own—had provided us with an enticing menu of international dishes.

Mexican Pulled Pork Tacos

SERVES 2

You can use the leftovers to make two of the following recipes:

- Easy Pork Enchiladas (page 192)
- Ramen with Pork, Shiitakes, and Spinach (page 192)
- Rustic Pork and White Bean Stew with Garlic Croutons (page 193)

Boneless pork butt is often sold as Boston butt. Trim the fat cap on the pork until it is about ⅛ inch thick. In addition to the traditional taco garnishes listed below, we recommend serving the pork with fresh guacamole, salsa, and sour cream.

PORK

- 1 (4-pound) boneless pork butt, trimmed and cut into 2-inch chunks (see note)
- 2 cups water
- 1 small onion, peeled and halved
- 2 tablespoons fresh lime juice
- 2 bay leaves
- 1 teaspoon ground cumin
- 1 teaspoon dried oregano
   Salt and pepper
- 1 orange, halved

TORTILLAS AND GARNISHES

4–6 (6-inch) corn tortillas, warmed (see page 190)
   Minced white or red onion
   Fresh cilantro leaves
   Thinly sliced radishes
   Lime wedges

1. Adjust an oven rack to the lower-middle position and heat the oven to 300 degrees.

2. Combine the pork, water, onion, lime juice, bay leaves, cumin, oregano, 1 teaspoon salt, and ½ teaspoon pepper in a large Dutch oven. Juice the orange into a bowl, remove any seeds, then add the juice and spent orange halves to the pot. Bring the mixture to a simmer over medium-high heat, stirring occasionally. Cover, transfer the pot to the oven, and cook until the meat is very tender and a fork inserted into the center meets little resistance, about 2 hours, flipping the meat halfway through cooking.

3. Remove the pot from the oven and turn the oven to broil. Using a slotted spoon, transfer the pork to a bowl. Discard the orange halves, onion, and bay leaves from the braising liquid (do not defat the liquid). Bring the liquid to a simmer over medium-high heat and cook, stirring often, until the liquid is syrupy and has reduced to about 1 cup, 8 to 12 minutes.

4. Using 2 forks, pull each piece of pork in half. Gently toss the reduced braising liquid with the pork and season with salt and pepper to taste. Spread the pork in an even layer on a wire rack set over a rimmed baking sheet.

5. Place the baking sheet on the lower-middle oven rack and broil until the top of the meat is well browned (but not charred) and the edges are slightly crisp, 10 to 16 minutes, flipping the meat halfway through cooking. *To make any two of the recipes on pages 192–193, reserve 1¼ pounds of the pork and refrigerate in an airtight container for up to 3 days.* Serve with the warm tortillas and garnishes.

Easy Pork Enchiladas

SERVES 2

The braised pork in this recipe is from Mexican Pulled Pork Tacos on page 191. In addition to the lime wedges, serve these enchiladas with sour cream, diced avocado, shredded lettuce, and hot sauce.

10	ounces braised pork (about 2 cups) (see note)
½	cup canned refried beans
1	(10-ounce) can enchilada sauce
1	(4-ounce) can chopped green chiles, drained
6	(6-inch) corn tortillas, warmed (see page 190)
½	cup chopped fresh cilantro
6	ounces cheddar cheese, shredded (1½ cups)
	Vegetable oil spray
	Lime wedges, for serving

1. Adjust an oven rack to the middle position and heat the oven to 450 degrees. Lightly coat an 8-inch square baking dish with vegetable oil spray.

2. Combine the pork, refried beans, ¼ cup of the enchilada sauce, and chiles in a microwave-safe bowl, cover, and microwave on high until hot, 1 to 3 minutes; set aside.

3. Spread the warm tortillas out on a clean counter. Stir the cilantro and ¾ cup of the cheese into the pork mixture. Divide the pork mixture evenly among the centers of the tortillas, about ½ cup of filling per enchilada. Tightly roll the tortillas around the filling and lay them, seam-side down, in the prepared baking dish.

4. Lightly coat the tops of the enchiladas with vegetable oil spray. Pour the remaining enchilada sauce over the top, covering the tortillas completely. Sprinkle the remaining ¾ cup cheese down the center of the enchiladas.

5. Cover the baking dish with foil and bake until the enchiladas are heated through, about 10 minutes. Remove the foil and continue to bake until the cheese is completely melted, about 5 minutes longer. Serve with the lime wedges.

Ramen with Pork, Shiitakes, and Spinach

SERVES 2

The braised pork in this recipe is from Mexican Pulled Pork Tacos on page 191. The sauce will seem a bit brothy when finished, but the noodles will quickly absorb the liquid.

4	teaspoons vegetable oil
3	garlic cloves, minced

1 tablespoon grated or minced fresh ginger

4 ounces shiitake mushrooms, stemmed and sliced thin

2 cups low-sodium chicken broth

1 teaspoon Asian chili-garlic sauce

2 (3-ounce) packages ramen noodles, seasoning packets discarded

1 tablespoon cider vinegar

1 tablespoon soy sauce

1 teaspoon sugar

10 ounces braised pork (about 2 cups) (see note)

3 ounces baby spinach (about 3 cups)

1. Mix 1 teaspoon of the oil, the garlic, and ginger together in a small bowl and set aside. Heat the remaining 1 tablespoon oil in a 12-inch nonstick skillet over high heat until just smoking. Add the mushrooms and cook until lightly browned, about 4 minutes.

2. Clear the center of the pan and add the garlic mixture. Cook, mashing the garlic mixture into the pan with the back of a spatula, until fragrant, about 30 seconds. Stir in the broth and chili sauce.

3. Break the bricks of ramen into small chunks and add to the skillet. Bring to a simmer and cook, tossing the ramen constantly with tongs to separate, until the ramen is just tender but there is still liquid in the pan, about 2 minutes.

4. Add the vinegar, soy sauce, and sugar. Stir in the pork and cook until heated through, about 2 minutes. Stir in the spinach, a handful at a time, until wilted. Serve.

NOTES FROM THE TEST KITCHEN

ALL ABOUT RAMEN

In Japan, the term *ramen* refers to a whole category of brothy noodle dishes, but in America we are limited to "instant ramen soup"—the dried blocks of thin, wavy wheat noodles sold in cellophane with a seasoning packet. Traditionally, ramen noodles are made from wheat flour and eggs, but in many instant varieties the eggs are replaced with chemical additives and yellow food coloring. Although you can find fresh ramen noodles, labeled *chukka soba* and *shina soba*, at Asian markets, we call for the supermarket staple of packaged ramen noodles (minus the flavoring packets) in our Ramen with Pork, Shiitakes, and Spinach.

Rustic Pork and White Bean Stew with Garlic Croutons

SERVES 2

The braised pork in this recipe is from Mexican Pulled Pork Tacos on page 191. Canned navy or great Northern beans can be substituted for the cannellini beans. See page 54 for a recipe to use up the leftover cannellini beans.

3 tablespoons olive oil

3 garlic cloves, minced (about 3 teaspoons)
Salt and pepper

2 ounces French or Italian bread, cut or torn into 1-inch cubes (about 1½ cups)

1 small onion, minced (about ½ cup)

1 carrot, peeled and cut into ¼-inch pieces

½ teaspoon dried thyme

1 bay leaf

½ cup dry white wine or vermouth

1¾ cups low-sodium chicken broth

¼ cup water

¾ cup drained and rinsed canned cannellini beans (see note)

1 tomato, cored and chopped medium

10 ounces braised pork (about 2 cups) (see note)

1 tablespoon chopped fresh parsley (optional)

1. Adjust an oven rack to the middle position and heat the oven to 400 degrees. Whisk 2 tablespoons of the oil, 1 teaspoon of the garlic, ⅛ teaspoon salt, and a pinch of pepper together in a large bowl. Add the bread, toss to coat, then spread out on a rimmed baking sheet. Bake the bread cubes until golden brown, 15 to 20 minutes.

2. Meanwhile, heat the remaining 1 tablespoon oil in a large saucepan over medium heat until shimmering. Add the onion, carrot, and ½ teaspoon salt and cook until softened, 5 to 7 minutes. Stir in the remaining 2 teaspoons garlic, thyme, and bay leaf and cook until fragrant, about 30 seconds. Stir in the wine and simmer for 1 minute.

3. Stir in the broth, water, beans, and tomato and simmer until the broth is flavorful and has thickened slightly, 15 to 20 minutes. Stir in the pork and cook until heated through, about 2 minutes. Stir in the parsley (if using). Sprinkle the croutons over individual portions before serving.

WOOD-GRILLED SALMON

CHAPTER 8

DINNER OFF THE GRILL

GRILLED BONE-IN CHICKEN BREASTS WITH CHERRY TOMATOES

THERE'S A LOT TO ADMIRE about a perfectly grilled chicken breast. Cooked bone-in with the skin on for extra flavor and juiciness, the smoke-infused meat should be tender and juicy and the skin golden and crisp. But don't let the everyday nature of this grill favorite fool you: This dish isn't that easy to get right. Skin that is intermittently both flabby and burnt, and meat that is sooty and parched are too often the reality. Despite these hurdles, we knew there had to be a reliable method to produce perfectly cooked chicken breasts with crisp skin on the grill. And since we would be grilling chicken breasts for just two people, we'd have plenty of extra space on the grill to add a vegetable, making our dish more of a meal.

Many recipes recommend grilling bone-in, skin-on chicken over a blazing hot single-level fire where the coals are spread evenly over the grill. We've learned from repeated failures that this approach doesn't work. Fat from the skin drips onto the coals, and before you know it, you have an inferno on your hands that dries out the meat and chars more skin every step of the way. Building what we call a half-grill fire was a more promising technique. Pushing all the coals to one side of the grill creates a hot area and a cool area. Food placed on the cool side can cook gently through indirect heat with the cover on, with no risk of flare-ups.

We put the indirect-heat technique to the test, laying the breasts on the grill's cooler half skin-side down (to better render the fat). To promote even cooking, we faced the thicker sides of the breasts toward the hot side of the grill and borrowed a trick we sometimes use when barbecuing large cuts of meat—covering the meat with a piece of foil before closing the lid. The foil creates a sort of oven within an oven, trapping a layer of heat against the meat that maintains a consistent temperature. After 30 minutes of cooking, the meat was uniformly tender and juicy, and tasters praised its grilled flavor and minimal char. But we still had a big problem: skin that was too flabby.

We decided we would have to start the breasts directly over the heat. We tried lightly browning all sides of the chicken on the grill's hot side, keeping it there for a total of less than 10 minutes before moving it to the cooler side. This short exposure to direct heat kept flare-ups to a minimum and helped crisp the skin. The skin was better, but our tasters wanted it to be even crisper. We couldn't brown it any longer on the hot side at the beginning of grilling; that would result in exactly what we had been trying to avoid, flare-ups and charred skin. But what about at the end of cooking? We took out a new batch of breasts, started them on the hot side, moved them to the cool side until they were almost done, then put them back on the hot side to finish cooking. This three-step dance was a success. Because the coals had cooled down and the chicken had rendered most of its fat, the skin gently crisped and turned golden, unhindered by flare-ups. And because we weren't grilling for a crowd, we had ample room on the grill to move the chicken around.

For our side dish to round out the meal, we settled on cherry tomatoes—their sweetness is a perfect complement to just about anything smoky from the grill, and they require very little prep or cooking time. We tossed the tomatoes with a little extra-virgin olive oil and skewered them. They were ready for the grill, but we waited until the last minute, when the chicken was off the grill and resting, to cook them. The slightly cooled coals provided the moderate blast of heat they needed without charring them. After about six minutes on the hotter side of the grill, and a few turns, the tomatoes were pleasantly blistered but still plump and fresh-tasting.

NOTES FROM THE TEST KITCHEN

THE BEST GRILL BRUSH
Anyone who has grilled a rack of sticky barbecued ribs has had to deal with the task of removing the sugary, burned-on mess that gets left behind. We set out to find a grill brush that could make the tedious task of cleaning a gunked-up cooking grate more efficient. What did we find? Brushes with stiffer bristles fared better than their softer counterparts, but none of them worked very well. The bristles on most bent after a few strokes and trapped large quantities of gunk, thereby decreasing their efficiency. Our favorite—the **Grill Wizard Grill Brush,** $9.99—has no brass bristles to bend, break, or clog with unwanted grease and grime. Instead, this brush has one large woven mesh stainless steel scrubbing pad, which is able to conform to any cooking grate's spacing, size, and material. Best of all, the pad is detachable, washable, and replaceable (a spare is included).

As for sauce, we decided to forgo thick glazes or barbecue sauces in favor of serving the chicken and tomatoes with a light dressing. A simple vinaigrette of extra-virgin olive oil, red wine vinegar, a little garlic, and some fresh basil was all that was needed to finish this simple and flavorful dinner from the grill.

Grilled Bone-In Chicken Breasts with Cherry Tomatoes

SERVES 2

If using kosher chicken, do not brine. If brining the chicken, do not season with salt in step 3. If desired, cilantro or tarragon can be substituted for the basil. You will need two to three 12-inch metal skewers for this recipe, depending on the size of your tomatoes.

- 12 ounces cherry tomatoes (about 2 cups)
- ¼ cup extra-virgin olive oil
- 1 tablespoon red wine vinegar
- 1 garlic clove, minced
  Salt and pepper
- 2 tablespoons chopped fresh basil (see note)
- 2 (12-ounce) bone-in, skin-on split chicken breasts, trimmed (see page 7) and brined if desired (see note; see page 76)

1. Toss the tomatoes with 1 tablespoon of the oil, then thread them onto two or three 12-inch metal skewers through the stem ends. Mix the remaining 3 tablespoons oil, vinegar, garlic, ¼ teaspoon salt, and ⅛ teaspoon pepper together in a small bowl, then stir in the basil and set aside for serving.

2A. FOR A CHARCOAL GRILL: Open the bottom grill vents completely. Light a large chimney starter filled with charcoal briquettes (100 briquettes; 6 quarts). When the coals are hot, pour them in an even layer over half the grill, leaving the other half empty. Set the cooking grate in place, cover, and open the lid vents completely. Heat the grill until hot, about 5 minutes.

2B. FOR A GAS GRILL: Turn all the burners to high, cover, and heat the grill until hot, about 15 minutes. Leave the primary burner on high and turn off the other burner(s). (Adjust the primary burner as needed to maintain a hot fire; see page 211.)

3. Clean and oil the cooking grate. Pat the chicken breasts dry with paper towels and season with salt and pepper. Place the chicken breasts on the hotter part of the grill and cook (covered if using gas) until lightly browned on both sides, 6 to 10 minutes, flipping them halfway through cooking. (If flare-ups occur, slide the chicken breasts to the cooler part of the grill and mist the fire with water from a spray bottle.)

4. Slide the chicken breasts, skin-side down, to the cooler part of the grill, with the thicker sides of the breasts facing the hotter part of the grill. Tent the chicken breasts loosely with foil, cover the grill, and continue cooking until the thickest part of the breasts registers 150 degrees on an instant-read thermometer, 15 to 25 minutes longer.

5. Return the chicken breasts to the hotter part of the grill and cook (covered if using gas) until well browned on both sides and the thickest part of the breasts registers 160 to 165 degrees, 6 to 10 minutes longer, flipping them halfway through cooking. Transfer the chicken breasts to a serving platter, tent loosely with foil, and let rest.

6. While the chicken rests, place the skewered tomatoes on the hotter part of the grill and cook until the skins begin to blister and wrinkle, 3 to 6 minutes, turning the skewers as needed. Remove the skewers from the grill and carefully slide the tomatoes off the skewers and onto the platter with the chicken breasts. Drizzle the vinaigrette over the chicken breasts and tomatoes and serve.

GRILLED CHICKEN FAJITAS

ORDER FAJITAS IN A RESTAURANT and you'll usually get a showy production of sizzling meats and vegetables. But once the theatrics die down, what's left is often a disappointment—dry, stringy meat and limp, tasteless vegetables. Worse yet, the proportions are typically off, and you're left with too much filling, not enough tortillas, and too little of the toppings you so desperately need to cover up the bland flavor of the main ingredients. When done right, though, fajitas need little adornment, and the smoky grilled meat and vegetables take center stage. We wanted to develop a recipe for really great chicken fajitas—after all, fajitas are one of the few items on a menu that you can typically order for two people, and boneless, skinless breasts are readily available in small quantities. We just needed to find the right proportions of ingredients and a way to keep the chicken from drying out.

The steak in classic beef fajitas has no need for a marinade to add juiciness or flavor, but lean boneless chicken breasts need some added moisture. Starting with a mixture of vegetable oil, lime juice, garlic, salt, and pepper as our base, we tried several marinating methods. Grilling the chicken plain and tossing the

NOTES FROM THE TEST KITCHEN

THE BEST BONELESS CHICKEN BREASTS

Boneless chicken breasts are a low-fat, no-fuss, virtually ready-to-use product, which makes them standard fare in many homes. Considering their popularity, we were curious to know if there was a difference in flavor among the confusing array of options in the market. We also wondered if terms like all-natural, organic, and kosher have any real bearing on the quality and flavor of the meat. To find out, we gathered six brands of boneless, skinless chicken breasts and tried them in casseroles and sautéed with a pan sauce. When it came to the casseroles, most tasters agreed that there was very little noticeable difference from brand to brand. However, on their own, we found that the kosher and all-natural breasts had flavor and texture that

were superior to those of the average supermarket brands. In the end, we preferred **Bell & Evans,** a naturally raised brand, for its clean, rich flavor and good texture.

THE BEST PROPANE LEVEL INDICATOR

You never want to run out of gas midway through grilling. To that end, we tested three propane level indicators, which are designed to show how much fuel you have in your tank. Our favorite, which we vastly preferred over the other models, is the **Original Grill Gauge**, $13.99, which looks like a car gas gauge. You hook the indicator to the collar of the tank; when you lift the tank 3 inches off the ground, it registers the gas level by weight. But if you don't have a gas gauge or propane level indicator, don't worry. There's an easy trick to figure out how much propane is left. Bring a cup or so of water to a boil in a saucepan or kettle and pour the water over the side of the tank. Where the water succeeds in warming the tank, the tank is empty; where the tank remains cool to the touch, there is propane inside.

cooked strips with the marinade (now really a sauce) gave the chicken only superficial flavor. Brining seasoned the chicken and kept it juicy, but tasters found the meat too moist and heavy. Soaking the chicken breasts directly in the marinade yielded the best results; used this way, the marinade contributed a bright, bold tang. The highly acidic mixture (we were using ¼ cup of lime juice—a lot for just two chicken breasts) not only added fresh citrus flavor but also reduced the marinating time to a mere 15 minutes—any longer and the proteins in the meat started to break down and coagulate.

Although moving in the right direction, the marinade still lacked depth. After trying numerous flavor additions, we finally hit upon Worcestershire sauce. One tablespoon was plenty, adding a welcome layer of saltiness and smoke. A bit of brown sugar helped round out the flavors, and minced jalapeño and cilantro added freshness.

While the chicken breasts marinated, we turned our attention to the vegetables. To keep things simple, we decided to stick with the traditional bell pepper and onion. One of each was just the right amount, and tasters preferred both red bell pepper and red onion for flavor and color. Quartering the pepper allowed it to lie flat on the grill and cook evenly on both sides. Onion wedges cooked unevenly, but rounds were both pretty and practical. Placing the vegetables on the grill with the chicken, we quickly discovered that the vegetables burned easily and required more moderate heat than the chicken to cook through properly.

In order to allow the chicken and vegetables to cook side by side at slightly different heat levels, we created a simple two-level fire with more coals on one side of the grill for a hotter fire and fewer on the other side for a cooler fire. Once the grill was ready, the chicken cooked for eight to 12 minutes on the hotter side of the grill, while the vegetables cooked safely on the cooler side in the same amount of time.

As for the flour tortillas, 8 to 10-inch rounds yielded too much tortilla in proportion to the filling; smaller 6-inch tortillas were the perfect size. Three per person was just the right amount to properly contain the amount of chicken and vegetables we were using. Heating each side of the tortillas for a brief 20 seconds on the cooler side of the grill—once the chicken and vegetables were pulled off—allowed them to puff up

GRILLED CHICKEN FAJITAS

and lose their raw, gummy texture. Quickly wrapping the warmed tortillas in a clean kitchen towel or foil prevented them from becoming dry and brittle.

With the warm tortillas steaming in their wrapper, we just had to separate the onion into rings and slice the bell pepper and chicken breasts into strips. But something was still missing. In the end, we decided to reserve some of our marinade to toss with the cooked chicken strips and vegetables for a final burst of bright, fresh flavor.

Grilled Chicken Fajitas

SERVES 2

Do not marinate the chicken for longer than 15 minutes, or the lime juice will turn the meat mushy. If you decide not to warm your tortillas on the grill, see page 190 for some other options. To make this dish spicier, add the chile seeds to the marinade. Serve with sour cream, shredded cheddar or Monterey Jack cheese, and lime wedges.

    5   tablespoons vegetable oil
    ¼   cup fresh lime juice from 2 limes
    2   tablespoons chopped fresh cilantro
    3   garlic cloves, minced
    1   tablespoon Worcestershire sauce
  1½   teaspoons brown sugar
    1   jalapeño chile, stemmed, seeded, and minced
        (see note)
        Salt and pepper
    2   (6 to 8-ounce) boneless, skinless chicken breasts,
        trimmed
    1   small red onion, sliced into ½-inch rings
        (do not separate the rings)
    1   red, yellow, or orange bell pepper, stemmed,
        seeded, and quartered
    6   (6-inch) flour tortillas (see note)

1. Combine ¼ cup of the oil, lime juice, cilantro, garlic, Worcestershire, brown sugar, jalapeño, ½ teaspoon salt, and ½ teaspoon pepper in a bowl. Measure out and reserve ¼ cup of the marinade for serving. Add ½ teaspoon more salt to the remaining marinade and pour it into a large zipper-lock bag. Add the chicken breasts, seal the bag tightly, and turn to coat. Marinate the chicken in the refrigerator for 15 minutes.

2A. FOR A CHARCOAL GRILL: Open the bottom grill vents completely. Light a large chimney starter filled with charcoal briquettes (100 briquettes; 6 quarts). When the coals are hot, spread two-thirds of them evenly over the grill, then pour the remaining coals over half the grill. Set the cooking grate in place, cover, and heat the grill until hot, about 5 minutes.

2B. FOR A GAS GRILL: Turn all the burners to high, cover, and heat the grill until hot, about 15 minutes. Leave the primary burner on high and turn the other burner(s) to medium. (Adjust the burners as needed to maintain a hot fire and a medium fire on separate sides of the grill; see page 211.)

3. Clean and oil the cooking grate. Remove the chicken from the marinade, place on the hotter part of the grill, and cook (covered if using gas) until well browned on both sides and the thickest part of the breasts registers 160 to 165 degrees on an instant-read thermometer, 8 to 12 minutes, flipping them halfway through cooking. Transfer the chicken to a carving board, tent loosely with foil, and let rest.

4. While the chicken cooks, brush the onion rings and bell pepper with the remaining 1 tablespoon oil and season with salt and pepper. Place the onion rings and bell pepper on the cooler part of the grill and cook (covered if using gas) until spottily charred on both sides, 8 to 12 minutes, flipping them halfway through cooking. Transfer the vegetables to the carving board and tent loosely with foil.

5. Working in batches, place a few of the tortillas in a single layer on the cooler part of the grill and cook until warmed and lightly browned, about 20 seconds per side. As the tortillas are done, wrap them in a kitchen towel or a large piece of foil.

6. Separate the onion rings and slice the bell pepper into ¼-inch strips. Toss the vegetables together in a bowl with half of the reserved ¼ cup marinade. Slice the chicken into ¼-inch strips and toss with the remaining marinade in a separate bowl. Arrange the chicken and vegetables on a platter and serve with the warm tortillas.

GRILLED BRATWURST WITH ONION AND PEPPERS

ON THE SURFACE, FEW THINGS SOUND EASIER THAN grilling up a few bratwurst—all you need is meat and a fire. Throw some onions and peppers into the mix and you've got an easy dinner for two. But we know from experience that nicely browned links with juicy interiors can be an elusive goal. Fatty sausages drip grease onto the coals, causing flare-ups that can quickly turn exteriors into carbon while the insides remain barely cooked. The onions usually wind up mostly raw with a few charred spots. We wanted a foolproof grilling method that would cook the sausages to perfection, and we hoped to offer sweet peppers and caramelized onions as part of the bargain.

The best grilled sausages with peppers and onions we've ever eaten have come from the street vendors just outside Fenway Park. They are organized on a large scale to serve hungry mobs, but perhaps we could adapt some of their strategies to serve just two. The secret to their technique is precooking the meat with the onions and peppers on a griddle that sits on the grill's cooking grate. The onions and peppers are sliced, spread over the griddle, topped with the sausages, and then placed over the fire. Once the vegetables are nearly done and full of flavor from the meat's dripping fat, the partially cooked sausages are put directly over the flames. Because most of the meat's fat has been rendered, flare-ups are minimal. The sausage can crisp and finish cooking all the way through without risk of blackening.

The closest thing we had to a griddle was our skillet, and we really didn't want to put it on top of a searing-hot grill. But we do often use a disposable aluminum roasting pan on the grill—and it seemed a promising option. A large sliced onion, two quartered peppers, and four sausages made two good-sized dinner portions, but our ingredients were hopelessly lost inside a standard 13 by 9-inch aluminum roasting pan. We needed a tighter vessel, so that the sausage drippings could thoroughly infuse the vegetables. The vegetables and sausages fit more snugly in a smaller 8 by 8-inch aluminum baking pan.

We placed the onion and peppers in the aluminum pan, topped them with the bratwurst, and covered the pan with foil to help speed up the cooking process. We then placed the pan over a single-level fire. After 10 minutes, the sausages and peppers were nearly cooked through, so we removed them from the pan and placed them directly over the coals (we opted to brown the peppers along with the sausages). Six minutes later, we had nicely browned links infused with onion flavor, and peppers with a nice amount of char and good texture. Unfortunately, however, the onions themselves left a lot to be desired. Some were tender, others still crunchy; none had caramelized flavor.

What if we tried a different approach and gave the onions a jump start before putting them on the grill? We tried sautéing them first, seasoned with a little salt and pepper, but it took nearly 15 minutes for them to soften. Although we'd never microwaved onions before, we figured it was worth a shot. As it turned out, the microwave achieved the same results as the skillet, but in just three minutes. We then layered the uncooked peppers and sausages over the hot onions in the disposable pan and placed the pan on the grill. This time around, all the onions were perfectly soft and tender. To deepen

GRILLED BRATWURST WITH ONION AND PEPPERS

their flavor, we allowed them to caramelize in the pan on the grill for an extra five to seven minutes after taking the sausages and peppers off.

With only a little more work than it takes to throw links on the fire, we now had juicy, browned grilled bratwurst, lightly charred peppers, and sweet caramelized onions as good as any we've eaten in the shadow of a ballpark.

Grilled Bratwurst with Onion and Peppers
SERVES 2

We prefer bratwurst, but this recipe will work with any raw, uncooked sausage.

    1   large onion, halved and sliced thin
    ¼   teaspoon salt
    ⅛   teaspoon pepper
    2   red bell peppers, stemmed, seeded, and quartered
    1   (8-inch square) disposable aluminum roasting pan
    1   pound bratwurst (about 2 links) (see note)
    2   hot dog buns, toasted

1. Combine the onion, salt, and pepper in a medium microwave-safe bowl. Cover with plastic wrap and microwave on high until the onion begins to soften and turn translucent at the edges, 3 to 6 minutes, stirring halfway through cooking (be careful of the steam). Transfer the onion, along with the bell peppers, to the disposable aluminum baking pan. Place the sausages in a single layer on the vegetables and cover the pan tightly with foil.

2A. FOR A CHARCOAL GRILL: Open the bottom grill vents completely. Light a large chimney starter filled with charcoal briquettes (100 briquettes; 6 quarts). When the coals are hot, pour them in an even layer over the grill. Set the cooking grate in place, cover, and open the lid vents completely. Heat the grill until hot, about 5 minutes.

2B. FOR A GAS GRILL: Turn all the burners to high, cover, and heat the grill until hot, about 15 minutes. (Adjust the burners as needed to maintain a hot fire; see page 211.)

3. Clean and oil the cooking grate. Place the disposable pan in the center of the grill, cover the grill, and cook for 10 minutes.

4. Slide the pan to one side of the grill and carefully remove the foil. Transfer the sausages and peppers directly to the cooking grate and cook (covered if using gas) until the sausages are well browned on all sides and the peppers are spottily charred, 5 to 7 minutes, turning them as needed. Transfer the sausages to a platter and tent loosely with foil. Transfer the peppers to a carving board and cut into ¼-inch strips.

5. Cover the grill and continue to cook the onion, stirring occasionally, until beginning to brown and the liquid has evaporated, 5 to 7 minutes longer. Return the sliced peppers to the pan with the onion and serve with the sausages in buns.

VARIATIONS
Grilled Bratwurst with Onion and Fennel
Follow the recipe for Grilled Bratwurst with Onion and Peppers, omitting the red bell peppers and adding 1 fennel bulb, halved, cored, and sliced thin, to the bowl with the onion before microwaving in step 1.

Grilled Bratwurst with Sauerkraut and Apples
Follow the recipe for Grilled Bratwurst with Onion and Peppers, omitting the onion and red bell peppers. Combine 2 Granny Smith apples, peeled and grated on the large holes of a box grater, 1 cup drained sauerkraut, and ⅛ teaspoon dried sage in the disposable pan (do not microwave). Place the sausages in a single layer on top of the sauerkraut mixture and cook as directed in step 4. Omit step 5 and serve the sausages with the sauerkraut mixture after the sausages are browned.

GRILLED PORK CHOPS WITH SWEET POTATOES

WHEN YOU'RE FIRING UP THE GRILL for just two people and pork is what you want, chops are the way to go; other cuts of pork (such as a shoulder roast) are typically all-day affairs and can easily feed a dozen hungry people. But because pork chops are relatively lean, they have a tendency to dry out on the grill. Thick sauces and glazes are often slathered on to mask the flavorless, leathery meat. We wanted a chop with a deeply browned crust, and meat that would be tender and juicy all the way to the bone. And although we have nothing against a flavorful glaze, we think it should complement the pork, not hide it.

For grilling, we knew bone-in thick-cut chops were the best choice. We like center-cut chops and rib chops, both of which are cut from the middle of the pig's loin. Both are tender and flavorful, but tasters preferred the rib chops, which were juicy and well marbled with fat.

We have found single-level fires to be problematic when cooking bone-in chicken breasts and T-bone steaks, and sure enough, they didn't work here either. The chops developed a beautiful bronze exterior within minutes, but when we checked their temperature they were completely raw inside. Leaving the chops on the grill longer would only burn our perfect crust before we'd even glazed them.

Next we tried a two-level fire, which is achieved by putting more hot coals on one side of the grill than on the other, thereby creating two different heat zones. This approach worked better—starting the chops over high heat to brown the exterior and then moving them to the cooler part of the grill to finish cooking—but it still failed to produce a thoroughly cooked interior in a reasonable amount of time. Thinking about our recipe for grilled bone-in chicken breasts (see page 197) in which we cover the breasts with foil for part of the cooking time, we decided to give this technique a try. We seared the chops over high heat, then moved them to the cooler part of the grill, brushed them with a basic glaze, and covered them loosely with foil before putting the lid on. Less than 10 minutes later (we flipped and glazed the chops after about five minutes), the interior of the chops registered between 140 and 145 degrees, so we took them off the grill to rest and finish coming up to temperature. This time we had a crisp crust underneath the glaze and flavorful, juicy meat.

Turning our attention to the glaze, we whipped up a few different flavor combinations for tasters to sample. They particularly liked the sweet-tangy combination of maple syrup and mustard. After testing a variety of mustards, we decided the glaze was best with two: Dijon for its sharp piquancy and whole-grain for its texture. Extra-virgin olive oil and a pinch of cayenne completed the glaze. Our glaze was not only flavorful, but quick and convenient as well—it was naturally thick so it required no reducing, and it consisted entirely of items we already had in our pantry.

Since we were cooking only two chops, we had a lot of free space on the grill and decided to add some sweet potatoes (a nice complement to pork) to complete our meal. We tried grilling them whole and halved; tasters unanimously preferred the dark grill marks and concentrated flavor of the halved potatoes. We rubbed the potatoes with oil, seasoned them with salt, and parcooked them in the microwave for several minutes to give them a head start, just as we have done with other types of potatoes before grilling.

While browning the chops on the hotter part of the grill, we placed the potatoes, cut-side down, on the

NOTES FROM THE TEST KITCHEN

THE BEST BASTING BRUSH
Pastry brushes can brush egg whites onto dough just fine, but they're poor at slathering barbecue sauce onto meat on a hot grill. We wanted a good barbecue basting brush that allowed us to neatly and safely baste our food. We found plenty of options made from myriad materials, with handles measuring everywhere from 6 to 15 inches. We tested seven brushes, and the **Precision Grill Tools Super BBQ Silicone Basting Brush,** $8.99, proved our favorite. With its angled brush head and good handle length, this brush let testers baste each food item comfortably and precisely, no matter the shape of the food or its location on the grill. The brush is easy to clean, both in the dishwasher and by hand.

THE BEST GRILL TONGS
For the most part, we pass on the new models of tongs that appear each grilling season and just rely on a traditional and effective pair. But to make sure that we weren't missing anything, we picked up a few of the latest on the market. Unfortunately, most looked and performed like medieval torture devices, with sharp, serrated edges and claw-like pincers that repeatedly nicked the surface of steaks and shredded fish into flakes. Our overall winner was a plain pair of **OXO Good Grips 16-Inch Locking Tongs,** $14.95. Not only do they grip, turn, and move food around the grill easily, but they are also long enough to keep hands a safe distance from the grill.

cooler part. Nicely browned on both sides and moist throughout by the time the chops were ready to eat, these sweet potatoes were delicious as they were, but they were even better when chopped up and gently coated with a light vinaigrette featuring balsamic vinegar, shallot, and chopped fresh tarragon for a quick warm potato salad.

Grilled Glazed Pork Chops with Tarragon Sweet Potatoes

SERVES 2

If the pork is "enhanced" (see page 80 for more information), do not brine. If brining the pork, do not season with salt in step 5. Toss the sweet potatoes with the vinaigrette while they are warm so they absorb maximum flavor.

SWEET POTATOES

- ¼ cup extra-virgin olive oil
- 2 tablespoons chopped fresh tarragon
- 1 tablespoon balsamic vinegar
- 1 small shallot, minced (about 1 tablespoon)
  Salt and pepper
  Pinch sugar
- 2 small sweet potatoes (8 ounces each), scrubbed and halved lengthwise

PORK CHOPS

- 2 tablespoons maple syrup
- 2 tablespoons Dijon mustard
- 2 tablespoons whole-grain mustard
- 2 tablespoons extra-virgin olive oil
  Pinch cayenne pepper
  Salt and pepper
- 2 (12 to 14-ounce) bone-in rib or center-cut pork chops, about 1½ inches thick, brined if desired (see note; see page 76)

1. FOR THE SWEET POTATOES: Combine 3 tablespoons of the oil, tarragon, vinegar, shallot, ¼ teaspoon salt, ⅛ teaspoon pepper, and sugar in a medium bowl and set aside for serving.

2. Place the sweet potatoes in a single layer on a large microwave-safe plate and poke each sweet potato several times with a skewer. Brush the sweet potatoes with the remaining 1 tablespoon oil and season with salt.

Microwave on high until the sweet potatoes soften but still hold their shape, 6 to 8 minutes, flipping them halfway through cooking.

3. FOR THE PORK CHOPS: Combine the maple syrup, mustards, oil, cayenne, a pinch of salt, and a pinch of pepper in a small bowl. Measure out and reserve ¼ cup of the glaze and set aside for serving.

4A. FOR A CHARCOAL GRILL: Open the bottom grill vents completely. Light a large chimney starter filled with charcoal briquettes (100 briquettes; 6 quarts). When the coals are hot, spread two-thirds of them evenly over the grill, then pour the remaining coals over half the grill. Set the cooking grate in place, cover, and open the lid vents completely. Heat the grill until hot, about 5 minutes.

4B. FOR A GAS GRILL: Turn all the burners to high, cover, and heat the grill until hot, about 15 minutes. Leave the primary burner on high and turn the other burner(s) to medium. (Adjust the burners as needed to maintain a hot fire and a medium fire on separate sides of the grill; see page 211.)

5. Clean and oil the cooking grate. Pat the pork chops dry with paper towels and season with salt and pepper. Place the pork chops on the hotter part of the grill and cook (covered if using gas) until well browned on both sides, 6 to 10 minutes, flipping them halfway through cooking.

6. Slide the pork chops to the cooler part of the grill, brush with the glaze, and tent loosely with foil. Cover the grill and continue to cook until the center of the chops registers 140 to 145 degrees on an instant-read thermometer, 7 to 9 minutes longer, flipping and brushing them with the glaze halfway through cooking. Transfer the pork chops to a serving platter, tent loosely with foil, and let rest until the center of the chops registers 150 degrees, 5 to 10 minutes.

7. While the pork chops cook on the hotter part of the grill, place the sweet potatoes, cut-side down, on the cooler part of the grill. Cook until well browned on both sides and the tip of a paring knife slips in and out of the sweet potatoes easily, 18 to 20 minutes, flipping them halfway through cooking.

8. Transfer the potatoes to a carving board and cut into 1-inch pieces, then add them to the bowl with the reserved vinaigrette and toss to coat. Transfer the sweet potatoes to the platter with the pork chops and serve, passing the reserved glaze separately.

GRILLED T-BONE STEAK

GRILLED PORTERHOUSE OR T-BONE STEAK WITH POTATOES

BOTH T-BONE AND PORTERHOUSE STEAKS contain a T-shaped bone down the middle that divides a beefy, tender New York strip steak on one side from a supple, buttery piece of tenderloin on the other—two great steaks in one. (The porterhouse contains a larger tenderloin, making it pricier.) One of these large steaks easily serves two and allows each person to sample both cuts of meat, so we naturally thought it would be a perfect fit for our grilling chapter. And with only one steak on the grill, why not throw on a side dish to complete the meal? We immediately thought of potatoes, a classic pairing with steak.

This sounded simple enough, but we knew we couldn't just throw a steak and some potatoes on the grill and hope for the best. The strip portion of a T-bone contains a fair amount of fat, which has a tendency to drip on the fire below it, causing flare-ups and charring the meat. Moving the steak periodically prevents charring, but it also keeps it from developing a good crust. Since we wanted it all—a dark crust, smoky aroma, and deep grill flavor—we had our work cut out for us. And we had a hunch that success would depend on the setup of our grill.

We knew a single-level fire (where the coals are spread evenly across the grill) was out. We wouldn't get the crust we wanted with all those flare-ups. We would need two levels of heat—a hotter zone to sear the outside of the steak and a cooler zone where the interior of the steak could finish cooking through. After lighting a full chimney of coals, we built a two-level fire by placing more coals on one side of the grill than on the other. When the grill was hot, we browned our steak on the side with more coals before sliding it to the cooler side. The results were encouraging. Flare-ups were reduced (the flare-ups on the cooler side were too small to touch the meat) and the steak had a pretty decent crust.

But we knew we could do better. We looked to refine our technique and tried placing all the coals on one half of the grill, leaving the other side empty. The steak took about six minutes per side to get an impressive sear on the hot side, and then we slid it over to the cooler side to allow the indirect heat to gently finish cooking the interior. This steak was by far the best yet.

One problem remained. Though tasters were impressed with the crust and the steak's grilled flavor, they found the coveted tenderloin section to be somewhat tough and dry. The solution turned out to be a simple one: Position the meat so that the tenderloin faced the cooler side of the grill. This allowed the delicate tenderloin to cook at a slightly slower rate and stay tender and juicy.

Now that our grilling technique for the steak was perfected, we addressed the potatoes. The test kitchen's established technique for grilling potatoes is to halve and skewer small red potatoes (which don't fall apart on the grill), parboil them, brush them with olive oil, and then quickly place them on the hot grill. Besides yielding perfectly cooked potatoes—charred (not burnt) exteriors, smooth and creamy interiors, and plenty of smoky flavor—the skewers hold them together, allowing for hassle-free transfer from pot to grill to serving platter.

Although this technique needed no improvement, it was a little more hassle than we wanted when grilling for two people. We decided to try precooking the skewered potatoes in the microwave. We brushed them with oil to prevent sticking, seasoned them with salt, microwaved them, and threw them on the grill. This streamlined approach worked great, except for one thing: The interiors of the potatoes remained unseasoned. Piercing each potato prior to microwaving encouraged the salt on the skin to migrate to the inside. We added a final boost of flavor by tossing the grilled potatoes with olive oil, chives, and garlic before serving.

Grilled Porterhouse or T-Bone Steak with Red Potatoes
SERVES 2

You will need two 12-inch wooden skewers for this recipe. We prefer this steak cooked to medium-rare, but if you prefer it more or less done, see our guidelines in "Testing Meat for Doneness" on page 208.

- 2 **tablespoons extra-virgin olive oil**
- 2 **tablespoons minced fresh chives**
- 1 **small garlic clove, minced**

TWO TYPES OF T-BONES

Both T-bone and porterhouse steaks contain a strip steak and a tenderloin steak connected by a T-shaped bone. Technically, a T-bone must have a tenderloin portion at least ½ inch across, and a porterhouse's tenderloin must measure at least 1¼ inches across.

T-BONE   **PORTERHOUSE**

CARVING PORTERHOUSE AND T-BONE STEAKS

1. After the meat has rested, start by slicing close to the bone to remove the strip section.

2. Turn the steak around and cut the tenderloin section off the bone.

3. Slice the strip and tenderloin crosswise ¼ to ½ inch thick.

SKEWERING POTATOES FOR THE GRILL

Place a potato half cut-side down on the counter and pierce it through the center with a skewer. Repeat, holding the already-skewered potatoes for better leverage.

TESTING MEAT FOR DONENESS

An instant-read thermometer is the most reliable method for checking the doneness of chicken, duck, beef, and pork, and a simple nick-and-peek test—making a small nick at the center of the fish and judging its color—works best for thick pieces of fish. Cutlets, thin fish fillets, shrimp, and scallops all cook too quickly for an actual doneness test and you should rely more on visual cues and cooking times.

To use an instant-read thermometer, simply insert it through the side of a chicken breast, steak, or pork chop. The chart below lists temperatures at which the meat should be removed from the heat; the temperature of the meat, with the exception of chicken and turkey, will continue to climb between 5 and 10 degrees as it rests before serving.

WHEN IS IT DONE?

MEAT	COOK UNTIL IT REGISTERS	SERVING TEMPERATURE
Chicken and Turkey Breasts	160 to 165 degrees	*
Chicken Thighs	175 degrees	*
Duck Breasts		
Medium-rare	120 to 125 degrees	130 degrees
Medium	130 to 135 degrees	140 degrees
Medium-well	140 to 145 degrees	150 degrees
Well-done	150 to 155 degrees	160 degrees
Pork	140 to 145 degrees	150 degrees
Beef and Lamb		
Rare	115 to 120 degrees	125 degrees
Medium-rare	120 to 125 degrees	130 degrees
Medium	130 to 135 degrees	140 degrees
Medium-well	140 to 145 degrees	150 degrees
Well-done	150 to 155 degrees	160 degrees

*Not applicable.

Salt and pepper

12 ounces small red potatoes (about 4), halved and skewered (see page 208)

1 (1¾-pound) porterhouse or T-bone steak, 1 to 1½ inches thick

1. Combine 1 tablespoon of the oil, chives, garlic, ¼ teaspoon salt, and ⅛ teaspoon pepper in a medium bowl and set aside for serving. Place the skewered potatoes on a large microwave-safe plate and poke each potato several times with a skewer. Brush the potatoes with the remaining 1 tablespoon oil and season with salt. Microwave on high until the potatoes soften but still hold their shape, 6 to 8 minutes, flipping them halfway through cooking.

2A. FOR A CHARCOAL GRILL: Open the bottom grill vents completely. Light a large chimney starter filled three-quarters with charcoal briquettes (75 briquettes; 4½ quarts). When the coals are hot, pour them in an even layer over half the grill, leaving the other half empty. Set the cooking grate in place, cover, and heat the grill until hot, about 5 minutes.

2B. FOR A GAS GRILL: Turn all the burners to high, cover, and heat the grill until hot, about 15 minutes. Leave the primary burner on high and turn the other burner(s) to low. (Adjust the burners as needed to maintain a hot fire and a low fire on separate sides of the grill; see page 211.)

3. Clean and oil the cooking grate. Pat the steak dry with paper towels and season with salt and pepper. Place the steak on the hotter part of the grill with the tenderloin side facing the cooler part of the grill. Cook (covered if using gas) until well browned on both sides, 10 to 15 minutes, flipping the steak halfway through cooking and turning so that the tenderloin is still facing the cooler part of the grill. (If flare-ups occur, slide the steak to the cooler part of the grill and mist the fire with water from a spray bottle.)

4. Slide the steak to the cooler part of the grill, with the bone side facing the hotter part of the grill. Cover and continue to cook until the center of the steak registers 125 degrees on an instant-read thermometer (for medium-rare), 2 to 6 minutes longer, flipping it halfway through cooking. Transfer the steak to a carving board, tent loosely with foil, and let rest.

5. While the steak cooks on the cooler part of the grill, place the potatoes, cut-side down, on the hotter part of the grill. Cover and cook until browned on both sides, 4 to 6 minutes, flipping them halfway through cooking. Slide the potatoes to the cooler part of the grill, cover, and continue to cook until the tip of a paring knife slips in and out of the potatoes easily, 4 to 6 minutes longer.

6. Remove the skewers from the grill, carefully slide the potatoes off the skewers into the bowl with the reserved oil mixture, and toss to combine. Following the photos on page 208, cut the strip and filet pieces of steak off the bone, then cut each piece crosswise into ¼ to ½-inch-thick slices. Serve with the potatoes.

GRILLED BEEF AND VEGETABLE KEBABS

BEEF AND VEGETABLE KEBABS ARE STANDARD GRILL fare. Unfortunately, many of us have come to accept mediocre kebabs as the norm. Recipes we came across in our research offered beef that was incinerated on the outside but raw on the inside, or so overcooked and dry that it was impossible to cut, let alone chew. And the veggies cooked at different rates, ending up charred in spots but still raw overall, or so overcooked and mushy that they fell apart. Still, there's plenty to like about kebabs: They're easy, they can be tailored to the number of diners, and they require minimal preparation. We just needed to find a way to preserve the juiciness and flavor of the beef while still obtaining a rich, caramelized exterior. And we needed to find the right combination of vegetables that would not only cook at the same rate, but would also give us enough variety without leaving us with a refrigerator full of half-used vegetables.

We knew that choosing the right cut of beef was essential. Given that we didn't want to pay top price for a premium cut, we considered which cheaper cuts of meat would be tender enough to use for kebabs. We also wanted a cut of meat that wasn't too hard to cut into smaller pieces. In some cuts of meat, fat and sinew are abundant, making it extremely hard to prepare evenly sized pieces for the skewer. We weren't about to spend an hour trimming and cutting intramuscular fat and connective tissue to make four skewers of kebabs. It had to be a simple, quick process.

GRILLED BEEF AND VEGETABLE KEBABS

The three cuts that fit these requirements were flank steak, blade steak, and sirloin steak tips (flap meat). We bought all three kinds, cut them into cubes, threaded the meat onto skewers, and placed them on the hot grill. The flank was plenty beefy, but it was tough unless it was thinly sliced against the grain. Blade steaks were beefy and tender, but they contained a line of gristle that, once removed, left strips of meat too thin to be cut into decent-sized (1½-inch) cubes. The steak tips met both criteria: They were very affordable and did not contain too much fat or connective tissue.

NOTES FROM THE TEST KITCHEN

HOW HOT IS YOUR FIRE?

To determine the heat level of the cooking grate itself, heat up the grill and hold your hand 5 inches above the cooking grate, counting how long you can comfortably keep it there. Note that this works with both charcoal and gas grills.

Hot fire	2 seconds
Medium-hot fire	3 to 4 seconds
Medium fire	5 to 6 seconds
Medium-low fire	7 seconds

FIGHTING FLARE-UPS

Flare-ups from the grill are a not-so-rare occurrence, caused primarily by fats melting into the fire. They are much more problematic with charcoal grills since the burners on gas grills often have covers to protect them. Regardless, sometimes there's just no avoiding them, so it's important to make sure a little flare-up doesn't turn into an out-of-control grease fire that ruins your meal. We recommend keeping a squirt bottle or plant mister filled with water near the grill. At the first sign of flames, pull foods to a cool part of the grill and douse the flames with water.

THE BEST SKEWERS

While developing our recipes, we learned a lot about which skewers were best—and worst—for grilling. Though wooden skewers are occasionally called for in a recipe, as in our Grilled Porterhouse or T-Bone Steak with Red Potatoes (page 207), in which the potatoes are microwaved on skewers, we generally prefer metal skewers since they're reusable and can handle the heartiest of kebabs. Just be sure to stay away from round skewers; they flip just fine, but the food stays in place. Flat skewers proved much more effective. Our favorites are **Norpro's 12-Inch Stainless Steel Skewers** (six skewers for $10). They never burn, last forever, and hold the food in place.

In the past we have employed a soy sauce marinade to keep our steak tips juicy. The sodium in the soy sauce acts like a brine and helps the meat retain moisture when cooked. Since steak tips have a lot of beefy flavor that we didn't want to mask, we kept our marinade simple with a combination of soy sauce, olive oil, garlic, and pepper. We then poked the meat with a fork to allow the marinade to penetrate deeply. After 10 to 15 minutes on a hot grill, the beef tasted great and was nicely browned.

Our beef was just how we wanted it, but now we had to choose the right vegetables to go with it. Since the beef and vegetables would be going on the same skewers, we knew the vegetables needed to be able to stand up to the heat of the grill for the same amount of time as the beef. This quickly ruled out cherry tomatoes; 10 minutes or more of grill time caused them to rupture and turn to mush. Onions, peppers, and mushrooms fared much better, and we were able to use them in quantities that didn't leave us with any leftovers—we needed just one onion, one pepper, and 5 ounces of mushrooms for four kebabs. But we found the vegetables to be a little bland and undercooked by the time the meat was done. Letting the vegetables soak in extra marinade improved their flavor a bit but didn't help them cook any faster, and cooking the vegetables on separate skewers from the meat did not allow the flavors of the meat and vegetables to meld together. We knew the vegetables had to be parcooked before hitting the grill, so we microwaved them—with the marinade for flavor—for a few minutes. Now when we skewered our meat and vegetables together, they finished cooking at the same rate, giving us a simple and satisfying meal for two.

Grilled Beef and Vegetable Kebabs

SERVES 2

Do not marinate the beef for more than 2 hours or it will become too salty. You will need four 12-inch metal skewers for this recipe. If you have pieces of meat smaller than 1½ inches, thread two small pieces together to approximate a 1½-inch cube.

⅓ cup olive oil
¼ cup soy sauce
2 garlic cloves, minced

½ teaspoon pepper

1 pound steak tips, poked all over with a fork and cut into 1½-inch chunks

1 red bell pepper, stemmed, seeded, and cut into 1½-inch pieces

1 small red onion, cut into 1½-inch pieces

5 ounces white mushrooms, stemmed

1. Mix the oil, soy sauce, garlic, and pepper together in a large microwave-safe bowl. Measure out ¼ cup of the soy sauce mixture and transfer to a large zipper-lock bag. Add the steak tips, seal the bag tightly, and turn to coat. Marinate the steak tips in the refrigerator for at least 1 hour or up to 2 hours.

2. Add the bell pepper, onion, and mushrooms to the bowl with the remaining soy sauce mixture and toss to coat. Cover with plastic wrap and marinate at room temperature for 30 minutes.

3. Microwave the vegetables on high until the onions begin to soften and turn translucent at the edges, 3 to 6 minutes, stirring halfway through cooking (be careful of the steam). Remove the plastic wrap from the bowl and set aside until the meat is marinated.

4. Thread the meat and vegetables evenly onto four 12-inch metal skewers, starting and ending with the meat.

5A. FOR A CHARCOAL GRILL: Open the bottom grill vents completely. Light a large chimney starter filled with charcoal briquettes (100 briquettes; 6 quarts). When the coals are hot, pour them in an even layer over the grill. Set the cooking grate in place, cover, and heat the grill until hot, about 5 minutes.

5B. FOR A GAS GRILL: Turn all the burners to high, cover, and heat the grill until hot, about 15 minutes. (Adjust the burners as needed to maintain a hot fire; see page 211.)

6. Clean and oil the cooking grate. Place the kebabs on the grill and cook (covered if using gas) until the meat is well browned on all sides and the vegetables are tender, 10 to 14 minutes, turning as needed. Remove the skewers from the grill, slide the beef and vegetables off the skewers onto a platter, and serve.

ARGENTINE-STYLE GRILLED BEEF SHORT RIBS

WE LOVE BEEF SHORT RIBS, but they are typically a time-consuming affair—slow, extended braising is usually the method of choice to make this cut of meat extremely yielding and tender. If you're going to spend that much time preparing short ribs, you might as well make them for a crowd. When we want to make short ribs for just two people, we turn to grilling—it's simple and it takes a fraction of the time that braising does. And one of our favorite ways to serve grilled beef short ribs is drizzled with chimichurri—a thick vinaigrette-like sauce bursting with the flavors of parsley and garlic that is popular in Argentina. We wanted to uncover a foolproof technique for cooking short ribs on the grill, and while we were at it we wanted to add some vegetables to make a complete meal for two.

With some short ribs ready for the grill, we pitted three grilling methods against one another, but none worked perfectly. Grilling the meat directly over a bed of hot coals (as we would a regular steak) merely burned the exterior before the thick middle portion was cooked through. Grilling over a more moderate fire worked a little better, but we still found the interior to be tough by the time the exterior was properly seared. Using a grill-roasting method in which the coals are banked on one side while the ribs lie on the opposite side, we hoped that the gentler indirect heat would solve our problems, but no such luck. After just half an hour of grill-roasting, the meat became dry and stringy. Worse, there were several layers of unrendered fat throughout each rib that were flabby and unappealing.

At this point, we wondered if it wasn't a butchering issue. Following the lead of some Asian recipes we've seen, we tried cutting down the ribs further before cooking. In effect, the meat is butterflied several times (slit crosswise and opened up like a book) until it is quite thin (between ¼ and ½ inch thick). Giving this a whirl, we threw the thinly cut short ribs over a hot grill, and presto! This was the meat we were looking for—tender with just a slight chew, a crisp crust, and fully rendered fat.

Now much thinner, our ribs were cooking extremely fast, in about five minutes, and we wondered how we

Herb Pesto

MAKES ABOUT ¼ CUP

Any combination of soft leaf herbs—parsley, cilantro, basil, tarragon, and chives—will work in this recipe. No more than 1 tablespoon of heartier herbs, such as thyme, rosemary, sage, and oregano, should be added. Walnuts, pecans, whole blanched almonds, skinned hazelnuts, unsalted pistachios, pine nuts, or any combination thereof can be used here. Toss the pesto with pasta, spread it on a sandwich, or use it to flavor dips and dressings. The pesto can be refrigerated in an airtight container for up to 4 days or frozen for up to 1 month.

- 1 cup packed fresh herbs (see note)
- 3 tablespoons extra-virgin olive oil
- 2 tablespoons nuts (see note), toasted (see page 226)
- 1 small garlic clove, minced
  Salt and pepper
- 2 tablespoons grated Parmesan or Pecorino Romano cheese

Process the herbs, oil, nuts, garlic, ¼ teaspoon salt, and ⅛ teaspoon pepper in a food processor until smooth, about 30 seconds, scraping down the bowl as needed. Transfer the pesto to a bowl, stir in the Parmesan, and season with salt and pepper to taste.

would coordinate their cooking time with the vegetables (we had settled on a simple mix of eggplant, zucchini, and red bell pepper), which required more moderate heat. Reducing the heat to accommodate the vegetables only caused the meat to turn pale and tough—it needed the quick sear from the high heat to cook properly. Creating two heat zones on the grill (what we call a two-level fire)—half that was hot enough to achieve the proper sear on the meat, and half that had a moderate heat level to cook the vegetables—was the answer. Once the grill was ready, the meat seared quickly on the hotter side of the grill, while the vegetables cooked safely on the cooler side. While the meat rested, we roughly chopped the vegetables and combined them in a bowl for a robust grilled salad, but we wanted something to brighten their flavor. Tossing the vegetables with a simple vinaigrette of oil, vinegar, and parsley was the perfect way to liven up our salad.

All that was left to do was work out the details of the chimichurri. Parsley and garlic are the heart of this flavorful sauce, and for more bite we added minced shallot and red pepper flakes for a little heat. Extra-virgin olive oil was favored over both regular olive oil and vegetable oil, for its ability to stand up to the boldness of the other ingredients, and red wine vinegar contributed just the right amount of acidity. We now had a unique and boldly flavored summer meal for two that can easily be prepared any night of the week.

Argentine-Style Grilled Beef Short Ribs with Summer Vegetables

SERVES 2

Italian eggplant is a smaller version of the large variety (sometimes labeled globe) that is commonly available; it has more delicate skin and flesh than larger eggplant. If you are unable to find an Italian eggplant, a slender Japanese or Asian eggplant can be substituted. Purchase English-style ribs with at least 1 inch of meat above the bone. If you choose flanken-style ribs, you will need a butcher to cut them thin enough for this recipe.

SAUCE

- ¼ cup chopped fresh parsley
- 2 tablespoons extra-virgin olive oil
- 1 small shallot, minced (about 1 tablespoon)
- 1 tablespoon red wine vinegar
- 1½ teaspoons water
- 1 garlic clove, minced
- ¼ teaspoon salt
  Pinch red pepper flakes

VEGETABLES AND SHORT RIBS

- 2 tablespoons extra-virgin olive oil
- 1 tablespoon chopped fresh parsley
- 1½ teaspoons red wine vinegar
  Salt and pepper

1 red bell pepper, stemmed, seeded,
and quartered

1 small zucchini, ends trimmed, halved lengthwise

1 small Italian eggplant, ends trimmed, halved
lengthwise (see note)

1½ pounds English-style short ribs, prepared following the
photos, or 1¼ pounds flanken-style short ribs, about
¼ inch thick (see note)

1. FOR THE SAUCE: Combine all of the ingredients in
a small bowl and let sit at room temperature while preparing the vegetables and short ribs, or cover and refrigerate for up to 2 days. (If refrigerated, let the sauce sit at
room temperature for 15 minutes before serving.)

2A. FOR A CHARCOAL GRILL: Open the bottom grill
vents completely. Light a large chimney starter filled
with charcoal briquettes (100 briquettes; 6 quarts). When
the coals are hot, spread two-thirds of them evenly over
the grill, then pour the remaining coals over half the
grill. Set the cooking grate in place, cover, and heat the
grill until hot, about 5 minutes.

2B. FOR A GAS GRILL: Turn all the burners to high,
cover, and heat the grill until hot, about 15 minutes.
Leave the primary burner on high and turn the other
burner(s) to medium. (Adjust the burners as needed to
maintain a hot fire and a medium fire on separate sides
of the grill; see page 211.)

3. FOR THE VEGETABLES AND SHORT RIBS: Combine
1 tablespoon of the oil, parsley, vinegar, ¼ teaspoon salt,
and ⅛ teaspoon pepper in a medium bowl, and set aside
for tossing with the vegetables.

4. Clean and oil the cooking grate. Brush the vegetables with the remaining 1 tablespoon oil and season
with salt and pepper. Place the vegetables on the cooler
part of the grill and cook (covered if using gas) until
spottily charred on both sides, 8 to 12 minutes, flipping
them halfway through cooking. Transfer the vegetables
to a carving board and tent loosely with foil.

5. While the vegetables cook, pat the short ribs dry
with paper towels and season with salt and pepper. Place
the short ribs on the hotter part of the grill and cook
(covered if using gas) until well browned on both sides,
4 to 6 minutes, flipping them halfway through cooking.
Transfer the short ribs to a platter, tent loosely with foil,
and let rest.

6. Cut the vegetables into 1-inch pieces, add them to
the bowl with the reserved vinaigrette, and toss to coat.
Serve the vegetables with the short ribs and sauce.

NOTES FROM THE TEST KITCHEN

BUYING SHORT RIBS

Short ribs are just what their name says they are: short ribs
cut from any location along the length of the cow's ribs. They
can come from the lower belly section or higher up toward
the back, from the shoulder (or chuck) area or the forward
midsection. Short ribs can be butchered in one of two ways.
Most likely you will see English-style short ribs—single ribs
surrounded by a thick, blocky chunk of meat. Flanken-style
short ribs are sliced across the bones, so that each piece is a
cross section of several bones surrounded by meat.

ENGLISH-STYLE   FLANKEN-STYLE

PREPARING ENGLISH-STYLE RIBS FOR THE GRILL

1. With a paring or
boning knife, trim the
surface fat and silver skin
from each rib.

2. Make a cut into the
meat right above the
bone. Continue cutting
almost but not quite all
the way through the meat.
Open the meat onto a
cutting board, as you
would open a book.

3. Make another cut into
the meat, parallel to the
board, making the lower
half of the section of meat
that you are slicing about
¼ inch thick, cutting
almost but not all the
way through to the end
of the meat.

4. Repeat step 3 as needed,
one or two more times,
until the meat is about
¼ inch thick throughout.
You should have a bone
connected to a long strip of
meat about ¼ inch thick.
Cut the meat off the bone
and discard the bone.

WOOD-GRILLED SALMON WITH ASPARAGUS

THE PREMISE OF WOOD-GRILLED SALMON IS SIMPLE: Salmon fillets are set on a soaked plank of aromatic cedar wood, which is then placed on the grill. Soaking the plank keeps the fish moist during cooking and prevents the soft, resinous cedar from smoking too heavily or, in the worst case, combusting. What makes this dish especially appealing is that because of the moderate amount of smoke, the fish is perfumed with subtle wood flavor instead of the heady, overpowering flavors that many smoked fish recipes suffer from. This characteristic of the dish also makes for a perfect pairing with a grilled vegetable instead of the typically rich sides that are meant to balance out boldly flavored smoked items. The resulting combination is an elegant grilled meal.

After taking a trip to pick up some cedar planks from our local specialty foods store, we settled in and got to work. We soaked the planks for an hour, topped them with salmon fillets, and put them on the cooking grate, covered, over high heat. With a bit of fiddling (and yes, we did ignite a plank during one failed, though memorable, test), we were able to produce moist salmon tinged with a nice wood flavor. Now that we knew what we were after, we wondered if we could achieve the same results without making a special trip for planks.

Wood chips are generally by our side throughout the grilling season and seemed like the best option. We knew we couldn't simply swap them for the plank because the chips would fall through the cooking grate, so we made two individual foil trays to hold the chips and the salmon—a technique that would be impractically time-consuming if serving a group, but easy enough for just two. We tossed a handful of soaked chips in each tray, laid our fillets on top, and set the trays on the grill's hot cooking grate.

The soaked chips lent some nice woody flavor to the fish, but they adhered to the salmon flesh, making for mangled fillets once cooked. To remedy this, we left the skin on the salmon, which protected the flesh from the chips; once the fish was cooked, we could easily separate the skin and discard it. The resulting moist, fully intact fillets had some wood flavor, but we wanted more. Poking a few holes in the bottom of the foil allowed even more heat to reach the wood chips, causing them to release more of their woody flavor without making our fish taste overly smoky.

Though the flavor and texture were now exactly where we wanted them to be, the fillets were unappealingly pale. Following the lead of a few recipes we had come across, we tried packing the fillets in a heavy coating of brown sugar before grilling them. This method of caramelizing the sugar produced an appealing golden hue, but it made the fish candy-sweet. A better solution was to coat each fillet with a thin layer of olive oil and a light sprinkling of granulated sugar. These fillets were perfectly golden, and the mildly sweet exterior surrounding the smoky-rich salmon tasted just as good as it looked.

Now that we had flavorful, perfectly cooked salmon, we wanted grilled vegetables to complement it. However, cooked over high heat along with the salmon, our vegetables were burning no matter which vegetables we used or how we adjusted the heat. The solution was to grill the vegetables after the salmon had finished cooking and was resting off the grill. Asparagus worked the best, in part because its flavor pairs well with salmon but also because it cooked quickly, ensuring our salmon would not have a chance to get cold. Cooked separately but served together, the combination of subtly smoky salmon and bright, crisp-tender asparagus makes for a winning meal from the grill.

Wood-Grilled Salmon with Asparagus
SERVES 2

Any variety of wood chips will work here, but we think aromatic woods such as cedar and alder contribute the best flavor. We prefer salmon cooked to medium, but if you prefer it more or less done, adjust the cooking time in step 3 accordingly.

- ¾ teaspoon sugar
  Salt and pepper
- 2 (6 to 8-ounce) skin-on salmon fillets, about 1½ inches thick
- 2 tablespoons olive oil
- 1 cup wood chips, soaked in water for 15 minutes and drained (see note)
- 1 bunch asparagus (about 1 pound), tough ends trimmed (see page 224)

1. Combine the sugar, ¼ teaspoon salt, and ⅛ teaspoon pepper in a bowl. Pat the salmon fillets dry with paper towels, then brush the flesh sides with 1 tablespoon of the oil and rub evenly with the sugar mixture. Following the photos, use heavy-duty foil to make two 7 by 5-inch trays. Perforate the bottom of each tray with the tip of a knife. Divide the wood chips between the trays and lay a salmon fillet, skin-side down, on top of the wood chips in each tray.

NOTES FROM THE TEST KITCHEN

CLEANING THE GRATE

After cleaning the grate with a grill brush, it is important to oil it to prevent food from sticking. Dip a large wad of paper towels in vegetable oil, using tongs, and wipe the cooking grate thoroughly several times.

MAKING WOOD-GRILLED SALMON

1. Cut out two rectangles of heavy-duty aluminum foil and crimp the edges until each tray measures 7 by 5 inches. Using a paring knife, poke small slits in the bottom of the trays. (These vents help heat the chips.)

2. Place the soaked wood chips in the foil trays and arrange the salmon skin-side down directly on top of the wood chips.

3. Once the salmon is cooked, slide a metal spatula between the flesh and the skin; the fish should release easily.

2A. FOR A CHARCOAL GRILL: Open the bottom grill vents completely. Light a large chimney starter filled with charcoal briquettes (100 briquettes; 6 quarts). When the coals are hot, pour them in an even layer over the grill. Set the cooking grate in place, cover, and heat the grill until hot, about 5 minutes.

2B. FOR A GAS GRILL: Turn all the burners to high, cover, and heat the grill until hot, about 15 minutes. (Adjust the burners as needed to maintain a hot fire; see page 211.)

3. Clean and oil the cooking grate. Place the trays on the grate, cover, and cook until the sides of the salmon fillets are opaque and the thickest part of the fillets registers 125 degrees on an instant-read thermometer, 10 to 15 minutes. Transfer the trays to a wire rack, tent loosely with foil, and let rest.

4. While the salmon rests, toss the asparagus with the remaining 1 tablespoon oil in a large bowl. Place the asparagus on the grill and cook until tender and spotty-brown, 3 to 6 minutes, turning it as needed. Transfer the asparagus to a platter.

5. Slide a metal spatula between the skin and the flesh of the salmon, transfer the fillets to the platter with the asparagus, and serve.

VARIATIONS

Chinese-Style Wood-Grilled Salmon
with Asparagus
Look for Chinese five-spice powder in either the spice aisle or the international aisle of the supermarket.

Follow the recipe for Wood-Grilled Salmon with Asparagus, adding ¾ teaspoon Chinese five-spice powder and ⅛ teaspoon cayenne pepper to the sugar mixture, and substituting 2 teaspoons hoisin sauce for the oil in step 1.

Barbecued Wood-Grilled Salmon with Asparagus
Follow the recipe for Wood-Grilled Salmon with Asparagus, adding ½ teaspoon chili powder and ⅛ teaspoon cayenne pepper to the sugar mixture, and substituting 1 teaspoon Dijon mustard mixed with 1 teaspoon maple syrup for the oil in step 1.

GRILLED FISH TACOS WITH CORN ON THE COB

POPULAR IN SOUTHERN CALIFORNIA and parts of Mexico, fish tacos consist of grilled pieces of fish and crisp shredded lettuce drizzled with a tangy white sauce, all wrapped up in warm, soft corn tortillas. An unlikely combination of flavors and textures, perhaps, but one bite and you're hooked. Although fish tacos are best eaten under the Pacific sun with your feet firmly planted in the sand, we wanted a recipe for this dish that we could make at home, one that offered the same great grilled flavor and bright, refreshing ingredients. And to make our fish tacos a meal for two, we decided to pair them with grilled corn for an unbeatable combination—both fish and corn are ideal ingredients when cooking for two, because you can buy just the amount you need and not have any left over.

Most of the recipes we found for fish tacos called for a sturdy white fish, so we tried halibut, swordfish, cod, and mahi-mahi. We found them all acceptable, although mahi-mahi was preferred for its meaty flavor and firm texture. For two people, a 12-ounce fillet was plenty, but it was awkward to prepare and even more difficult to grill—it simply fell apart when we tried to flip it. Two 6-ounce fillets were a better choice, each of which we could easily cut into three pieces (to give us one piece per taco).

We first refrigerated the fish on a wire rack set over a baking sheet until our grill was ready—this helped the fillets firm up and remain in one piece when cooked. Because fish cooks relatively quickly, we knew a hot single-level fire, one with an even amount of heat over the entire grill, would be our best bet. This would allow our fish a chance to develop a nicely crisped exterior in a short amount of time without the interior being overcooked. We did note that we had to be thorough when cleaning and oiling the cooking grate; otherwise, the fish stuck and tore apart. Off the grill, we topped our fish with shredded lettuce and a basic mayo-based sauce and rolled it all up in a corn tortilla. This fish taco was good, but tasters all agreed the fish needed a flavor boost. Salt and pepper weren't enough, so we put together a boldly flavored rub of chili powder, coriander, and cumin, which gave us well-seasoned, flavorful fish.

Happy with our grilled mahi-mahi, we turned our attention to the accompaniments. Up to this point, our working taco sauce was pretty simple—nothing more than the traditional mayonnaise mixed with lime juice. Looking to add another flavor dimension, we mixed in some garlic and fresh cilantro, as well as minced chipotle chiles for their smoky heat. Although shredded lettuce is the traditional topping for fish tacos, we found that it was bland and turned limp in a matter of seconds when added to the warm fish. Shredded cabbage was a much better bet. The crisp, raw cabbage retained its crunch, although it was still a bit bland. Tossing it with a few extra ingredients—chopped cilantro, lime juice, salt, and a touch of oil—easily solved the problem. With our tacos complete, all we needed now was some grilled corn to go with them.

USE IT UP: CABBAGE

Creamy New York Deli Coleslaw
SERVES 4

If using caraway seeds, toast them in a dry skillet over medium heat, stirring frequently, until fragrant, about 3 minutes. The slaw can be stored in an airtight container in the refrigerator for up to 2 days.

- ¾ small head green cabbage (12 ounces), cored and shredded (about 6 cups) (see page 219)
- 1 carrot, peeled and grated on the large holes of a box grater
- Salt
- ½ cup mayonnaise
- 1 shallot, minced (about 3 tablespoons)
- 1 tablespoon white vinegar
- ½ teaspoon Dijon mustard
- ½ teaspoon sugar
- ½ teaspoon caraway seeds (optional), toasted (see note)
- Pepper

1. Toss the cabbage and carrot with ½ teaspoon salt in a colander set over a bowl. Let sit until wilted, about 1 hour. Rinse the cabbage mixture with cold water, then drain and dry well with paper towels. Transfer to a medium bowl.

2. Stir the mayonnaise, shallot, vinegar, mustard, sugar, caraway seeds (if using), and ⅛ teaspoon pepper into the cabbage. Cover and refrigerate until chilled, at least 30 minutes or up to 2 days. Season with salt and pepper to taste and serve.

GRILLED FISH TACOS WITH CORN ON THE COB

We placed two large ears of corn on the grill while the fish cooked, and we were happy to find that we could grill both items over the same heat and in the same amount of time. Sitting back with our fish tacos and grilled corn, we had created a little bit of paradise right in our own kitchen.

Grilled Fish Tacos with Corn on the Cob

SERVES 2

Halibut, swordfish, or red snapper can be substituted for the mahi-mahi; if the fish fillets are thicker or thinner, they will have slightly different cooking times. Be sure to oil the cooking grate well in step 4; fish is delicate and tends to stick on the grill. If you decide not to warm your tortillas on the grill, see page 190 for some other options. To make this dish more or less spicy, adjust the amount of chipotle chiles. See page 217 for a recipe to use up the leftover cabbage.

¼ small head green cabbage (4 ounces), cored and shredded (about 2 cups) (see photos)

3 tablespoons chopped fresh cilantro

1½ tablespoons fresh lime juice

1 tablespoon vegetable oil

Salt and pepper

⅓ cup mayonnaise

1-2 teaspoons minced canned chipotle chiles in adobo sauce (see note)

1 small garlic clove, minced

1 teaspoon chili powder

2 (6 to 8-ounce) skinless mahi-mahi fillets, about 1 inch thick (see note)

2 large ears fresh corn, husks and silk removed

2 tablespoons unsalted butter, softened

6 (6-inch) corn tortillas, warmed (see note)

Lime wedges, for serving

1. Toss the cabbage, 2 tablespoons of the cilantro, 1 tablespoon of the lime juice, 1 teaspoon of the oil, ⅛ teaspoon salt, and a pinch of pepper together in a bowl and set aside for serving. In a separate bowl, combine the remaining 1 tablespoon cilantro and remaining 1½ teaspoons lime juice with the mayonnaise, chipotles, and garlic. Season with salt and pepper to taste and set aside for serving.

2. Combine the chili powder, ¼ teaspoon salt, and ⅛ teaspoon pepper in a bowl. Pat the mahi-mahi fillets

dry with paper towels, then brush with 1 teaspoon more oil and rub evenly with the spice mixture.

3A. FOR A CHARCOAL GRILL: Open the bottom grill vents completely. Light a large chimney starter filled with charcoal briquettes (100 briquettes; 6 quarts). When the coals are hot, pour them in an even layer

ALL ABOUT CHIPOTLE CHILES

Smoky, sweet, and moderately spicy, chipotle chiles are jalapeño chiles that have been smoked over aromatic wood and dried. They are sold as is—wrinkly, reddish-brown, and leathery—or canned in adobo, a tangy, oily, tomato-and-herb sauce. We recommend purchasing canned chipotles because they are already reconstituted by the adobo and, consequently, are easier to use. Most recipes call for just a chile or two, as they are so potent, but the remaining chiles keep indefinitely if stored in an airtight container in the refrigerator, or they may be frozen. To freeze chipotles, spoon them out, each with a couple of teaspoons of adobo sauce, onto different areas of a baking sheet lined with wax paper, then place in the freezer. Once they are frozen, remove the chiles to a zipper-lock freezer bag, store in the freezer, and use as needed.

SHREDDING CABBAGE

1. Cut the cabbage into quarters, then trim and discard the hard core.

2. Separate the cabbage into small stacks of leaves that flatten when pressed.

3. Use a chef's knife to cut each stack of cabbage leaves into thin shreds.

over the grill. Set the cooking grate in place, cover, and heat the grill until hot, about 5 minutes.

3B. FOR A GAS GRILL: Turn all the burners to high, cover, and heat the grill until hot, about 15 minutes. (Adjust the burners as needed to maintain a hot fire; see page 211.)

4. Clean and oil the cooking grate. Gently place the mahi-mahi on the grill and cook (covered if using gas) until the fish is opaque and flakes apart when gently prodded with a paring knife, 10 to 14 minutes, gently flipping the fillets halfway through cooking with two spatulas. Transfer the fish to a carving board, tent loosely with foil, and let rest.

5. While the fish cooks, brush the corn with the remaining 1 teaspoon oil and season with salt and pepper. Place the corn on the grill and cook until the kernels are lightly charred on all sides, 6 to 10 minutes, turning the corn as needed. Remove from the grill and brush with the butter.

6. Working in batches, place a few of the tortillas in a single layer on the grill and cook until warmed and lightly browned, about 10 seconds per side. As the tortillas are done, wrap them in a kitchen towel or a large piece of foil.

7. Cut each mahi-mahi fillet into 3 equal pieces. Smear each warm tortilla with the mayonnaise mixture, top with the cabbage and a piece of fish, and serve with the corn and lime wedges.

GRILLED GLAZED TOFU WITH CABBAGE

WHETHER YOU ARE A VEGETARIAN OR NOT, tofu is great to have on hand when cooking for two because you can purchase it in small blocks, it stays fresh much longer than raw meat, and it's quick-cooking. We had come across some recipes for grilled tofu and were intrigued—we've pan-fried tofu but never thought about grilling it. We wondered if there was a way to make grilled tofu a complete meal for two. Thinking back to a tofu and cabbage combination that was a big hit as a stir-fry in the test kitchen, we decided to bring this pairing together on the grill.

First we needed to find the best way to prepare tofu for the grill. Starting with 14-ounce blocks, we cut planks, strips, and triangles, as well as 1-inch cubes that we

CUTTING TOFU FOR THE GRILL

Carefully cut the tofu in half horizontally to make two 4 by 3 by 1-inch planks before draining it on paper towels.

skewered with the hope that this might make the task of flipping the delicate tofu easier. We rubbed them all with oil and threw them on the grill to see how they fared. The skewers were a failure; the tofu cubes were no easier to flip, and the small cubes stuck to the cooking grate. We found it was best to cut the tofu horizontally into two thin, long planks. This shape maximized surface contact with the grill with the least amount of flipping.

Next we tested types of tofu. We grilled soft, medium-firm, firm, and extra-firm tofu and had tasters try them side by side. The extra-firm tofu was the easiest to grill, but it had a dry, crumbly texture that most tasters found unappealing. The others were all well liked for their smooth, custardy texture. Since the soft and medium-firm tofus tended to stick to the grill unless they were pressed first, we chose firm, which we could cut into planks and simply let drain on paper towels.

We knew adding enough flavor to the tofu—which is very mild-tasting on its own—would be key to the success of this recipe. Marinating seemed promising, but after an hour the marinade had not permeated far enough into the tofu to flavor it significantly, and the excess moisture it absorbed made it messy to grill. What about a thick glaze, applied toward the end of cooking?

Back in the kitchen, we made a basic glaze of soy sauce, sugar, mirin (a sweet Japanese rice wine), and water, which diluted the saltiness of the soy sauce without muting its rich flavor. To thicken our glaze we added a bit of cornstarch and simmered it for a few minutes until it developed a clingy, syrupy texture. The addition of garlic and ginger gave our glaze a final flavor boost.

To prepare our tofu for the grill, we simply brushed it with oil and seasoned it with pepper. Once the grill was nice and hot, we placed the tofu on a well-oiled cooking grate (important to prevent sticking) and allowed our tofu planks to sear on both sides, carefully flipping them once. Our well-browned tofu looked pretty, but the exterior had become thick and leathery, and the interior was chewy and dried out. Next we grilled the tofu until it was only lightly browned on both sides, then brushed it with a thin layer of glaze. The sugar in the glaze quickly caramelized and gave us the flavorful, dark brown crust we were after in a minimal amount of time, allowing the tofu to remain moist inside. We finished it with a thick slather of glaze off the grill as well.

For the cabbage, we chose napa cabbage for its thin, crisp leaves and delicate, mild flavor—one small head was just the right amount for two people. We found it was best to quarter the cabbage and grill it until the tips of the outer leaves were charred. We then sliced it and tossed it, still warm, with a dressing made from some of our glaze ingredients, sesame oil, and rice vinegar—simple enough, and tasters were won over. The final touch was the addition of cilantro (a generous ¼ cup) to brighten the flavors of this salad and cut through the sweetness of the glazed tofu.

Grilled Glazed Tofu with Warm Cabbage Slaw
SERVES 2

Mirin is a sweet Japanese rice wine available in the international aisle of most supermarkets; sherry or white wine can be substituted. Do not remove the core from the cabbage; it will help keep the leaves together on the grill.

1	(14-ounce) block firm tofu, cut horizontally into two planks (see page 220)
⅓	cup soy sauce
2	tablespoons mirin (see note)
1½	teaspoons grated or minced fresh ginger
1	garlic clove, minced
¼	cup chopped fresh cilantro
2	teaspoons toasted sesame oil
1	teaspoon rice vinegar
⅓	cup water
3	tablespoons sugar
½	teaspoon cornstarch
1	small head napa cabbage (1 pound), quartered lengthwise through the core (see note)
2	tablespoons vegetable oil
	Pepper

1. Spread the tofu out on several layers of paper towels and let sit for 20 minutes to drain.

2. Meanwhile, combine the soy sauce, mirin, ginger, and garlic in a small saucepan. Measure out 2 tablespoons of the soy sauce mixture, stir in the cilantro, sesame oil, and vinegar, and reserve for serving with the cabbage. Whisk the water, sugar, and cornstarch into the remaining soy sauce mixture in the saucepan. Bring to a simmer over medium-high heat and cook until thickened and reduced to ⅓ cup, about 5 minutes. Set aside.

3A. FOR A CHARCOAL GRILL: Open the bottom grill vents completely. Light a large chimney starter filled with charcoal briquettes (100 briquettes; 6 quarts). When the coals are hot, spread two-thirds of them evenly over the grill, then pour the remaining coals over half the grill. Set the cooking grate in place, cover, and heat the grill until hot, about 5 minutes.

3B. FOR A GAS GRILL: Turn all the burners to high, cover, and heat the grill until hot, about 15 minutes. (Adjust the burners as needed to maintain a hot fire; see page 211.)

4. Clean and oil the cooking grate. Brush the cabbage with 1 tablespoon of the vegetable oil and season with pepper. Place the cabbage on the grill (on the hotter part of the grill if using charcoal), cut-side down, and cook (covered if using gas) until slightly wilted and browned on all sides, 6 to 10 minutes, turning as needed. Transfer to a plate and tent loosely with foil.

5. While the cabbage cooks, pat the tofu dry with paper towels, brush with the remaining 1 tablespoon vegetable oil, and season with pepper. Gently place the tofu on the grill (on the hotter part of the grill if using charcoal) and cook (covered if using gas) until lightly browned on both sides, 6 to 10 minutes, gently flipping it halfway through cooking with two spatulas.

6. Slide the tofu to the cooler part of the grill if using charcoal, or turn all the burners to medium (adjust the burners as needed to maintain a medium fire; see page 211) if using gas. Brush the tofu with some of the glaze and cook until well browned on both sides, 2 to 4 minutes, flipping and brushing the tofu with more glaze halfway through cooking. Transfer the tofu to a plate, brush with the remaining glaze, and tent loosely with foil.

7. Cut the cabbage crosswise into thin strips, discarding the core. Transfer the cabbage to the bowl with the reserved dressing and toss to combine. Divide the cabbage between individual plates, top with the tofu, and serve.

PAN-ROASTED ASPARAGUS WITH TOASTED GARLIC AND PARMESAN

SIDE DISHES

PAN-ROASTED ASPARAGUS

ASPARAGUS IS PERFECT FOR A FAST SIDE DISH FOR TWO. It's easy to prepare, easy to shop for (one bunch makes two generous portions), and it cooks quickly. Our goal was straightforward: We wanted a simple stovetop method that would deliver crisp, nicely browned spears.

After a bit of research, we turned up several promising recipes, but the results were disappointing. In most cases, the spears were indeed browned but also limp, greasy, and shriveled. Many of the recipes we consulted suggested laying the spears in a skillet in a single layer, then individually rotating them to ensure even browning. This seemed awfully fussy for a single bunch of asparagus. We put this method on the back burner for the time being and began by testing different-sized spears, heat levels, pan types, and cooking fats.

The first thing that became obvious was that thinner spears would have to be eliminated, as they overcooked so quickly that there was no way to get a proper sear. Selecting thicker spears helped to solve this problem, but we were still a long way from getting them to brown properly. Over moderate heat, the spears took so long to develop a crisp, browned exterior that they overcooked. But cranking up the burner was not a good alternative—the spears skipped brown altogether and went straight to spotty and blackened.

We knew that in restaurants line cooks blanch pounds of asparagus before service, then toss them into the pan or onto the grill for a quick sear. They do this primarily to save time, but we wondered if this method of parcooking would also enhance browning. We tried searing some asparagus spears that had first been quickly blanched in boiling water. Sure enough, they quickly developed a crisp, golden brown crust. Our science editor explained that the exterior of raw asparagus is dry and waxy, and the sugars necessary for browning reactions are locked up inside the plant's tough cell walls. Some prior cooking is required to release these sugars, as is the case with sliced onions, which need to sweat before they caramelize.

We were reluctant to call for this extra step but wondered if covering the pan at the start of cooking would have the same effect. We cooked two more batches, covering each skillet for the first seven minutes and adding a few tablespoons of water to one of them. The batch with water added was definitely steamed, but it needed more browning. The asparagus in the other skillet, which contained nothing else besides olive oil, steamed

very little. When we replaced the oil with butter, however, the results were quite different: A small cloud of steam escaped the pan when the lid was lifted, and the asparagus had softened and turned bright green.

Evidently, the small amount of moisture in the butter (olive oil is 100 percent fat and contains no water, but butter is roughly 20 percent water) was enough to start steaming the asparagus, which then began to release its own moisture to help the process along. Tasters agreed that asparagus cooked in a mixture of olive oil and butter had the best combination of flavor and browning.

NOTES FROM THE TEST KITCHEN

TRIMMING ASPARAGUS SPEARS

1. Before cooking asparagus, it's important to remove the tough ends. Remove one asparagus spear from the bunch and snap off the end.

2. Using the broken asparagus as a guide, trim off the ends of the remaining spears using a chef's knife.

STORING ASPARAGUS

In-season asparagus should be tender, sweet, and flavorful. But sometimes the supermarket pickings are less than stellar—usually because they've been stored too long. We wondered if there was a way to rescue those tired stalks. We tried refrigerating bunches of asparagus three ways (always beginning by trimming an inch off the ends): wrapped in damp paper towels in an unsealed zipper-lock bag, cut-side down in a cup of water with an unsealed bag over the top, and cut-side down in a cup of sugar water with an unsealed bag over the top. The next day we steamed and tasted all three samples. Both water-soaked batches were sweeter and juicier than the towel-wrapped one, which had the toughest stalks and a slightly bitter flavor. We couldn't detect any significant difference between the asparagus soaked in sugar water and its plain-water counterpart. So if you end up with asparagus that needs some sprucing up, trim the ends and store the stalks in cool water overnight—they will wake up the next day refreshed and ready to go.

Once the lid was removed, however, it was a race against the clock to try to get all the spears turned and evenly browned before they overcooked and turned limp. Even with very thick asparagus, it was a race we almost always lost. In the course of this round of tests, however, we made a fortunate discovery. Citing the pleasing contrast of textures, tasters actually preferred the spears that were browned on one side only and remained bright green on the other—and these half-browned spears never went limp. Now we didn't have to worry about spending time meticulously flipping every spear.

During our tests, we noticed that arranging the spears so that half of them pointed in one direction and the other half pointed in the opposite direction promoted even browning on the one side. Now just a light stir to switch the spears from outside in and vice versa was enough to ensure that all of them became partially browned. With only a light seasoning of salt and pepper, our asparagus was crisp, green, and delicious.

Pan-Roasted Asparagus

SERVES 2

This recipe works best with asparagus that is at least ½ inch thick near the base. Do not use pencil-thin asparagus because it cannot withstand the heat and overcooks too easily.

- 1 tablespoon unsalted butter
- 2 teaspoons olive oil
- 1 bunch thick (see note) asparagus (about 1 pound), tough ends trimmed (see page 224)
  Salt and pepper
- 1 teaspoon fresh lemon juice

1. Heat the butter and oil together in a 12-inch skillet over medium heat until the butter is melted. Add half of the asparagus to the skillet with the tips pointed in one direction and the other half with the tips pointed in the opposite direction. Using tongs, distribute the spears in an even layer, cover, and cook until the asparagus is bright green and still crisp, about 7 minutes.

2. Uncover, increase the heat to medium-high, and cook until the asparagus is tender and well browned on one side, 3 to 4 minutes, using tongs to transfer the spears from the center of the pan to the edge of the pan to ensure even browning.

3. Transfer the asparagus to a serving dish. Season with salt and pepper to taste, drizzle the lemon juice over the top, and serve.

VARIATION

Pan-Roasted Asparagus with Toasted Garlic and Parmesan

Cook 2 garlic cloves, sliced thin, in 2 teaspoons olive oil in the skillet over medium heat until crisp and golden, about 4 minutes. Transfer the garlic to a paper towel–lined plate and set aside, leaving the oil in the skillet. Follow the recipe for Pan-Roasted Asparagus, omitting the oil and adding the butter to the oil left in the skillet from cooking the garlic. Sprinkle the toasted garlic and 2 tablespoons grated Parmesan cheese over the asparagus before serving.

GARLICKY GREEN BEANS

PREPARING SAUTÉED GREEN BEANS usually requires parboiling the beans, shocking them in ice water, drying them with towels, and finally sautéing them. We have always appreciated this technique because it allows you to do most of the prep work ahead of time. But when cooking for two on weekday evenings, we don't want to bother with a process that involves two pots, a colander, and an ice-water bath, just to prepare simple, unassuming green beans. We were after a streamlined process that still produced lightly browned, crisp-tender, fresh-tasting beans and a recipe that could be prepared quickly using only one pan. Just because we were cooking for two didn't mean we'd have to miss out on flavor, so we decided to roast some garlic and add it to the dish for a little oomph.

We first looked at methods for roasting garlic, since this could take a good chunk of time. Roasting garlic tames its bite and intensifies its sweet flavor; unfortunately, it also takes about an hour. For our simple green bean side dish, we were hoping to find a faster way to achieve the nutty flavor and buttery texture of roasted garlic. Slowly heating peeled garlic cloves in a skillet filled with oil took way too long, and the garlic browned unevenly before it was softened on the inside. The microwave proved to be a better tool to quickly and evenly cook the garlic through to its center. We peeled six cloves, cut them in half, and placed them in a small bowl with oil (to almost cover them) and a little sugar (to promote caramelization). Then we microwaved the mixture on high for one minute. The garlic now had that creamy texture we were looking for, and we were doubly rewarded with intensely flavored garlic oil that we could use when preparing the green beans.

Now that the garlic was ready, it was time to try sautéing our green beans. For our first test, we sautéed some beans in a skillet with oil without parboiling them—big mistake. The dry heat took too long to penetrate the beans, so that by the time they were tender and cooked, their exteriors were blackened—similar to Chinese stir-fried green beans. Not bad, but not exactly fresh-tasting either.

Our next thought was to try a combination of steaming and sautéing in oil, a method that had worked well for our Pan-Roasted Asparagus (page 225). But, unlike the pan-roasted asparagus, we didn't want to use butter as the moisture for steaming our beans since we would have a good amount of garlic oil to use. Instead, we heated 2 teaspoons of the garlic oil in a 12-inch skillet, added the green beans and 2 tablespoons of water, covered the skillet, and cooked the beans until they were bright green. We then added the remaining garlic and oil to infuse the beans with more flavor and cooked the beans until they were almost tender. To get the browning we wanted, we removed the lid to let any remaining moisture evaporate (leaving only the oil behind) and cooked the beans until they were spotty brown.

These beans hit the mark—they were fresh-tasting and had a great toasted flavor from the browning. We now had perfectly cooked beans studded with soft, nutty "roasted" garlic—all in about 10 minutes. All that was needed was a splash of vinegar to help finish the dish.

With so much extra time on our hands, we were free to develop a couple of variations. First we created a green bean dish enhanced with bright lemon juice and

zest; toasted sliced almonds added a nice crunch. For a second variation, we combined maple syrup and whole-grain mustard for a sweet and tangy side dish.

Garlicky Green Beans
SERVES 2

Microwave temperatures can vary, so be sure to check the garlic after 30 seconds to see if it has softened.

- **6 garlic cloves, peeled and halved lengthwise (see note)**
- **1 tablespoon extra-virgin olive oil**
  Pinch sugar
- **8 ounces green beans, trimmed (see page 150)**
- **2 tablespoons water**
- **1½ teaspoons red or white wine vinegar**
  Salt and pepper

1. Microwave the garlic, oil, and sugar, uncovered, in a small microwave-safe bowl until the garlic is softened and fragrant, 30 seconds to 1 minute.

2. Heat 2 teaspoons of the garlic oil in a 12-inch nonstick skillet over medium heat until shimmering. Reserve the remaining garlic mixture. Add the green beans and water, bring to a simmer, cover, and cook until bright green, about 3 minutes. Add the reserved garlic mixture to the skillet; do not stir. Continue to cook, covered, until the green beans are almost tender, about 2 minutes.

3. Uncover and cook, stirring occasionally, until the green beans are spotty brown and the garlic is golden, 3 to 4 minutes. Off the heat, stir in the vinegar, season with salt and pepper to taste, and serve.

VARIATIONS
Lemony Green Beans with Toasted Almonds
Follow the recipe for Garlicky Green Beans, omitting the garlic, sugar, and step 1. Proceed with the recipe, heating 1 tablespoon extra-virgin olive oil in the skillet in step 2 and replacing the vinegar with 1½ teaspoons fresh lemon juice and ⅛ teaspoon grated lemon zest in step 3. Sprinkle 2 tablespoons sliced almonds, toasted, over the beans just before serving.

Maple-Mustard Green Beans
Combine 2 teaspoons maple syrup, 2 teaspoons whole-grain mustard, and a pinch of cayenne in a small bowl.

NOTES FROM THE TEST KITCHEN

HOW TO TOAST NUTS
In order for nuts and seeds to contribute the most flavor, they need to be toasted. To toast a small amount (under 1 cup) of nuts or seeds, put them in a dry skillet over medium heat. Simply shake the skillet occasionally to prevent scorching and toast until they are lightly browned and fragrant, 3 to 8 minutes. Watch the nuts closely because they can go from golden to burnt very quickly.

Follow the recipe for Garlicky Green Beans, omitting the garlic, sugar, and step 1. Proceed with the recipe, heating 1 tablespoon extra-virgin olive oil in the skillet in step 2 and adding the mustard-maple mixture to the green beans with the vinegar in step 3.

BRAISED BRUSSELS SPROUTS

BRUSSELS SPROUTS, WHEN PROPERLY COOKED, have crisp outer leaves and a tender interior and boast a nutty flavor. They are also a convenient vegetable to work with because they are sold either loose or in small quantities—meaning you buy only what you need and there are no unwanted leftovers in the fridge (a big plus when you're cooking for just two). With these great selling points, why don't they show up on more dinner tables? The biggest problem is that Brussels sprouts are almost always poorly prepared—many home cooks don't know what to do with them, often transforming them into limp and bitter or flavorless rounds. We wanted to change that by finding a foolproof method for preparing Brussels sprouts that would keep their crispness and flavor intact.

There are numerous options for cooking Brussels sprouts: steaming, boiling, roasting, and braising. Steaming and boiling tend to make for waterlogged sprouts; roasting is really the best way to draw out their flavor and create a nice crispness in the leaves. But on a weeknight, who has time to roast Brussels sprouts on a big baking sheet for 45 minutes? We decided to go with braising; these mini cabbages could cook quickly and easily on the stovetop, leaving the oven available for the main course, and we could then reduce the remaining braising liquid to create a simple but flavorful sauce.

We began by selecting our Brussels sprouts; half a pound seemed like just the right amount for two servings. We trimmed the stems and removed the outer, discolored leaves, then cut each sprout in half. In a 12-inch skillet, we sautéed a minced shallot in a tablespoon of butter (the butter would help to thicken our sauce), then added our halved Brussels sprouts and ¾ cup of water and covered the skillet, leaving the sprouts to braise. We removed the lid after seven minutes to find a disappointing scene—there was no liquid left in the skillet and our sprouts had burned. We tried

again, this time using a smaller skillet but keeping the same amount of liquid, which we would utilize to make the sauce once the sprouts were done. This time, we watched the sprouts more closely; when they were bright green and almost tender, we removed the lid to let the sprouts cook through and the liquid reduce.

After another five minutes, the Brussels sprouts were tender and the remaining liquid had cooked down to a nice sauce that coated the sprouts. These Brussels sprouts met all the criteria we were looking for—they were tender and bright green and had a nice nutty flavor. But, because we used water alone for the braising liquid, the sauce was lacking in flavor.

For our next test, we replaced the water with chicken broth, which we had used before to braise other vegetables. This was a winning move, adding more flavor to both the vegetable and the sauce. We wondered if the addition of a little wine would further enhance the flavor of the dish. However, when we tested this theory, we found that the sprouts braised in wine and chicken broth didn't taste much different from the ones braised in just broth, so we decided to skip the wine and keep our ingredient list short. With a great method in hand, we then developed a simple variation for curried Brussels sprouts with currants.

Braised Brussels Sprouts
SERVES 2

When buying Brussels sprouts, choose those with small, tight heads, no more than 1½ inches in diameter. Be careful not to cut too much off the stem end when trimming the sprouts, or the leaves will fall away from the core.

- 1 tablespoon unsalted butter
- 1 small shallot, minced (about 1 tablespoon)
   Salt
- 8 ounces small Brussels sprouts, stem ends trimmed, discolored leaves removed, and halved through the stems (see note)
- ¾ cup low-sodium chicken broth
   Pepper

1. Melt the butter in a 10-inch nonstick skillet over medium heat. Add the shallot and ⅛ teaspoon salt, and cook until softened, about 2 minutes. Add the sprouts, broth, and a pinch of pepper and bring to a simmer.

Cover and cook until the sprouts are bright green and almost tender, 7 to 10 minutes.

2. Uncover and continue to cook until the sprouts are tender and the liquid is slightly thickened, 3 to 5 minutes. Season with salt and pepper to taste and serve.

VARIATION

Braised Brussels Sprouts with Curry and Currants
If currants are unavailable, substitute an equal amount of coarsely chopped raisins.

Follow the recipe for Braised Brussels Sprouts, adding ¾ teaspoon curry powder with the shallot and 1 tablespoon currants with the broth in step 1.

GLAZED CARROTS

MOST HOME COOKS ALWAYS HAVE A BAG OF CARROTS in the crisper drawer, generally reserved for sautéing with onion and celery to form the base of a bigger dish. But carrots should not be so readily overlooked. This vegetable, when not chopped or cut into lunchtime snack sticks, makes an easy and delicious answer to the question of what *else* is for dinner, after you've solved the entrée dilemma. We think glazed carrots are an especially attractive option, since a light sauce nicely complements the carrots' natural sweetness, and they pair well with just about any meat. With a few handfuls of carrots in hand—we wouldn't need more than that to serve two—we set out to develop a surefire recipe for glazed carrots.

To start, we looked at how best to cut the carrots. Matchsticks were out from the get-go—we were looking for simplicity, not to improve our knife skills. Instead, we peeled regular loose carrots and cut them on the bias into ovals; this elegant shape, we thought, would help to dress up any main course.

Most recipes suggest that carrots should be steamed, parboiled, or blanched prior to glazing, resulting in a pile of dirtied utensils and sometimes an extra pot to clean. We opted to take a streamlined path and put the carrots, ½ cup of water, and a bit of sugar in a 10-inch skillet—nonstick, for the sake of easy cleanup. Then we covered the skillet and let the carrots simmer for five minutes. Mission accomplished: The carrots were cooked through without much ado. The flavor, however, was a bit watered down.

To amp up the flavor, we swapped out the water for chicken broth; the broth lent the carrots a savory backbone and a full, round flavor, whereas water left them hollow. We then experimented with more compelling sweeteners, substituting brown sugar, maple syrup, and honey for the sugar in separate tests. But we found the brown sugar imparted a muddied note to the dish, maple syrup was too assertive, and honey was too floral. We stood by clean, pure, easy-to-measure granulated sugar.

Finally, we moved on to finessing the glaze. After the carrots had simmered for a few minutes and were just on the verge of tender—they would see more heat during glazing, so we simmered them until they were just shy of done—we lifted the lid from the skillet, stepped up the heat, and let the liquid reduce so it wasn't thin and watery. Finally, we added a tablespoon of butter (cut into small pieces for quick melting) and a teaspoon more sugar to encourage glaze formation and increase sweetness. All of this resulted in a light, clingy glaze that with a few more minutes of cooking took on a pale amber hue and a light caramel flavor.

A sprinkle of fresh lemon juice gave the dish sparkle, and a twist of freshly ground black pepper provided depth. We were as surprised as our tasters that glazed carrots could be this good and this easy. Looking to add some spice to our carrots, we created two potent variations—one with ginger and another with curry.

Glazed Carrots

SERVES 2

You will need a 10-inch nonstick skillet with a tight-fitting lid to make this recipe. Glazed carrots are a good accompaniment to any type of meat—beef, pork, lamb, or poultry.

- 3 carrots, peeled and sliced ¼ inch thick on the bias (see page 230)
- ½ cup low-sodium chicken broth
- 1 tablespoon sugar
- 1 tablespoon unsalted butter, cut into 4 pieces
- 1 teaspoon fresh lemon juice
  Salt and pepper

1. Bring the carrots, broth, and 2 teaspoons of the sugar to a boil in a 10-inch nonstick skillet over medium-high heat. Reduce the heat to medium, cover, and simmer,

GLAZED CURRIED CARROTS WITH CURRANTS AND ALMONDS

stirring occasionally, until the carrots are almost tender when poked with the tip of a paring knife, about 5 minutes.

2. Uncover, increase the heat to medium-high, and simmer, stirring occasionally, until the liquid is reduced to about 1 tablespoon, 1 to 2 minutes. Stir in the remaining 1 teaspoon sugar and butter, and cook, stirring frequently, until the carrots are completely tender and the glaze is light gold, 1 to 2 minutes.

3. Off the heat, stir in the lemon juice and season with salt and pepper to taste. Transfer the carrots to a serving dish, scraping the glaze from the pan, and serve.

VARIATIONS

Glazed Carrots with Ginger and Rosemary

Cut a ½-inch piece of fresh ginger in half. Follow the recipe for Glazed Carrots, adding the ginger to the skillet with the carrots in step 1, and ¼ teaspoon minced fresh rosemary with the butter in step 2. Discard the ginger pieces before serving.

Glazed Curried Carrots with Currants and Almonds

Lightly toasting the curry powder in a warm, dry skillet brings forth its full flavor. If currants are unavailable, substitute an equal amount of coarsely chopped raisins.

Toast ½ teaspoon curry powder in a 10-inch nonstick skillet over medium heat until fragrant, about 30 seconds. Follow the recipe for Glazed Carrots, adding the carrots, broth, and sugar to the skillet with the curry powder in step 1. Add 2 tablespoons currants with the butter in step 2, and sprinkle 2 tablespoons sliced almonds, toasted (see page 226), over the carrots before serving.

NOTES FROM THE TEST KITCHEN

SLICING CARROTS ON THE BIAS

For a more elegant presentation, we cut our carrots on the bias into ovals about ¼ inch thick and 2 inches long.

CREAMY PEAS WITH BACON AND GOAT CHEESE

WE ACTUALLY PREFER TO BUY PEAS FROZEN rather than fresh. They are picked and frozen at the height of ripeness, unlike the fresh peas in supermarkets, which can be days old. This means they are always a reliable option for the home cook—there's no waiting for the summer harvest, as the same good quality is available year-round. Plus they're another great speedy vegetable for two with no waste—just use what you need and put the rest back in the freezer. The sad thing is that most cooks simply boil or microwave peas in water, but these methods of preparation don't add much in the way of flavor, nor do they showcase the naturally sweet taste of the peas. We wanted to find a better method for cooking peas and incorporate some rich flavor to complement their sweetness.

In our research, we came across many recipes for creamy peas—a simple dish of peas and reduced heavy cream—and we liked the idea of this quick and easy yet elegant side dish. When we tried a few recipes, though, tasters seemed to want more than just cream and peas. So we decided to dress up our creamy peas even more with the addition of goat cheese and bacon.

Frozen peas merely need to be heated through to be at their finest, so we looked at how best to prepare our dish to prevent overcooking the peas (a common mistake made with frozen peas). We began by cooking the peas in the cream in a nonstick skillet, and then simply stirred some goat cheese into the mixture off the heat. Tasters complained that the resulting texture was grainy and too thick. Keeping the pan on the stove and adding the cheese to melt resulted in overcooking the peas, so this plan of action was out. Maybe we were overthinking the method for our simple dish. Instead of staggering the addition of our ingredients, we tried combining the peas, cream, and goat cheese in the pan right from the start. This worked like a dream—when the peas were cooked through, the cheese was melted, and the cream had thickened slightly.

We had created a dish with perfectly plump peas in a nice creamy sauce, but tasters felt it needed textural contrast. To add more flavor and some texture, we decided to include two slices of bacon. To keep the bacon crisp, we cooked it in the skillet first and set it aside to be sprinkled over the cooked peas just before serving. Tasters were thrilled with this combination but still felt that it needed another subtle flavor.

Since bacon and scallion make such a classic pairing, we thought we would try sprinkling some thinly sliced scallions over the peas along with the bacon. Unfortunately, the raw scallions overwhelmed the delicate flavor of the peas. Since our peas were on the stove for only a few minutes, we thought that adding the scallions to cook along with the peas might just mellow them enough to work with the peas. We were right.

Now our simple weeknight peas were perfect, with scallions and bacon adding just the right flavor subtlety and a nice crispness to this easy accompaniment.

NOTES FROM THE TEST KITCHEN

THE BEST BACON

We've been hearing a lot about small producers of premium bacon using old-fashioned curing methods and hand labor. But premium bacon can cost double or even triple the price of ordinary bacon. Could such a dramatic difference in price really be worth it? To find out, we bought six artisanal bacons by mail order in a single style (applewood-smoked) and two high-end grocery store bacons. The results? We were amazed to find that two of the four highest-rated bacons were not premium mail-order bacons at all, but supermarket brands. **Applegate Farms Uncured Sunday Bacon** (top) and **Farmland/Carando Apple Cider Cured Bacon, Applewood Smoked** (bottom), were a step up from the usual mass-produced bacon, straddling the gap between artisanal and more mainstream supermarket styles. Although these bacons didn't receive quite the raves of the two top-ranked premium bacons, tasters praised them both for good meaty flavor and mild smokiness.

GIVE (FROZEN) PEAS A CHANCE

In the test kitchen, we've come to depend on frozen peas. Not only are they more convenient than their fresh comrades in the pod, but they also taste better. In test after test, we've found that frozen peas are tender and sweet, whereas fresh peas are starchy and bland. Finding good frozen peas is not hard. After tasting peas from the major national brands, including Birds Eye and Green Giant, along with organically grown peas from Cascadian Farm, our panel found little difference in flavor or texture. All of the peas were sweet and fresh, with a bright green color.

Creamy Peas with Bacon and Goat Cheese
SERVES 2

Do not thaw the peas before adding them to the skillet in step 2. Be sure to serve the peas right away, as this dish will thicken slightly as it cools.

   2 slices bacon, cut into ¼-inch pieces
1½ cups frozen peas (6 ounces) (see note)
   ¼ cup heavy cream
   1 ounce goat cheese, cut into 4 pieces
   2 scallions, sliced thin
      Salt and pepper

1. Cook the bacon in a 10-inch nonstick skillet over medium–low heat until crisp, about 10 minutes. Using a slotted spoon, transfer the bacon to a paper towel–lined plate. Pour off the fat from the skillet, then wipe out the skillet with a wad of paper towels.

2. Add the peas, cream, goat cheese, and scallions to the skillet, cover, and cook, stirring often, until the peas are heated through and the cheese is melted, 2 to 4 minutes. Season with salt and pepper to taste. Transfer to a serving dish and sprinkle the bacon over the top before serving.

CHERRY TOMATO SALADS

IN THE COOKING-FOR-TWO KITCHEN, we think cherry tomatoes are essential ingredients. These multipurpose salad staples frequently make appearances in baked or roasted chicken dishes, on crudité platters, or as a simple sautéed side dish. But when making recipes that yield two servings, you generally need only ½ pint, or 1 cup, of cherry tomatoes. Sure, the extra tomatoes can keep for days, but we wanted to use them to create a simple tomato salad with a light dressing that would showcase their naturally sweet flavor. Because these tomatoes are available year-round—meaning they're still appealing in winter—we knew this recipe would be a keeper, perfect for both summery picnics and cold January nights, when the tomatoes would provide a hint of warmer weather to come. We knew from experience, however, that we couldn't merely slice them in half, toss them with vinaigrette, and call it a salad. Like bigger, meatier beefsteak and plum varieties, cherry tomatoes exude lots of liquid when cut, quickly turning a salad into soup. We were determined to avoid this misstep.

In the test kitchen, we often utilize salt to remove water from large tomatoes: We slice the tomatoes, sprinkle them with salt, and allow them to drain to remove liquid and concentrate flavors (even in-season tomatoes benefit from this process). Following suit, we tossed our ½ pint of halved cherry tomatoes with ¼ teaspoon of salt, plus a pinch of sugar to accentuate sweetness, and let them drain in a colander. After 30 minutes, only a paltry 2 teaspoons of liquid had leached out. What if we exposed even more of the tomatoes' surface area to salt? We tried again with a fresh batch of cherry tomatoes, cutting each one along the equator and then in half again. We were thrilled to see we had made progress—the salted, quartered tomatoes netted 1 tablespoon of liquid. But even this wasn't enough to prevent the salad from turning soggy when we tossed the tomatoes with oil and vinegar.

Some tomato salad recipes call for removing the watery seed pockets of the tomatoes, thus eliminating a major source of liquid. We weren't about to cut open a pile of cherry tomatoes and painstakingly push out the jelly and seeds with our thumbs; we needed a more efficient method. That's when we thought of a salad spinner. The centrifugal force of the whirling bowl spins water off lettuce and herbs, so we thought it would

have the same effect on our tomatoes. We were right—spinning salted and drained tomatoes resulted in the release of 3 tablespoons of liquid.

Our tomatoes were no longer liquidy, but when we tossed them with a light dressing, we noticed they tasted a little dull. This was not too surprising, as the jelly is the most flavorful part of the tomato, and we had stripped it away. We decided to reduce the jelly to concentrate its flavor, then use the reduction in our dressing. We strained the seeds from the jelly and then boiled 2 tablespoons of it in a small saucepan with a chopped shallot and balsamic vinegar. After cooling the mixture and combining it with olive oil, we tossed it with the cherry tomatoes. This time we had nailed it: Every bite of the salad delivered sweet tomato flavor.

Tasters fully appreciated the flavor of the tomatoes, but to dress up our salad and take the acidity down a notch, we stirred in ½ cup fresh mozzarella and some chopped fresh basil. Now the flavors were evenly balanced and incredibly fresh. Our cherry tomato salad was reminiscent of a luscious summer caprese, but it was even better because it could be made any time of the year.

Cherry Tomato Salad with Basil and Fresh Mozzarella
SERVES 2

If cherry tomatoes are unavailable, substitute grape tomatoes; cut the grape tomatoes in half along the equator rather than quartering them. You will need a salad spinner for this recipe. See page 70 for a recipe to use up the leftover cherry tomatoes.

- 6 **ounces cherry tomatoes (see note), quartered (about 1 cup)**
- ½ **teaspoon sugar**
  Salt
- 1 **small shallot, minced (about 1 tablespoon)**
- 1 **teaspoon balsamic vinegar**
- 2 **teaspoons extra-virgin olive oil**
- 2 **ounces fresh mozzarella, cut into ½-inch chunks and patted dry with paper towels (about ½ cup)**
- ¼ **cup chopped fresh basil**
  Pepper

1. Toss the tomatoes, sugar, and ¼ teaspoon salt together in a medium bowl and let sit for 30 minutes.

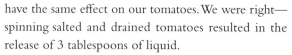

Transfer the tomatoes to a salad spinner and spin until most of the seeds and excess liquid have been removed, 45 to 60 seconds, stirring frequently to redistribute the tomatoes. Return the tomatoes to the bowl and set aside. Strain the tomato liquid through a fine-mesh strainer, pressing on the solids to extract as much liquid as possible. Discard the solids.

2. Bring 2 tablespoons of the tomato liquid (discard any extra), shallot, and vinegar to a simmer in a small saucepan over medium heat, and cook until reduced to about 1 tablespoon, 2 to 3 minutes. Transfer the mixture to a small bowl and cool to room temperature. Whisk in the oil until combined.

3. Stir the mozzarella and basil into the tomatoes. Pour the dressing over the tomato mixture and toss to combine. Season with salt and pepper to taste and serve.

VARIATION

Cherry Tomato Salad with Tarragon and Blue Cheese
Toasted chopped pecans or walnuts make a nice addition to this salad.

Follow the recipe for Cherry Tomato Salad with Basil and Fresh Mozzarella, substituting 1 ounce crumbled blue cheese (about ¼ cup) for the mozzarella and cider vinegar for the balsamic vinegar. Add 1 teaspoon Dijon mustard and 2 teaspoons honey to the tomato liquid with the oil in step 2, and substitute 2 teaspoons chopped fresh tarragon for the basil.

WILTED SPINACH SALADS

THE TRADITIONAL WILTED SPINACH SALAD, tossed with a warm bacon dressing, makes for an appealing and elegant salad. With few ingredients, it's easy to borrow this dish from restaurants and prepare it yourself. Unfortunately, many times, the resulting homemade salads are soggy masses of dark green spinach, bogged down from too much oil and too much heat. We decided it was time to take matters into our own hands and create a foolproof recipe for a wilted spinach salad that would serve two and would provide a nice alternative to basic greens dressed with store-bought vinaigrette.

First we experimented with various types of spinach. We tossed flat-leaf, baby, and curly-leaf spinach with a warm vinaigrette to see how they held up under the heat. We found that the flat-leaf and baby spinach became soft and mushy, but the heartier curly-leaf variety stood up to the heat much better. We also discovered during this testing that tasters much preferred spinach that was just beginning to wilt, because it seemed less bogged down by the dressing.

With the spinach variety settled, we set about making a dressing. We wanted to build the dressing on a base of fruity extra-virgin olive oil, which we thought would add a nice freshness and good flavor to our salad. To make the dressing, we began by heating 2 tablespoons

NOTES FROM THE TEST KITCHEN

SPINACH THAT CAN TAKE THE HEAT
For our wilted spinach salads, we found that tender flat-leaf and baby spinach became soft and mushy when tossed with hot dressing. But the heartier curly-leaf variety, wilted until just tender, stands up to the heat just fine.

STORING BAGGED SPINACH
Fresh spinach used to come in perforated plastic bags that allowed the greens to breathe and stay fresh longer. These days, the bags of greens we buy no longer have the holes. Why the change? Plastic bag technology has come a long way over the years. Though they appear solid, the bags in which spinach and other greens are now sold are made of a polymer that allows the ripening gases that all produce emits to pass through freely. Because of this, leftover packaged spinach or greens will do much better when stored in their original bags than when stored in ordinary plastic ones. To ensure freshness for as long as possible, fold the bag over and tape it shut.

ZESTING CITRUS FRUIT WITH A VEGETABLE PEELER

A vegetable peeler is a great tool for removing the zest from citrus fruit. Gently peel away a 1-inch piece of zest, trying to avoid any of the bitter white pith beneath it.

SPINACH SALAD WITH RADISHES, FETA, AND PISTACHIOS

of olive oil in a Dutch oven along with some minced shallot. We opted against incorporating the ubiquitous bacon—which usually settles on the bottom of the bowl anyway—and went for a brighter flavor instead, ditching sharp vinegar in favor of fresh lemon juice, which we added to the warmed oil.

The citrus flavor was such a hit with our tasters that we tried adding grated lemon zest to the dressing; tasters loved the flavor of the little bits of zest, but they weren't crazy about the texture. Since we were already heating the oil to make the dressing, we realized that adding a strip of lemon zest to the hot oil was the perfect way

to infuse the dressing with more citrus flavor. Then we could remove the strip of zest, pour in the lemon juice, and add the spinach to lightly wilt in the hot dressing. We found the dressing also needed a hit of sugar to balance the citrus and the earthy flavor of the spinach. We were definitely on the right track, but we wanted to add a few interesting ingredients to the mix since our salad was fairly lightweight at this point.

We tested various vegetable options—tomatoes became watery under heat, bell peppers didn't add any new flavors, and carrots were a little ordinary for our restaurant-style salad—before settling on the clean flavor of sliced radishes. This was a good start, but the salad needed a bit more presence, perhaps in the form of cheese. Crumbled feta cheese was a clear winner, except that it kept melting under the heat of the dressing. To remedy this, we froze the cheese until it was slightly firm to prevent it from melting so quickly and added it to the spinach only after our salad was moved to a serving bowl. To complete our updated version of wilted spinach salad, we added chopped pistachios for a nice crunch.

With a great wilted spinach salad recipe in our back pocket, we turned to making a couple of simple but sophisticated variations, one using raisins, blue cheese, and pecans, and another with goat cheese, dried cherries, and almonds.

USE IT UP: SPINACH

Creamed Spinach

SERVES 2

This classic side dish is excellent with roast chicken or grilled steaks.

- 1 teaspoon olive oil
- 5 ounces curly-leaf spinach (about 4 cups), stemmed and torn into bite-sized pieces
- 1 tablespoon unsalted butter
- 1 small shallot, minced (about 1 tablespoon)
  Salt
- ¼ cup heavy cream
- 1 tomato, cored, seeded, and cut into ½-inch pieces
- ½ ounce Parmesan cheese, grated (about ¼ cup)
  Pepper

1. Heat the oil in a large saucepan over medium-high heat until shimmering. Add the spinach, a handful at a time, until wilted. Continue to cook, stirring frequently, until the spinach is uniformly wilted and glossy, about 40 seconds. Drain the spinach in a colander and press on the leaves using the back of a large spoon to release any extra liquid.

2. Wipe out the saucepan with paper towels. Melt the butter in the saucepan over medium heat. Add the shallot and ¼ teaspoon salt and cook until softened, about 2 minutes. Stir in the cream and cook just until warm, about 30 seconds. Off the heat, stir in the drained spinach, tomato, and Parmesan. Season with salt and pepper to taste and serve.

Spinach Salad with Radishes, Feta, and Pistachios

SERVES 2

Be sure to cook the spinach just until it begins to wilt; any longer and the leaves will overcook and clump.

- 2 tablespoons crumbled feta cheese
- 2 tablespoons extra-virgin olive oil
- 1 (1-inch) strip lemon zest plus 2 teaspoons fresh lemon juice
- 1 small shallot, minced (about 1 tablespoon)
- 1 teaspoon sugar
- 5 ounces curly-leaf spinach (about 4 cups), stemmed and torn into bite-sized pieces
- 3 radishes, sliced thin
- 2 tablespoons chopped unsalted pistachios, toasted (see page 226)
  Salt and pepper

1. Place the cheese on a plate and freeze until slightly firm, about 15 minutes.

2. Heat the oil, zest, shallot, and sugar in a Dutch oven over medium-low heat until the shallot is softened, 2 to 4 minutes. Discard the zest and stir in the lemon juice. Add the spinach, cover, and cook until the spinach is just beginning to wilt, about 30 seconds.

3. Transfer the spinach and hot dressing to a large bowl. Add the cheese, radishes, and pistachios and toss to combine. Season with salt and pepper to taste and serve.

VARIATIONS

Spinach Salad with Raisins, Blue Cheese, and Pecans

Follow the recipe for Spinach Salad with Radishes, Feta, and Pistachios, substituting crumbled blue cheese for the feta cheese, orange zest for the lemon zest, orange juice plus ½ teaspoon white vinegar for the lemon juice, 2 tablespoons raisins for the radishes, and chopped pecans, toasted (see page 226), for the pistachios.

Spinach Salad with Cherries, Goat Cheese, and Almonds

Follow the recipe for Spinach Salad with Radishes, Feta, and Pistachios, substituting crumbled goat cheese for the feta cheese, grapefruit zest for the lemon zest, grapefruit juice for the lemon juice, 2 tablespoons dried cherries for the radishes, and sliced almonds, toasted (see page 226), for the pistachios.

FENNEL SALAD

ALTHOUGH FENNEL IS WIDELY AVAILABLE, it's not always an obvious choice for a simple side dish. Sure, it's great when roasted with other vegetables or included in a pasta dish or a stew to add depth of flavor. But with its light, sweet anise flavor and crunchy texture, it also makes a great salad. And since one medium bulb is just enough to make a side salad for two, we decided to explore the salad route.

Our research turned up several recipes that featured fennel with oranges and olives, so we decided to take this simple approach highlighting Mediterranean flavors. Because this salad would be so simple, we knew it would be important to both choose each ingredient carefully and make sure each one was of the highest quality.

Beginning with the olives—the most potent ingredient on our list—we looked at the three basic types found at the supermarket: brine-cured green, brine-cured black, and salt-cured black (often labeled "oil-cured"). Curing is the process that removes the bitter compounds from olives to make them suitable for consumption. Brine-cured olives are soaked in a salt solution; salt-cured olives are packed in salt until nearly all their liquid has been extracted, then covered in oil to be replumped. Both processes traditionally take weeks or even months.

To find out which olive type would be right for our salad, we made a salad with each of them. Tasters found both the green olives and the brine-cured black olives too acidic for this simple salad, especially when they were combined with a vinaigrette and orange pieces. Salt-cured olives won the tasting, but they needed to be thinly sliced so that they didn't overwhelm the other flavors in the salad.

Next, we focused on the fennel and orange. One of each was sufficient to make two servings of salad. As we ran through our tests, we realized that we liked the fennel best when it was sliced as thin as possible. Also, we noticed that the orange had to be cut into bite-sized pieces. We first trimmed the outer rind and bitter white pith from the orange with a paring knife, then cut the orange into quarters and crosswise through each quarter across the segments. This resulted in nice, tidy pieces and prevented the orange segments from falling apart as the salad was tossed, because the segment borders and connective tissue kept them together (see page 237).

With our main players set, we moved on to the vinaigrette. We began by using our usual 4-to-1 ratio of oil to acid and tested different acid options. We tried using lemon juice and white wine, red wine, and cider vinegars. The overall favorite was red wine vinegar, which tasters praised for its complex acidic notes and its nonfruity flavor (they felt that the orange added enough fruity flavor). The only problem was that tasters wanted more vinegar, so we adjusted our ratio slightly, then tossed in some salt and pepper to balance the flavors of our salad.

To finish, we added 2 tablespoons of chopped fresh mint—just enough to make our fennel salad refreshing in addition to light. Our salad was full of bright, nuanced flavors—everything we had set out to make. This quick salad would be a welcome change any night of the week.

SHOPPING FOR FENNEL
Thinly sliced fennel adds a nice anise flavor to salads. When shopping, look for fennel with its long, thin stalks still attached, and be sure that the fennel bulb is creamy white and not bruised or discolored. Fennel is sometimes labeled as anise in the supermarket produce aisle, so don't be stumped when there's no sign for fennel.

CUTTING AN ORANGE

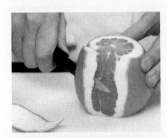

1. Cut away the rind and pith from the orange using a paring knife.

2. Quarter the peeled orange, then slice each quarter crosswise into ¼-inch-thick pieces.

THE BEST RED WINE VINEGAR
Red wine vinegar has a sharp but clean flavor, making it a versatile choice for salad dressings. While acidity is the obvious key factor in vinegar, it is actually the inherent sweetness of the grapes used to make this vinegar that makes its flavor appealing to the palate. Curious whether or not flavor is dependent on price, we pitted ten supermarket brands against four high-end brands. **Spectrum Naturals Organic Red Wine Vinegar,** a slightly more expensive brand, won hands-down for its peppery, sweet, and full-bodied flavors. However, if you can't find this brand, there is a supermarket deal to be had in our second-place winner, Pompeian Red Wine Vinegar, which is easier to find and boasted bright and fruity flavors.

Fennel, Orange, and Olive Salad
SERVES 2

If you can find one, a blood orange, with its reddish-orange flesh, makes a colorful alternative to a regular orange. This salad pairs well with simply prepared fish and chicken dishes.

- 1 fennel bulb (about 12 ounces), trimmed of stalks, cored, and sliced thin (see page 71)
- 1 orange (see note), peeled, quartered, and cut into ¼-inch pieces (see photos)
- 2 tablespoons chopped fresh mint
- 1 tablespoon chopped pitted oil-cured black olives
- 2 tablespoons extra-virgin olive oil
- 2 teaspoons red wine vinegar
- ¼ teaspoon salt
  Pepper

Toss the fennel, orange, mint, and olives together in a medium bowl. Whisk the oil, vinegar, salt, and ⅛ teaspoon pepper together, then pour over the fennel mixture and toss to coat. Season with pepper to taste and serve.

SUMMER VEGETABLE GRATIN

BRIGHTLY COLORED VEGETABLE GRATINS make an enticing dinner party option; they're incredibly elegant, can be assembled ahead of time, and, with the perfect mix of melted cheese and juicy tomatoes and squash, they definitely satisfy a crowd. But if you're cooking for less than a crowd, do you have to write them off the menu? We didn't think so, so we set out to make a smaller gratin, full of ripe summer vegetables, that could be simply and easily prepared. Knowing that we'd be able to scale back on preparation time and ingredients, we suspected our smaller gratin would be even easier and faster than the regular size.

Getting started, we spent a day in the test kitchen trying out a few sample gratin recipes, hoping to find one that was successful. But it wasn't meant to be—most of them produced gratins so flooded with vegetable juices that we had to serve them with a slotted spoon. One even called for slices of sourdough bread

SUMMER VEGETABLE GRATIN

to be layered among the vegetables, presumably to soak up some of the juices. But even with a cup of spongy bread cubes, a deluge of liquid still ruined the dish. And with the release of juices, along went the flavor—the gratins were bland and watery.

Before we could outline a dehydration plan, we had to determine exactly which vegetables to include. After some experimentation, we decided to stick with a fairly typical combination of tomato, zucchini, and summer squash, and one of each was all we needed, keeping the grocery list nice and tidy. The other common choices, eggplant and bell peppers, fell by the wayside. Eggplant was simply too mushy and spongy, and bell peppers looked pretty but took on a steamed flavor unless they were roasted before being added to the gratin.

With our vegetables selected, we focused on our baking dish. We chose a shallow 8½ by 5½-inch casserole dish—the perfect size to make two servings—and its low sides exposed more of the gratin's surface, which we knew would speed up evaporation of the vegetable juices. We sliced our vegetables thin, layered them evenly in the casserole, drizzled a bit of olive oil and some herbs on top, and moved the dish to the oven. We kept the dish uncovered, thinking this step, combined with the low sides of the casserole dish, would lead to a perfectly cooked gratin with the right amount of juices evaporated. Unfortunately, our gratin was still waterlogged.

To rid the zucchini and squash of some of their liquid, precooking methods such as grilling, broiling, or sautéing came to mind. Although these methods were workable, we didn't want to spend all day at the grill, oven, or stove just to make a side dish for two. Salting, a technique frequently used to draw moisture from vegetables, made more sense. This method, which took just 30 minutes, worked like a charm on the zucchini and summer squash, drying them out and thoroughly seasoning them as well. The salted tomatoes, however, were still exuding more liquid than we wanted.

In our testing, we found that the spots where the edges of the tomatoes had peeked through the layers of zucchini were particularly good, having taken on the appealing qualities of oven-roasted tomatoes. To capitalize on this effect, we remodeled the organization of our gratin, moving the tomatoes to a single top layer where they could really roast and caramelize. This worked well, especially when we drizzled the tomatoes with aromatic olive oil mixed with minced garlic and dried thyme.

This fragrant oil was so good that we decided to toss the salted zucchini and squash in it as well before we baked the gratin. To add another layer of complexity, we caramelized a thinly sliced onion and inserted these flavorful onion slices between the zucchini-squash and tomato layers. We tested various baking times and temperatures and found that a 400-degree oven for 40 minutes produced the right mix of juiciness in the bottom part of our gratin and roasted bites in the top part.

To promote crispness on the top layer and add a nice saltiness, we sprinkled the gratin with grated Parmesan about 10 minutes before it was finished. When we pulled it out of the oven, we added some chopped fresh basil and let it cool for a few minutes. No longer a waterlogged mess, our downsized gratin was now perfectly juicy and full of flavorful vegetables.

Summer Vegetable Gratin

SERVES 2

Buy zucchini and summer squash of roughly the same diameter. We like the visual contrast zucchini and summer squash bring to the dish, but you can also use just one or the other. You will need a shallow 8½ by 5½-inch baking dish with sides that are no more than 2 inches high for this recipe (see page 3). Serve with grilled fish or meat and accompanied by bread to soak up the flavorful juices.

2 tablespoons extra-virgin olive oil

1 small zucchini (4 ounces), ends trimmed, sliced crosswise into ¼-inch-thick rounds (see note)

1 small yellow summer squash (4 ounces), ends trimmed, sliced crosswise into ¼-inch-thick rounds (see note)

¾ teaspoon salt

1 tomato, sliced ¼ inch thick

1 onion, halved and sliced thin

1 garlic clove, minced

½ teaspoon pepper

¼ teaspoon dried thyme

1 ounce Parmesan cheese, grated (about ½ cup)

2 tablespoons chopped fresh basil

1. Adjust an oven rack to the upper-middle position and heat the oven to 400 degrees. Brush an 8½ by 5½-inch baking dish with 1 teaspoon of the oil and set aside.

2. Toss the zucchini and summer squash with ½ teaspoon of the salt in a colander set over a bowl, and let sit for 30 minutes. Spread the zucchini and summer squash slices out on several layers of paper towels. Gently press the tops of the slices dry with more paper towels.

3. Meanwhile, spread the tomato slices out on several more layers of paper towels, sprinkle with the remaining ¼ teaspoon salt, and let sit for 30 minutes. Gently press the tops of the tomato slices dry with more paper towels.

4. While the vegetables sit, heat 2 teaspoons more oil in a 10-inch nonstick skillet over medium heat until shimmering. Add the onion, cover, and cook, stirring occasionally, until softened, 5 to 7 minutes. Uncover and continue to cook, stirring often, until the onion is softened and deep golden brown, about 10 minutes longer. Transfer the onion to a bowl and set aside.

5. Combine the remaining 1 tablespoon oil, garlic, pepper, and thyme in a small bowl. In a large bowl, toss the dried zucchini and summer squash with half of the oil-garlic mixture, then arrange in the prepared casserole. Arrange the caramelized onions in an even layer over the squash. Slightly overlap the tomato slices in a single layer on top of the onion. Spoon the remaining oil-garlic mixture evenly over the tomato slices.

6. Bake until the vegetables are tender and the tomato slices are starting to brown around the edges, 30 to 35 minutes. Sprinkle with the cheese and continue to bake until the vegetables are bubbling and the cheese is lightly browned, about 10 minutes longer. Let the gratin sit for 10 minutes and sprinkle with the basil before serving.

CREAMY VEGETABLE GRATINS

CREAMY VEGETABLE GRATINS are the perfect complement to a large roast or a holiday ham, so most recipes generally serve a crowd and require a fair amount of prep work as a result. We wanted a repertoire of these comfort classics scaled down to serve just two and made easy enough to prepare on a busy weeknight.

Most gratins are made with a heavy cream sauce, topped with cheese, and then baked in a shallow dish until the vegetables are bound together and the topping becomes appealingly brown. More often than not, however, they contain mushy or undercooked vegetables and an unappetizing and curdled or gloppy sauce. We set out to fix these problems.

Starting our testing with potato gratin, we tried two common methods we encountered in several published recipes. For one, we rubbed our shallow dish with garlic, sliced a large russet potato—the perfect amount for a scaled-down gratin—and laid the slices in rows. We then topped them with a preliminary mixture of heavy cream and cheese and placed the dish in the oven to bake. We also tried recipes that called for parboiling the sliced potatoes in cream on the stove before dumping them into a shallow casserole dish, sprinkling them with cheese, and finishing the dish in the oven. Both versions presented problems.

We liked the ease of simply slicing and baking the vegetables, but most of the recipes that took this approach resulted in a sauce that broke, leaving us with cottage cheese–like curds floating in a watery sauce. On the other hand, when the recipes called for precooking, the potatoes were coated with a rich, creamy sauce; it turns out that the potatoes release some of their starch into the cooking liquid, which acts as a natural thickening agent to keep the sauce from breaking. But precooking the potatoes also meant they had to be stirred, which required diligent attention and can cause the potatoes to break apart. We set out to combine the best elements of these two methods and create a potato gratin that would let the oven do the work while still rewarding us with a creamy sauce.

We knew that we needed a sauce that was stable enough to withstand about 30 to 40 minutes in the oven without breaking. With baked macaroni and cheese (bound together with a sauce of milk and flour) as our inspiration, we made a quick sauce on the stovetop using 3 teaspoons of flour and ¾ cup of whole milk, tossed the potatoes in it, and transferred the mixture to the casserole dish to bake. The gratin came out of the oven with a silky smooth, creamy sauce. Tasters' only complaint was that the sauce wasn't quite rich enough, so we decided to use heavy cream in place of the milk and reduced the flour amount to 2 teaspoons to prevent an overly thick sauce. The resulting sauce pleased tasters, but it still needed a few flavor tweaks. We didn't think that rubbing the baking dish with garlic was imparting enough garlicky flavor, so we omitted that step. Instead, we cooked some shallot in a little butter before adding garlic, fresh thyme, and a pinch each of cayenne pepper and nutmeg. We then built the sauce in the same pot with the aromatics.

With our sauce in place, we focused on the potatoes. We tried making the gratin with russet, all-purpose, and Yukon Gold varieties. Yukon Gold and all-purpose potatoes weren't bad, but tasters found them a bit waxy. The traditional russet, with its tender bite and earthy flavor, was the unanimous favorite. The russet also formed tighter, more cohesive layers owing to its higher starch content.

As with our Summer Vegetable Gratin (page 239), we found that a smaller baking dish was the right cooking vessel; the shallow sides would allow the proper amount of evaporation (leaving us with a thick, creamy dish) and also help the cheese on top to brown more quickly (preventing a long cooking time that would cause the sauce to break). So we set the individual ramekins and loaf pans aside and reached for an oval baking dish measuring 8½ by 5½ inches with sides that were 2 inches high. Any shape will do, but for the best gratin, the baking dish should be roughly this size.

Up until now, we had been using the tiresome technique of carefully layering the sauce-coated raw potato slices one at a time in our baking dish. We decided to speed up the process and simply poured the potatoes into the dish, gently pressing them to remove any air pockets that formed. We covered the dish with foil and baked it in a 400-degree oven for 40 minutes, after which we sprinkled the potatoes with ¼ cup Gruyère and let the gratin cook uncovered for 10 minutes longer so the cheese would brown. The potatoes emerged from the oven bubbling hot with a golden crown. Although the casserole was quite loose straight out of the oven, a 10-minute rest was all it needed to cool off a bit and become a cohesive dish.

Once we had our basic technique down, we came up with a variation by swapping the potatoes for cauliflower. Following the technique we used for the potatoes, and using the same size casserole dish, we started by cutting the cauliflower florets into 1-inch pieces. We quickly learned that since cauliflower has more moisture and less starch than potatoes, we would have to make a thicker sauce. We reduced the amount of cream from ¾ cup to ¼ cup and cut the flour in half to just 1 teaspoon. The resulting sauce coated the florets nicely,

---

USE IT UP: CAULIFLOWER

Roasted Cauliflower
SERVES 2

This dish stands well on its own, but for a variation try stirring 1 teaspoon of either curry powder or chili powder into the oil before seasoning the cauliflower in step 1.

- ½ head cauliflower (about 1 pound), trimmed and stem cut flush with the bottom
- 3 tablespoons extra-virgin olive oil
- Salt and pepper

1. Adjust an oven rack to the lowest position and heat the oven to 475 degrees. Cut the cauliflower into 4 equal wedges so that the core and florets remain intact. In a medium bowl, combine the olive oil, ¼ teaspoon salt, and ¼ teaspoon pepper and add the wedges, tossing them with the oil. Place the wedges cut-side down on a foil-lined rimmed baking sheet.

2. Cover the baking sheet tightly with foil and cook for 10 minutes. Remove the foil and continue to cook until the bottoms of the cauliflower pieces are golden, 8 to 12 minutes longer.

3. Working quickly, remove the baking sheet from the oven and carefully flip the wedges. Continue to roast until the cauliflower is golden all over, 8 to 12 minutes longer. Season with salt and pepper to taste and serve.

but after sampling our finished cauliflower gratin, we found that reducing the amount of cream also cut back on the flavor of our dish.

We tried another cauliflower gratin, but this time we doubled the amount of grated Gruyère, thinking that we could make up for some of the lost fat and flavor with cheese. The cauliflower cooked in the oven, covered with foil, and released its moisture, loosening the sauce to the perfect creamy consistency. Then, as we had done with the potatoes, we added the cheese—½ cup this time—for the final 10 minutes of cooking. But before we sprinkled the cheese on top, we stirred the cauliflower to coat it evenly with the sauce. Now when we pulled the finished dish out of the oven, the cauliflower was covered in a rich, creamy sauce and had a beautiful, golden brown top.

Potato Gratin

SERVES 2

Prepare and assemble all of the ingredients before slicing the potatoes or the potatoes will begin to turn brown (do not store the sliced potatoes in water). Slicing the potatoes ⅛ inch thick is crucial for the success of this dish; use a mandoline, a V-slicer, or a food processor fitted with a ⅛-inch-thick slicing blade. You will need a shallow 8½ by 5½-inch baking dish with sides that are no more than 2 inches high for this recipe (see page 3). Parmesan can be substituted for the Gruyère, if desired.

- 1 large russet potato (about 12 ounces), peeled and sliced ⅛ inch thick (see note)
- 1 tablespoon unsalted butter
- 1 small shallot, minced (about 1 tablespoon)
- ½ teaspoon salt
- 1 garlic clove, minced
- 1 teaspoon minced fresh thyme or ¼ teaspoon dried
- ¼ teaspoon pepper
  Pinch ground nutmeg
  Pinch cayenne pepper
- 2 teaspoons unbleached all-purpose flour
- ¾ cup heavy cream
- ¼ cup grated Gruyère cheese (see note)

1. Adjust an oven rack to the upper-middle position and heat the oven to 400 degrees. Coat an 8½ by 5½-inch baking dish with vegetable oil spray. Place the potatoes in a medium bowl and set aside.

2. Melt the butter in a small saucepan over medium heat. Add the shallot and salt and cook until softened, about 2 minutes. Stir in the garlic, thyme, pepper, nutmeg, and cayenne and cook until fragrant, about 30 seconds. Stir in the flour and cook until incorporated, about 10 seconds. Whisk in the cream, bring to a simmer, and cook until beginning to thicken, about 30 seconds.

3. Pour the sauce over the potatoes and toss to coat thoroughly. Transfer the mixture to the prepared dish and gently pack the potatoes into an even layer, removing any air pockets. Cover the dish with foil and bake until the potatoes are almost tender, 35 to 40 minutes.

4. Remove the foil and sprinkle with the cheese. Continue to bake, uncovered, until the cheese is lightly browned and the potatoes are tender, about 10 minutes longer. Let the gratin sit for 10 minutes before serving.

NOTES FROM THE TEST KITCHEN

THE BEST MANDOLINE

If you don't own a food processor, a mandoline can make quick work of turning out piles of identically sliced vegetables. We wanted to test the range of models being marketed to home cooks and were shocked by the assortment of sizes and prices (anywhere from $25 to $400). We gathered 13 mandolines and put them to the test. We preferred models with a V-shaped blade and rimmed, long-pronged hand guards. If we were going to own a mandoline, we figured it should be able to do the works—slice, julienne, and waffle-cut—while keeping our hands safe. We found our winner in the **OXO V-Blade Mandoline Slicer.** Testers liked its wide, sturdy gripper guard, and its razor-sharp blade made short work of a variety of fruits and vegetables. Plus, it wasn't anywhere near $400—this savvy slicer sells for $49.99.

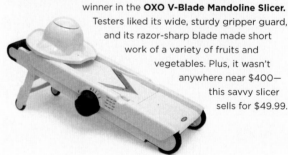

POTATO GRATIN

Cauliflower Gratin

SERVES 2

Parmesan cheese can be substituted for the Gruyère, if desired. You will need a shallow 8½ by 5½-inch baking dish with sides that are no more than 2 inches high for this recipe (see page 3). Serve with steaks or pork chops. See page 241 for a recipe to use up the leftover cauliflower.

- ½ head cauliflower (about 1 pound), trimmed, cored, and cut into 1-inch pieces (about 4 cups) (see photos)
- 1 tablespoon unsalted butter
- 1 small shallot, minced (about 1 tablespoon)
- ½ teaspoon salt
- 1 garlic clove, minced
- ½ teaspoon minced fresh thyme or pinch dried
- ⅛ teaspoon pepper
- Pinch ground nutmeg
- Pinch cayenne pepper
- 1 teaspoon unbleached all-purpose flour
- ¼ cup heavy cream
- 1 ounce Gruyère cheese (see note), grated (about ½ cup)

1. Adjust an oven rack to the upper-middle position and heat the oven to 400 degrees. Coat an 8½ by 5½-inch baking dish with vegetable oil spray. Place the cauliflower in a medium bowl and set aside.

2. Melt the butter in a small saucepan over medium heat. Add the shallot and salt and cook until softened, about 2 minutes. Stir in the garlic, thyme, pepper, nutmeg, and cayenne and cook until fragrant, about 30 seconds. Stir in the flour and cook until incorporated, about 10 seconds. Whisk in the cream, bring to a simmer, and cook until beginning to thicken, about 30 seconds.

3. Pour the sauce over the cauliflower and toss to coat thoroughly. Transfer the mixture to the prepared dish and gently pack the cauliflower into an even layer, removing any air pockets. Cover the dish with foil and bake until the cauliflower is almost tender, 30 to 35 minutes.

4. Remove the foil, stir the cauliflower to coat with the sauce, and sprinkle with the cheese. Continue to bake, uncovered, until the cheese is lightly browned and the cauliflower is tender, about 10 minutes longer. Let the gratin sit for 10 minutes before serving.

NOTES FROM THE TEST KITCHEN

PREPARING CAULIFLOWER

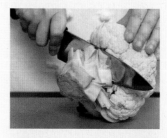

1. After pulling off the outer leaves, trim off the stem near the base of the head.

2. Turn the cauliflower upside down so the stem is facing up. Using a sharp knife, cut around the core to remove it.

3. Using the tip of a knife, separate the florets from the inner stem.

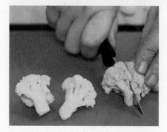

4. Cut the florets in half, or in quarters if necessary, so that individual pieces measure about 1 inch.

MASHED POTATOES AND ROOT VEGETABLES

BECAUSE MASHED POTATOES ARE RELATIVELY SIMPLE, many recipes introduce root vegetables to the mix. The sweet and earthy flavors of carrots or parsnips added to plain mashed potatoes is certainly appealing, and the combination presents a nice change from regular old mashed potatoes. The trouble is that mashed potatoes and root vegetables often make enough to feed an army. We knew that we would have to choose just one root vegetable—preferably a small one—to keep our mash from yielding too much, but first we would have to get the ratio of root vegetable to potato just right.

In early rounds of recipe testing, we'd concluded that a 1-to-1 ratio of root vegetables to potatoes was much too heavy on the vegetable side. We decided to experiment with a 1-to-3 ratio, while also significantly reducing the total amount of vegetables to make a serving for two, not 10. We tried boiling 4 ounces of carrot (we developed our mash with carrot, but found parsnip to be equally appealing) and 12 ounces of Yukon Gold potatoes, which are waxy and low in starch, together in the same pot, draining them, mashing them with a potato masher, and stirring in cream and melted butter. This time both the consistency and serving size were right, but with only 4 ounces of carrot to 12 ounces of potato, the distinctive flavor of the carrot was barely recognizable.

If we wanted to maintain an agreeable texture, we had to find a way to make the most of a small amount of vegetables. Could we enhance their character by cooking them separately to bolster their flavor? We tried sautéing the carrots in butter until caramelized—for rich flavor—and then mashing them with boiled potatoes. This mash was definitely moving in the right direction with its sweet and nutty vegetable flavor, but we were sure we could come up with a more convenient one-burner, one-pot recipe. We thought that sautéing the carrot first in a saucepan before adding the raw potato and braising the two together in the same saucepan might do the trick.

We sautéed a carrot in a generous amount of butter (2 tablespoons) until the butter browned and the vegetable had caramelized. Next, we added a peeled and sliced potato to the pot, along with ⅓ cup water and a dash of salt. After 15 minutes of gentle cooking, the potato and carrot were completely tender and all of the water had been absorbed. The flavor was spot-on: rich, earthy, and well balanced. Swapping the water for chicken broth—preferred over vegetable broth for its richer flavor—allowed the potatoes to soak up even more savory notes. As for dairy options, tasters didn't deviate from the test kitchen's usual choice of half-and-half, preferring it to milk and cream. We mashed the vegetables and let them drink up as much half-and-half as they could, which was ⅓ cup.

The flavor of our recipe was finally just right, but the texture had been thrown off in the meantime. When potatoes are boiled, some of their starch leaches out into the cooking water, never making it into the finished dish. With our unusual procedure, however, the starch could not escape and ended up being incorporated into the mash. The result was an overly starchy, almost gluey texture. Thinking things over, we realized we needed to get rid of some starch before we cooked the potatoes.

Our solution was rinsing the potato; in just a couple of minutes, we rinsed our peeled, sliced potato in several changes of water and watched the cloudy, starch-filled rinsing liquid run down the drain. Once the potato pieces were cooked and mashed, we knew that we'd found our solution—the starchiness was gone.

To finish off the potatoes, a sprinkling of fresh herbs was in order. The delicate onion flavor of minced chives

NOTES FROM THE TEST KITCHEN

RINSING POTATOES

Rinsing peeled, sliced potatoes in several changes of water removes excess starch and prevents gumminess once the potatoes are cooked and mashed.

offered a nice counterpoint to the earthy vegetables. At last, we had a standout recipe for mashed potatoes and root vegetables that was perfectly portioned for two.

Mashed Potatoes and Root Vegetables

SERVES 2

A russet potato will yield a slightly fluffier, less creamy mash, but it can be used in place of the Yukon Gold potato if desired. It is important to cut the vegetables into equal-sized pieces so they cook at the same rate. Be sure to rinse the potato in 3 or 4 changes of cold water to remove the excess starch.

> 2   tablespoons unsalted butter
> 1   medium carrot or parsnip, peeled,
>   halved lengthwise, and cut into ¼-inch-thick
>   half-moons
> 1   large Yukon Gold potato (about 12 ounces),
>   peeled, cut into ¼-inch pieces, rinsed, and drained
>   (see note)
> ⅓   cup low-sodium chicken broth
>   Salt
> ⅓   cup half-and-half, warmed, plus more as needed
> 1   tablespoon minced fresh chives (optional)
>   Pepper

1. Melt the butter in a medium saucepan over medium heat. Add the carrot and cook, stirring occasionally, until the butter is browned and the carrot is caramelized, 5 to 10 minutes.

2. Add the potato, broth, and ¼ teaspoon salt to the pan, and bring to a simmer. Cover and cook over medium-low heat, stirring occasionally, until the potato pieces fall apart easily when poked with a fork and all the liquid has been absorbed, 10 to 15 minutes. Remove the pan from the heat, uncover, and let the steam escape for 2 minutes.

3. Mash the potato and carrot in the saucepan with a potato masher. Gently fold in the half-and-half and chives (if using). (If the mixture is too thick, add 1 to 2 tablespoons more half-and-half as needed.) Season with salt and pepper to taste and serve.

SMASHED POTATOES

SILKY-SMOOTH MASHED POTATOES are at their best when topped with rich holiday gravy or a highly seasoned pan sauce. But there are times when there is no gravy to be had, and that's when smashed potatoes are just the thing. Their bold flavors and rustic, chunky texture give them the brawn to stand on their own, whether served with a grilled steak or a roast chicken.

Unfortunately, most recipes for this dish are plagued by a multitude of variations and refinements. Running the gamut from lean and mean to might-as-well-be-mashed—no skin, no texture, no oomph—smashed potatoes suffer from an identity crisis. We wanted chunks of potato textured with skins and bound by rich, creamy puree. And we wanted to make just enough that we wouldn't be eating leftover potatoes with dinner for the next week.

Using the test kitchen's standard add-ins—melted butter and half-and-half—we smashed our way through four different varieties of potato: russet, all-purpose, Yukon Gold, and medium-sized Red Bliss. The russets and all-purpose potatoes had strong potato flavor, but their dry texture caused them to crumble quickly when smashed, and their skins were too thick and tough against the soft, mealy flesh. The texture of the waxy Yukon Golds was slightly firmer, but these potatoes broke down too much when smashed. The moist, low-starch red potatoes won out with their pleasantly tender thin skins, which worked nicely in a chunky potato side.

We then looked at how many potatoes to cook to yield a serving for two. We reasoned that if one large russet (about 8 ounces) was enough to serve one as a baked potato, then a pound should do it for two. But when we tested that theory with our red potatoes, we were left with almost enough smashed potatoes for a family of four. So we settled on 12 ounces (about four small potatoes) as the perfect amount for two.

Next we had to decide how to cook the potatoes. We tried cooking them both whole and cut into 1-inch chunks. Even though cutting the potatoes reduced the cooking time, the end result was leaden, soggy smashed potatoes with diluted potato flavor. Cooked whole, the potatoes retained their naturally creamy texture, as less potato surface was exposed to the water. To add complementary flavor and depth to our potatoes, we added a bay leaf and salt to the water to season the potatoes as they cooked.

Although a potato masher and fork are good tools for making chunky mashed potatoes, they took our smashed potatoes a little too far, smoothing out the rough, uneven chunks of potato that define this dish. We took a cue from the recipe name, grabbed a plain old wooden spoon, and began smashing each potato with the back of it. If they were cooked just right, they burst apart, splitting their skins when they broke. This task was even easier once the potatoes had dried for a few minutes and their skins were no longer slippery.

Now we turned to the other component that would make these potatoes really stand out: the dairy. Using only butter and half-and-half with the mildly flavored red potatoes resulted in flat-tasting smashed potatoes. To boost the flavor, we tried sour cream, trusted partner of the baked potato. Sour cream alone didn't give the potatoes enough body, so we tried supplementing it with both half-and-half and heavy cream. Both of these additions served only to dull the acidity of the sour cream—which we liked. After making batches of sour, watery potatoes, we realized this was the wrong approach. We needed something tangy yet creamy that would bind the potatoes in terms of both flavor and texture. A fellow test cook suggested the rather unconventional cream cheese. Surprisingly, 3 tablespoons of cream cheese—and no sour cream or half-and-half—gave these savory potatoes just the right touch of tang and creaminess. All they needed now was some butter to add richness, and a single tablespoon was just the right amount for a deeper flavor without greasiness.

In our standard mashed potato recipe, we found it important to add the melted butter before the half-and-half; the butter coats the potatoes' starch with fat, which keeps them from soaking up too much liquid from the half-and-half and turning leaden. We wondered if the order in which we added the cream cheese and butter to the smashed potatoes would make a difference. It did—we quickly learned that it was better to mix the two together first, with a bit of the cooking water, and then gently fold them into the smashed potatoes all at once. This also acted to incorporate more flavor from the cooking water, which was nicely seasoned with the salt and bay leaf.

Unfortunately, after our sensational smashed potatoes sat in the pan for a few minutes—and we were ready to dish them out—their luscious texture went from creamy and smooth to dry and unpalatable. The potatoes had quickly absorbed what little moisture the butter and cream cheese had to offer. Not wanting to make the potatoes any richer, we decided to use some more of the potato cooking water to thin out the potatoes. We started with 1 tablespoon and added more as needed until we had a unified and creamy consistency. Just thick enough to be scooped up with a fork, these potatoes were thinner in terms of texture but not flavor.

To finish seasoning the potatoes, we added a little more salt and a dash of freshly ground black pepper. Tasters thought something green and fresh would be nice, so we mixed some chopped fresh chives with our cream cheese mixture; this move brightened the flavor just enough. Finally, we had perfected the uncomplicated but exciting alternative to plain old mashed potatoes.

NOTES FROM THE TEST KITCHEN

STORING POTATOES

Since potatoes seem almost indestructible compared with other vegetables, little thought is generally given to their storage. But after testing potatoes stored in four different environments—a cool, dark place, in the refrigerator, near a sunlit window, and in a warm, dark place—for four weeks, we had our answer. As expected, the potatoes stored in a cool, dark spot were the winners. They were still firm, had not sprouted, and were crisp and moist when cut. To push things even further, we then tested whether we could achieve even better results by storing potatoes in a cool, dark place with an apple—a common old wives' tale that we wanted to put to the test. We found that due to the ethylene gas the apple released, it did indeed boost the storage time; these potatoes lasted almost two weeks longer.

THE BEST WOODEN SPOON

Wooden spoons are such basic utensils. Is there really any difference between one wooden spoon and another? After using 10 models to caramelize onions and stir pots of vegetable curry, we can confidently say yes. To test durability, we also tried snapping each spoon in half. The qualities we liked include thin edges (which scrape more effectively than thick edges), a strong but not bulky handle, and a broad bowl that covers a lot of surface area and can reach into the corners of a pot. Our favorite is the **Mario Batali 13-Inch Wooden Spoon** ($4.95), which is strong but lightweight and has a comfortable grip.

SERVES 2

White potatoes can be used instead of red, but their skins lack the rosy color. Serve with chicken or beef.

- 12 **ounces red potatoes (about 4 small), scrubbed (see note)**
-      **Salt**
- 1   **bay leaf**
- 3   **tablespoons cream cheese, softened**
- 1   **tablespoon unsalted butter, melted**
-      **Pepper**
- 1   **tablespoon minced fresh chives (optional)**

1. Bring the potatoes, ½ teaspoon salt, bay leaf, and 2 quarts water to a simmer in a medium saucepan, and cook until tender, 10 to 15 minutes. Reserve ½ cup of the potato cooking water, then drain the potatoes. Return the potatoes to the pot, discard the bay leaf, and let the steam escape for 2 minutes.

2. While the potatoes dry, whisk the softened cream cheese and melted butter together in a small bowl until smooth and fully incorporated. Stir in 2 tablespoons of the reserved cooking water, ¼ teaspoon salt, ¼ teaspoon pepper, and chives (if using).

3. Using the back of a wooden spoon, smash the potatoes just enough to break the skins. Fold in the cream cheese mixture until most of the liquid has been absorbed and chunks of potatoes remain. Add more cooking water, 1 tablespoon at a time as needed, until the potatoes are slightly looser than desired (the potatoes will thicken slightly). Season with salt and pepper to taste and serve.

VARIATION

Garlic-Rosemary Smashed Potatoes

Melt 2 tablespoons unsalted butter in a small skillet over medium heat. Add 2 garlic cloves, minced, and ¼ teaspoon minced fresh rosemary, and cook until fragrant, about 30 seconds, then transfer to a small bowl and set aside. Follow the recipe for Smashed Potatoes, substituting the butter-garlic mixture for the melted butter in step 2 and omitting the chives.

RICE PILAF

WHEN MADE PROPERLY, RICE PILAF IS FRAGRANT and fluffy, but it often turns up as an overly cooked, clumpy mess. Getting rice pilaf just right is dependent upon getting the ratio of water to rice correct, so we felt this common side—which can be tricky to scale down—was the perfect candidate for downsizing for two.

We began by deciding on the best type of rice for pilaf. We immediately limited our testing to long-grain rice, since medium- and short-grain rice produce a rather sticky, starchy product and we were looking for fluffy, separate grains. Plain long-grain white rice worked well in our pilaf, but basmati rice was even better: Each grain was separate, long, and fluffy, and the rice had a fresh, delicate fragrance. That said, you can use plain long-grain rice if basmati is not available.

Most important to our testing was deciding how much rice would serve two. The test kitchen has found in past tests that 1½ cups of long-grain rice serve four, so we tried simply cutting that amount in half to ¾ cup. But dividing by two didn't work quite as well for the water. Our usual amount of water is 2¼ cups (for 1½ cups rice), but we found that we couldn't simply divide the water amount in half (to 1⅛ cups); instead, we found we needed a bit more water, 1¼ cups, to yield fully cooked rice.

With our rice-to-water ratio set, we were ready to test the traditional cooking method, which calls for rinsing the rice, sautéing it in some fat, then adding a hot liquid and simmering. Various recipes we researched declared all these steps to be essential in producing the ultimate pilaf with separated light and fluffy grains. We did find that rinsing the rice made a slight difference in texture, and the grains were more separated and shiny. Sautéing the rice, however, had an important impact on both the flavor and the texture of the pilaf—it added a pleasant toasty flavor and worked to keep the grains separate. We liked the flavor of rice sautéed in a tablespoon of butter best, but there are certainly times when oil is preferred (for example, when serving the pilaf with Asian food). We also liked the added flavor dimension of sautéing a shallot in the fat before adding the rice.

Most recipes for rice pilaf call for cooking the rice in the water until the water is gone (at which point the rice is still underdone), then removing the pan from the heat and letting the rice steam until tender. We tried letting the rice steam for 10 minutes after being removed from the heat. We wondered if a longer or shorter steaming time would make much of a difference in the resulting pilaf. We made a few batches of pilaf, allowing it to steam for five minutes, 10 minutes, and 15 minutes. The pilaf that steamed for five minutes was heavy and wet. The batch that steamed for 15 minutes was the lightest and least watery, but it was still somewhat heavy.

We realized we needed a way to absorb the excess water that was evaporating in the covered pan before it could be reabsorbed by the rice. We decided to try placing a clean kitchen towel between the pan and the lid right after we took the rice off the stove. The towel, we reasoned, would prevent condensation and absorb the water. We found this produced the best results of all, and it reduced the steaming time to only 10 minutes.

At last, we had a great recipe for flavorful and fluffy rice pilaf that would pair well with anything.

NOTES FROM THE TEST KITCHEN

THE BEST BASMATI RICE
Prized for its nutty flavor and sweet aroma, basmati rice is eaten worldwide in pilafs and biryanis and as an accompaniment to curries. The best Indian-grown rice is said to come from the Himalayan foothills, where the snow-flooded soil and humid climate offer ideal growing conditions. Choosing among the multitude of boxes, bags, and burlap sacks available today on supermarket shelves can be confusing. To find a truly great grain, we steamed seven brands, five from India and two domestic options.

Matched against Indian imports, domestic brands suffered. Indian basmati is aged for a minimum of a year, though often much longer, before being packaged. Aging dehydrates the rice, which translates into grains that, once cooked, expand greatly, more so than any other long-grain rice. American-grown basmati is not aged and hence doesn't expand as much as Indian-grown rice. American basmati proved to be not nearly as aromatic as Indian-grown basmati, and the cooked grains were soft and stubby. Although all of the imported brands were acceptable, tasters' top pick was **Tilda,** which was "wonderfully textured."

Rice Pilaf
SERVES 2

Oil can be substituted for the butter, depending on what you are serving with the pilaf. You will need a small saucepan with a tight-fitting lid to make this recipe.

1¼   **cups water**
¼   **teaspoon salt**
⅛   **teaspoon pepper**
1   **tablespoon unsalted butter (see note)**
1   **small shallot, minced (about 1 tablespoon)**
¾   **cup basmati or long-grain rice, rinsed
     (see page 20)**

1. Bring the water to a boil, covered, in a small saucepan over medium-high heat. Add the salt and pepper, and cover to keep hot.

2. Meanwhile, melt the butter in a second small saucepan over medium heat. Add the shallot and cook until softened, about 2 minutes. Stir in the rice and cook until the edges of the grains begin to turn translucent, about 2 minutes. Stir the hot, seasoned water into the rice. Return to a boil, then reduce the heat to low, cover, and simmer until all the water is absorbed, 12 to 15 minutes.

3. Off the heat, uncover the saucepan and place a clean kitchen towel folded in half over it, then replace the lid. Let the rice stand for 10 minutes, then fluff with a fork and serve.

VARIATIONS
Rice Pilaf with Pine Nuts, Basil, and Lemon Zest
Follow the recipe for Rice Pilaf, stirring ¼ cup shredded fresh basil, 2 tablespoons pine nuts, toasted (see page 226), and ¼ teaspoon grated lemon zest into the rice just before serving.

Rice Pilaf with Saffron and Toasted Almonds
Follow the recipe for Rice Pilaf, stirring a pinch of saffron into the butter with the shallot in step 2. Stir 2 tablespoons sliced almonds, toasted (see page 226), into the rice just before serving.

BLUEBERRY CRUMBLE

DESSERTS

STRAWBERRY SHORTCAKES

SHORTCAKES MAY SEEM SIMILAR TO OTHER FRUIT desserts such as crisps and cobblers, but there is one important difference—the fruit is not cooked. For a true shortcake, sweetened fruit, usually strawberries, is spread between halves of a split biscuit. A dollop or two of whipped cream is also added. The contrast of the cool fruit, warm and crisp biscuit, and chilled whipped cream places this dessert in a category by itself. And unlike fruit desserts that are baked in one large dish, shortcakes are assembled individually—so naturally we thought they would make an ideal dessert for two.

Because the fruit is not cooked, frozen fruit is not an option. The fruit must be ripe as well. Half-ripe berries might be fine in a pandowdy but will make a second-rate shortcake. Also, because the fruit is not baked, only softer fruits are appropriate. A pear or apple shortcake does not make sense. Strawberries are soft enough and have enough flavor to be used uncooked.

Our first order of business was to figure out how to prepare the strawberries. Quartered or sliced strawberries in shortcakes often slide off the split biscuits, and crushed fruit stays put but doesn't look as appealing. We found a happy compromise by slicing most of the strawberries and then crushing the remaining portion to unify the sliced fruit. The thick puree anchors the sliced fruit so that it won't slip off the biscuit. We found that a pint of strawberries was the perfect amount for two people, and a few teaspoons of sugar contributed just the right amount of sweetness. Our testing for this recipe revolved mostly around the biscuits and figuring out the best way to scale down a standard recipe. Strawberry shortcake requires a substantial biscuit—it should be dense, cakey, and sturdy enough to withstand splitting and layering with juicy fruit and whipped cream. We assumed that a richer biscuit—that is, one made with eggs—would work best.

To make sure, we tried four very different sweetened biscuits—a baking powder version with fat cut into flour, baking powder, salt, and sugar and then moistened with milk; buttermilk biscuits, with buttermilk in place of milk and baking soda substituted for part of the baking powder; cream biscuits, with heavy cream standing in for the milk and some of the fat; and egg-enriched cream biscuits, with an egg and half-and-half

replacing the milk. After sampling each, we felt that the egg-enriched biscuits had the advantage. The baking powder and buttermilk biscuits weren't rich enough. The cream biscuits were good-looking but gummy inside. The egg and half-and-half biscuits were finer-textured and more cake-like.

With our general direction settled, we began to test individual ingredients as well as their amounts. Because biscuits should be tender, we assumed that low-protein cake flour would deliver the best results. But to our surprise, the cake flour biscuit came in last, with a meltingly tender yet powdery and dry texture that was too much like shortbread. There was not enough gluten in this flour to support all the fat. Shortcakes made with all-purpose flour (⅔ cup was just right) were tender, moist, and cakey, making them our clear favorite.

We then experimented with liquids, figuring that the egg might be crucial but maybe not the half-and-half. Buttermilk made the biscuits too savory, and heavy cream made them squat and dense. Milk was fine, but the richer flavor of half-and-half made it our first choice. Most recipes that yield six biscuits include only one egg, but using less than one egg for our scaled-down recipe would obviously be difficult. Instead we reduced the amount of half-and-half so we could use one egg and still keep the proper ratio of wet to dry ingredients— just 2 tablespoons of half-and-half did the trick.

We already knew that mixing biscuit dough in a food processor, our preferred method, is foolproof. For cooks without a food processor, we suggest freezing the butter and then using a box grater to shave the butter into bits before cutting it into the flour.

When shaping the dough, we challenged the test kitchen's established method for biscuits. We traditionally advocate using a biscuit cutter to stamp out the dough rounds, to avoid overworking the dough, since warm hands can cause the dough's surface butter to melt. Using a biscuit cutter requires less handling with larger amounts of dough. When making just two biscuits, however, there is such a small quantity of dough that very little handling is needed. Patting the dough into a square, then stamping out just two biscuits, wasted too much dough—shaping the biscuits by hand proved the better method. Dividing the dough in half and shaping each piece into a 2½-inch circle that was about 1 inch thick on a floured work surface was fast and simple. Flouring our hands as we worked helped to minimize overworking the dough. These biscuits were attractive, rustic, and tender—a perfect complement to the strawberries and whipped cream.

Easy Strawberry Shortcakes
MAKES 2

Fresh blueberries, raspberries, or halved blackberries can be substituted for some or all of the strawberries. Fresh fruit is key to the success of these shortcakes, so do not substitute frozen. Preparing the fruit first gives it a chance to become truly juicy—just what you want on freshly made shortcakes.

SHORTCAKES

- ⅔ cup (3¼ ounces) unbleached all-purpose flour, plus extra for the counter
- 2 tablespoons sugar
- 1 teaspoon baking powder
- ⅛ teaspoon salt
- 4 tablespoons (½ stick) unsalted butter, cut into ½-inch pieces and chilled
- 2 tablespoons half-and-half
- 1 large egg, at room temperature
- 1 large egg white, lightly beaten

FRUIT

- 2 cups (10 ounces) fresh strawberries, hulled (see note)
- 5 teaspoons sugar
- 1 recipe Whipped Cream (recipe follows)

1. FOR THE SHORTCAKES: Adjust an oven rack to the middle position and heat the oven to 425 degrees. Line a rimmed baking sheet with parchment paper.

2. Pulse the flour, 5 teaspoons of the sugar, baking powder, and salt together in a food processor until combined, about 3 pulses. Sprinkle the butter pieces over the top and pulse until the mixture resembles coarse cornmeal, about 15 pulses. Transfer the mixture to a medium bowl. Whisk the half-and-half and whole egg together, then stir into the flour mixture with a rubber spatula until large clumps form.

3. Turn the mixture out onto a well-floured counter. Divide the dough into two even pieces, then, with

well-floured hands, shape each into a 2½-inch circle, about 1 inch thick.

4. Arrange the shortcakes on the prepared baking sheet. Brush the tops with the egg white and sprinkle with the remaining 1 teaspoon sugar. Bake the shortcakes until golden brown, 10 to 12 minutes, rotating the baking sheet halfway through baking. Transfer the shortcakes to a wire rack and let cool for 15 minutes. (The shortcakes can be cooled completely and stored in a zipper-lock bag at room temperature for up to 3 days or frozen for up to 1 month. Before serving, refresh in a 350-degree oven for 3 to 5 minutes if not frozen and 7 to 10 minutes if frozen.)

5. FOR THE FRUIT: Meanwhile, crush ¾ cup of the strawberries with a potato masher in a medium bowl. Slice the remaining 1¼ cups berries and fold them into the crushed berries along with the sugar. Let the berry mixture sit at room temperature until the sugar has dissolved and the berries are juicy, about 10 minutes.

6. Split each shortcake in half and lay the bottoms on individual serving plates. Spoon the fruit over each bottom, dollop with the whipped cream, and cap with the shortcake tops. Serve.

NOTES FROM THE TEST KITCHEN

HULLING STRAWBERRIES

If you don't own a strawberry huller, you can improvise with a plastic straw. Push the straw through the bottom of the berry and up through the leafy stem end. The straw will remove the core as well as the leafy top.

STORING EGGS

Although perishable, properly stored eggs will last up to three months, but both the yolks and the whites will become looser and their flavor will begin to fade. To be sure that you have fresh eggs, check the sell-by date on the side of the carton. By law, the sell-by date must be no more than 30 days after the packaging date. To ensure freshness, store eggs in the back of the refrigerator (the coldest area), not in the door (which is actually the warmest part of the refrigerator), and keep them in the carton. It holds in moisture and keeps eggs from drying out; the carton also protects the eggs from odor.

Whipped Cream

MAKES ABOUT ¾ CUP

The whipped cream can be refrigerated in a fine-mesh strainer set over a small bowl, wrapped tightly with plastic wrap, for up to 8 hours.

⅓ **cup heavy cream, chilled**
1 **teaspoon sugar**
¼ **teaspoon vanilla extract**

Whip the cream, sugar, and vanilla together in a large bowl with an electric mixer on medium-low speed until frothy, about 1 minute. Increase the speed to high and continue to whip the cream to soft peaks, 1 to 3 minutes.

BLUEBERRY CRUMBLE

BLUEBERRY CRUMBLE MAY BE A SIMPLE DISH—sweetened blueberries baked under a crunchy streusel topping—but that doesn't mean it's foolproof. All too often, the filling is soupy. That's because the thick layer of streusel on top of the fruit prevents the excess moisture in the berries from evaporating. The filling soaks into the topping, leaving both components compromised. We wanted to make a crumble that featured a thick, fresh-tasting blueberry filling topped with a contrasting layer of crunchy streusel.

Crumbles are so named because they were originally vehicles for using up stale cake or cookies, which were crumbled over the fruit before baking. Modern recipes typically use a streusel topping of flour, butter, sugar, and oats over a simple filling of blueberries, sugar, and spices. (A crisp is similar but contains nuts.) We were not impressed by any of the blueberry crumble recipes we tested, so we decided to build our own from scratch.

Two cups of fresh blueberries were an ample amount for two people. We baked batches of untopped filling (we'd get to the streusel later) to test granulated sugar against light brown and dark brown sugars. The results were clear: The brown sugars competed with the fresh berry flavor. To the white sugar we added cinnamon, nutmeg, and cloves in varying amounts and combinations, but we were surprised to find that tasters

preferred no spice at all—sugar and a pinch of salt were all the seasonings the filling needed.

There were two ways we could firm up the filling: precooking the berries or adding a thickener. Simmering the mixture on the stovetop thickened the filling, but it also reduced the blueberries to mush and cooked out their fresh flavor. Moving on to the thickeners, we tried tossing the sugared berries with flour, tapioca, and cornstarch. The flour worked but made the filling pasty. Tapioca needed at least 40 minutes in the oven to thicken, which was too much cooking time for the berries, especially since we were using such a small amount. A mere 1½ teaspoons of cornstarch were enough to quickly thicken the filling without muting the flavor of the berries.

We diligently tested the traditional crumble toppings of cookies (their texture was never truly crunchy and too many crumbs sank into the filling) and cake crumbs (which were impractical—we don't usually have extra cake sitting around). Disappointed, we decided to stick with making our own streusel by combining flour, butter, sugar, and oats. Our tasters liked a modestly flavored filling (with the berries taking center stage), but they wanted more flavor in the streusel, so we replaced the granulated sugar with light brown sugar and added a touch of cinnamon for spice. Although we would normally combine a streusel topping in a food processor, with such small ingredient quantities we found it easier to simply mix them together by hand.

But when we sprinkled our topping onto the filling, it sank and became quite soggy. We wondered if the size of the crumble pieces was the problem. Rather than combining the ingredients until the mixture was fine, we cut the cold butter into the dry streusel ingredients just until they clumped together into rough dime-sized pieces. This streusel baked up crisp and crunchy—tasters were pleased. However, there was still one nagging problem: The blueberry filling was bubbling up and over the topping in places. Maybe it was time to revisit our baking vessel.

Up to this point, we had been baking the crumble in a small 8½ by 5½-inch casserole dish. This was working OK, but maybe baking the crumble in individual ramekins would help solve the problem. Two 12-ounce ramekins proved the perfect remedy—the smaller individual baking dishes allowed us to create a thicker layer of topping, which in turn prevented the filling from bubbling over. We finally had a foolproof blueberry crumble, just for two.

Blueberry Crumble

MAKES 2

Avoid instant or quick oats here—they are too soft and will make the crumble mushy. In step 2, do not press the topping into the berry mixture or it may sink and become soggy. Frozen berries do not work in this recipe because they shed too much liquid. You will need two 12-ounce ramekins for this recipe (see page 3). The crumble can also be prepared in an 8½ by 5½-inch baking dish. Serve with vanilla ice cream or Whipped Cream (page 254).

¼–⅓ cup (1¾ to 2⅓ ounces) granulated sugar

1½ teaspoons cornstarch

Salt

2 cups (10 ounces) fresh blueberries (see note)

½ cup (2½ ounces) unbleached all-purpose flour

⅓ cup old-fashioned oats (see note)

¼ cup packed (1¾ ounces) light brown sugar

¼ teaspoon ground cinnamon

4 tablespoons (½ stick) unsalted butter, cut into 4 pieces and chilled

1. Adjust an oven rack to the lower-middle position and heat the oven to 375 degrees. Combine ¼ cup of the granulated sugar, cornstarch, and a pinch of salt in a medium bowl. Gently toss the berries with the sugar mixture. (If the fruit tastes tart, add up to 1½ tablespoons more sugar.) Divide the berries evenly between two 12-ounce ramekins.

2. Mix the flour, oats, brown sugar, cinnamon, and a pinch of salt together in a medium bowl. Add the butter to the bowl and, using your fingers, blend the butter into the dry ingredients until dime-sized clumps form. Pinch together any powdery parts, then sprinkle the topping evenly over the berries.

3. Place the crumbles on a rimmed baking sheet and bake until the filling is bubbling around the edges and the topping is deep golden brown, about 30 minutes, rotating the baking sheet halfway through baking. Let the crumbles cool on a wire rack for 15 minutes before serving.

AN EASY WAY TO WASH BERRIES

It's important to wash berries to rid them of any dirt and debris, but they can break under the pressure of the water or drying. We figured out a two-step method that treats berries gently.

1. Place the berries in a colander and place under running water for about 30 seconds.

2. Line a salad spinner with a couple of layers of paper towels and carefully disperse the berries. Spin until the berries are dry, about 20 spins.

THE BEST VANILLA ICE CREAM

The perfect complement to cobblers and crisps, vanilla ice cream has a universal appeal. Yet we're often stumped when selecting ice cream at the supermarket. To find out which brand is best, we tasted 18 varieties, including 10 French-style (with egg yolks) and eight regular (yolkless) vanilla ice creams.

The side-by-side comparison was striking. Some ice creams were fluffy and light; others were dense and rich. Upon examining the labels, we learned that high fat content and egg yolks can give ice cream a rich, creamy texture, but stabilizers and emulsifiers go a long way toward improving the texture.

A few of our samples had assertive vanilla notes that reminded tasters of "frozen, boozy eggnog," but others seemed to be lacking in vanilla flavor altogether. Flavor is generally contributed by vanilla beans, imitation vanilla extract, or compounds derived from natural vanilla extract.

Our top-rated ice creams, which scored high for both creamy texture and flavor (both use natural vanilla compounds), were **Turkey Hill Vanilla Bean** and **Edy's Dreamery Vanilla**. For a smooth, subtle, and balanced vanilla ice cream, Turkey Hill is our top choice; the second-place Edy's Dreamery has a good vanilla flavor that packs more of a punch.

PEAR CRISP

WITH ITS SWEET FILLING AND CRUNCHY, BUTTERY topping, a fruit crisp is a simple baked dessert, at least in theory. Apples are usually the fruit of choice for a crisp, but the delicate texture and subtle flavor of pears make this homey dessert a little more sophisticated. Believing that pears and apples are similar enough, we figured scaling down a crisp recipe to serve two—and substituting pears for apples—would not be much of a stretch.

No other way to say it: We paid for our culinary naïveté. Instead of a fruit crisp, our first attempt resulted in a watery pear sauce slathered with a gummy mixture of raw flour and soggy nuts. Other recipes we prepared didn't fare much better. Many consisted of hard, starchy chunks of pear with chewy, granola bar–like toppings. It was obvious from our initial tests that pears react quite differently from apples when baked in a crisp. Further testing taught us that pear varieties, unlike many kinds of apples, are not always interchangeable. In the end, we found that Bartletts (two, of course, was the perfect quantity) are best suited to a crisp.

Our first step toward perfecting our crisp recipe was to determine why pears react to baking so differently from apples. Our science editor explained that pears and apples contain almost the same amount of moisture, but their cell walls are of very different strengths. During the ripening process, enzymes begin to break down the moisture-retaining cell walls in pears much faster than in apples. Cooking accelerates this process, which is why our impulse to use ripe pears for their more intense flavor resulted in mush. Using pears at the cusp of ripeness is key; at this point, they have converted most of their starches into sugar but don't exude all of their juice when cooked.

Using ripe yet firm Bartlett pears reduced the wateriness, but our filling was still coming out too mushy, with a topping that tasted raw because it never completely cooked through. We thought about baking the filling and topping separately, but this seemed like too much trouble for such a simple dessert. It occurred to us that maybe the pears weren't solely to blame. Was the sugar in the filling acting as an enabler, drawing out excess liquid? And wasn't the sugar turning to liquid itself when heated? Perhaps we needed to use even less than

we already were for our smaller recipe. When we tried omitting it, we were pleased to find that the amount of liquid in the bottom of the baking dish was significantly reduced and the topping was much drier. After some testing, we found the best balance between sweetness and moistness, for our reduced filling of two pears, to be just 1 tablespoon of sugar.

As a final refinement, we experimented with thickening the filling. Taking a cue from our Blueberry Crumble (see page 255), we used cornstarch; just ¼ teaspoon mixed with the sugar and a little lemon juice thickened the juice exuded from two pears just enough, without leaving a starchy taste or texture.

Every crisp needs a crunchy, sweet topping to provide textural contrast to the softer fruit. Our standard apple crisp topping—consisting of cold butter cut into sugar, flour, and nuts—was dry and powdery when used with pears. Because pears release more juice than apples, the flour from the topping was being washed down into the filling. What we needed was a sturdier topping that would remain on top of the filling when baked.

Borrowing from an old crumb cake recipe, we tried a streusel topping, in which melted butter is incorporated into flour (as opposed to cold butter being cut in), which helps to bind the flour to the other topping ingredients. Now when we took the dessert out of the oven, it had a crunchy topping that defined it as a true crisp. Mixing the topping by hand was easy enough because we were working with so few ingredients—the only precaution we had to take was to make sure the nuts were finely chopped.

In our pear crisp adventure, we learned that small details make all the difference. We increased the oven temperature from 375 to 425 degrees, which made the topping even crunchier. Admittedly, this is a minor adjustment, but it is this kind of small detail that makes a great pear crisp.

One last word on baking dishes—we did most of our testing for this recipe in a small 8½ by 5½-inch baking dish, which worked well. But taking one more lesson from our blueberry crumble, we tried dividing the crisp between two individual 12-ounce ramekins and liked it even better. The smaller cooking vessels made the topping more compact, giving us a bit more crunch in each bite.

PEAR CRISP

Pear Crisp

MAKES 2

For this crisp, the pears should be ripe but firm, which means the flesh at the base of the stem should give slightly when gently pressed with a finger. You will need two 12-ounce ramekins for this recipe (see page 3). The crisp can also be prepared in an 8½ by 5½-inch baking dish.

- **2 tablespoons granulated sugar**
- **1 teaspoon fresh lemon juice**
- **¼ teaspoon cornstarch**
- **Salt**
- **2 ripe but firm Bartlett or Bosc pears (see note), peeled, halved, cored, and cut into 1½-inch chunks (see photos)**
- **⅓ cup finely chopped almonds or pecans**
- **¼ cup (1¼ ounces) unbleached all-purpose flour**
- **2 tablespoons light brown sugar**
- **⅛ teaspoon ground cinnamon**
- **Pinch ground nutmeg**
- **3 tablespoons unsalted butter, melted and cooled**

1. Adjust an oven rack to the lower-middle position and heat the oven to 425 degrees. Whisk 1 tablespoon of the granulated sugar, lemon juice, cornstarch, and a pinch of salt together in a medium bowl. Gently toss the pears with the sugar mixture and divide evenly between two 12-ounce ramekins.

2. Mix the nuts, flour, brown sugar, remaining 1 tablespoon granulated sugar, cinnamon, nutmeg, and a pinch of salt together in a medium bowl until combined. Drizzle the melted butter over the top and combine until the mixture resembles crumbly wet sand. Pinch between your fingers into small pea-sized pieces (with some smaller loose bits).

3. Sprinkle the topping evenly over the pears, breaking up any large chunks. Place the crisps on a rimmed baking sheet and bake until the filling is bubbling around the edges and the topping is deep golden brown, 20 to 25 minutes, rotating the baking sheet halfway through baking. Let the crisps cool on a wire rack for 15 minutes before serving.

VARIATIONS

Pear Crisp with Oat Topping

Follow the recipe for Pear Crisp, reducing the amount of nuts to 3 tablespoons. After adding the butter to the flour mixture in step 2, add ¼ cup old-fashioned oats and mix until evenly incorporated.

Triple-Ginger Pear Crisp

Follow the recipe for Pear Crisp, using almonds and replacing the cinnamon and nutmeg with ¼ teaspoon ground ginger. Reduce the amount of lemon juice to ½ teaspoon and add ½ teaspoon grated or minced fresh ginger to the sugar-cornstarch mixture in step 1. Add 1 tablespoon finely chopped crystallized ginger with the nuts and flour in step 2.

NOTES FROM THE TEST KITCHEN

HOW TO CORE PEARS

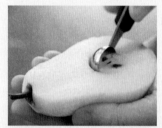

1. Halve the pears from stem to blossom end and then remove the core using a melon baller for a clean look.

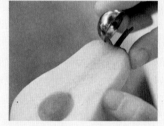

2. After removing the core, use the edge of the melon baller to scrape away the interior stem of the pear, from the core to the stem.

GETTING THE TOPPING RIGHT

Because pears exude so much juice when cooked, a traditional loose and sandy crisp topping will sink into the filling and won't get crunchy. We used a streusel technique that unified the ingredients to make a firmer topping that stays on top of the pears.

SOGGY CRISP
A sandy topping made with cold butter sinks into the filling.

CRISPY CRISP
A topping made with melted butter is more cohesive and stays in place.

CHERRY CLAFOUTI

FEW DISHES EXEMPLIFY HOMEY FRENCH COOKING quite as well as cherry clafouti, a creamy and light baked custard studded with whole fruit. Though simple in theory—it's just fruit and batter, after all—this dessert is actually notoriously finicky and can suffer from all manner of problems in both flavor and texture. We hoped to develop a foolproof recipe for cherry clafouti that would serve two—and that we could make any time of year, not just during cherry season.

Clafouti batter typically contains little but eggs, flour, milk or cream, sugar, and a flavoring or two. The ratios of those ingredients, however, can vary a great deal from recipe to recipe, producing clafoutis with textures ranging from moist, airy, and delicate like an omelet, to dense, squat, and chewy like a torte, and everywhere in between. We whipped up a half-dozen recipes, and tasters preferred clafouti that was rich and full-flavored yet light in texture; they didn't care for those that tasted particularly eggy or starchy.

Since eggs and dairy are the primary components of the batter, we focused our attention there. Eggs contribute structure, moisture, and flavor to clafouti, and recipes typically include anywhere from four to eight eggs for a clafouti serving six to eight people. Recipes with too many eggs resulted in a rubbery texture; with too few eggs, the clafouti was too soft to cut neatly, and the flavor was too mild. Not pleased with the flavor or texture of a scaled-down working recipe using two whole eggs, we tried varying amounts of whole eggs and egg yolks and settled on a combination of one whole egg and one yolk. Firm-textured and yet not rubbery, rich but not eggy, our clafouti was progressing in the right direction.

As for the dairy component, we tried milk and cream alone, as well as a combination of the two. By itself, milk tasted too lean; a blend of milk and cream was better, but cream alone made the best clafouti by far, rich-tasting and with a substantial—but not dense—texture.

Flour typically binds the clafouti batter and creates the structure necessary to support the fruit. But because we were working with such a small amount of batter to begin with, the flour had a tendency to make the batter stiff and sticky as the flour's protein developed into tough gluten—great for bread but not so for tender custard. Adding less flour to the batter kept the texture tender, but a distinct gumminess persisted.

Reviewing the initial testing recipes, we found a few where the flour was cut or completely replaced with cornstarch. After experimenting, we determined that using all cornstarch (just 1 tablespoon was all we needed) produced the best clafouti yet: light, creamy, and not the least bit gummy.

Few of the clafoutis that we prepared were particularly sweet, and these weren't even very enjoyable. Sugar should be used in a clafouti as a complement to the tart cherries. Any more than 3 tablespoons of sugar made the clafouti cloyingly sweet and muted the flavor of the fruit.

Finally pleased with the batter, we could now move on to the star of the show: the cherries. Authentic recipes claim that unpitted tart cherries are a must, as the pits intensify the fruit's flavor. However, we didn't find that to be the case, and picking the pits out of each mouthful—and the accompanying risk of a cracked tooth—took some of the joy out of this dessert. Pitted cherries tasted just fine, especially when the batter's flavor was boosted by some vanilla and a splash of amaretto liqueur. Fresh sour cherries are hard to find, even in season, so we decided to test jarred and canned cherries as well and to develop our recipe using them. Our favorite sour cherry variety is the deep purple Morello, which holds up quite well when preserved.

Some recipes insist on a cast-iron baking pan for clafouti, but we wanted to find another option, one more accessible to all cooks and one that was the right size for clafouti for two. We tested a few possibilities and found that a small 8½ by 5½-inch baking dish worked just fine. Perfection may be in the eye of the beholder, but we like to think that our clafouti turned out pretty close. Simple and satisfying, this is an easy weeknight dessert for two.

NOTES FROM THE TEST KITCHEN

SOUR CHERRIES

It's important to track down sour cherries for a great-tasting Cherry Clafouti because sweet cherries lose their flavor once cooked. There are several types of both light and dark sour cherries, but our favorites are deep purple Morello cherries. You may be able to find fresh Morello cherries in season in some regions of the country, but most of us need to use jarred or canned cherries. Luckily, Morellos preserve quite well, retaining their very tart flavor and meaty texture. We like to use jarred Morello cherries.

Cherry Clafouti

SERVES 2

Fresh sour cherries can be hard to find, even in season, so we developed this recipe using jarred Morello cherries. If you are lucky enough to find them, an equal amount of pitted fresh cherries can be used. You will need an 8½ by 5½-inch baking dish for this recipe (see page 3).

> 3 tablespoons granulated sugar
>
> 1 tablespoon cornstarch
>
> Pinch salt
>
> ⅔ cup heavy cream, at room temperature
>
> 1 large egg, at room temperature
>
> 1 large egg yolk, at room temperature
>
> 1½ teaspoons amaretto
>
> 1 teaspoon vanilla extract
>
> ¾ cup (5 ounces) drained jarred pitted Morello cherries, halved and patted dry (see note)
>
> Confectioners' sugar, for dusting

1. Adjust an oven rack to the middle position and heat the oven to 350 degrees. Whisk the granulated sugar, cornstarch, and salt together in a medium bowl until combined. Whisk in the cream, egg, egg yolk, amaretto, and vanilla until smooth and thoroughly combined.

2. Arrange the cherries in an even layer in an 8½ by 5½-inch baking dish and pour the cream mixture over the top. Bake the clafouti until a toothpick inserted into the center comes out just barely clean, 30 to 35 minutes, rotating the baking dish halfway through baking.

3. Let the clafouti cool on a wire rack until the custard has set up, about 10 minutes. Dust with confectioners' sugar before serving.

VARIATION

Plum Clafouti

For a nice presentation, fan the plum slices out over the bottom of the dish before pouring in the custard.

Follow the recipe for Cherry Clafouti, substituting cognac for the amaretto and 1 plum, pitted and sliced into ¼-inch wedges, for the cherries.

USE IT UP: JARRED MORELLO CHERRIES

Cherry Sauce

MAKES ABOUT 1 CUP

Serve this sauce with vanilla ice cream or pound cake. The sauce can be refrigerated in an airtight container for up to 1 week. If desired, reheat before serving.

> 2 tablespoons sugar
>
> 1¼ teaspoons cornstarch
>
> Pinch salt
>
> 1¼ cups (7 ounces) drained jarred pitted Morello cherries, ¼ cup juice reserved
>
> 2 tablespoons dry red wine
>
> ½ cinnamon stick

Stir the sugar, cornstarch, and salt together in a small saucepan. Whisk in the reserved cherry juice and wine. Add the cinnamon stick, bring to a simmer over medium-high heat, and cook, whisking frequently, until the mixture thickens, 2 to 3 minutes. Discard the cinnamon stick. Stir in the cherries and return to a brief simmer. Serve warm or at room temperature.

FREE-FORM APPLE TARTLETS

THE FREE-FORM APPLE TART IS RELATIVELY EASY to make, as far as pastries go—a single layer of buttery pie dough in the shape of a thin, flat round is simply folded up over fresh apples. But as every cook knows, simple doesn't always translate easily to success. The pastry can crack or crumble, the apples can taste bland or starchy, and the filling can dry out from exposure to the oven's high heat (since there is no top crust to seal in moisture). With these considerations in mind, we set out to create a recipe that would be easy to put together, make use of readily available ingredients, and produce two individual tartlets with rich apple flavor, moist filling, and tender, flaky crust.

We started with the dough. From past experience we knew that pastry can crack and leak juice, which results in soggy bottoms. A quick glance at a couple dozen recipes revealed that many bakers solve this problem by making a sturdier (read: tougher) dough. Several recipes skirted the tough crust issue by utilizing a different sort of dough. Cookie-like crusts, short and sandy in texture, were common. However, these recipes usually include sour cream, cream cheese, egg yolk, and/or cornmeal—ingredients that mask the pure flavor of simple pie dough. Because we were keen on a flaky, delicate pie pastry, we knew we had our work cut out for us.

Reverting to a standard formula of flour, fat, and water, we made crusts with both shortening and butter and with butter alone. We preferred the latter, but there was a limit to just how much butter we could use. A ratio of 1 part butter to 2 parts flour resulted in a weak, leaky crust, which we attributed to too much fat and too little flour. We settled on 5 tablespoons of butter to ¾ cup of flour, which provided the most buttery flavor and tender texture without compromising the structure.

We tried mixing the dough with a food processor, with a standing mixer, and by hand. The latter two methods mashed the butter into the flour and produced a less flaky crust. Quick pulses with the food processor "cut" the butter into the flour so that it remained in distinct pieces. After this step, we added water 1 tablespoon at a time until the dough held its shape when pinched together.

Further testing revealed that doughs with large lumps of butter needed a lot of water to come together. Once baked, these crusts were very flaky but weak; as soon as the chunks of butter melted, the fruit juice found its escape hatch. By contrast, doughs in which the butter was processed to fine crumbs required very little water. They yielded crusts that were sturdier but also short and mealy (similar to the cookie-like crusts). Because we were after the long, fine layering of a flaky crust without a lot of leaking, we mixed in the butter until it was about the size of coarse cornmeal—just big enough to create the steamed spaces needed for flakiness. Now we had the ideal crust: flaky but strong enough to contain the bubbling fruit juice during baking.

We next moved on to the filling. The test kitchen has done years of testing with apple varieties, and a combination of sweet and tart apples has always been the clear winner for a dessert of this nature. This recipe was no exception. Using one small McIntosh and one small Granny Smith proved to be the right combination and amount. The moisture in the mild McIntosh prevented the more tart Granny Smith from drying out, but overall the filling was still a bit dry.

Some recipes suggest cooking the apples first, but with simplicity as a goal, this seemed too fussy for our two individual tartlets. We then tried slicing the apples thinner and increasing the oven temperature. These changes were an improvement; the thinner apple slices cooked more quickly at the higher temperature and were, therefore, moister—but they still weren't perfect. At the suggestion of a colleague, we sprinkled a teaspoon of sugar and a few dots of butter over the top of the tartlets. This turned out to be a great idea, helping to keep the apples from drying out while they baked.

We moved on to the assembly of our apple tartlets. We rolled out multiple dough rounds to varying diameters and found that a 7-inch circle was ideal: thick enough to contain the apples but thin enough to bake evenly and thoroughly. We stacked the apples in the center, leaving a 1½-inch border. The dough was then lifted up and back over the fruit (the center of the tart remains exposed) and loosely pleated to allow for shrinkage. One of our most important discoveries came at this step. Leaving a ½-inch border between the apples and the folded edge of the tartlet shells further prevents the apple juice from leaking through the folds in the dough.

The last small but significant step toward a crisp crust was to cool the tarts on a wire rack; this kept the crust from steaming itself as it cooled. For the effort expended, the reward was remarkable: a satisfyingly flaky crust crackling around each bite of tender apples.

Free-Form Apple Tartlets

MAKES 2

If preparing the dough in a very warm kitchen, refrigerate all of the ingredients before making the dough. To prevent the tarts from leaking, it is crucial to leave a ½-inch border of dough around the fruit. Serve with vanilla ice cream or Whipped Cream (page 254).

TART DOUGH

¾ **cup (3¾ ounces) unbleached all-purpose flour**

¼ **teaspoon salt**

CORING AND SLICING APPLES

1. A quick way to core and slice apples for baking if you don't own an apple corer is to cut the sides of the apple squarely away from the core.

2. Cut each piece of apple into ¼-inch-thick slices.

MAKING FREE-FORM APPLE TARTLETS

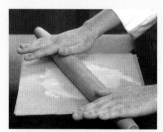

1. Roll each chilled disk of dough into a 7-inch circle between 2 small sheets of lightly floured parchment paper. Slide the dough rounds with the parchment onto a rimmed baking sheet and refrigerate until firm.

2. Discard the top pieces of parchment paper. Stack the apple slices into a circular wall, leaving a 1½-inch border of dough. Fill the center with the remaining apples.

3. Fold 1 inch of the dough up over the fruit, leaving a ½-inch border between the fruit and the edge of the tart shell, and pleat the dough. Brush with the egg white, sprinkle with sugar, and dot evenly with the butter.

5 tablespoons unsalted butter, cut into ¼-inch pieces and chilled

2–3 tablespoons ice water

FILLING

1 small Granny Smith apple, peeled, cored, halved, and sliced ¼ inch thick (see photos)

1 small McIntosh apple, peeled, cored, halved, and sliced ¼ inch thick (see photos)

3 tablespoons plus 1 teaspoon sugar

1 teaspoon fresh lemon juice
   Pinch ground cinnamon

1 egg white, lightly beaten

1 tablespoon unsalted butter, cut into ¼-inch pieces

1. FOR THE TART DOUGH: Process the flour and salt together in a food processor until combined. Scatter the butter pieces over the top and pulse until the mixture resembles coarse cornmeal, about 15 pulses. Continue to pulse, adding the water through the feed tube 1 tablespoon at a time, until the dough comes together and forms a ball, about 10 pulses.

2. Divide the dough into 2 even pieces. Turn each piece of dough onto a sheet of plastic wrap and flatten each into a 3-inch disk. Wrap each piece tightly in the plastic wrap and refrigerate for 1 hour. Before rolling out the dough, let it sit on the counter to soften slightly, about 10 minutes. (The wrapped dough can be refrigerated for up to 2 days or frozen for up to 1 month. If frozen, let the dough thaw completely on the counter before rolling it out.)

3. FOR THE FILLING: Adjust an oven rack to the middle position and heat the oven to 400 degrees. Working with one disk at a time, roll out the chilled dough into a 7-inch circle between 2 small sheets of lightly floured parchment paper. Slide the two dough rounds, still between the parchment paper, onto a rimmed baking sheet and refrigerate until firm, about 20 minutes.

4. Toss the apples, 3 tablespoons of the sugar, lemon juice, and cinnamon together in a medium bowl. Remove the top sheet of parchment paper from each dough round. Following the photos, stack one-half of the apples into a circular wall on one of the dough rounds, leaving a 1½-inch border of dough around the edge and reserving a few apple slices to fill in the middle of the tart. Fill in the middle of the tart with the reserved apple slices. Being careful to leave

½ inch of dough around the apples, fold the outermost 1 inch of dough over the fruit, pleating it every 1 to 2 inches as needed. Repeat with the remaining apples and dough round.

5. Lightly brush the dough with the egg white and sprinkle the tartlets evenly with the remaining 1 teaspoon sugar. Dot the tartlets evenly with the butter. Bake the tartlets until the crust is golden and crisp and the apples are tender, 35 to 40 minutes, rotating the baking sheet halfway through baking.

6. Let the tartlets cool slightly on the baking sheet for 5 minutes, then transfer to a wire rack and let sit until the apple juice has thickened, about 10 minutes. Serve warm or at room temperature.

APPLE DUMPLINGS

HOT APPLE DUMPLINGS, FRESH FROM THE OVEN, are a soul-satisfying dessert that showcases the arrival of one of fall's best offerings. But preparing dumplings from scratch—starting with homemade pastry dough—can be labor-intensive and hardly seems worth the effort when cooking for two. Frozen puff pastry from the supermarket makes dumplings easier to prepare, but for a recipe that requires relatively few ingredients— apples, cinnamon, sugar, sometimes raisins, and the dough—finding just the right proportions would be key in scaling down our recipe.

For the apple filling, there were two main questions: What type of apple would be best in our dumplings, and how should the apple be cut? We gathered and tested the most commonly available apples. After a bake-off, we agreed that Granny Smiths, Galas, and McIntoshes retained the most distinct apple flavor when baked. When we took texture into account, however, one apple proved the clear winner. The McIntosh turned to mush by the time the puff pastry had turned golden brown, and the Gala fared only slightly better. Granny Smiths held their shape and texture the best, and their tart flavor was a nice foil to the delicate pastry.

In some recipes, apples were sliced into wedges; in others, they were simply peeled, cored, and left whole. We found that if the apples were sliced, they cooked down too much before the pastry had a chance to cook through. Left whole, however, the apples didn't soften properly by the time the pastry reached a golden brown color.

Since we needed only one apple for two dumplings, the solution was to core the apple, then cut it crosswise, and place one half in each dumpling. The apple halves became tender but still retained their shape. A pat of butter and a little cinnamon sugar were all that was needed (tasters felt that raisins were distracting).

Over the years, we've learned that puff pastry works well, as long as you play by its rules. For the perfect puff, the pastry must be cold and the oven hot. We cut the pastry sheet in half, reserving half for another use. We cut the remaining pastry in half, lightly rolled each piece into a 6-inch square, and placed an apple half, cut-side down, on each sheet. Though we still had to work quickly—puff pastry becomes impossible to work with if it gets too warm—making only two dumplings certainly simplified the task.

Our biggest problem was that our dumplings split at the seams while they baked, which exposed the apple halves and caused them to dry out. We needed a better method for sealing our pastry bundles. After many rounds of tests, we arrived at pulling the four corners of the dough up and around the apple and twisting them into a knot. A little water brushed along the edges went a long way toward helping the seams stay put while baking. In a 400-degree oven, the apple and pastry cooked at the same rate, resulting in tender fruit and golden brown, flaky pastry.

To finish our dessert, we created a simple cider and brown sugar reduction. We drizzled the cider glaze over the apple dumplings, and with the first bite we knew we had developed a dumpling recipe we would be making again and again.

Apple Dumplings
MAKES 2

This recipe uses half of a standard 9-inch square sheet of puff pastry. Be sure to let the pastry thaw on the counter before cutting. If the dough starts to separate at the seams before you cut it, simply rejoin the seams by rolling them smooth with a rolling pin. See page 102 for a recipe to use up the leftover pastry, or you can refreeze it or refrigerate it for up to 2 days. Serve with vanilla ice cream or a drizzle of heavy cream.

½ **(9-inch square) sheet frozen puff pastry, thawed**
  and cut in half widthwise to make two squares
  (see note) (see page 101)

1   medium Granny Smith apple, peeled, cored, and halved crosswise (see photo)

1   tablespoon unsalted butter, cut into 2 pieces

¼   cup packed (1¾ ounces) plus 1 teaspoon light brown sugar

⅛   teaspoon ground cinnamon

    Water, for brushing the dough

½   cup apple cider

1. Adjust an oven rack to the middle position and heat the oven to 400 degrees. Line a rimmed baking sheet with parchment paper.

2. Following the photo, roll each piece of pastry dough into a 6-inch square on a lightly floured counter. Carefully transfer the dough squares to the prepared baking sheet.

3. Place an apple half, cut-side down, in the center of each dough square and place a piece of butter in the center of each apple. Toss 1 teaspoon of the brown sugar with the cinnamon and sprinkle over the apples. Working with one dumpling at a time, brush the edges of the dough lightly with water. Pull the dough up over the apple, twisting the dough ends to form a knot at the top. Pinch the edges of the 4 seams of dough together, using more water if necessary, to create a tight seal.

4. Bake the dumplings until the crust is golden brown and the apples are tender but not mushy, 18 to 22 minutes, rotating the baking sheet halfway through baking.

5. While the dumplings bake, simmer the apple cider and the remaining ¼ cup brown sugar together in a small saucepan over medium-low heat until the sauce is slightly thickened and measures ¼ cup, 10 to 12 minutes.

6. Immediately transfer the baked dumplings to individual serving plates or shallow bowls. Pour 2 tablespoons of the cider sauce over each dumpling and serve.

MAKING APPLE DUMPLINGS

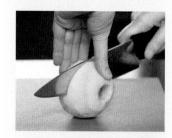

1. After peeling and coring the apples, cut each apple in half crosswise.

2. On a lightly floured counter, roll each 4½-inch square of dough into a 6-inch square, then carefully transfer the dough squares to a parchment paper–lined rimmed baking sheet.

3. After placing an apple half in the center of each square, and adding butter and cinnamon sugar, brush the edges of the dough with water and pull them up over the apple, twisting the ends to form a knot.

4. Pinch the edges of the 4 seams of dough together, using more water if necessary, to create a tight seal.

THE BEST APPLE CORER

Rather than slicing an apple and then removing the core and seeds from each piece, we'd rather reach for an apple corer, which does the job in one fell swoop. Testing five models, we found those with narrow blade diameters (less than ¾ inch) struggled to cut through firmer apples, and stubby metal tubes (less than 3½ inches) were too short for large apples. We had much better results with the reasonably priced **OXO Good Grips Corer,** $7.95, and testers appreciated its comfortable grip.

RASPBERRY-NECTARINE PIE

ALTHOUGH PEACH PIE IS A SUMMER CLASSIC, we wanted to try and highlight a few of our other favorite summer fruits in a simple pie for two. Nectarines can be every bit as intoxicating as peaches when ripe, and they're even easier to prepare—no fussy peeling necessary. Raspberries add a tart-sweet counterpoint to the nectarines, and when cooked, they break down slightly, creating a thick and vibrant filling. Even ripe nectarines, however, vary in juiciness from season to season and from nectarine to nectarine, making it difficult to know just how much thickener or sweetener a pie will need. We wanted to create a filling that was juicy but not swimming in liquid, its flavors neither muscled out by spices nor overwhelmed by thickeners. And we wanted a double crust, one that would be buttery, flaky, and well browned.

Our first challenge was to decide what size pie plate to use, then scale back the dough ingredients accordingly. After hunting around some local bakeware shops, we determined that a 6-inch pie plate would be just right for two servings. Hoping to avoid spending too much time fiddling with the proportions of the pie dough, we started our testing with the test kitchen's traditional single-crust pie dough. Chilled, divided in half, and rolled out, it proved to be the perfect amount of dough for a small double-crust pie.

We now moved on to the filling. Experimenting with different sugars, we were surprised to discover that both light and dark brown sugar bullied the nectarines, whereas granulated sugar complemented them. Lemon juice brightened the flavor of the nectarines and raspberries, and a dash of salt rounded out the filling.

Our next challenge was to find a thickener that would leave the fruits' color and flavor uncompromised. As with our other fruit desserts for two, cornstarch was the decisive winner—flour made our pie filling somewhat gummy, and tapioca did not have enough time to properly dissolve in the short baking time for our small pie. Just 2 teaspoons of cornstarch achieved the proper consistency for our filling.

As we continued our testing, however, the filling was not consistent. One batch would be just thick enough and the next would be relatively soupy. We realized the ripeness and juiciness of the nectarines were the culprits. We found our solution in macerating the nectarines along with the raspberries and sugar for 20 minutes, then draining all but 1 tablespoon of the juice to stir back into the fruit. The sugar draws out much of the fruit's liquid, so when the pie bakes, it doesn't turn into raspberry-nectarine soup. Cutting vent holes (three worked well in our mini pie) into the top crust also helps excess steam escape, which in turn helps keep the pie from getting soggy.

Trying different oven rack levels and temperatures to satisfy the browning requirements of both the top and bottom crusts, we found that baking the pie on a low rack at an initial high heat of 425 degrees, then a moderately high heat of 375 degrees, worked best. We also found that preheating a baking sheet, and baking the pie on it, gave us a pleasantly firm and browned bottom crust.

Raspberry-Nectarine Pie

SERVES 2

If you don't have a food processor, see "Hand Mixing Pie Dough" on page 267. You will need one 6-inch pie plate for this recipe (see page 3).

PIE DOUGH

- 1¼ cups (6¼ ounces) unbleached all-purpose flour
- 1 tablespoon sugar
- ½ teaspoon salt
- 3 tablespoons vegetable shortening, cut into ½-inch pieces and chilled
- 5 tablespoons unsalted butter, cut into ¼-inch pieces and chilled
- 4–6 tablespoons ice water

FILLING

- 2 nectarines, pitted and sliced ⅓ inch thick
- 1 cup (5 ounces) fresh raspberries
- ¼–⅓ cup (1¾ to 2⅓ ounces) plus 1 teaspoon sugar
- 2 teaspoons cornstarch
- ¾ teaspoon fresh lemon juice plus ¼ teaspoon grated lemon zest
- Pinch salt
- 1 large egg white, lightly beaten

1. FOR THE PIE DOUGH: Process the flour, sugar, and salt together in a food processor until combined. Scatter the shortening over the top and process until the mixture resembles coarse cornmeal, about 10 seconds.

RASPBERRY-NECTARINE PIE

Scatter the butter pieces over the top and pulse until the mixture resembles coarse crumbs, about 10 pulses. Transfer the mixture to a medium bowl.

2. Sprinkle 4 tablespoons of the ice water over the mixture. Stir and press the dough together, using a stiff rubber spatula, until the dough sticks together. If the dough does not come together, stir in the remaining water, 1 tablespoon at a time, until it does.

3. Divide the dough into 2 even pieces. Turn each piece of dough onto a sheet of plastic wrap and flatten each into a 3-inch disk. Wrap each piece tightly in the plastic wrap and refrigerate for 1 hour. Before rolling out the dough, let it sit on the counter to soften slightly, about 10 minutes. (The wrapped dough can be refrigerated for up to 2 days or frozen for up to 1 month. If frozen, let the dough thaw completely on the counter before rolling it out.)

4. Adjust an oven rack to the lowest position, place a foil-lined rimmed baking sheet on the rack, and heat the oven to 425 degrees. Roll out one disk of dough into a 9-inch circle on a lightly floured counter, then fit it into a 6-inch pie plate, letting the excess dough hang over the edge; cover with plastic wrap and refrigerate until firm, about 30 minutes. Roll out the other disk of dough into a 9-inch circle on a lightly floured counter, then transfer to a parchment paper–lined plate; cover with plastic wrap and refrigerate until firm, about 30 minutes.

5. FOR THE FILLING: Meanwhile, toss the nectarines, raspberries, and ¼ cup of the sugar together in a medium bowl, and let sit, tossing occasionally, until the fruit releases its juice, about 20 minutes.

6. Drain the fruit thoroughly through a colander, reserving 1 tablespoon of the juice. In a medium bowl, toss the drained fruit, reserved juice, cornstarch, lemon juice, lemon zest, and salt together until well combined. (If the fruit tastes tart, add up to 1½ tablespoons more sugar.)

7. Spread the fruit in the dough-lined pie plate, mounding it slightly in the middle. Following the photos, gently arrange the second piece of pie dough over the pie. Trim, fold, and crimp the edges, and cut 3 vent holes in the top. Brush the crust with the egg white and sprinkle with the remaining 1 teaspoon sugar.

8. Place the pie on the heated baking sheet and bake until the top crust is golden brown, about 20 minutes. Reduce the oven temperature to 375 degrees, rotate the baking sheet, and continue to bake until the juices

are bubbling and the crust is deep golden brown, 20 to 25 minutes longer. Let the pie cool on a wire rack until the filling has set, about 1½ hours. Serve slightly warm or at room temperature.

NOTES FROM THE TEST KITCHEN

HAND MIXING PIE DOUGH

If you don't have a food processor, follow this method for mixing pie dough by hand. Freeze the butter in its stick form until very firm. Whisk together the flour, sugar, and salt in a large bowl. Add the chilled shortening and press it into the flour using a fork. Grate the frozen butter on the large holes of a box grater into the flour mixture, then cut the mixture together, using two butter or dinner knives, until the mixture resembles coarse crumbs. Add the water as directed.

MAKING A RASPBERRY-NECTARINE PIE

1. After rolling out the top crust, gently arrange it over the filled pie crust bottom.

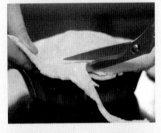
2. Using scissors, trim all but ½ inch of the dough overhanging the edge of the pie plate.

3. Press the top and bottom crusts together, then tuck the edges underneath.

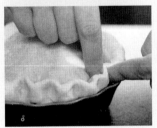
4. Crimp the dough evenly around the edge of the pie, using your fingers. Cut 3 vent holes attractively in the center of the top crust with a paring knife.

LEMON BUTTERMILK SHEET CAKE

A SWEET-TART LEMON SHEET CAKE holds a lot of promise as a light summer dessert—a single bite should offer a punch of bright and sweet lemon flavor—like a gulp of great lemonade. But most recipes we tried missed the mark. The lemon flavor was either too fleeting or overpowering, and sheet cakes are often hard to bake evenly. And although sheet cakes are usually made in a 13 by 9-inch pan to feed a crowd, we wanted to develop a recipe for a small sheet cake, one that easily served two—with maybe a snack-sized piece for leftovers.

Before we addressed flavor and size issues, we needed a solid foundation. We started by preparing batches of the test kitchen's white and yellow sheet cakes (white cakes use only egg whites, whereas yellow cakes include whole eggs), replacing a few tablespoons of the milk in each recipe with lemon juice. Tasters much preferred the denser yellow cake, as the richness of the whole eggs balanced the acidity of the lemon. This recipe uses cake flour for a fine, velvety crumb and utilizes the traditional creaming method (beating butter and sugar before adding the wet and dry ingredients) to develop structure and height in the cake.

After numerous tests, we adjusted the ingredient amounts for this standard-sized sheet cake and cut the yield of the batter by about two-thirds—which fit nicely into a 7¼ by 5¼-inch baking dish. Tasters liked the flavor and texture of this cake, but we weren't pleased with the domed top and sloping sides. Adding the lemon juice had changed the chemistry of the recipe. Replacing some of the baking powder with baking soda helped, as did reducing the baking temperature from 350 to 325 degrees—the slower baking meant that the edges and interior of the cake set at the same time, resulting in a perfectly flat top. Now it was time to address the lemon flavor.

The best way to bright, clean lemon flavor was on the path we had already started down—swapping out some of the milk for freshly squeezed lemon juice. But with our small amount of batter, we could go up to only 1 tablespoon of lemon juice before the cake started tasting too tart. We added 2 teaspoons of lemon zest to round out the lemon flavor and used a test kitchen trick

of beating the zest with sugar to create a homemade lemon sugar that lent a wallop of lemony richness to the cake. Replacing the remaining milk with buttermilk (and once again adjusting the ratio of baking powder to baking soda) added extra tang that reinforced the lemon flavor.

Other recipes weigh down this light and tender cake with heavy buttercream or cream cheese frostings, but we found nothing was easier—or better—than glazing the warm cake with a simple mixture of confectioners' sugar, buttermilk, and lemon juice. The glaze started out relatively thin and weak on flavor. Reducing the amount of buttermilk in the glaze allowed the lemon flavor to come through, and the glaze thickened and clung to the cake, which tasters preferred. A sprinkle of some reserved lemon sugar added crunch and a final flourish of lemon flavor and color.

Lemon Buttermilk Sheet Cake
SERVES 2

We recommend using a small offset spatula to easily and neatly glaze the warm cake. You will need a 7¼ by 5¼-inch baking pan or a dish of similar size for this recipe (see page 3).

CAKE

- ⅔ cup (2¾ ounces) cake flour
- ¼ teaspoon baking powder
- ⅛ teaspoon baking soda
- ⅛ teaspoon salt
- 3 tablespoons buttermilk, at room temperature
- 1 tablespoon fresh lemon juice plus 2 teaspoons grated lemon zest
- ¼ teaspoon vanilla extract
- ⅓ cup (2⅓ ounces) granulated sugar
- 3 tablespoons unsalted butter, softened
- 1 large egg, at room temperature

GLAZE

- ¾ cup (3 ounces) confectioners' sugar
- 1 tablespoon fresh lemon juice
- 1 teaspoon buttermilk

1. FOR THE CAKE: Adjust an oven rack to the middle position and heat the oven to 325 degrees. Grease and flour a 7¼ by 5¼-inch baking dish. Combine the flour, baking powder, baking soda, and salt in a medium bowl. Combine the buttermilk, lemon juice, and vanilla in a small bowl.

2. In a medium bowl, beat the sugar and lemon zest together with an electric mixer on medium speed until moist and fragrant, 30 to 60 seconds, scraping down the bowl as needed. Measure out and reserve 1 tablespoon of the lemon sugar, cover, and set aside. Add the butter to the remaining lemon sugar and beat until light and smooth, 2 to 4 minutes, scraping down the bowl as needed. Beat in the egg until incorporated. Reduce the mixer speed to low and beat in one-half of the flour mixture, followed by all of the buttermilk mixture, scraping down the bowl as needed. Beat in the remaining flour mixture until just incorporated.

3. Give the batter a final stir with a rubber spatula to make sure it is thoroughly combined. Scrape the batter into the prepared pan, smooth the top, and gently tap the pan on the counter to settle the batter. Bake the cake until the top is golden brown and a toothpick inserted into the center comes out with a few crumbs attached, 25 to 28 minutes, rotating the pan halfway through baking. Transfer the cake to a wire rack and let cool for 10 minutes.

4. FOR THE GLAZE: Meanwhile, whisk the confectioners' sugar, lemon juice, and buttermilk together until smooth. Gently spread the glaze over the warm cake and sprinkle evenly with the reserved lemon sugar. Let the cake cool completely, about 1½ hours, before serving.

NOTES FROM THE TEST KITCHEN

OFFSET SPATULAS
Unlike a regular spatula, the blade of an offset spatula dips down at the handle, keeping your fingers and knuckles out of the way. We recommend having two, even though they come in many sizes. The 8½-inch Ateco Offset Spatula, $5, is perfect for spreading brownie and cake batter, and even transferring cookies from baking sheets. For smaller jobs, like frosting cupcakes, we like the **4½-inch Wilton Angled Comfort Grip Spatula,** $4.50, which scored ahead of the pack.

RUSTIC PEACH CAKE

THERE ARE COUNTLESS STYLES OF CAKES made with fresh peaches, but one of our favorite peach cakes is a rustic single-layer yellow cake studded with chunks of fresh peaches. We gathered a dozen recipes for this style of cake, bought a crate of peaches, and got baking. This style of cake is usually baked in a large springform pan, making it easy to remove the delicate cake from the pan when ready to serve. After doing a bit of research, we were able to find springform pans in two smaller sizes—we could use an 8-inch pan or a 4½-inch pan. We liked the idea of individual cakes, so we settled on using two 4½-inch pans.

Recipes for rustic peach cake had big problems. Some cakes were made mushy and wet by an excess of peach juice, and others featured chunks of bloated peaches that sank to the bottom of the pan and steamed. Since putting peaches inside the cake was causing so many problems, we decided to start with one recipe we had seen where the peaches were put on top of the cake. We found that just one peeled, pitted, and sliced peach was enough to cover the top of our two springform pans and give the cake a good peach-to-cake ratio. The portion of the cake where the fruit met the cake was soggy, but we could fix that problem later.

Our plan was to make the necessary adjustments to the test kitchen's basic recipe for yellow cake to make it work with fresh peaches, and to scale it down for two. Our first move was to replace the cake flour in the yellow cake with all-purpose flour to create a sturdier crumb that could better support the fruit on top. Instead of milk, we used just 1 tablespoon of sour cream for a denser, heartier texture. And because the peaches were so sweet, we cut back the amount of sugar to ¼ cup, using a mixture of granulated and light brown sugars for more flavor. Scaling back to one egg and 4 tablespoons of butter worked well, and our batter fit neatly in our two individual springform pans.

Now that we had a rich but sturdy cake base, we could concentrate on fine-tuning the texture of the peaches. To reduce the moisture they were shedding, we tried precooking the peaches, but that muted their fresh flavor. Some recipes call for sugaring the peaches and letting them exude liquid before adding them to the cake, but the peaches continued to weep moisture into the cake no matter how long we let them sit. Tossing the peaches with thickeners only made them gluey.

Since we needed something dry to absorb excess moisture from the peaches, we wondered if dried peaches might work. We chopped a handful of dried peaches and scattered them on top of the cake batter before layering on the sliced fresh peaches. The dried peaches softened beautifully in the oven as they soaked up the flavorful juice from the fresh fruit, resulting in a moist—but not soggy—cake bursting with two layers of peach flavor. And since dried peaches aren't always available, we tried using dried apricots and got the same great flavor and results.

Rustic Peach Cake

MAKES 2

Since overly ripe peaches will make this cake soggy, look for barely ripe peaches that give slightly to the touch. You will need two 4½-inch springform pans for this recipe (see page 3). Serve with vanilla ice cream or Whipped Cream (page 254).

PEACHES

- 2 tablespoons granulated sugar
- ⅛ teaspoon ground cinnamon
- 1 medium peach, peeled, pitted, and cut into 8 wedges (see note)

CAKE

- ½ cup (2½ ounces) unbleached all-purpose flour
- ½ teaspoon baking powder
- ⅛ teaspoon salt
- 4 tablespoons (½ stick) unsalted butter, softened
- 2 tablespoons granulated sugar
- 2 tablespoons light brown sugar
- 1 large egg
- 1 tablespoon sour cream
- ½ teaspoon vanilla extract
- 3 tablespoons finely chopped dried peaches or apricots

1. FOR THE PEACHES: Adjust an oven rack to the middle position and heat the oven to 350 degrees. Grease two 4½-inch springform pans. Combine the granulated sugar and cinnamon in a medium bowl. Measure out and reserve 1 tablespoon of the cinnamon sugar and

set aside. Add the peach wedges to the bowl with the remaining cinnamon sugar and toss to coat.

2. FOR THE CAKE: Whisk the flour, baking powder, and salt together in a small bowl, and set aside. In a medium bowl, beat the butter and sugars together with an electric mixer on medium speed until light and smooth, 2 to 4 minutes, scraping down the bowl as needed. Beat in the egg, sour cream, and vanilla until combined, scraping down the bowl as needed. Reduce the mixer speed to low and slowly add the flour mixture until just incorporated, 30 to 60 seconds.

3. Give the batter a final stir with a rubber spatula to make sure it is thoroughly combined. Divide the batter evenly between the prepared pans, smooth the tops, and gently tap the pans on the counter to settle the batter. Scatter the dried peaches evenly over the batter, then arrange 4 sugared peach wedges in a pinwheel pattern over the top in each pan. Sprinkle the reserved sugar mixture evenly over the peaches.

4. Place the cakes on a rimmed baking sheet and bake until the tops are golden brown and a toothpick

---

NOTES FROM THE TEST KITCHEN

EASY PEACH PEELING

After serrated peelers arrived on the market, we all but renounced our usual fruit-peeling tricks (including blanching the fruit briefly in boiling water to loosen the skin). Similar to regular vegetable peelers, these specialized gadgets (with miniature serrations) make quick work of separating tough, thick skin from delicate fruit such as peaches and tomatoes. But which brand is best? Less-than-stellar blades plagued a few of our models, and the extra force required left our hands sticky when we skinned peaches with these peelers. Sharp blades, by contrast, seemed to do most of the work for us. Our favorite, the **Messermeister Serrated Swivel Peeler**, $5.50, dazzled testers with its supremely sharp blade, which was eminently gentle, even on the ripest peach in the crate.

CHOPPING DRIED FRUIT

Dried fruits (like the dried peaches or apricots in our Rustic Peach Cake) and knives have a very sticky relationship. An easy way to avoid sticking when chopping dried fruit is to give your knife a quick spritz with vegetable oil spray before getting started.

inserted into the centers comes out with a few moist crumbs attached, 30 to 35 minutes, rotating the baking sheet halfway through baking. Let the cakes cool completely on a wire rack, about 1½ hours.

5. Remove the sides of the pans and carefully slide the cakes onto individual serving plates. Serve.

RICH CHOCOLATE BUNDT CAKE

A BUNDT CAKE IS THE PINNACLE OF CAKE-BAKING simplicity. With its decorative shape, this cake doesn't require frosting or fussy finishing techniques. What chocolate Bundt cakes do require, it turns out, is a major boost in flavor. Despite their tantalizing looks, most of these cakes have at best a muted chocolate presence. A chocolate Bundt cake should taste every bit as good as it looks, with a fine crumb, moist texture, and rich chocolate flavor in every bite.

Bundt cakes require a specific pan for baking, and up to this point we had only seen large Bundt pans that make enough cake to feed a crowd. But with a little research, we found that there are actually individual Bundt pans. We would need to scale our cake batter down significantly to make the right amount for two.

After sampling several chocolate Bundt cakes (all seriously lacking in chocolate flavor), we liked the texture of one made with sour cream that resembled a pound cake. Using it as our starting point, we developed a recipe using roughly the same proportions of butter, sugar, eggs, and flour and using the traditional method of creaming the butter and sugar (beating them together) before adding the other ingredients. Numerous attempts to scale down the recipe failed, resulting in too much batter and baked cakes overflowing our individual Bundt pans. After much trial and error, we finally reached our optimal yield: 2 tablespoons butter, ⅓ cup sugar, one egg, and ⅓ cup flour.

We then focused on boosting the virtually nonexistent chocolate flavor. The recipe included a small amount of cocoa powder, and to that we added some bittersweet chocolate. Now we had more chocolate flavor, but we wanted a deeper, more complex taste. This time, more cocoa powder seemed like a logical solution. We replaced a portion of the flour in our recipe with

PREPARING A BUNDT PAN

A Bundt cake is attractive only if you get it out of the pan in one piece. After unmolding lots of Bundt cakes unsuccessfully, we came up with a foolproof solution. This method works much better than the standard technique of greasing and flouring, which isn't as foolproof and often results in a cake with an unsightly pasty white film from the flour.

Make a simple paste from 1 tablespoon melted butter and 1 tablespoon cocoa powder. Apply the paste to the inside of the Bundt pans with a pastry brush, taking care to reach all the nooks and crannies.

DARK CHOCOLATE

Semisweet and bittersweet chocolate, also called dark chocolate, must contain at least 35 percent chocolate liquor (a combination of chocolate solids and cocoa butter), although most contain more than 55 percent and some can go as high as 99 percent. Many brands have distinctive flavors that tasters liked in particular desserts, but two brands, **Callebaut Intense Dark Chocolate** and **Ghirardelli Bittersweet Chocolate,** consistently produced great results in all types of baked goods. Note that both of these chocolates contain 60 percent cacao— the type most recipes calling for dark chocolate have been developed to use. (Chocolates containing 70 percent or more cacao usually require recipe adjustments to get good results.)

an equal amount of cocoa powder. But we came upon the real trick to developing deep chocolate flavor when we borrowed a technique that we've used for devil's food cake. We poured boiling water over the cocoa and chocolate to dissolve and melt them, a step that not only disperses the cocoa particles throughout the batter but also blooms the flavor.

Now we had great, complex chocolate flavor, but the cake was still a bit too dry. Our first thought was to decrease the amount of flour in the cake, but this compromised its structure and added minimal moisture. We had better success switching from granulated sugar to light brown sugar, which added moisture and dramatically improved flavor. Finally, we increased the amount of boiling water added with the cocoa powder and chocolate from 1 tablespoon to 2. This small difference made the batter looser and the baked cake significantly more moist—moist enough to finally satisfy our goal.

To finish the recipe, we dissolved a small amount of espresso powder along with the chocolate and cocoa and also added a dose of vanilla extract. Both flavors complemented the floral nuances of the chocolate. With the pans chosen and the batter scaled, we turned our attention to oven temperatures, baking the cakes at 325, 350, and 375 degrees. At the highest temperature, the cakes developed a thick upper crust and uneven crumb. Finding little difference in the cakes baked at the other two temperatures, we opted for 350 degrees (and a slightly faster baking time). At long last, we had reached chocolate heaven.

Rich Chocolate Bundt Cake

MAKES 2

We prefer the flavor of Dutch-processed cocoa powder, but you can substitute natural (regular) cocoa powder if necessary. You will need two 1-cup Bundt pans for this recipe (see page 3). For an accurate measurement of boiling water, bring a kettle of water to a boil, then measure out the desired amount. Don't be tempted to make the cake in another pan; the heavy batter was designed to work in a Bundt pan that has a center tube to facilitate baking. Dust with confectioners' sugar before serving, if desired.

 2 tablespoons unsalted butter, cut into chunks and softened, plus 1 tablespoon melted butter for brushing the pans
 3 tablespoons Dutch-processed cocoa powder (see note)
 ⅓ cup (1⅝ ounces) unbleached all-purpose flour
 ¼ teaspoon salt
 ¼ teaspoon baking soda
 1½ ounces bittersweet chocolate, chopped fine

 ¼ teaspoon instant espresso or instant coffee
 2 tablespoons boiling water (see note)
 3 tablespoons sour cream, at room temperature
 ½ teaspoon vanilla extract
 ⅓ cup packed (2⅓ ounces) light brown sugar
 1 large egg, at room temperature

1. Adjust an oven rack to the middle position and heat the oven to 350 degrees. Following the photo on page 271, use 1 tablespoon melted butter and 1 tablespoon of the cocoa powder to prepare two 1-cup Bundt pans. Whisk the flour, salt, and baking soda together in a small bowl.

2. Combine the chocolate, remaining 2 tablespoons cocoa, and instant espresso in a small bowl. Pour the boiling water over the top, cover, and let sit until the chocolate is melted, 3 to 5 minutes. Whisk the mixture until smooth and set aside to cool. When cool, whisk in the sour cream and vanilla.

3. In a medium bowl, beat the brown sugar and 2 tablespoons softened butter together with an electric mixer on medium speed until light and smooth, 2 to 4 minutes, scraping down the bowl as needed. Beat in the egg until combined, about 15 seconds. (The batter may look curdled.)

4. Reduce the mixer speed to low and slowly add one-half of the flour mixture, followed by all of the chocolate mixture, scraping down the bowl as needed. Beat in the remaining flour mixture until just combined.

5. Give the batter a final stir with a rubber spatula to make sure it is thoroughly combined. Divide the batter evenly between the prepared pans, smooth the tops, and gently tap each pan on the counter to settle the batter. Wipe any drops of batter off the sides of the pans. Place the pans on a rimmed baking sheet and bake the cakes until a toothpick inserted into the centers comes out with a few moist crumbs attached, 20 to 22 minutes, rotating the baking sheet halfway through baking.

6. Let the cakes cool in the pans for 10 minutes, then flip out onto a wire rack. Let the cakes cool completely, about 1½ hours, before serving.

FLUFFY YELLOW LAYER CAKE WITH CHOCOLATE FROSTING

ALMOST EVERY BIRTHDAY PARTY we ever attended when we were growing up served a yellow layer cake. Moist, light, and fluffy, it practically melted on the tongue. The secret behind this addictive cake? It almost always came from a box. Although we still have fond memories of this chemically engineered confection, we couldn't help but wonder: Was it possible to create a yellow layer cake with the same ethereal texture and supreme fluffiness but also the great flavor of natural ingredients? Unlocking the secret to moist and fluffy yellow cake would be our first order of business; we would then try to find a way to downsize the recipe to serve two. After all, there are times when a birthday celebration demands fluffy yellow layer cake (preferably with chocolate frosting!), but you don't need a cake that serves a crowd.

After several months of testing, we finally perfected a fluffy yellow cake, reminiscent of the boxed cake-mix variety—without the cloyingly sweet chemical flavor. The secret to success came in combining a chiffon-cake method (whipping egg whites separately and folding them into the cake batter at the end to lighten the batter) with butter-cake ingredients (butter as the fat, fewer eggs, a greater proportion of flour, and a liquid, usually some type of dairy). After adding extra egg yolks to enrich the crumb, we had a light, porous cake that still had enough heft to hold a frosting. The few final refinements were replacing some of the butter with oil and increasing the amount of sugar, both of which helped achieve a moister cake. Replacing the milk with buttermilk produced a porous, fine crumb. We now had a cake that was so moist and fluffy that we could almost patent it.

Now for our next challenge: Could we scale back this fluffy yellow cake without compromising the cake's moist, fluffy identity? The first decision was what pan to use. We started our testing with a 6-inch cake pan—the idea was to make one cake and slice it in half horizontally, thereby creating two layers from one cake.

We adjusted the ingredients to one-third of the original recipe, with a few minor areas where we needed to round up or down. After we whipped up our batter and poured it into our cake pan, we had high hopes. As we pulled the cake out of the oven, however, disappointment struck. The cake had domed, creating an unattractive top layer. Worse yet, when we sliced into the cake, we encountered a dense, moist center—a far cry from the original fluffy yellow cake. What had gone wrong?

In reviewing the possible culprits, we came up with a few possibilities. Sugar is added to the egg white during whipping to help stabilize it, and give the cake lift. If there is not enough sugar, the egg white can easily deflate when folded into the batter. When downsizing the recipe, we had reserved only 1 tablespoon of sugar to whip with the white. In our next test we increased the sugar to 2 tablespoons, and the results were immediately noticeable. The whipped white was more stable, and the resulting cake had more lift; however, we were still faced with an unpleasantly dense center.

Our pastry expert in the test kitchen advised us that maybe our cake pan was overfilled with batter. Because the cake relied on lift from the whipped egg whites, if there was too much batter in the pan, the cake would not be able to rise properly. (This could also be contributing to the domed top, which we had yet to address.) Sure enough, our cake pan was a little over three-quarters full, and cake pans should not be more than one-half full. Furthermore, our cake was taking about 28 minutes to cook, much too long for this small cake—another indicator that we had too much batter in the pan.

As we reviewed our ingredients, it did not seem feasible to reduce them any further without compromising their delicate ratios. Our solution was to divide the batter between two 6-inch round cake pans. This worked wonders. Each cake rose beautifully, had a perfectly flat top, and cooked far more quickly, because we now had two relatively thin layers. We assembled and frosted the cake, sliced into it, and knew we had found the answer. Our mini fluffy yellow cake was now worthy of its name—we had recaptured its moist, tender, feathery allure.

Reducing the yield on our chocolate frosting was a breeze in comparison. Easy to make, with a rich chocolate flavor and a light, satiny texture, this frosting was truly the icing on the cake.

FLUFFY YELLOW LAYER CAKE WITH CHOCOLATE FROSTING

Fluffy Yellow Layer Cake with Chocolate Frosting

SERVES 2

We prefer the flavor of Dutch-processed cocoa powder, but you can substitute natural (regular) cocoa powder if necessary. This frosting may be made with milk, semi-sweet, or bittersweet chocolate, but we prefer a frosting made with milk chocolate. Bring all of the ingredients to room temperature before making the cake. You will need two 6-inch round cake pans for this recipe (see page 3). To keep the cake platter clean while you assemble the cake, line the edges with strips of parchment paper and remove them before serving.

CAKE

- ¾ cup (3 ounces) cake flour
- ½ cup (3½ ounces) granulated sugar
- ½ teaspoon baking powder
- ¼ teaspoon salt
- ⅛ teaspoon baking soda
- ⅓ cup buttermilk, at room temperature
- 3 tablespoons unsalted butter, melted and cooled slightly
- 2 large egg yolks, at room temperature
- 1 tablespoon vegetable oil
- ¾ teaspoon vanilla extract
- 1 large egg white, at room temperature

FROSTING

- 7 tablespoons unsalted butter, softened
- ⅓ cup (1⅓ ounces) confectioners' sugar
- ¼ cup (¾ ounce) Dutch-processed cocoa powder (see note)
- Pinch salt
- ¼ cup light corn syrup
- ½ teaspoon vanilla extract
- 3 ounces chocolate, melted and cooled slightly (see note)

1. FOR THE CAKE: Adjust an oven rack to the middle position and heat the oven to 350 degrees. Grease and flour two 6-inch round cake pans, then line the bottoms with parchment paper. Whisk the flour, 6 tablespoons of the granulated sugar, baking powder, salt, and baking soda together in a medium bowl and set aside. Whisk the buttermilk, melted butter, egg yolks, oil, and vanilla together in a small bowl.

2. In a medium bowl, whip the egg white with an

electric mixer on medium-high speed until foamy, 30 to 60 seconds. Gradually whip in the remaining 2 tablespoons granulated sugar and continue to whip until stiff peaks just form, 2 to 3 minutes, scraping down the bowl as needed (the whites should hold a peak but the mixture should appear moist). Set aside.

3. Add the flour mixture to a second medium bowl. With the electric mixer on low speed, gradually pour in the butter mixture and mix until almost incorporated (a few streaks of dry flour will remain), 15 to 30 seconds, scraping down the bowl as needed. Increase the speed to medium-low and beat until smooth and fully incorporated, 10 to 15 seconds, scraping down the bowl as needed.

4. Using a rubber spatula, stir one-third of the whipped egg white into the batter to lighten, then gently fold in the remaining egg white until no white streaks remain. Divide the batter between the prepared pans, smooth the tops, and gently tap the pans on the counter to settle the batter.

5. Bake the cakes until a toothpick inserted into the centers comes out with a few crumbs attached, 16 to 18 minutes. Let the cakes cool in the pans for 10 minutes. Run a small knife around the edge of the cakes, then flip them out onto a wire rack. Peel off the parchment paper, flip the cakes right-side up, and let cool completely before frosting, about 1½ hours.

6. FOR THE FROSTING: While the cakes cool, process the butter, confectioners' sugar, cocoa, and salt in a food processor until smooth, about 10 seconds, scraping down the bowl as needed. Add the corn syrup and vanilla, and process until just combined, 5 to 10 seconds. Scrape down the bowl, then add the chocolate and pulse until smooth and creamy, 5 to 10 seconds. (The frosting can be made up to 3 hours in advance and left at room temperature, or refrigerated in an airtight container for up to 3 days. If refrigerated, let sit at room temperature for 1 hour before using.)

7. TO ASSEMBLE: Place one of the cakes on a cake platter or large plate. Spread ¼ cup of the frosting over the cake, right to the edges. Place the remaining cake layer on top and press lightly to adhere. Frost the cake with the remaining frosting and serve.

ALMOND CAKE

ALMONDS HAVE BEEN A CULINARY STAPLE in countries around the Mediterranean for centuries, used in place of flour for cakes and for thickening sauces. The sweet almond is the star ingredient in almond cake, a simple Italian dessert. Like pound cake, almond cake is a versatile dessert that is as good plain as it is with a simple sauce, whipped cream, or fresh berries.

There are many types of almond cakes, some using marzipan (sweetened almond paste), and others using polenta, or cornmeal, to add texture. To get the lay of the land, we tasted several of these cakes side by side—both baking some recipes we found and ordering some cakes from reputable local Italian bakeries. Some of the cakes were downright unpalatable, with flavors so sickly sweet that we could barely choke them down, and others were so incredibly dense they required a serrated knife to cut. There were a few, however, that offered a simple, coarse pound cake–like texture and a clean, lightly sweetened almond flavor. These were the cakes that tasters homed in on as their favorites, and although they had

some serious textural and flavor problems of their own, they held promise. Could we uncover the secret to great almond cake and scale it down to serve just two?

We were first intrigued by the complete absence of flour in some of the recipes we found. In fact, many of the recipes used nothing but finely ground almonds as the base. Our first goal was to determine if we were going to add any flour to our cake, or let the almonds really speak for themselves. Testing different ratios of almonds (ground fine in a food processor) and all-purpose flour, we started with a batter made of half flour and half almonds. Tasters complained that the almond flavor was too faint and the cake too light. Working our way toward more almonds and less flour, we settled on ¼ cup of flour and 1 cup of almonds. Any more flour and the cakes lost their appealing rustic texture, but any less and they were too moist and heavy. A final substitution of cake flour for the all-purpose flour gave our almond cakes a welcome lightness without sacrificing pure almond flavor.

Next we focused our attention on the sugar. We already knew we wanted granulated sugar in this cake recipe, not only for its pure sweetness, but because we knew brown sugar would add moisture that this cake definitely didn't need (it already had plenty of moisture from the oil in the almonds). Our challenge was to figure out just how much sugar was necessary. Starting with ½ cup, we added some to the almonds when we ground them in the food processor—to prevent them from turning into nut butter. A mere 2 tablespoons did the trick. We then creamed 6 tablespoons with the butter before adding the other ingredients. The resulting cake was flavorful and the sugar really brought out the almond flavor, but the crust that formed was almost like candy. Reducing the amount of sugar by 1 tablespoon worked perfectly.

Most almond cakes that we found in our research (that fed eight people) called for three eggs. Knowing that it would be hard to put any less than one egg in the cake, we hoped that one would be the winning number. Indeed, we were happy to find that one egg was exactly right—any less and the cake sagged in the middle. Now the cake had good structure, with a light spring and tender crumb.

Up to this point, our batter was coming together pretty easily, but the end result was thick and required a spatula to spread it in the pans. Taking a cue from past cake recipes, we started adding liquid to thin the batter out. Two tablespoons of water worked great, making the batter pourable. But it also dulled the flavor of the cake just a bit—we'd worked so hard to get the right balance of flavors it seemed counterintuitive to now water them down. But substituting milk for water satisfied all our tasters.

Up to this point, we had been cooking the cakes in 6-ounce ramekins. We were finding that the cakes were rising above the rims and doming, making for an unattractive presentation. We didn't think we could reduce the ingredients any further without compromising the texture of the cake. We found the solution in individual 4½-inch springform pans that were wider than the ramekins we had been using. The cakes now rose perfectly, with just a slight dome—these small almond cakes were finally where we wanted them to be.

Almond Cake

MAKES 2

Be careful not to overtoast the almonds or the cakes will have a dry, crumbly texture. You will need two 4½-inch springform pans for this recipe (see page 3). These cakes have a dense, pound cake–like texture and taste great when served with Whipped Cream (page 254) and fresh berries.

> 1 cup (4 ounces) slivered almonds, toasted (see note; see page 226)
> 7 tablespoons (3 ounces) granulated sugar
>   Pinch salt
> ¼ cup (1 ounce) cake flour
> ¼ teaspoon baking powder
> 2 tablespoons unsalted butter, cut into 2 pieces and softened
> 1 large egg, at room temperature
> 2 tablespoons whole milk, at room temperature
>   Confectioners' sugar, for dusting

1. Adjust an oven rack to the middle position and heat the oven to 325 degrees. Grease two 4½-inch springform pans.

2. Process the almonds, 2 tablespoons of the sugar, and salt together in a food processor until very finely ground, about 15 seconds. Add the flour and baking powder, and pulse to incorporate, about 5 pulses.

3. Beat the remaining 5 tablespoons sugar and butter together in a medium bowl with an electric mixer on medium speed until light and smooth, 2 to 4 minutes, scraping down the bowl as needed. Beat in the egg until combined, 15 to 30 seconds. Reduce the mixer speed to low and slowly add the ground almond mixture until incorporated, 15 to 30 seconds, scraping down the bowl as needed. Beat in the milk until combined, 15 to 30 seconds.

4. Give the batter a final stir with a rubber spatula to make sure it is thoroughly combined. Divide the batter evenly between the prepared pans, smooth the tops, and gently tap the pans on the counter to settle the batter. Place the cakes on a rimmed baking sheet and bake until the tops are golden brown and a toothpick inserted into the centers comes out with a few crumbs attached, 25 to 30 minutes, rotating the baking sheet halfway through baking.

5. Let the cakes cool in the pans for 10 minutes. Run a small knife around the edge of each cake, then remove the sides of the pans. Carefully transfer the cakes to a wire rack and let cool slightly, about 30 minutes.

6. Carefully slide the cakes onto individual serving plates. Dust with confectioners' sugar before serving warm.

NEW ORLEANS BOURBON BREAD PUDDING

THE BEST BOURBON BREAD PUDDING is a rich, scoopable custard that envelops the bread with a perfect balance of sweet spiciness and musky bourbon flavor. The history behind New Orleans's most famous dessert is as eclectic as the city itself. The basic custard and bread combination is of English origin. The bread—which in New Orleans is almost always a baguette—is from France. The addition of raisins to the custard can be credited to German settlers, and it was the Irish who infused the cream base with various liquors. The bourbon, of course, originally came from Kentucky traders.

We decided to stick to a custard-based recipe with raisins because it seemed both traditional and easy; unfortunately, the bread puddings we made in our initial test of five published recipes were awful. We encountered a wide range of problems, from harsh bourbon flavor to curdled eggs to rock-hard raisins to slimy bread swimming in a river of custard. These bread puddings were nothing like the New Orleans ideal.

NEW ORLEANS BOURBON BREAD PUDDING

Some recipes have you cube the bread and stale it overnight, but these bread puddings looked more like the cobblestone streets in the French Quarter than something we'd like to eat for dessert. We wanted a more rustic look and had much better results tearing the bread into ragged pieces. As one baguette was far too much bread for two people, we found that two rustic French rolls gave us the perfect amount for two 12-ounce ramekins. Toasting the torn pieces to a deep golden brown enriched their flavor and gave the bread a crispness that helped to prevent the finished dish from turning soggy.

The ratio of eggs to dairy (one egg to ½ cup dairy) in the custard is time-tested, and we found that a mixture of 3 parts cream to 1 part milk was rich but not over the top. We arrived at two eggs, ¾ cup cream, and ¼ cup milk to achieve the right yield for our two individual puddings. Tasters preferred the caramel flavor of brown sugar (rather than the usual white sugar) to sweeten the custard.

Now it was time to tackle the most problematic aspect of this dish: the curdling custard. Setting the ramekins with the pudding in a roasting pan filled with hot water (called a water bath) was one way to moderate the oven heat and keep the eggs from curdling, but we wondered if there was an easier way. We found that replacing the traditional whole eggs with just egg yolks helped stave off curdling. (We later found out that's because the whites set faster than the yolks.) Also helpful in curdle-proofing the pudding was lowering the oven temperature (to 300 degrees) and covering the ramekins with foil.

But with a foil cover, our pudding never formed much of a toasted top. Taking inspiration from pie recipes in which cinnamon and sugar are sprinkled on the dough to form a crunchy topping, we adapted this idea for our individual bread puddings. Before the custard had fully set up in the oven, we removed the foil, added the cinnamon, sugar, and some butter, and let the puddings bake for another 15 minutes. Then we increased the temperature and, after 10 more minutes, the topping had caramelized and formed a golden crust.

There's no doubt that bourbon bread pudding is an adult dessert. It should have enough robust bourbon flavor to warm you up, but not so much that it knocks you down. Two tablespoons to plump the raisins (which solved the rock-hard raisin problem from earlier tests) and an additional tablespoon in the custard gave our bread puddings just enough bourbon punch. And for a real taste of New Orleans, we drizzled our bread puddings with a warm bourbon-based cream sauce.

New Orleans Bourbon Bread Pudding
MAKES 2

Six ounces of French bread can be substituted for the rolls. You will need two 12-ounce ramekins for this recipe. The bread pudding can also be prepared in an 8½ by 5½-inch baking dish (see page 3).

BREAD PUDDING
- 2 rustic French rolls (about 3 ounces each), torn into 1-inch pieces (about 3 cups) (see note)
- ¼ cup golden raisins
- 3 tablespoons bourbon
- ¾ cup heavy cream
- ⅓ cup packed (2⅓ ounces) light brown sugar
- ¼ cup whole milk
- 2 large egg yolks, at room temperature
- 1 teaspoon vanilla extract
- ½ teaspoon ground cinnamon
- Pinch ground nutmeg
- Pinch salt
- 1 tablespoon granulated sugar
- 2 tablespoons unsalted butter, cut into ¼-inch pieces and chilled

BOURBON SAUCE
- 1 tablespoon bourbon
- ½ teaspoon cornstarch
- 3 tablespoons heavy cream
- 2 teaspoons granulated sugar
- Pinch salt

1. FOR THE BREAD PUDDING: Adjust an oven rack to the middle position and heat the oven to 450 degrees. Grease two 12-ounce ramekins. Spread the bread out on a rimmed baking sheet and toast until crisp and browned, stirring occasionally, 10 to 12 minutes. Let the bread cool completely. Reduce the oven temperature to 300 degrees.

2. Bring the raisins and 2 tablespoons of the bourbon to a simmer in a small saucepan over medium-high heat, and cook for 1 minute. Strain the raisins, reserving the liquid.

3. Whisk the reserved raisin soaking liquid, remaining 1 tablespoon bourbon, cream, brown sugar, milk, egg yolks, vanilla, ¼ teaspoon of the cinnamon, nutmeg, and salt together in a medium bowl. Add the toasted bread and toss until evenly coated. Let the mixture sit, tossing occasionally, until the bread begins to absorb the custard and is softened, 20 to 25 minutes.

4. Stir the reserved raisins into the bread mixture until combined. Divide the bread mixture evenly between the prepared ramekins and cover each ramekin with foil. Place the bread puddings on a rimmed baking sheet and bake for 30 minutes.

5. Meanwhile, in a small bowl, mix the remaining ¼ teaspoon cinnamon and granulated sugar together.

Using your fingers, work the butter into the sugar mixture until small pea-sized pieces form. Remove the foil from the bread puddings and sprinkle with the butter mixture. Rotate the baking sheet and continue to bake, uncovered, until the custard is just set, about 15 minutes. Increase the oven temperature to 450 degrees and bake until the top is crisp and golden brown, about 10 minutes. Let the bread puddings cool for 30 minutes.

6. FOR THE BOURBON SAUCE: Whisk 1½ teaspoons of the bourbon and the cornstarch together in a small bowl until well combined. Place the cream and sugar in a small saucepan, and stir to moisten the sugar. Heat over medium heat until the sugar dissolves. Whisk in the cornstarch mixture and bring to a boil. Reduce the heat to low and cook until the sauce thickens, 30 to 60 seconds. Off the heat, stir in the remaining 1½ teaspoons bourbon and salt. Drizzle the warm sauce over each bread pudding and serve.

VARIATION

Bourbon Bread Pudding with Chocolate
We like the flavor of bittersweet chips here, but semisweet chips can be substituted.

Follow the recipe for New Orleans Bourbon Bread Pudding, adding all the bourbon in step 3 and substituting ⅓ cup bittersweet chocolate chips for the raisins.

NEW YORK CHEESECAKE

NEW YORK CHEESECAKE SHOULD BE A TALL, BRONZE-skinned, and dense affair—and an orchestration of different textures and an exercise in flavor restraint. At the core, it should be cool, thick, satiny, and creamy; radiating outward, it goes gradually from velvety to suede-like, then, finally, about the edges, it is cake-like and fine-pored. The flavor should be simple, sweet and tangy, and rich. Because cheesecake is so rich, you don't necessarily want to be faced with a huge portion of leftovers. Our goal, therefore, would be to develop a recipe for two small cheesecakes, using two 4½-inch springform pans.

We decided to start with the crust and work our way up. Some recipes claim that a pastry crust was the crust of choice for the original New York cheesecake.

We tried one, but after a lot of expended effort, a pastry crust only became soggy beneath the filling. Cookie and cracker crumbs were tasty and more practical options. A graham cracker crust (made with three graham crackers—pulsed to crumbs—some sugar, and melted butter) divided and pressed into the bottom of the pans, then prebaked until it was fragrant and browning around the edges, was ideal.

A great New York cheesecake should be of great stature—which means ample amounts of cream cheese—and our individual ones were no exception. Made with ½ pound of cream cheese, they were not tall enough. We threw in another 2 ounces—the springform pans each reached maximum capacity, but the cheesecakes stood appropriately tall. With the sugar at ⅓ cup, these cheesecakes struck a perfect balance of sweet and tangy.

Cheesecakes always require a dairy supplement to the cream cheese—usually either heavy cream or sour cream, or sometimes both. Additional dairy loosens up the texture of the cream cheese, giving the cake a smoother, more luxurious feel. Sour cream beat out heavy cream; with a tang of its own, sour cream supplemented the tangy quality of the cream cheese (rather than dulling it as the heavy cream did). Tasters preferred a relatively small amount of sour cream—just 4 teaspoons. This was enough to contribute its tangy flavor and smooth, creamy texture without advertising its presence.

Eggs help bind the cheesecake, make it cohesive, and give it structure. They also help achieve a smooth, creamy texture. Recipes for New York cheesecake seem to agree that yolks in addition to whole eggs help give it the proper velvety, lush texture. Our testing bore this out, and, ultimately, we concluded that one whole egg plus one yolk for our scaled-down version yielded cheesecake of unparalleled texture: dense but not heavy, firm but not rigid, and perfectly rich.

Perfecting the flavor of the cheesecake was easy. A touch of lemon juice, a pinch of salt, and a small dose of vanilla extract were all it needed. Everyone in the test kitchen appreciated this minimalist cheesecake.

Although cheesecake comes together easily, care must be used when mixing the ingredients lest the batter contain small nodules of unmixed cream cheese that can mar the smoothness of the baked cake. Frequent and thorough scraping of the bowl during mixing is key to ensuring that every spot of cream cheese is incorporated, but starting with semisoftened cream cheese is certainly helpful.

There are many ways to bake a cheesecake: in a moderate oven, in a low oven, in a water bath, and in accordance with the New York method—500 degrees for about 10 minutes, then 200 degrees for about an hour (which appears to be a standard technique). We tried them all, but the New York method was the only one that yielded the nut-brown surface that is a distinguishing mark of an exemplary New York cheesecake. This dual-temperature, no-water-bath baking method also produced a lovely graded texture—soft and creamy at the center and firm and dry at the periphery.

Larger cheesecakes take over an hour to bake to the proper consistency, but we were surprised to find that once we turned the oven down to 200 degrees (we needed only five minutes at 500 degrees), our cheesecakes were done within 10 to 15 minutes. After being chilled, they were cheesecake perfection. When sliced into, the cakes kept their shape and had just the right texture. We do caution against taking the cheesecake beyond an internal temperature of 160 degrees. The few that we did were hideously and hopelessly cracked.

NEW YORK CHEESECAKE

Uptight though it may seem, an instant-read thermometer inserted into the cake is the most reliable means of judging the doneness of the cheesecake.

New York Cheesecake

MAKES 2

You will need two 4½-inch springform pans for this recipe (see page 3). Serve as is or with fresh berries.

CRUST

- **3 whole graham crackers, broken into 1-inch pieces**
- **3 tablespoons unsalted butter, melted and cooled**
- **1 tablespoon sugar**

FILLING

- **10 ounces cream cheese, cut into chunks and softened**
- **⅓ cup (2⅓ ounces) sugar**
- **Pinch salt**
- **4 teaspoons sour cream**
- **½ teaspoon fresh lemon juice**
- **½ teaspoon vanilla extract**
- **1 large egg**
- **1 large egg yolk**

1. FOR THE CRUST: Adjust an oven rack to the middle position and heat the oven to 325 degrees. Process the graham cracker pieces in a food processor to fine, even crumbs, about 30 seconds. Drizzle 2 tablespoons of the butter and sprinkle the sugar over the crumbs, and pulse to incorporate. Divide the mixture evenly between two 4½-inch springform pans. Following the photo on page 281, press the crumbs firmly into an even layer using the bottom of a spoon. Bake the crusts until fragrant and beginning to brown, about 10 minutes. Let the crusts cool to room temperature, about 15 minutes.

2. FOR THE FILLING: Meanwhile, increase the oven temperature to 500 degrees. In a large bowl, beat the cream cheese with an electric mixer on medium-low speed until smooth, 1 to 2 minutes, scraping down the bowl as needed.

3. Beat in ¼ cup of the sugar and salt until incorporated, 30 to 60 seconds. Beat in the remaining sugar until incorporated, 30 to 60 seconds, scraping down the bowl as needed. Beat in the sour cream, lemon juice, and vanilla until incorporated, 15 to 30 seconds. Beat in

the egg and egg yolk until combined, 30 to 60 seconds, scraping down the bowl as needed.

4. Being careful not to disturb the baked crusts, brush the inside of the prepared springform pans with the remaining 1 tablespoon butter. Carefully divide the filling evenly between the two pans and smooth the tops. Place the cheesecakes on a rimmed baking sheet and bake for 5 minutes.

5. Without opening the oven door, reduce the oven temperature to 200 degrees and continue to bake the cheesecakes until an instant-read thermometer inserted into the centers registers 150 degrees, 10 to 15 minutes, rotating the baking sheet halfway through baking.

6. Transfer the cheesecakes to a wire rack and run a small knife around the edge of each cake. Let the cheesecakes cool until just barely warm, about 1 hour. Wrap the pans tightly in plastic wrap and refrigerate until cold, at least 2 hours or up to 4 days.

7. Remove the sides of the pans and carefully slide the cheesecakes onto individual serving plates. Let the cheesecakes sit at room temperature for 30 minutes before serving.

FLAN

FLAN IS A DECEPTIVELY SIMPLE SPANISH DESSERT. Made with just a few ingredients that are readily available (sugar, eggs, and milk), it is similar in construction and flavor to other baked custards from around the world. This dessert is slightly lighter than a standard baked custard, with an ultra-creamy and tender texture. It also sports a thin layer of sweet caramel that pools over the custard once unmolded. The perfect flan is mellow in flavor, neither too sweet nor too eggy. It should also be firm enough to unmold on a serving plate without collapsing. Wanting to make just enough flan for two, we set out to develop a recipe for flan that could be baked in individual 6-ounce ramekins, rather than a 9-inch round cake pan as many recipes use.

Since eggs are integral to flan, we started there. Not all recipes found in our research agreed on the number of eggs or the proportion of egg yolks to egg whites. Here's what we found when we started baking: Too many whites produced a custard that was almost solid and rubbery; too few egg whites, on the other hand, and our custard collapsed—egg whites, we discovered, give the custard structure. Egg yolks provide richness—with too few the flan tasted lean, and too many left the flan tasting, well, too eggy. After much tinkering, we came up with what we consider the ideal ratio for a two-serving flan: one white to two yolks. The resulting custard was tender yet not overly rich, and firm enough to unmold easily.

Next we looked at the milk. We made our initial custard using whole milk (1 cup was the right amount for two individual flans), but it tasted too thin and the egg flavor dominated. Next we augmented the milk with heavy cream, but the flan's richness seemed out of place and too close to its French neighbor, crème caramel. We reviewed recipes from Spanish and Latin American cookbooks and found that some include sweetened condensed milk, which is rich and creamy, without the intense fat of heavy cream. This made sense, so we replaced some of the whole milk with sweetened condensed milk, using an equal ratio of ½ cup whole milk to ½ cup condensed milk. The resulting flan was more in line with the best flan we've eaten, but still a bit too rich. This was easily fixed by switching to 2 percent milk. We also enjoyed an extra bonus from the condensed milk—because it's sweetened, it made our dessert sweet enough that we didn't need to include sugar.

Refining the flavors of the flan was easy. We first tested varying amounts of vanilla, which tasters found somewhat unremarkable. Then we tried adding grated lemon zest, a traditional flavoring in this dessert, and tasters loved the citrus undertones. A mere ⅛ teaspoon was all this dessert needed.

Finally, the crowning touch—the caramel. There are basically two methods of making caramel. In the dry method, you use only sugar, cooking it slowly until it melts and caramelizes. The wet method uses a combination of water and sugar. The sugar begins to dissolve in the water, then the mixture is simmered until the water evaporates and the sugar caramelizes. The dry method can be tricky to pull off, so we opted for the wet as a way of increasing the margin of success for the home cook.

Some recipes instruct you to pour the caramel into the mold (we were using two 6-ounce ramekins) and then tilt the pan to coat the sides, but we ended up

burning our fingers. Because caramel is hot enough to cause serious burns, we rethought this method. Instead, we decided to coat only the bottom of the ramekins, reasoning that the caramel sinks to the bottom of the ramekin while baking anyway. When we unmolded the custard, the caramel still poured evenly over the top.

How you bake flan and how long you bake it can make the difference between a great dessert and a mediocre, or even disappointing, one. After considerable experimentation, we determined that baking the custards at 350 degrees in a water bath, to maintain an

NOTES FROM THE TEST KITCHEN

MAKING FLAN

1. Cook the caramel until it is a dark amber color and registers about 350 degrees on a candy or instant-read thermometer.

2. Slowly pour the caramel into the prepared ramekins, being careful not to splash caramel onto yourself or the outside of the ramekins. Caramel is extremely hot so care must be taken.

3. Place the baking pan in the oven and carefully pour enough boiling water into the pan to reach halfway up the sides of the ramekins.

4. To unmold the baked flan, run a knife around the edges to loosen them. Place an inverted serving plate over the top and quickly flip the custard onto the plate, drizzling extra caramel on top.

even, gentle heating environment, produced custards that were creamy and smooth. This involves simply placing the ramekins in a square baking pan, then filling the baking pan with boiling water until it reaches partway up the sides of the ramekins of custard. We also found that lining the baking pan first with a towel further ensures that the bottom of the custard won't overcook.

Flan

MAKES 2

We prefer to use low-fat milk in this recipe, although any type of milk (even skim) can be used, resulting in varying degrees of richness. Note that the custard will look barely set once it is ready to be removed from the oven. You will need two 6-ounce ramekins for this recipe (see page 3).

- 3 tablespoons water
- 3 tablespoons sugar
- 1 large egg, at room temperature
- 1 large egg yolk, at room temperature
- ½ cup low-fat milk (see note)
- ½ cup sweetened condensed milk
- ⅛ teaspoon grated lemon zest

1. Adjust an oven rack to the middle position and heat the oven to 350 degrees. Bring a kettle of water to a boil. Place a kitchen towel in the bottom of a metal 8-inch square baking pan. Grease two 6-ounce ramekins and place them on the towel.

2. Pour the water into a small saucepan, then pour the sugar into the center of the pan (don't let it hit the pan sides). Gently stir the sugar with a clean spatula to wet it thoroughly. Bring to a boil over medium-high heat and cook, without stirring, until the sugar has dissolved completely and the liquid has a faint golden color (and registers about 300 degrees on a candy or instant-read thermometer), 3 to 4 minutes.

3. Following the photos on page 284, reduce the heat to medium-low and continue to cook, stirring occasionally, until the caramel has a dark amber color (and registers about 350 degrees on a candy or instant-read thermometer), 1 to 2 minutes longer. Carefully divide the caramel between the two ramekins and let cool slightly until hardened.

4. Whisk the egg and egg yolk together in a medium bowl. Whisk in the milk, sweetened condensed milk, and lemon zest until thoroughly combined. Divide the custard evenly between the two ramekins.

5. Place the baking pan in the oven and carefully pour enough boiling water into the pan to reach halfway up the sides of the ramekins. Bake the custards until the centers are just barely set, 25 to 30 minutes.

6. Carefully remove the ramekins from the water bath and let the custards cool to room temperature, about 1 hour. Cover the ramekins tightly with plastic wrap and refrigerate until cold, at least 2 hours or up to 1 day.

7. Run a small knife around one of the ramekins to loosen the custard. Place an inverted serving plate over the top and quickly flip the custard onto the plate, drizzling any extra caramel sauce over the top (some caramel will remain stuck in the ramekin). Repeat with the remaining custard and serve.

USE IT UP: SWEETENED CONDENSED MILK

Dulce de Leche

MAKES ABOUT 1 CUP

Dulce de leche is a Latin American sauce with a deep caramel flavor. Be sure to stir the sauce frequently as it cooks to prevent it from burning. Serve this sauce warm, drizzled over ice cream or pound cake, or at room temperature, spread on crusty bread. The sauce can be stored in an airtight container for up to 1 week. Reheat, if desired.

- ¾ cup sweetened condensed milk
- 1 cup whole milk, warmed

1. Cook the sweetened condensed milk in a small saucepan over medium-high heat, stirring often with a wooden spoon, until it comes to a boil, about 3 minutes. Reduce the heat to medium-low and continue to cook, stirring constantly, until deep golden brown and very thick, 10 to 12 minutes.

2. Slowly stir in the warmed milk (the mixture may seize at first). Continue to cook over medium-low heat, stirring occasionally, until the sauce is completely smooth, about 10 minutes. Serve warm or at room temperature.

Conversions & Equivalencies

SOME SAY COOKING IS A SCIENCE AND AN ART. We would say that geography has a hand in it, too. Flour milled in the United Kingdom and elsewhere will feel and taste different from flour milled in the United States. So, while we cannot promise that the loaf of bread you bake in Canada or England will taste the same as a loaf baked in the States, we can offer guidelines for converting weights and measures. We also recommend that you rely on your instincts when making our recipes. Refer to the visual cues provided. If the bread dough hasn't "come together in a ball," as described,

you may need to add more flour—even if the recipe doesn't tell you so. You be the judge.

The recipes in this book were developed using standard U.S. measures following U.S. government guidelines. The charts below offer equivalents for U.S., metric, and Imperial (U.K.) measures. All conversions are approximate and have been rounded up or down to the nearest whole number. For example:

1 teaspoon = 4.929 milliliters, rounded up to 5 milliliters
1 ounce = 28.349 grams, rounded down to 28 grams

VOLUME CONVERSIONS

U.S.	METRIC
1 teaspoon	5 milliliters
2 teaspoons	10 milliliters
1 tablespoon	15 milliliters
2 tablespoons	30 milliliters
¼ cup	59 milliliters
⅓ cup	79 milliliters
½ cup	118 milliliters
¾ cup	177 milliliters
1 cup	237 milliliters
1¼ cups	296 milliliters
1½ cups	355 milliliters
2 cups	473 milliliters
2½ cups	592 milliliters
3 cups	710 milliliters
4 cups (1 quart)	0.946 liter
1.06 quarts	1 liter
4 quarts (1 gallon)	3.8 liters

WEIGHT CONVERSIONS

OUNCES	GRAMS
½	14
¾	21
1	28
1½	43
2	57
2½	71
3	85
3½	99
4	113
4½	128
5	142
6	170
7	198
8	227
9	255
10	283
12	340
16 (1 pound)	454

CONVERSIONS FOR INGREDIENTS COMMONLY USED IN BAKING

Baking is an exacting science. Because measuring by weight is far more accurate than measuring by volume, and thus more likely to achieve reliable results, in our recipes we provide ounce measures in addition to cup measures for many ingredients. Refer to the chart below to convert these measures into grams.

INGREDIENT	OUNCES	GRAMS
1 cup all-purpose flour*	5	142
1 cup cake flour	4	113
1 cup whole wheat flour	5½	156
1 cup granulated (white) sugar	7	198
1 cup packed brown sugar (light or dark)	7	198
1 cup confectioners' sugar	4	113
1 cup cocoa powder	3	85
Butter†		
4 tablespoons (½ stick, or ¼ cup)	2	57
8 tablespoons (1 stick, or ½ cup)	4	113
16 tablespoons (2 sticks, or 1 cup)	8	227

* U.S. all-purpose flour, the most frequently used flour in this book, does not contain leaveners, as some European flours do. These leavened flours are called self-rising or self-raising. If you are using self-rising flour, take this into consideration before adding leavening to a recipe.
† In the United States, butter is sold both salted and unsalted. We generally recommend unsalted butter. If you are using salted butter, take this into consideration before adding salt to a recipe.

OVEN TEMPERATURES

FAHRENHEIT	CELSIUS	GAS MARK (imperial)
225	105	¼
250	120	½
275	130	1
300	150	2
325	165	3
350	180	4
375	190	5
400	200	6
425	220	7
450	230	8
475	245	9

CONVERTING TEMPERATURES FROM AN INSTANT-READ THERMOMETER

We include doneness temperatures in many of our recipes, such as those for poultry, meat, and bread. We recommend an instant-read thermometer for the job. Refer to the table above to convert Fahrenheit degrees to Celsius. Or, for temperatures not represented in the chart, use this simple formula:

Subtract 32 degrees from the Fahrenheit reading, then divide the result by 1.8 to find the Celsius reading.

EXAMPLE:

"Roast until the juice runs clear when the chicken is cut with a paring knife or the thickest part of the breast registers 160 degrees on an instant-read thermometer." To convert:

160° F − 32 = 128°
128° ÷ 1.8 = 71° C (rounded down from 71.11)

Index

L

Lamb
 domestic, flavor of, 99
 imported, flavor of, 99
 Pita Sandwiches, Greek-Style, with Tzatziki Sauce, 25–28
 rack of, preparing, 99
 Roast Rack of, with Whiskey Sauce, 98–99
 testing for doneness, 208
Lasagna, 58–61, *60*
Lasagna noodles, no-boil, taste tests on, 59
Leeks, buying, 153
Lemon(s)
 Basil, and Shrimp, Spaghetti with, 58
 and Basil, Spaghetti with, 57–58
 Buttermilk Sheet Cake, 268–69
 Lemony Green Beans with Toasted Almonds, 226
Lettuce, iceberg, storing, 25
Lighter Chicken Parmesan, 126–27
Lighter Meat Loaf, 138–39
Lighter New England Clam Chowder, 142–43
Lobster
 Fresh Fettuccine with, 118–19
 hard-shell and soft-shell, 119
 preparing, 119

M

Main dishes (everyday)
 Burgers, Old-Fashioned, 80–83, *81*
 Chicken
  Bake, Simple, with Fennel, Orange,
   and Oil-Cured Olives, 72
  Bake, Simple, with Fennel, Tomatoes, and Olives, 70–72
  Mole, 75–77
  Tikka Masala, 72–75, *74*
 Crab Cakes, Pan-Fried, 90–92, *91*
 Eggplant, Stuffed, 93–94
 Mussels, Steamed
  in Coconut Milk with Cilantro, 90
  with Tomato and Basil, 90
  in White Wine with Parsley, 88–89
 Pork Chops
  Crunchy Baked, *68,* 78–80
  Crunchy Baked, with Prosciutto and Asiago Cheese, 80
  Thick-Cut, Sweet and Spicy, 77–78
 Salmon, Oven-Roasted, 85–87, *86*
 Shrimp, Pan-Seared, with Chipotle Sauce, 83–85
 Shrimp Tikka Masala, 75
 Tofu, Crispy, with Sweet Chili Sauce, 94–95
Main dishes (fancy)
 Beef Wellingtons, Individual,
  with Madeira Sauce, *96,* 100–102
 Chicken Kiev, 111–14, *113*
 Cornish Game Hens, Roast,
  with Couscous Stuffing, 107–10, *108*
 Duck Breasts, Pan-Roasted,
  with Dried Cherry Sauce, 110–11

Main dishes (fancy) *(cont.)*
 Lamb, Roast Rack of, with Whiskey Sauce, 98–99
 Lobster, Fresh Fettuccine with, 118–19
 Paella, 116–17
 Pork Tenderloin, Herbed Roast, 105–7
 Prime Rib, Herb-Roasted, with Potatoes, 102–5, *103*
 Ricotta Gnocchi with Browned Butter
  and Sage Sauce, 120–21
 Scallops, Broiled, with Creamy Mushroom Sauce, 114–16
Main dishes (from the pantry)
 Corn Chowder, Pantry, 163–66, *164*
 Frittata, Bacon, Potato, and Cheddar, 156–57
 Frittata, Sun-Dried Tomato, Potato,
  and Mozzarella, *154,* 157
 Pasta e Fagioli, 167–69, *168*
 Pasta with Tuna and Garlic, 162–63
 Quesadillas, Bean and Cheese, 171
 Quesadillas, Cheese and Bacon, 170–71
 Skillet Strata with Cheddar and Thyme, 157–59
 Skillet Strata with Sausage and Gruyère, 159
 Soufflé, Cheese, 171–73
 Soufflé, Spinach, 173
 Spaghetti with Fried Eggs, 159–62, *160*
 White Bean Soup, Tuscan, 166–67
Main dishes (grilled)
 Beef
  Porterhouse or T-Bone Steak
   with Red Potatoes, *206,* 207–9
  Short Ribs, Argentine-Style,
   with Summer Vegetables, 212–14
  and Vegetable Kebabs, 209–12, *210*
 Bratwurst
  with Onion and Fennel, 203
  with Onions and Peppers, 201–3, *202*
  with Sauerkraut and Apples, 203
 Chicken Breasts, Bone-In,
  with Cherry Tomatoes, 196–97
 Chicken Fajitas, 197–200, *199*
 Fish Tacos with Corn on the Cob, 217–20, *218*
 Pork Chops, Glazed,
  with Tarragon Sweet Potatoes, 203–5
 Salmon, Wood-Grilled
  with Asparagus, *194,* 215–16
  Barbecued with Asparagus, 216
  Chinese-Style with Asparagus, 216
 Tofu, Glazed, with Warm Cabbage Slaw, 220–21
Main dishes (one roast, three meals)
 Beef
  and Barley Stew, Hearty, 189
  Pot Roast, French-Style, *174,* 185–87
  Ragù, Rigatoni with, 187
  Shepherd's Pie, *188,* 189
 Chicken
  Breasts, Pan-Roasted, with Lemon
   and Caper Sauce, 176–77
  Cherry Tomatoes, and Olives, Penne with, 177–78
  Salad Wraps, Crispy, 178–79
  Warm Roast, and Bread Salad with Arugula, 179